YOUR PLAYBOOK FOR MOLD CLAIMS

TOXIC MOLD LITIGATION IN AMERICA

Strategy, Science & Settlements in a High-Stakes Field

NGOZI E. BOLIN, ESQ.

Book Cover by James Olen

Legal Disclaimer

Important Notice to Readers

THIS BOOK IS PROVIDED FOR INFORMATIONAL AND EDUCATIONAL PURPOSES ONLY AND IS NOT INTENDED TO CONSTITUTE LEGAL ADVICE.

No Attorney-Client Relationship

The information contained in this book does not create an attorney-client relationship between the author, publisher, and any reader or user of this material. Reading this book, accessing its content, or using any information contained herein does not establish any professional relationship or create any duties or obligations on the part of the author or publisher to any reader.

Not a Substitute for Professional Legal Counsel

The content of this book is general in nature and may not apply to your specific situation. Legal matters are highly fact-specific and jurisdiction-dependent. Laws, regulations, court decisions, and legal interpretations change frequently and vary significantly between jurisdictions. Nothing in this book should be used as a substitute for competent legal advice from a licensed attorney in your jurisdiction who is familiar with the specific facts of your case.

YOU SHOULD ALWAYS CONSULT WITH A QUALIFIED ATTORNEY BEFORE MAKING ANY LEGAL DECISIONS OR TAKING ANY ACTION BASED ON INFORMATION CONTAINED IN THIS BOOK.

Accuracy and Currency of Information

While every effort has been made to ensure the accuracy of the information contained in this book at the time of publication, the author and publisher make no representations or warranties regarding the completeness, accuracy, reliability, or currency of the information provided. Laws and legal precedents change constantly, and what may have been accurate at the time of writing may no longer be current or applicable.

The information in this book reflects the law as understood by the author as of the publication date. Legal developments occurring after the publication date are not reflected in this material.

Jurisdictional Limitations

Laws vary significantly among different countries, states, provinces, and localities. The information in this book may be based primarily on the laws of specific jurisdictions and may not be applicable in your location. Local laws should always be consulted, and local legal counsel should be retained for matters involving specific jurisdictions.

Limitation of Liability

TO THE FULLEST EXTENT PERMITTED BY LAW, THE AUTHOR, PUBLISHER, EDITORS, CONTRIBUTORS, AND DISTRIBUTORS OF THIS BOOK DISCLAIM ALL LIABILITY FOR ANY LOSS, DAMAGE, OR INJURY ARISING FROM THE USE OF OR RELIANCE ON THE INFORMATION CONTAINED HEREIN, WHETHER SUCH LIABILITY ARISES IN CONTRACT, TORT, STRICT LIABILITY, OR OTHERWISE.

This limitation applies to all damages or injuries, including but not limited to:

- Direct, indirect, incidental, and consequential damages
- Lost profits or business opportunities
- Legal fees and costs

- Punitive or exemplary damages
- Any other economic or non-economic losses

No Warranties

THIS BOOK IS PROVIDED "AS IS" WITHOUT WARRANTY OF ANY KIND, EXPRESS OR IMPLIED, INCLUDING BUT NOT LIMITED TO WARRANTIES OF MERCHANTABILITY, FITNESS FOR A PARTICULAR PURPOSE, OR NON-INFRINGEMENT.

Individual Circumstances

Every legal situation is unique. The examples, case studies, and scenarios presented in this book are for illustrative purposes only and may not reflect the full complexity of actual legal situations. The outcomes described may not be achievable in your circumstances, and past results do not guarantee future outcomes.

Updates and Revisions

The author and publisher are under no obligation to update or revise the content of this book to reflect changes in the law or legal practice. Readers are encouraged to verify all information with current legal sources and qualified legal professionals.

Third-Party Content and References

Any references to third-party materials, websites, organizations, or publications are provided for informational purposes only and do not constitute an endorsement of such materials or entities. The author and publisher are not responsible for the content, accuracy, or availability of third-party materials.

Compliance with Professional Rules

Readers who are legal professionals should ensure that their use of any information in this book complies with applicable professional conduct rules, ethical requirements, and licensing obligations in their jurisdiction.

Intellectual Property Notice

This book is protected by copyright and other intellectual property laws. The information provided is for personal, educational, and non-commercial use only. Any commercial use, reproduction, or distribution requires express written permission from the copyright holder.

Severability

If any portion of this disclaimer is held to be invalid or unenforceable, the remaining portions shall remain in full force and effect.

BY READING AND USING THIS BOOK, YOU ACKNOWLEDGE THAT YOU HAVE READ, UNDERSTOOD, AND AGREE TO BE BOUND BY THE TERMS OF THIS DISCLAIMER.

IF YOU DO NOT AGREE WITH THESE TERMS, DO NOT USE THIS BOOK.

Contents

Introduction

On a humid July morning in 2024, a young military family living in government housing at Fort Cavazos, Texas, opened their hallway closet to retrieve winter clothes they'd stored months earlier. Behind the stacked boxes, stretching from floor to ceiling, they discovered a wall of black staining so extensive it seemed to pulse in the dim light. The smell (musty, organic, wrong) explained why their three-year-old daughter had been hospitalized twice that month for pneumonia that wouldn't respond to treatment.

They reported the problem immediately. The property manager documented the complaint, promised an inspection, and did nothing. For six months, the family lived with deteriorating conditions while their daughter's breathing grew more labored and their own health declined. They submitted fourteen written maintenance requests. Twelve went unanswered. Two received responses stating the issue would be "evaluated."

Then their attorney obtained the internal emails.

Management had known about the roof leak for thirteen months. A contractor had warned them in writing that moisture intrusion was "creating conditions for significant mold amplification." The regional supervisor had responded: "Remediation budget is tapped out this quarter. Can we push to Q3?" Another email, three months later, referenced the family's complaints with a single line: "They haven't mentioned legal action yet."

The case settled six months later for $10 million.

This is not your grandfather's landlord-tenant dispute. This is not a minor maintenance disagreement over bathroom tile discoloration. And this is not speculative "toxic mold syndrome" litigation from the sensationalized early 2000s.

Toxic mold litigation in the United States has entered a decisive new phase.

The Modern Landscape: High Stakes and Higher Standards

By 2026, toxic mold litigation is neither a fleeting trend nor an uncontrollable mass tort. It has matured into a technically complex, jurisdiction-sensitive, and scientifically scrutinized practice area defined by substantial financial exposure and exacting evidentiary standards.

The attorneys who succeed in this space are not general litigators reacting to alarming photographs of black discoloration. They are specialists who understand building science, medical causation requirements, insurance policy construction, and evidentiary gatekeeping. They know the difference between Stachybotrys and Aspergillus, and more importantly, they know which battles courts will let them fight and which they'll lose at summary judgment.

The early panic gave way to discipline. Courts demanded proof. Legislatures clarified duties. Insurers refined exclusions. And practitioners learned that mold cases are won not by rhetoric about invisible toxins, but by rigorous causation analysis and strategic framing of preventable moisture intrusion.

Recent years confirm that toxic mold litigation remains not only viable but increasingly significant. Between 2024 and 2025, several major settlements underscored the continued viability (and substantial value) of well-developed mold claims:

$10 million resolution involving Army housing conditions at Fort Cavazos

$6.6 million Las Vegas residential exposure case

$6.5 million New York City housing authority settlement

These results illustrate defining trends that separate today's mold litigation from the speculative claims of two decades ago:

Rising Settlement Values When Liability Evidence is Strong. High-value outcomes are associated with documented moisture intrusion over extended periods, internal communications demonstrating delayed remediation, vulnerable plaintiffs (children, elderly, immunocompromised residents), and clear property damage alongside health complaints. These settlements are not typical. They represent cases where negligence is undeniable and medical proof survives strict admissibility challenges.

Expansion Beyond Landlord-Tenant Disputes. Modern mold litigation frequently includes property managers, architects and engineers, general contractors, subcontractors, lumber and building material manufacturers, and coating and paint product companies. This expansion reflects growing recognition that mold is often a symptom of systemic building envelope failures, design defects, or construction errors, not merely negligent maintenance.

Sophisticated Defense Strategies. Defendants now routinely challenge specific medical causation under Daubert or Frye standards, limit damages to allergy or asthma exacerbation, contest sampling methodologies, and attribute symptoms to alternative environmental factors. As a result, mold litigation has become increasingly science-driven, with outcomes hinging on expert admissibility rather than jury sympathy.

The Central Battle: Proof Over Panic

If one principle defines modern toxic mold litigation, it is this: **General fear is no longer enough. Specific proof is decisive.**

The family at Fort Cavazos didn't win $10 million because jurors were afraid of black mold. They won because their attorney could prove:

The property manager received fourteen documented complaints

Internal emails showed deliberate delay for budgetary reasons

Environmental testing revealed Stachybotrys concentrations forty times outdoor baseline levels

Medical records documented temporal correlation between exposure and illness

A pediatric pulmonologist could testify (and survive Daubert scrutiny) that the child's pneumonia was causally related to documented fungal exposure

Building envelope analysis proved the roof defect was both identifiable and inexcusably ignored

Remove any two of those elements, and the settlement value would have dropped by millions. Remove four, and the case might not have survived summary judgment.

This is the reality of toxic mold litigation in 2026. Courts increasingly require plaintiffs to demonstrate:

Reliable evidence of mold presence and species identification

Meaningful exposure levels, not mere visibility

A scientifically supported connection between that exposure and the specific plaintiff's medical condition

A differential diagnosis ruling out alternative causes

Documentation proving the defendant knew or should have known about the moisture problem

Evidence that response time was unreasonable under the circumstances

Defense experts often concede that mold can cause allergic reactions or asthma exacerbation. But they vigorously contest claims of systemic toxicity, neurological impairment, or immune dysfunction absent strong peer-reviewed support and measurable dose evidence.

As a result, damages are frequently limited to respiratory symptoms, allergy-related conditions, temporary displacement costs, and property loss. Large verdicts and settlements arise when liability evidence is overwhelming, medical proof survives strict admissibility scrutiny, and (critically) when defendants' own records reveal conscious indifference or deliberate concealment.

Why This Field Endures and Evolves

Unlike the predicted mass tort explosion that never materialized, toxic mold litigation persists for structural reasons that ensure its continued relevance:

1. Aging Housing Stock. Deferred maintenance in rental properties, public housing, and older residential developments increases moisture problems. As buildings age without capital improvements, water intrusion becomes not a possibility but a probability.

2. Climate Change. More frequent flooding, increased humidity patterns, atmospheric river events, and extreme weather create mold-prone environments at accelerating rates. What was once a regional concern in humid climates now affects properties nationwide.

3. Urban Density. Multi-family housing amplifies remediation failures. When one unit's moisture problem spreads to adjacent units through shared walls and HVAC systems, individual complaints become coordinated litigation.

4. Insurance Market Dynamics. Tightening mold exclusions, sub-limits on remediation coverage, and aggressive application of anti-concurrent causation clauses generate secondary litigation over coverage interpretation and bad faith claims handling.

5. Public Awareness. Tenants and homeowners are increasingly informed about indoor air quality rights, habitability standards, and disclosure obligations. Post-pandemic attention to ventilation and air quality has heightened sensitivity to environmental conditions.

Unlike asbestos, which was tied to specific products and historical industries, mold is a recurring condition arising wherever moisture meets organic building material. That biological reality ensures continued litigation exposure across all property types, in all jurisdictions, for the foreseeable future.

The Myth and the Reality

The early narrative suggested mold litigation would either collapse as junk science or dominate the courts as the next asbestos.

Neither occurred.

The reality in 2026 is more nuanced and more interesting:

Mold cases are viable but fact-intensive. Success requires mastery of multiple disciplines.

High-value settlements exist but are not routine. They reflect compelling evidence, not fear.

Scientific skepticism limits expansive injury theories. Courts demand peer-reviewed support.

Insurance policy language shapes outcomes as much as liability law. Coverage disputes drive settlement dynamics.

Toxic mold litigation has become a disciplined practice area requiring integration of building science, medical evidence, insurance coverage analysis, statutory compliance, and strategic trial planning.

Consider what actually happened between 2001 and 2026: Mold litigation evolved from speculative toxic tort to specialized construction and property dispute. The field didn't explode. It professionalized.

Attorneys who treat mold as generic premises liability fail. Their cases are dismissed at summary judgment or settle for nuisance value. Those who master building science, environmental sampling protocols, Daubert gatekeeping, and insurance policy interpretation succeed. The difference in outcomes is measured in millions of dollars.

It is not driven by fear but by proof. Not by speculation but by documentation. Not by sensational "black mold" narratives but by evidence that property owners, managers, or contractors knew about preventable moisture intrusion and failed to respond reasonably.

What This Book Provides

This book is written for attorneys, judges, mediators, risk managers, property professionals, and insurance claims specialists who recognize that toxic mold litigation is neither fad nor fringe. It is a durable, evolving field shaped by science, statutory reform, and economic stakes.

Across twenty chapters, this book examines toxic mold litigation from foundation to verdict:

Part I: Scientific and Medical Foundations

The science underlying mold exposure claims and why building science often matters more than mycology

The challenge of proving specific medical causation under modern evidentiary standards

What courts accept, what they question, and what they routinely exclude

Part II: Regulatory and Legislative Frameworks

Federal regulatory guidance and its indirect influence on litigation

The California model and state-by-state legislative evolution

How building codes, disclosure statutes, and rental laws create duty and define breach

Part III: Core Legal Theories and Expanding Liability

Breach of warranty of habitability: the most reliable claim in residential cases

Negligence and construction defect theories when mold signals systemic failure

Failure to disclose in real estate transactions, where honesty matters more than toxicity

Insurance coverage battles and the modern landscape of mold exclusions

Insurance bad faith and the expanding liability of carriers who mishandle claims

The growing roster of defendants: architects, engineers, contractors, and manufacturers

Part IV: Institutional and Large-Scale Litigation

Commercial and multi-family housing claims where scale changes everything

Military housing and government contractor liability amid sovereign immunity complexities

Public housing litigation and the intersection with disability rights

Part V: Trial Practice and Valuation

Damages analysis: from modest respiratory claims to eight-figure settlements

Expert battles and evidentiary strategy: winning the admissibility war

Settlement trends and case valuation in the modern market

Judicial skepticism and how to navigate resistance to expansive injury theories

Trial presentation: translating science into persuasive narrative

Part VI: The Future

Climate change, aging infrastructure, and the forces sustaining this field

Technology, artificial intelligence in environmental testing, and data-driven litigation

Insurance market evolution and legislative possibilities

Predictions for the next decade of mold litigation practice

A Balanced Perspective Without Advocacy Bias

Importantly, this manuscript approaches toxic mold litigation without advocacy bias. It acknowledges both the legitimacy of serious indoor air quality failures and the judicial caution surrounding expansive toxic injury theories that lack scientific validation.

The objective is not to amplify fear of mold nor to dismiss documented harm. Rather, it is to analyze the field as it stands in 2026: technical, fact-intensive, jurisdictionally nuanced, and highly dependent on strategic litigation design.

This book recognizes that:

Some mold cases involve genuine, preventable harm to vulnerable occupants and deserve substantial compensation

Some mold claims rest on speculative causation theories that courts appropriately exclude

Most cases fall somewhere between these extremes, where outcomes depend on evidence quality, expert credibility, and litigation strategy

Success in toxic mold litigation today requires more than photographs of visible growth or reports of persistent odor. It demands environmental testing protocols that withstand cross-examination. It requires medical testimony grounded in reliable methodology and peer-reviewed literature. It depends upon navigating building codes, lease obligations, disclosure statutes, and insurance policy language with precision.

And above all, it requires understanding that mold cases are won not by rhetoric about invisible dangers but by proof of preventable moisture intrusion, unreasonable response, and documented consequences.

Why This Matters Now

As climate-driven moisture events increase, aging housing stock deteriorates, and insurers tighten policy language, toxic mold litigation will continue to evolve. Whether it remains a sustained high-value niche practice or expands into broader systemic reform will depend on the courts, legislatures, insurers, and practitioners who shape it in the coming decade.

For attorneys considering whether to accept a mold case, this book provides the analytical framework to distinguish viable claims from speculative ones. For property managers and developers, it offers insight into prevention strategies and documentation practices that reduce litigation risk. For insurance professionals, it clarifies the coverage and bad faith issues that drive settlement dynamics. For judges and mediators, it explains the scientific and evidentiary complexities that define case value.

The modern toxic mold case is rarely about whether mold exists. Courts and juries understand that mold grows when moisture persists. The question is whether the defendant knew about the moisture problem, whether the response was reasonable, whether exposure caused measurable harm, and whether the claim can survive rigorous scientific scrutiny.

When the answer to all four questions is "yes" (supported by documentation, expert testimony that survives Daubert challenges, and evidence of institutional indifference), settlements can reach eight figures.

When the answer to any one question is "no," case value contracts rapidly, often to property damage and relocation costs alone.

Understanding which cases fall into which category is worth millions of dollars.

The Strategic Roadmap

This book provides that strategic roadmap.

It begins with science because without understanding what mold is, how it grows, and what health effects are medically defensible, no litigation strategy can succeed. It then examines the regulatory and legislative frameworks that define duty and shape reasonable response expectations. From there, it analyzes the core legal theories that drive mold claims, the expanding universe of potential defendants, and the insurance dynamics that often determine settlement feasibility.

The later chapters address trial practice, expert selection, damages valuation, and the evidentiary battles that separate cases that settle for millions from those dismissed at summary judgment. The book concludes by examining the future of this field: how climate change, technology, and evolving insurance markets will shape mold litigation in the years ahead.

Throughout, the emphasis remains constant: **discipline over drama, evidence over emotion, proof over panic.**

The family at Fort Cavazos received $10 million not because their attorney scared a jury with talk of "toxic black mold." They received it because their attorney could prove (with emails, expert testimony, medical records, environmental data, and building science analysis) that their daughter's illness was the direct, foreseeable, and preventable consequence of thirteen months of documented neglect.

That is modern toxic mold litigation.

That is what this book teaches you to recognize, evaluate, and either pursue vigorously or decline strategically.

Welcome to the field. The stakes are high, the science is demanding, and the outcomes are increasingly predictable for those who understand the rules.

Let's begin.

PART I: Scientific and Medical Foundations

1

The Rise of Toxic Mold Litigation in the United States

I. From Sensational Prediction to Specialized Practice

In March 2001, a Texas jury awarded Melinda Ballard $32 million in a mold case against her insurance carrier. The verdict made national headlines. Time Magazine ran a cover story. CNN aired special reports. Insurance companies panicked. Property owners braced for impact. Legal commentators confidently predicted toxic mold would become "the next asbestos."

The tidal wave never came.

Instead, something more interesting happened. Toxic mold litigation evolved.

By 2026, mold litigation in the United States is neither a fleeting trend nor an uncontrollable mass tort. It has matured into a technically complex, jurisdiction-sensitive, and scientifically scrutinized niche practice area. The attorneys who succeed in this space are not general litigators reacting to alarming photographs of black staining. They are specialists who understand building science, medical causation standards, insurance policy construction, and evidentiary gatekeeping.

The journey from sensational panic to disciplined practice reveals essential lessons about how environmental litigation actually develops in American courts. The early predictions weren't entirely wrong. They were premature and oversimplified. Mold litigation did grow. It did generate substantial settlements. It did expand beyond simple landlord-tenant disputes. But it did so in a way that rewarded technical mastery over dramatic rhetoric.

The early panic gave way to discipline. Courts demanded proof. Legislatures clarified duties. Insurers refined exclusions. And practitioners learned that mold cases are won not by rhetoric, but by rigorous causation analysis and strategic framing.

II. The Modern Mold Case: 2024-2026 Trends

Recent years confirm that toxic mold litigation remains a high-stakes field. Between 2024 and 2025, several major settlements underscored the continued viability of well-developed mold claims:

- **$10 million** resolution involving Army housing conditions at Fort Cavazos
- **$6.6 million** Las Vegas residential exposure case
- **$6.5 million** New York City housing violation settlement

But these numbers tell only part of the story. What makes these cases exceptional is not the presence of mold (thousands of properties have mold) but the convergence of specific factors that courts and insurers recognize as creating genuine liability exposure.

The Fort Cavazos case illustrates the pattern perfectly. The settlement wasn't driven by fear of "toxic black mold." It was driven by:

- Fourteen documented tenant complaints over six months
- Internal emails showing management knew about the roof leak for thirteen months
- A contractor's written warning that moisture intrusion was "creating conditions for significant mold amplification"
- Email evidence that remediation was delayed for budgetary reasons

- Medical records showing a three-year-old hospitalized twice for pneumonia during the exposure period
- Environmental testing revealing Stachybotrys concentrations forty times outdoor baseline
- A pediatric pulmonologist whose causation testimony could survive Daubert scrutiny
- Clear building envelope analysis proving the roof defect was both identifiable and inexcusably ignored

Remove half of those elements, and the case value drops by millions. Remove all but two or three, and the case might not survive summary judgment.

These results illustrate several defining trends in modern mold litigation:

1. Rising Settlement Values (But Only When Evidence is Overwhelming)

High-value outcomes are generally associated with:

- Documented moisture intrusion over extended periods (months or years, not days or weeks)
- Internal communications demonstrating delayed remediation (emails, texts, work orders showing knowledge and inaction)
- Vulnerable plaintiffs (children, elderly, immunocompromised residents, pregnant women)
- Clear property damage alongside health complaints (not health claims alone)
- Multiple corroborating evidence sources (not just tenant testimony)

However, these settlements are not typical. They represent the top tier of mold litigation where liability evidence is undeniable and medical proof survives strict admissibility challenges. The average mold case settles for far less, often for property damage, relocation costs, and modest compensation for temporary respiratory symptoms.

Understanding this distribution is critical. Attorneys who approach every visible mold condition expecting seven-figure outcomes will quickly learn that courts and insurance carriers have become sophisticated at distinguishing cases with genuine systemic negligence from routine maintenance disputes.

2. Expansion Beyond Landlord-Tenant Disputes

Modern mold litigation frequently includes:

- Property managers and management companies
- Architects and engineers who designed building systems
- General contractors responsible for construction oversight
- Subcontractors who installed specific building components
- Lumber and building material manufacturers whose products failed
- Coating and paint product companies marketing "mold-resistant" materials
- HVAC designers and installers whose systems created condensation problems
- Waterproofing contractors whose work proved defective

This expansion reflects the growing recognition that mold is often a symptom of systemic building envelope failures, design defects, or construction errors, not merely negligent maintenance. When moisture intrusion results from improper flashing installation during construction, the liability chain extends far beyond the landlord who discovers the problem years later.

In a 2024 Las Vegas case that settled for $6.6 million, the defendant list included not just the property owner but the original developer, the general contractor, the window installation subcontractor, the architect who specified the building envelope system, and the manufacturer of the exterior cladding material. Each defendant had insurance coverage. Each had documentation showing knowledge of moisture management requirements. Each pointed fingers at the others. The resulting settlement reflected the aggregate exposure across multiple parties, not just one negligent landlord.

This multi-party reality has transformed mold litigation from simple premises liability into complex construction defect and products liability cases requiring coordination among multiple expert disciplines and sophisticated allocation analysis.

3. Sophisticated Defense Strategies That Narrow Claims

Defendants now routinely:

- Challenge specific medical causation under Daubert (*Daubert v. Merrell Dow Pharmaceuticals., Inc.*, 509 U.S. 579 (1993)) or Frye (*Frye v. United States*, 293 F. 1013 (D.C. Cir. 1923)) standards
- Limit damages to allergy or asthma exacerbation (excluding systemic injury claims)
- Contest sampling methodologies (timing, protocol, chain of custody)
- Attribute symptoms to alternative environmental factors (seasonal allergies, dust mites, pet dander, smoking)
- Emphasize the absence of federal exposure thresholds
- Present peer-reviewed literature showing limited evidence of systemic toxicity
- Demonstrate prompt response to complaints (when documentation supports it)

As a result, mold litigation has become increasingly science-driven. The dramatic photographs of black staining that once swayed juries now serve merely as evidence that moisture intrusion occurred. The real battle takes place in expert depositions, Daubert hearings, and motion practice over what that moisture intrusion actually caused.

A 2025 case in Ohio illustrates the trend. Plaintiffs discovered extensive Stachybotrys growth behind kitchen cabinets in a rental home. Photographs were disturbing. The landlord had ignored multiple complaints. Environmental testing confirmed significant indoor amplification. The case appeared strong until the defense moved to exclude the plaintiff's medical expert (a clinical ecologist whose causation methodology relied on unvalidated laboratory tests and lacked peer-reviewed support). The court granted the motion. Without admissible medical testimony, the case settled for $75,000, covering property loss and relocation expenses but no medical damages. Five years earlier, the same case might have settled for $500,000 based on jury fear alone.

This represents the maturation of the field. Courts have seen enough mold cases to distinguish between legitimate respiratory injury claims grounded in reliable science and speculative systemic toxicity theories lacking empirical support.

III. Legislative Framework: The California Model and Beyond

No discussion of toxic mold litigation is complete without examining the legislative response that shaped modern practice.

The California Toxic Mold Protection Act (enacted in 2001) remains one of the most frequently cited statutory models. Enacted to address concerns over indoor mold exposure, it directed the development of permissible exposure limits and provided regulatory structure for remediation standards.

But here's what the Act did not do: It did not create automatic liability. It did not establish numeric exposure thresholds that could trigger per se negligence. It did not transform mold litigation into a strict liability regime.

What the Act accomplished was more subtle and more lasting:

It formalized state recognition of mold as a legitimate public health issue. Before the Act, defendants could argue that mold concerns were exaggerated media panic. After the Act, that argument became harder to sustain. The statute acknowledged that indoor mold exposure could pose health risks, even without defining precise thresholds.

It encouraged development of remediation guidelines. While not creating enforceable standards, the Act influenced professional practices. Contractors, property managers, and insurance adjusters could no longer claim ignorance of appropriate response protocols. Industry standards evolved in the statute's wake, creating benchmarks against which conduct could be measured.

It influenced disclosure obligations. The Act heightened awareness that mold and moisture problems constituted material conditions requiring disclosure in real estate transactions. Even though the Act didn't directly create disclosure duties, it shifted expectations about what sellers and landlords should reveal.

It shaped landlord response expectations in habitability disputes. California courts interpreting the implied warranty of habitability increasingly referenced the legislative recognition of mold as a significant environmental concern. The Act didn't create new causes of action, but it strengthened existing ones.

While the Act did not create an automatic private cause of action, it significantly influenced:

- Disclosure obligations in real estate transactions
- Habitability standards in rental housing
- Landlord remediation practices and response timelines
- Building code enforcement priorities and inspection protocols

Other states have taken varied approaches. Some have revised rental statutes to impose clearer moisture-control obligations. Others have strengthened disclosure requirements in real estate transactions. Several jurisdictions are updating building codes to address water intrusion prevention and ventilation standards.

Texas adopted a more structured regulatory approach, implementing licensing requirements for mold assessors and remediators, creating remediation protocols, and requiring certificates of mold remediation following work completion. While some regulatory components evolved over time, Texas continues to emphasize procedural compliance as a key element of reasonable response.

Nevada focused on clarifying landlord maintenance obligations, strengthening tenant remedies for uninhabitable conditions, and enhancing disclosure expectations in residential sales.

New York's approach reflects its dense urban environment, emphasizing municipal housing code enforcement, administrative violation tracking systems, and heightened public scrutiny of delayed remediation in multi-family and public housing contexts.

The legislative trend is clear: prevention and remediation standards are tightening, even if medical causation standards in court remain demanding. States are not defining toxic mold numerically. They are defining reasonable response procedurally.

This shift aligns perfectly with how courts actually evaluate these cases. Judges and juries focus less on parts-per-million measurements and more on whether the property owner responded promptly and reasonably once aware of moisture intrusion.

IV. Insurance Market Retrenchment

In the early 2000s, insurers reacted aggressively to mold litigation by introducing broad mold exclusions. The Ballard verdict and similar high-profile cases triggered what can only be described as panic in the insurance industry.

Over time, these exclusions have evolved into increasingly technical policy language, including:

- Absolute mold exclusions (barring all mold-related coverage regardless of cause)
- Pollution exclusion cross-references (classifying mold as a "pollutant")
- Anti-concurrent causation clauses (denying coverage if an excluded cause contributes in any way)
- Sub-limits for mold-related remediation (capping coverage at $5,000 or $10,000)
- Narrow resulting-loss provisions (defining precisely what consequential damage is covered)

By 2026, insurance coverage disputes are often as significant as the underlying liability claims. In many cases, the insurance battle is the case.

Attorneys must now analyze:

- Whether water damage constitutes a covered peril under the specific policy language
- Whether mold is a "resulting loss" from covered water damage
- Whether remediation costs fall within coverage or within a restrictive sub-limit
- Whether the insurer's handling of the claim constitutes bad faith
- Whether anti-concurrent causation clauses apply when both covered and excluded perils contribute
- Whether pollution exclusions encompass mold or apply only to traditional environmental contaminants

The Fort Cavazos case involved not just the underlying negligence claim but a parallel insurance coverage dispute over whether the property management company's general liability policy covered mold-related claims. The carrier initially denied coverage based on a pollution exclusion. The property management company filed a declaratory judgment action. The underlying plaintiffs asserted bad faith claims. The case ultimately settled with contributions from multiple insurance policies after two years of coverage litigation.

Mold litigation frequently becomes two lawsuits in one: liability and coverage. Understanding both is essential to realistic case evaluation.

The insurance dimension has also influenced case selection. Plaintiffs' attorneys now routinely investigate insurance coverage before filing suit. A strong liability case against an uninsured or underinsured defendant may not be economically viable. Conversely, a modest liability case with clear insurance coverage and potential bad faith exposure may justify aggressive litigation.

V. The Central Battle: Specific Medical Causation

If one principle defines modern toxic mold litigation, it is this:

General causation is rarely enough. Specific causation is decisive.

Courts increasingly require plaintiffs to demonstrate:

1. Reliable evidence of mold presence (not just discoloration but actual species identification)
2. Meaningful exposure levels (not just presence but dose)
3. A scientifically supported connection between that exposure and the specific plaintiff's condition (not just temporal association)
4. A differential diagnosis ruling out alternative causes (systematically addressing other possible explanations)

Defense experts often concede that mold can cause allergic reactions or asthma exacerbation. This concession is strategic. By acknowledging what science clearly supports, defense experts establish credibility before contesting claims they believe lack scientific foundation.

But they vigorously contest claims of systemic toxicity, neurological impairment, or immune dysfunction absent strong peer-reviewed support. The battle lines are clearly drawn:

Generally Accepted by Courts:

- Allergic rhinitis (nasal congestion, sneezing, watery eyes)
- Asthma exacerbation in individuals with pre-existing asthma
- Respiratory irritation (coughing, wheezing, throat irritation)
- Hypersensitivity pneumonitis (in rare, well-documented cases)

Frequently Challenged and Often Excluded:

- Cognitive impairment or "brain fog" attributed to mold exposure
- Chronic inflammatory response syndrome (CIRS)
- Broad immune dysfunction
- Neurological injury absent invasive fungal infection
- Systemic toxicity theories based on mycotoxin exposure

The gap between these categories represents millions of dollars in potential damages. A case limited to allergic symptoms might settle for $25,000 to $75,000. A case involving documented, admissible evidence of chronic respiratory disease caused by prolonged exposure might settle for $250,000 to $750,000. A case involving a child with permanent lung injury supported by unimpeachable medical testimony might reach seven figures.

But a case alleging cognitive impairment, immune dysfunction, and systemic toxicity without peer-reviewed support will likely fail at the expert admissibility stage, regardless of how disturbing the photographs or how sympathetic the plaintiff.

As a result, damages are frequently limited to:

- Respiratory symptoms and their treatment costs
- Allergy-related conditions requiring ongoing management
- Temporary displacement and relocation expenses
- Property loss (personal belongings damaged by mold or remediation)

- Emotional distress tied to living conditions (in jurisdictions permitting such claims)

Large verdicts generally arise when liability evidence is overwhelming and medical proof survives admissibility scrutiny. The combination is rarer than most new practitioners expect.

VI. Jurisdictional Nuance: Why Location Matters More Than Mold Species

Not all jurisdictions treat mold claims equally. Forum selection can materially impact case valuation in ways that have nothing to do with the underlying facts.

Some courts:

- Permit broader expert testimony under more lenient admissibility standards
- Allow emotional distress claims without requiring physical injury
- Interpret habitability statutes expansively, creating strong tenant protections
- Apply plaintiff-friendly causation presumptions in certain contexts
- Award attorney's fees routinely in landlord-tenant disputes

Others:

- Apply strict Daubert standards that exclude speculative medical theories
- Limit non-economic damages through statutory caps or restrictive judicial interpretation
- Dismiss systemic illness theories at summary judgment absent extraordinary scientific support
- Enforce insurance exclusions broadly, limiting coverage-driven settlements
- Require physical injury before permitting emotional distress recovery

Consider two hypothetical cases with identical facts:

Case A: Filed in California state court in San Francisco

- Strong tenant protection statutes
- Habitability doctrine interpreted broadly
- Emotional distress damages available without physical injury
- Daubert standard applied but with some flexibility for clinical judgment
- Attorney's fees recoverable under landlord-tenant statute
- Jury pool with high cost-of-living awareness
- Settlement value: $300,000 to $500,000

Case B: Filed in rural Texas state court

- More limited tenant statutory protections
- Habitability claims viable but narrowly construed
- Emotional distress requires physical injury in most circumstances
- Strict application of reliability standards to medical causation
- Attorney's fees generally not recoverable absent specific statutory provision
- Jury pool with lower damage expectations
- Settlement value: $75,000 to $150,000

Same mold. Same moisture intrusion. Same health complaints. Different outcomes based purely on jurisdiction.

For practitioners, forum selection (where permissible) can materially impact case value. For defendants, understanding jurisdictional differences helps calibrate settlement authority. For insurers, geographic exposure varies substantially based on local law.

VII. Why Mold Litigation Endures: The Structural Forces

Toxic mold litigation continues to grow for reasons that have nothing to do with litigation trends and everything to do with structural realities:

1. Aging Housing Stock

Deferred maintenance increases moisture problems. As buildings age without capital improvements, roofs deteriorate, plumbing systems fail, building envelopes degrade, and ventilation systems become inadequate. The average age of U.S. housing stock continues to increase. So does the probability of moisture intrusion.

In public housing, budget constraints often force maintenance deferrals. In private rental housing, property owners may delay capital improvements to maximize short-term returns. In condominium developments, homeowners associations may underfund reserve accounts, leaving critical repairs unaddressed until failures become catastrophic.

This creates a predictable pipeline of future mold litigation. The buildings most likely to generate mold claims in 2030 already exist. They're aging today.

2. Climate Change

More flooding, humidity, and extreme weather events create mold-prone environments. What was once a regional concern in humid coastal areas now affects properties nationwide.

Atmospheric river events on the West Coast, increased hurricane intensity in the Southeast and Gulf regions, more frequent severe storms in the Midwest, and rapid freeze-thaw cycles in northern states all contribute to moisture intrusion that building envelopes designed decades ago cannot handle.

Climate-driven moisture events are not speculative. They're documented, accelerating, and creating exactly the conditions (prolonged moisture exposure to organic building materials) that generate mold growth and litigation.

3. Urban Density

Multi-family housing amplifies remediation failures. When moisture intrusion affects one unit in a 200-unit apartment complex, inadequate response can spread contamination through shared walls, common HVAC systems, and building-wide plumbing stacks.

Single-family detached homes contain moisture problems within one structure. Multi-family buildings can transform isolated failures into systemic exposure affecting dozens of families, creating the pattern evidence and aggregate damages that drive high-value settlements.

4. Insurance Limitations

Coverage disputes generate secondary litigation. As insurers continue tightening mold exclusions and sub-limits, property owners face larger out-of-pocket exposure. This creates incentives to litigate coverage issues aggressively. It also creates bad faith exposure when carriers deny arguably covered claims.

The insurance dimension ensures that even when underlying liability is modest, coverage disputes can drive extended litigation and substantial settlements.

5. Public Awareness

Tenants and homeowners are increasingly informed about indoor air quality rights. Post-pandemic attention to ventilation, air filtration, and indoor environmental conditions has heightened awareness of mold as a legitimate concern (though not necessarily as the toxic threat early media coverage suggested).

Tenants now understand habitability standards. Homeowners know about disclosure obligations. Buyers expect transparency about moisture history. This awareness translates into earlier reporting of problems, documentation of complaints, and willingness to pursue legal remedies when response is inadequate.

Unlike asbestos, mold is not tied to a single product or historical industry. It is a recurring condition arising wherever moisture meets organic building material. That reality ensures continued litigation exposure.

The question is not whether mold litigation will continue. It will. The question is whether individual cases are prosecuted competently, with realistic expectations grounded in scientific and legal realities.

VIII. The Myth and the Reality: What Actually Happened

The early narrative suggested mold litigation would either collapse as junk science or dominate the courts as a mass tort.

Neither occurred.

Instead, something more interesting happened. The field professionalized.

Consider what actually happened between 2001 and 2026: Mold litigation evolved from speculative toxic tort to specialized construction and property dispute. Attorneys who treat mold as generic premises liability fail. Their cases are dismissed at summary judgment or settle for nuisance value. Those who master building science, environmental sampling protocols, Daubert gatekeeping, and insurance policy interpretation succeed. The difference in outcomes is measured in millions of dollars.

The reality in 2026 is more nuanced:

- Mold cases are viable but fact-intensive (success requires documentation, not just allegations)
- High-value settlements exist but are not routine (they reflect overwhelming evidence of negligence plus admissible medical causation)
- Scientific skepticism limits expansive injury theories (courts demand peer-reviewed support, not clinical judgment alone)
- Insurance policy language shapes outcomes as much as liability law (coverage determines whether settlement funds are available)

Toxic mold litigation has become a disciplined practice area requiring integration of:

- Building science (understanding how water moves through building assemblies)
- Medical evidence (distinguishing accepted respiratory effects from speculative systemic claims)
- Insurance coverage analysis (interpreting complex exclusions and resulting-loss provisions)
- Statutory compliance (navigating state-specific landlord-tenant, disclosure, and building code requirements)
- Strategic trial planning (knowing when to settle, when to fight, and

when to walk away)

- It is not driven by fear but by proof. Not by speculation but by documentation. Not by sensational "black mold" narratives but by evidence that property owners knew about preventable moisture intrusion and failed to respond reasonably.

This evolution has been positive for the field's legitimacy but challenging for attorneys expecting easy recoveries. The cases that settle for millions are winnable precisely because they deserve to. The cases that fail at summary judgment generally should fail. The system, over time, has separated legitimate claims from speculative ones with increasing accuracy.

IX. A Roadmap for the Chapters Ahead

This book examines toxic mold litigation from foundation to verdict:

Chapters 2-3 establish the scientific and medical foundations, explaining what mold is, how courts evaluate exposure evidence, and why specific medical causation is the battlefield that determines case value.

Chapters 4-6 analyze the regulatory and legislative landscape, from federal guidance to state-specific statutes, showing how legal duties arise and what "reasonable response" actually means.

Chapters 7-12 examine core legal theories (habitability, negligence, construction defect, failure to disclose, insurance coverage, and bad faith), showing how different claims apply in different contexts and which defendants face exposure.

Chapters 13-14 address institutional and large-scale litigation, where military housing, public housing, and multi-family developments present unique challenges and opportunities.

Chapters 15-19 focus on valuation, expert strategy, settlement dynamics, judicial skepticism, and trial presentation, providing practical guidance for navigating cases from filing through verdict.

Chapter 20 examines the future, considering how climate change, technology, insurance market evolution, and legislative trends will shape mold litigation in the coming decade.

Chapter 1 establishes the context: toxic mold litigation in America is no longer speculative, sensational, or simplistic. It is a specialized, evolving field defined by high evidentiary standards and substantial financial exposure.

But it is also a field where competent practitioners with realistic expectations and disciplined case development can achieve meaningful results for clients harmed by preventable moisture intrusion and institutional indifference.

The chapters that follow provide the tools to navigate it successfully.

Understanding that mold litigation has matured from panic to professionalism is the first step. The second step is mastering the science that courts now demand. That's where Chapter 2 begins.

2

The Science of Mold and Indoor Air Quality

Foundations for Toxic Mold Litigation

I. When Science Determines Everything

The environmental consultant's report showed Stachybotrys concentrations forty times outdoor baseline levels. The photographs were disturbing: black staining covering an entire bedroom wall behind a dresser that hadn't been moved in two years. The medical records documented three emergency room visits for respiratory distress. The landlord's own text messages acknowledged the roof leak had persisted "for months, maybe longer."

The case was dismissed before trial.

Why? Because the plaintiff's medical expert testified that mycotoxins from Stachybotrys had caused "systemic immune dysfunction and neurological impairment." When pressed on cross-examination about measurable mycotoxin levels in the apartment, he admitted no air sampling for toxins had been conducted. When asked about peer-reviewed studies supporting his causation theory in residential exposure scenarios, he cited case reports and clinical experience. When confronted with the absence of federal exposure standards, he stated that "the presence of toxic mold speaks for itself."

The court excluded his testimony under Daubert. Without admissible medical causation evidence, the case collapsed to a property damage claim that settled for $18,000.

Had the same expert limited his testimony to respiratory irritation and allergic rhinitis (both well-supported by the environmental and medical evidence), the case would likely have survived summary judgment and settled for $150,000 to $250,000. The overreach cost the plaintiff over $100,000 in potential recovery.

This chapter exists to prevent that outcome. In modern toxic mold litigation, science is not peripheral. It is determinative. Unlike traditional premises liability cases, toxic mold claims require proof of exposure, dose, biological mechanism, and medical consequence. The courtroom becomes a forum for microbiology, building science, immunology, toxicology, and epidemiology.

Without scientific credibility, even the most visually disturbing evidence of mold growth rarely sustains significant verdicts. Courts increasingly demand reliable methodology and measurable proof. Accordingly, attorneys must understand not only legal doctrine but the underlying environmental and medical science that drives admissibility and valuation.

Understanding mold litigation begins with understanding mold itself.

II. What Mold Is (and Is Not)

Mold is a naturally occurring fungus that reproduces through microscopic spores. Spores are ubiquitous in both indoor and outdoor environments. Their mere presence does not establish contamination, toxicity, or liability.

Walk outside on any given day and you are inhaling mold spores. Open your windows and spores drift inside. This is normal. This is unavoidable. This is not actionable.

Instead, litigation typically centers on **indoor amplification** caused by sustained moisture intrusion. The key question is not whether mold spores are present (they always are) but whether conditions inside the property allowed dramatic proliferation that created exposure levels substantially exceeding normal background concentrations.

Common genera referenced in toxic mold cases include:

- *Stachybotrys* (often referred to as "black mold")
- *Aspergillus*
- *Penicillium*
- *Cladosporium*
- *Alternaria*

Each has distinct environmental behaviors and medical implications. Understanding these differences matters in litigation because defense experts will exploit imprecise claims that lump all "toxic mold" together.

Stachybotrys chartarum

Often identified as *Stachybotrys chartarum*, this mold became widely known as "toxic black mold" during the litigation wave of the early 2000s. The name stuck, though it's scientifically misleading. Not all black-appearing mold is Stachybotrys. Not all Stachybotrys produces toxins. And the color is irrelevant to toxicity.

Stachybotrys thrives on cellulose-rich building materials such as drywall and ceiling tiles when exposed to prolonged moisture. It requires sustained wet conditions (not just dampness but saturation) and grows relatively slowly compared to other mold species. It became notorious due to alleged mycotoxin production, particularly trichothecenes.

However, its presence alone does not establish airborne toxicity. Stachybotrys typically requires sustained wet conditions and physical disturbance to aerosolize spores. Unlike some mold species that release spores readily into the air, Stachybotrys spores tend to remain attached to surfaces unless disturbed through demolition, aggressive cleaning, or remediation activities.

This matters in litigation. Defense experts will argue that visible Stachybotrys growth on an undisturbed wall does not necessarily create significant airborne exposure. They will point out that spore trap air samples may show relatively low Stachybotrys counts even when surface growth is extensive. They will emphasize that mycotoxin production requires specific moisture and nutrient conditions that may or may not exist in a given property.

Plaintiffs must be prepared to counter these arguments with evidence of disturbance (ongoing water intrusion, occupant activity near contaminated areas, HVAC systems pulling spores from wall cavities) or with surface sampling demonstrating the extent of colonization even if airborne levels appear modest.

Aspergillus

A common indoor and outdoor mold, *Aspergillus* species are frequently associated with allergic responses and asthma exacerbation. In immunocompromised individuals, certain species (particularly *Aspergillus fumigatus*) may cause invasive infections (aspergillosis) that can be life-threatening.

In litigation, defense experts often concede Aspergillus's allergenic potential while disputing claims of systemic toxicity in otherwise healthy individuals. This strategic concession allows defense counsel to acknowledge that something real happened (the plaintiff experienced respiratory symptoms) while limiting the scope of compensable injury.

Aspergillus is so common in both indoor and outdoor environments that its presence alone rarely establishes negligence. The question becomes whether indoor concentrations significantly exceeded outdoor baselines and whether those elevated levels persisted long enough to cause the plaintiff's specific symptoms.

Penicillium

Widely present in indoor environments following water intrusion, *Penicillium* species can proliferate rapidly on a variety of materials including wallpaper, carpet, mattresses, and upholstered furniture. They are commonly identified in air sampling reports and frequently cited in habitability disputes.

Like Aspergillus, Penicillium is ubiquitous. Its presence is expected in virtually all indoor environments at low levels. Litigation focuses on whether moisture intrusion allowed amplification to levels that materially affected habitability and health.

Cladosporium and Alternaria

These outdoor molds frequently enter buildings through open windows and doors. They can also grow indoors on damp surfaces. They are common allergens but rarely associated with serious illness in healthy individuals.

Defense experts often point to elevated Cladosporium or Alternaria levels as evidence that the plaintiff's symptoms may be caused by seasonal outdoor allergens rather than indoor mold growth related to moisture intrusion. This argument is particularly effective when air sampling was conducted during spring or fall when outdoor mold spore counts peak naturally.

Plaintiffs must be prepared to distinguish between transient outdoor mold that happens to be detected in indoor samples and actual indoor amplification caused by water damage.

III. Mold vs. Moisture: The Critical Legal Distinction

Scientifically, mold growth requires three conditions:

1. Moisture (relative humidity above 60% or actual water presence)
2. Organic substrate (wood, drywall, ceiling tiles, carpet, fabric)
3. Suitable temperature (typically between 40°F and 100°F, which includes most inhabited spaces)

Eliminate any one of these three conditions and mold cannot grow. Add all three and mold growth is inevitable, usually within 24 to 48 hours of water intrusion.

Legally, the root cause (moisture intrusion) is often more significant than the fungal organism itself.

Courts frequently focus on:

- Plumbing leaks (burst pipes, slow leaks, condensation)
- Roof failures (missing shingles, deteriorated flashing, damaged membranes)
- Improper flashing or window installation (allowing water penetration at building envelope transitions)
- HVAC condensation (improperly sized or maintained systems creating moisture)
- Flooding or storm damage (natural disasters or drainage failures)
- Building envelope defects (systemic design or construction failures allowing chronic intrusion)

In many cases, mold is evidence of an underlying construction defect or negligent maintenance rather than an independent harm. As a result, successful litigation often hinges on proving the source, duration, and foreseeability of water intrusion.

Case in Focus: The Window Installation Defect

In a 2024 Nevada case, a homeowner discovered extensive mold growth in wall cavities behind bedroom drywall. Environmental testing identified multiple species including Stachybotrys and Aspergillus. The homeowner's attorney initially focused on the mold itself, retaining a medical expert to testify about mycotoxin exposure.

During discovery, a building envelope expert traced the moisture source to improperly installed windows. The original contractor had failed to install flashing according to manufacturer specifications and building code requirements. For seven years, rainwater had been slowly penetrating the building envelope during storms, saturating the wall cavity insulation and creating perfect conditions for mold growth.

The case ultimately settled for $450,000. But the settlement was driven not by mycotoxin testimony (which was never offered) but by building science evidence proving:

- The window installation violated code
- The defect was identifiable and should have been caught during construction inspection
- The chronic moisture intrusion was the direct result of the installation failure
- The mold growth was the inevitable consequence of that sustained moisture

The mold was the symptom. The construction defect was the cause. The litigation strategy shifted accordingly, and the result followed.

IV. Mycotoxins and the Controversy Over "Toxic Mold"

Mycotoxins are secondary metabolites produced by certain mold species under specific environmental conditions. They form the scientific basis for claims alleging systemic illness from indoor exposure beyond simple allergic responses.

Understanding mycotoxins requires understanding what they are and (equally important) what the science actually says about residential exposure.

Mycotoxins are toxic compounds produced by fungi, primarily as byproducts of mold metabolism. They include:

- **Trichothecenes** (produced by some Stachybotrys strains)
- **Aflatoxins** (produced by some Aspergillus species, primarily in agricultural settings)
- **Ochratoxin A** (produced by some Aspergillus and Penicillium species)
- **Fumonisins** (produced primarily by Fusarium species in agricultural settings)

These compounds are well-documented toxins in certain contexts. Agricultural workers exposed to moldy grain can experience acute illness. Food contaminated with aflatoxins poses cancer risks. Laboratory animals exposed to high doses of purified mycotoxins show toxic effects.

But translating these findings to typical residential exposure scenarios involves enormous scientific leaps that courts increasingly scrutinize.

However, mycotoxin-based claims face substantial evidentiary challenges:

- **Lack of established indoor exposure thresholds.** No regulatory agency has defined what concentration of airborne mycotoxins in residential settings constitutes a health hazard. Without established thresholds, experts cannot testify that measured levels (assuming measurement even occurred) exceeded safe limits.
- **Limited dose-response data in residential settings.** Most mycotoxin research involves agricultural or industrial exposures, ingestion of contaminated food, or laboratory studies using purified toxins at concentrations far exceeding residential scenarios. Extrapolating from these contexts to a family living in a home with visible mold growth requires assumptions that defense experts effectively challenge.
- **Variability in laboratory testing methodologies.** Testing for airborne mycotoxins is technically challenging and expensive.

Different laboratories use different methodologies. Results are difficult to interpret without established reference ranges. Chain of custody issues arise frequently.

- **Difficulty proving biologically significant airborne concentrations.** Even when mycotoxins are detected in dust samples or air samples, establishing that concentrations were sufficient to cause the plaintiff's specific symptoms is extraordinarily difficult. Defense experts will point out that detection does not equal toxicity, that mycotoxins degrade over time, and that the timing of sampling relative to exposure is often unclear.

Courts increasingly require plaintiffs to demonstrate not only the presence of a mold species capable of producing toxins but measurable exposure levels sufficient to cause the alleged medical condition through a biologically plausible mechanism.

Defense experts frequently argue that:

- Most residential mold exposure produces allergic or irritant effects (which are real and compensable but do not support claims of systemic toxicity)
- Severe systemic toxicity from airborne mycotoxin exposure is rare in typical indoor environments absent extraordinary circumstances
- Environmental sampling does not reliably establish dose (a snapshot air sample does not reflect chronic exposure)
- Laboratory detection of mycotoxins in dust or bulk samples does not prove airborne inhalation at toxic levels

Accordingly, expansive "toxic mold syndrome" theories often encounter admissibility challenges under modern evidentiary standards.

Practitioner Warning:

ADMISSIBILITY ALERT

Never promise systemic mycotoxin injury damages before your medical expert has been thoroughly vetted for Daubert/Frye admissibility. The words "toxic mold" in a complaint set expectations that may be impossible to meet scientifically. Consider framing claims around documented respiratory effects and property damage first. Mycotoxin theories can be added if expert review confirms they will survive scrutiny, but leading with them risks case-killing exclusion orders.

V. Indoor Air Quality Testing: Tools and Limitations

Environmental consultants employ various testing methodologies. Each has strengths and limitations that become focal points in litigation. Understanding what each test can and cannot prove is essential for both evaluating expert reports and cross-examining opposing experts.

1. Air Sampling

Common methods include:

Spore Trap Sampling (Non-viable): Captures airborne particles on a sticky surface inside a collection device. Laboratory analysis identifies and counts spore types by microscopic examination. Results are typically expressed as spores per cubic meter of air (spores/m^3).

Culture-Based Sampling (Viable): Collects airborne spores on growth media. Viable spores germinate and are counted after incubation. This method identifies living spores capable of reproduction but may undercount total exposure because not all spores are viable.

Results are typically compared to outdoor baseline counts or to reference databases showing typical indoor levels in non-water-damaged buildings.

Strengths:

- Provides quantitative data on airborne spore concentrations
- Can identify dominant mold species present
- Comparison to outdoor samples helps identify indoor amplification
- Results are relatively easy to explain to juries (numbers matter)

Limitations:

- **Snapshot-in-time measurements:** A single air sample represents 5-10 minutes of air collection. It does not reflect conditions hours earlier or days later. Mold levels fluctuate based on occupant activity, HVAC operation, weather, and countless other variables.

- **Variability based on occupant activity or disturbance:** Walking near contaminated areas, opening doors, running fans, or conducting cleaning activities can temporarily elevate spore counts dramatically. Conversely, leaving a property vacant and undisturbed can produce artificially low readings.
- **Absence of universally accepted "safe" indoor thresholds:** There is no OSHA permissible exposure limit for mold spores in residential settings. There is no EPA numerical standard. Professional organizations provide general guidance (e.g., indoor levels should not significantly exceed outdoor levels), but these are not enforceable regulations.
- **Timing relative to remediation:** Sampling conducted after partial remediation may show reduced levels that do not reflect historic exposure. Sampling conducted during active remediation may show elevated levels that overstate typical occupant exposure.

Air sampling can suggest amplification, but rarely proves toxic dose. It establishes that something was present in measurable quantities at the moment of sampling. It does not, by itself, prove causation.

2. Surface Sampling

Tape Lifts: Adhesive tape is pressed against a surface, capturing mold growth. The sample is examined microscopically to identify mold species present.

Swab Samples: A sterile swab is rubbed across a surface and submitted for laboratory analysis (either microscopic examination or culture).

Bulk Samples: Pieces of contaminated material (drywall, carpet, insulation) are collected and analyzed.

Strengths:

- Confirms species identification of visible growth
- Useful for documenting extent of contamination
- Can identify hidden growth when wall cavities are accessed
- Directly demonstrates that specific materials are contaminated

Limitations:

- Does not demonstrate airborne exposure
- Does not prove health risk (surface contamination may not become airborne)
- Presence on surfaces does not necessarily correlate with breathing zone concentrations

Surface sampling can confirm visible growth but does not necessarily demonstrate airborne exposure or medical risk. It answers the question "what is growing here?" but not "did the plaintiff breathe harmful levels?"

3. Moisture Mapping

Moisture Meters: Handheld devices measure moisture content in building materials. Readings indicate whether materials are dry, damp, or wet.

Infrared Thermography: Thermal imaging cameras detect temperature differences that may indicate hidden moisture (wet materials appear cooler due to evaporative cooling).

Hygrometers: Measure relative humidity in the air.

From a liability perspective, moisture mapping often carries more weight than spore counts because it establishes the existence and duration of water intrusion. It provides objective evidence that the conditions necessary for mold growth existed.

Strengths:

- Identifies active moisture problems requiring immediate attention
- Locates hidden leaks and intrusion sources
- Provides visual documentation (thermal images are compelling)
- Demonstrates scope of water damage

Limitations:

- Does not directly prove mold growth or health effects
- Requires interpretation by qualified inspector
- Single measurements do not establish duration of moisture problem

In litigation, moisture documentation is often the strongest evidence because it proves the landlord, property owner, or contractor had (or should have had) reason to know that conditions conducive to mold growth existed.

Case in Focus: When Moisture Evidence Drives Settlement

A 2025 Maryland case involved a family living in a rental home with periodic musty odors and visible discoloration in one bedroom corner. Air sampling showed Penicillium and Cladosporium at levels only slightly above outdoor baseline. The landlord argued the levels were insignificant and that outdoor allergens explained the family's symptoms.

During inspection, moisture mapping revealed that the corner wall cavity had a moisture content of 35% (normal is below 15%). Infrared imaging showed moisture intrusion extending behind drywall across a 6-foot section. Further investigation traced the moisture to a slow plumbing leak that had been active for at least eighteen months based on visible water staining on floor joists in the basement directly below.

The case settled for $185,000. The settlement was driven not by dramatic spore counts but by objective moisture evidence proving:

- Long-term water intrusion existed
- The landlord had been notified of plumbing issues previously
- The conditions necessary for mold growth had persisted for over a year
- Remediation required substantial demolition and reconstruction

The moisture data established breach. The medical evidence (limited to respiratory irritation) established damages. The combination was sufficient.

VI. In Litigation: How Environmental Reports Are Scrutinized

Environmental reports are scrutinized for:

- **Proper sampling protocol:** Did the consultant follow recognized industry standards (AIHA, ACGIH, IICRC)? Were samples collected systematically or haphazardly?
- **Chain of custody documentation:** Can the samples be traced

from collection to laboratory analysis without breaks that might compromise results?

- **Laboratory accreditation:** Is the laboratory AIHA-LAP, LLC accredited or otherwise recognized? Are quality control procedures documented?
- **Consistency with industry standards:** Are methods and interpretations consistent with guidelines from organizations like AIHA (American Industrial Hygiene Association), ACGIH (American Conference of Governmental Industrial Hygienists), or IICRC (Institute of Inspection, Cleaning and Restoration Certification)?
- **Qualifications of the inspector:** Is the consultant a certified industrial hygienist (CIH), certified mold inspector, or otherwise qualified? What is their training and experience?
- **Sampling conditions:** Were samples collected during normal occupancy conditions or under artificially disturbed conditions? Were outdoor samples collected for comparison? Were weather conditions noted?

Reports lacking methodological rigor are vulnerable to exclusion or diminished weight. Defense experts will dissect every aspect of environmental testing, looking for grounds to argue that results are unreliable, unrepresentative, or scientifically meaningless.

Conversely, a thoroughly documented environmental report following recognized protocols becomes a powerful litigation tool that withstands even aggressive cross-examination.

VII. Health Effects: Accepted and Contested

The most widely accepted health effects associated with indoor mold exposure include:

Generally Accepted by Courts:

Allergic Rhinitis: Nasal congestion, sneezing, runny nose, itchy eyes. This is by far the most common mold-related health complaint. Courts routinely accept that mold exposure can cause or exacerbate allergic symptoms in sensitized individuals.

Asthma Exacerbation: Worsening of pre-existing asthma symptoms including wheezing, shortness of breath, chest tightness, and coughing. The Institute of Medicine (now the National Academy of Medicine) found sufficient evidence linking indoor dampness and mold to asthma exacerbation.

Irritant Symptoms: Eye, nose, and throat irritation in individuals exposed to high concentrations of mold spores, even without allergic sensitization. These symptoms result from physical irritation rather than immune response.

Hypersensitivity Pneumonitis: A rare inflammatory lung condition caused by repeated inhalation of specific antigens. In the mold context, it typically requires heavy occupational exposure but can occur in residential settings with extreme contamination. This condition requires clear clinical diagnosis, not just symptoms.

These conditions align with established immunologic and irritant responses to mold spores. Expert testimony supporting these diagnoses generally survives admissibility challenges when properly documented.

Less Widely Accepted and Frequently Challenged:

Cognitive Impairment: Claims of "brain fog," memory problems, difficulty concentrating, or other neurological symptoms attributed to mold exposure. Courts are skeptical absent evidence of invasive fungal infection reaching the central nervous system (extraordinarily rare in immunocompetent individuals).

Chronic Inflammatory Response Syndrome (CIRS): A controversial diagnosis involving a constellation of symptoms allegedly caused by exposure to water-damaged buildings. Some practitioners believe this represents a legitimate biotoxin-mediated illness. Most courts view it with skepticism due to limited peer-reviewed validation and lack of generally accepted diagnostic criteria.

Broad Immune Dysfunction: Claims that mold exposure caused general immune system compromise, increased susceptibility to infections, or autoimmune conditions. These claims typically lack sufficient scientific support in residential exposure contexts.

Neurological Injury Absent Invasive Infection: Claims of peripheral neuropathy, balance problems, or other neurological deficits attributed to mycotoxin exposure. Absent documented invasive fungal infection (which requires severe immunocompromise), these claims face substantial admissibility challenges.

Courts increasingly require peer-reviewed support and reliable differential diagnosis before permitting systemic injury theories to reach a jury. The gap between accepted respiratory effects and contested systemic illness represents the battleground where most mold cases are won or lost.

What Mold Actually Feels Like: Testimony That Survives Cross-Examination

When plaintiffs testify about their symptoms, credibility and specificity matter. Compare these two approaches:

Ineffective Testimony (Too Vague, Easily Challenged): "I felt sick all the time. I had headaches and couldn't think straight. I knew it was the mold making me toxic. I could feel the toxins in my body."

This testimony invites devastating cross-examination about alternative causes, subjective attribution, and lack of medical foundation.

Effective Testimony (Specific, Temporal, Documented): "Before we discovered the mold in July 2024, I had no history of respiratory problems. Within two weeks of moving into the apartment, I started waking up congested every morning. I'd cough for the first hour after waking. My symptoms were worst in the bedroom where we later found the wall contamination. When I spent weekends at my parents' house, my symptoms improved. I saw Dr. Martinez three times between August and October. He prescribed allergy medication and a rescue inhaler. When we moved out in November, my symptoms resolved within a week."

This testimony demonstrates temporal correlation, specificity, medical treatment, and improvement upon cessation of exposure. It's harder to challenge because it sticks to observable facts rather than speculative causation theories.

VIII. A Defensible Medical Case Requires:

- **Documented temporal relationship between exposure and symptoms:** Did symptoms begin after exposure started? Did they improve upon relocation? Did they recur upon re-entry? Temporal association alone is not sufficient, but its absence is often fatal.

- **Clinical findings consistent with known mold-related conditions:** Are the symptoms (congestion, wheezing, coughing, eye irritation) consistent with allergic rhinitis or asthma? Or are they vague complaints (fatigue, malaise, "brain fog") that could have countless causes?

- **Exclusion of alternative causes:** Did the physician consider and rule out seasonal allergies, dust mite exposure, pet dander, smoking, occupational exposures, viral illness, pre-existing conditions, and other common causes of respiratory symptoms? A differential diagnosis that fails to address obvious alternatives is vulnerable to exclusion.

- **Treatment consistent with diagnosis:** Did the physician prescribe medications appropriate for mold-related allergic or asthma symptoms? Or did they recommend unproven treatments or laboratory tests lacking scientific validation?

- **Peer-reviewed support for causation theory:** Can the expert cite published literature supporting the connection between residential mold exposure and the plaintiff's specific condition? Or does the opinion rest solely on clinical judgment and case reports?

Without this foundation, damages may be limited to temporary respiratory symptoms or relocation expenses. With it, medical damages can substantially increase case value.

IX. The Absence of Federal Exposure Standards: Why This Matters

One of the defining challenges in toxic mold litigation is the absence of federal indoor mold exposure limits.

There is no OSHA residential permissible exposure limit for mold spores. Federal agencies provide remediation guidance but do not establish enforceable numerical standards. The EPA has explicitly stated it does not have authority to regulate mold in indoor air and has not set federal standards.

This regulatory vacuum creates litigation ambiguity:

Plaintiffs argue that significant indoor amplification is inherently unsafe. They point to professional guidelines suggesting indoor levels should not substantially exceed outdoor levels. They emphasize that visible mold growth indicates a moisture problem requiring correction. They argue that the absence of standards should not shield defendants from liability for obvious contamination.

Defendants argue that without defined thresholds, claims of toxicity are speculative. They emphasize that detection of mold (which is ubiquitous) does not equal danger. They point out that professional organizations deliberately avoided setting numeric thresholds because scientific evidence does not support them. They argue that litigation should not impose standards that regulators declined to establish.

As a result, expert testimony becomes the primary mechanism for defining risk. The battle is not over whether spore counts exceeded a regulatory limit (no such limit exists) but over whether the environmental conditions were unreasonable and whether exposure caused the plaintiff's specific symptoms.

This is why building science and moisture documentation often matter more than spore counts. Courts understand that preventing prolonged moisture intrusion is reasonable. They understand that ignoring roof leaks or plumbing failures is negligent. They are less persuaded by arguments that a specific spore concentration crossed an invisible threshold into toxicity.

X. Building Science: The Often Decisive Discipline

In many mold cases, the most influential expert is not a physician but a building envelope specialist.

Key areas of analysis include:

- **Flashing and waterproofing systems:** How was the building envelope designed to shed water? Were transitions between materials (window to wall, roof to wall, balcony to interior) properly detailed? Was flashing installed according to manufacturer specifications and building code?
- **Drainage plane design:** Does the building envelope include proper drainage planes to channel water away from interior cavities? Are weep holes or drainage channels present and functional?

- **Vapor barrier integrity:** Are vapor barriers installed on the correct side of the insulation for the climate zone? Are they continuous or compromised by penetrations?

- **HVAC sizing and ventilation:** Is the HVAC system properly sized for the space? Does it provide adequate ventilation to control humidity? Are condensate drain lines clear and functional?

- **Condensation control:** In climate-controlled spaces, are there cold surfaces (single-pane windows, uninsulated exterior walls) where condensation forms during temperature differentials?

- **Window and roofing installation:** Were windows installed according to manufacturers' installation instructions? Are roof penetrations (vents, chimneys, skylights) properly flashed?

A scientifically grounded building science evaluation can establish:

- **Source of intrusion:** Where exactly is water entering the building envelope? Is it from above (roof), from the side (windows, walls), or from below (foundation, plumbing)?

- **Duration of exposure:** How long has moisture been present? Can the expert determine this from wood rot patterns, rust staining, mold growth extent, or other forensic indicators?

- **Scope of contamination:** How many wall cavities are affected? Is the problem isolated or systemic? Does it affect multiple units in a multi-family building?

- **Reasonableness of remediation efforts:** Were repairs adequate? Was the moisture source corrected? Was contaminated material properly removed? Were industry protocols followed?

Absent credible engineering analysis, medical causation arguments often lack structural foundation. Courts and juries want to understand how water got into the building and why it wasn't fixed. Building science answers those questions more persuasively than mycotoxin theories.

Case in Focus: Building Science Trumps Mycotoxin Claims

A 2024 Washington case involved a family claiming serious health effects from Stachybotrys exposure in their rental home. The plaintiff's medical expert offered testimony about mycotoxin-induced immune dysfunction. The defendant moved to exclude the testimony as unreliable.

Before the Daubert hearing occurred, the plaintiff's building envelope expert testified at deposition. He explained that the moisture intrusion resulted from a defective roof valley installation that violated both manufacturer specifications and building code requirements. He demonstrated that the landlord had received complaints about roof leaks three years earlier, had performed superficial patching, but had never addressed the underlying installation defect. He showed photographs of extensive water staining on roof decking, indicating years of chronic leakage. He calculated that proper repair and remediation would cost $125,000.

The case settled for $340,000 before the medical expert was ever deposed. The building science testimony alone created sufficient liability exposure that the insurance carrier recommended settlement to avoid trial on negligence and breach of habitability claims. The mycotoxin testimony became irrelevant because the case settled on construction defect and property damage theories.

This pattern repeats frequently. Strong building science evidence often drives settlement even when medical causation is contested.

XI. Remediation Standards and Secondary Liability

Professional remediation typically involves:

- **Isolation and containment:** Creating negative pressure barriers to prevent spore migration to unaffected areas
- **Negative air pressure:** Using HEPA-filtered air scrubbers to maintain pressure differentials
- **HEPA filtration:** Filtering air to remove airborne spores during demolition and removal
- **Removal of porous materials:** Discarding contaminated drywall, insulation, carpet, and other materials that cannot be adequately cleaned
- **Post-remediation clearance testing:** Conducting air sampling after work completion to verify that spore levels have returned to acceptable baselines

Improper remediation can spread contamination and create independent negligence claims against contractors. Common remediation errors include:

- Failing to isolate work areas (allowing spores to spread throughout the building)
- Failing to correct moisture source before remediating mold (resulting in recurrence)
- Inadequate removal of contaminated materials (leaving hidden growth in wall cavities)
- Improper disposal of contaminated materials (creating environmental hazards)
- Lack of personal protective equipment for workers
- No post-remediation verification

Although industry standards (such as IICRC S520 Standard for Professional Mold Remediation) are not statutory mandates, courts frequently examine whether remediation efforts were consistent with recognized professional guidelines.

Insurance disputes often hinge on whether remediation was performed according to accepted protocols. Carriers may deny claims for negligent remediation that made problems worse. Property owners may sue remediation contractors for incomplete work that failed to solve the problem.

This creates additional litigation complexity where multiple parties bear potential responsibility for contamination, remediation failures, and resulting harm.

XII. Litigation Implications of Mold Science

The science of mold exposure produces several consistent legal realities:

1. **Visible mold does not establish toxic exposure.** Jurors may assume that black staining means danger. Science shows that visibility and toxicity are not correlated. Defense experts will educate juries that appearance is irrelevant to health risk.
2. **Presence of spores does not prove medical causation.** Detection and dose are different concepts. Courts require evidence that exposure levels were sufficient to cause the plaintiff's specific injury through a biologically plausible mechanism.

3. **Mycotoxin claims require rigorous dose evidence.** Asserting that a mold species is "capable of producing" toxins is insufficient. Plaintiffs must prove production occurred, toxins became airborne, the plaintiff inhaled meaningful quantities, and those quantities caused specific injuries.

4. **Building science often drives liability more than microbiology.** Proving that a roof leaked for two years due to negligent maintenance often matters more than proving a specific mold species was present.

5. **Courts demand reliable methodology and peer-reviewed support.** Speculation, clinical judgment unsupported by literature, and novel theories lacking general acceptance face exclusion.

By 2026, toxic mold litigation is no longer driven by fear of discoloration on drywall. It is governed by exposure assessment, medical reliability, engineering analysis, and evidentiary discipline.

Scientific credibility determines admissibility.
Admissibility determines leverage.
Leverage determines value.

An attorney who understands these scientific principles can distinguish viable cases from speculative ones during initial consultation. An attorney who ignores them will file cases that collapse at summary judgment, wasting resources and harming clients.

XIII. Practical Takeaways for Litigators

For Plaintiffs' Counsel:

✓ Retain environmental consultants who follow AIHA or IICRC protocols
✓ Ensure air sampling includes outdoor comparison samples
✓ Prioritize moisture documentation over spore species identification
✓ Limit medical claims to conditions with peer-reviewed support
✓ Prepare experts for aggressive Daubert/Frye challenges
✓ Focus on building science to establish breach
✓Document temporal correlation between exposure and symptoms
✓ Obtain medical records showing treatment consistent with mold-related conditions

For Defense Counsel:

✓ Challenge sampling methodology and timing
✓ Emphasize absence of federal exposure standards
✓ Identify alternative causes of plaintiff's symptoms
✓ Retain allergists and toxicologists to narrow injury claims
✓ Obtain building envelope analysis showing proper design or prompt response
✓ Document remediation efforts following professional protocols
✓ Move early to exclude speculative medical causation theories
✓ Focus on comparative outdoor mold levels to minimize indoor findings

XIV. Conclusion: Science as the Foundation

Understanding mold science is not optional in modern toxic mold litigation. It is foundational. Every strategic decision flows from scientific realities:

- **Case selection** depends on whether environmental conditions support viable claims
- **Expert retention** requires vetting consultants who understand industry protocols
- **Damage valuation** hinges on which medical conditions courts accept
- **Settlement negotiations** reflect whether causation will survive admissibility challenges
- **Trial strategy** must translate complex science into comprehensible narrative

Attorneys who master this science gain decisive advantages. They recognize strong cases early. They avoid investing resources in claims that will fail. They prepare experts who withstand cross-examination. They negotiate from positions of scientific credibility rather than legal bluster.

Attorneys who ignore this science handicap themselves and their clients. They file cases based on dramatic photographs rather than admissible evidence. They retain experts who cannot survive Daubert. They make promises they cannot keep and face malpractice exposure when cases collapse.

The field rewards scientific literacy. Chapter 3 builds on this foundation by examining the central battlefield where science meets law: proving specific medical causation under modern evidentiary standards.

3

Proving Specific Medical Causation in Toxic Mold Litigation

Where Cases Live or Die

Three things kill more mold cases than anything else:

1. **Assumptions about exposure without measurement** ("There was visible mold, so exposure must have been toxic")
2. **Medical experts who overreach beyond peer-reviewed support** ("This mold caused systemic immune dysfunction and neurological damage")
3. **Failure to eliminate alternative causes systematically** ("The symptoms started after moving in, so the mold must be responsible")

This chapter shows you how to avoid all three.

Consider a 2024 case from Pennsylvania. The environmental consultant's report documented Stachybotrys, Aspergillus, and Penicillium at concentrations substantially exceeding outdoor baseline levels. Photographs showed extensive black staining across bedroom walls. The landlord had ignored fourteen maintenance requests over eight months. Medical records documented three urgent care visits for respiratory symptoms during occupancy.

The plaintiff's medical expert, a board-certified internist with twenty years of clinical experience, testified that the mold exposure caused "chronic inflammatory response syndrome with cognitive impairment, immune dysregulation, and persistent respiratory dysfunction." When asked about the scientific basis for this diagnosis, he cited his clinical observations, referenced the Shoemaker CIRS protocol, and stated that the "temporal relationship speaks for itself."

The defense moved to exclude the testimony under Daubert. The court granted the motion, finding:

- The CIRS diagnosis lacked general acceptance in the relevant scientific community
- The expert could not cite peer-reviewed studies establishing causation between residential mold exposure and the claimed systemic injuries
- The differential diagnosis failed to adequately address alternative causes including seasonal allergies, anxiety, and sleep disruption
- The expert acknowledged he had not measured actual mycotoxin exposure levels
- No objective medical findings supported the claimed immune dysregulation

Without medical causation testimony, the case settled three weeks later for $42,000 (covering property loss, relocation costs, and minimal respiratory treatment expenses).

Had the same expert limited his testimony to allergic rhinitis and mild asthma exacerbation (both clearly supported by the medical records and peer-reviewed literature), the case would likely have survived summary judgment and settled for $175,000 to $250,000. The overreach cost the plaintiff approximately $150,000 in potential recovery.

This outcome was entirely preventable. And it happens with disturbing frequency.

I. The Central Battlefield: Specific Causation

If Chapter 2 established that science governs toxic mold litigation, Chapter 3 addresses the legal crucible where science is tested: **specific medical causation**.

Modern mold cases rarely fail because mold was not present. They fail because plaintiffs cannot prove that *this* plaintiff's *specific* medical condition was caused by *this* exposure at *this* property.

Courts increasingly separate causation into two distinct inquiries:

1. General Causation: Can mold exposure cause the type of injury alleged? Is there scientific support for the proposition that mold can cause allergic rhinitis? Asthma exacerbation? Cognitive impairment? Immune dysfunction?

2. Specific Causation: Did mold exposure in this case cause this plaintiff's injury? Not whether mold *can* cause harm in general, but whether it *did* cause harm to this particular person under these particular circumstances.

General causation may be supported by medical literature recognizing mold as an allergen or asthma trigger. But specific causation requires far more:

- Measurable exposure (not just presence but dose)
- Temporal connection (symptoms began after exposure, improved after removal)
- Biologically plausible mechanism (how the exposure caused the specific injury)
- Exclusion of alternative causes (ruling out other explanations systematically)

In 2026, toxic mold litigation is defined by this distinction. Understanding it separates successful practitioners from those who file cases that inevitably fail.

II. The Gatekeeping Function: Daubert and Frye

In federal courts and most states, expert testimony must satisfy reliability standards under *Daubert v. Merrell Dow Pharmaceuticals, Inc.*, 509 U.S. 579 (1993) Some jurisdictions apply the older *Frye* "general acceptance" standard. Regardless of framework, judges serve as gatekeepers who exclude unreliable expert testimony before it reaches the jury.

Common judicial concerns in mold cases include:

Whether the expert relies on peer-reviewed literature. Has the causation theory been published in recognized scientific journals? Has it been subjected to peer review and scrutiny? Or does it rest solely on the expert's clinical experience and anecdotal observations?

Whether exposure levels were measured or assumed. Did the expert review actual environmental testing showing spore concentrations, or did the expert simply assume that visible mold equals toxic exposure?

Whether methodology is testable and reproducible. Can other experts using the same methodology reach the same conclusions? Or is the opinion based on subjective clinical judgment that cannot be verified?

Whether differential diagnosis was properly conducted. Did the expert systematically consider and rule out alternative causes? Or did the expert leap to a mold causation conclusion without adequate analysis?

Whether the expert extrapolates beyond established science. Agricultural studies showing mycotoxin effects on farm workers do not automatically translate to residential exposure. Laboratory studies using purified toxins at high doses do not necessarily predict effects of low-level residential exposure.

Experts who rely on anecdotal reports, unvalidated laboratory tests, or speculative toxin theories often face exclusion. When an expert is excluded, the case changes fundamentally. Without medical testimony connecting exposure to injury, plaintiffs typically cannot recover medical damages.

Exclusion of a medical expert frequently ends the case.

Or more precisely, it transforms a potential high-value personal injury case into a modest property damage and relocation expense claim. The difference is measured in hundreds of thousands of dollars.

III. Differential Diagnosis: Necessary but Not Sufficient

Plaintiffs often rely on differential diagnosis, a clinical method in which physicians identify possible causes of a patient's symptoms and systematically rule out alternatives until arriving at the most likely explanation.

In toxic mold litigation, a physician might testify:

"I considered the patient's respiratory symptoms. I evaluated whether they could be caused by seasonal allergies, dust mite exposure, pet dander, smoking, occupational exposures, viral illness, or pre-existing asthma. I ruled out seasonal allergies because symptoms persisted year-round. I ruled out dust mites because symptoms improved dramatically after the patient relocated. I ruled out smoking because the patient is a non-smoker. After eliminating alternative causes, I concluded that mold exposure was the most likely cause of the patient's symptoms."

Courts accept differential diagnosis when:

The underlying causal theory is scientifically valid. The physician must establish that mold *can* cause the type of symptoms observed. If the underlying theory (e.g., that residential mold exposure causes cognitive impairment) lacks scientific support, the differential diagnosis fails regardless of how thorough it appears.

Exposure is documented. The physician cannot diagnose mold-related illness without evidence that meaningful mold exposure actually occurred. Visual observation of mold or reports of musty odors may suffice for allergic symptoms, but systemic injury claims typically require quantitative exposure data.

Alternative causes are meaningfully addressed. A differential diagnosis that lists alternative causes but provides no analysis of why they were excluded is inadequate. The physician must explain the reasoning behind each elimination.

Courts reject differential diagnosis when:

The expert assumes exposure without measurement. "The patient lived in a moldy house, so exposure must have occurred" is insufficient when systemic injury is claimed.

Alternative causes are ignored or inadequately analyzed. If the patient smokes, has seasonal allergies, works in a dusty environment, and owns three cats, the physician cannot simply ignore these factors and attribute all symptoms to mold.

The theory of mold toxicity lacks general scientific support. Even perfect differential diagnosis cannot salvage a causation theory that is fundamentally unreliable.

In toxic mold litigation, differential diagnosis cannot compensate for weak exposure evidence or contested causal theories. It is necessary but not sufficient.

Case in Focus: When Differential Diagnosis Fails

A 2025 Oregon case involved a tenant claiming that mold exposure caused chronic fatigue, difficulty concentrating, joint pain, and frequent infections. The plaintiff's physician conducted a differential diagnosis, ruling out:

- Chronic fatigue syndrome (patient didn't meet diagnostic criteria)
- Fibromyalgia (tender point examination was negative)
- Lyme disease (testing was negative)
- Autoimmune conditions (antibody tests were negative)

The physician concluded that "toxic mold exposure" was the remaining explanation.

The defense expert testified that:

- The symptoms (fatigue, cognitive complaints, pain, infections) are extraordinarily non-specific and have hundreds of potential causes
- The plaintiff's differential diagnosis failed to adequately consider depression, anxiety, sleep disorders, hormonal imbalances, medication effects, and numerous other common conditions
- The temporal relationship was weak (symptoms began before the mold was discovered)
- No objective findings supported the claimed immune dysfunction
- Peer-reviewed literature does not support a causal connection between residential mold exposure and the constellation of

symptoms alleged

The court excluded the plaintiff's causation testimony. The case was dismissed on summary judgment.

The lesson: Differential diagnosis must be comprehensive, methodologically sound, and grounded in scientifically accepted causal relationships. Listing a few alternatives and eliminating them superficially is insufficient.

IV. Establishing Exposure: The Dose Problem

Causation requires more than identifying mold species. Plaintiffs must demonstrate:

Duration of exposure: How long was the plaintiff exposed? Days? Weeks? Months? Years? Acute effects require different exposure than chronic effects.

Intensity of exposure: What were the spore concentrations? How do they compare to outdoor baseline levels? To levels in non-water-damaged buildings?

Route of exposure: Was exposure primarily inhalation (breathing airborne spores)? Dermal contact (touching contaminated surfaces)? Ingestion (though this is rarely relevant in mold cases)?

Biologically plausible dose-response relationship: Is there scientific literature supporting that the measured exposure levels can cause the alleged injury? Or do the claimed effects require exposures far exceeding what environmental testing documented?

One of the greatest evidentiary obstacles is the absence of defined indoor exposure thresholds. Without regulatory limits, experts must rely on:

- Comparative spore counts (indoor vs. outdoor)
- Professional guidelines (though these are advisory, not regulatory)
- Moisture history and duration
- Medical correlation (temporal relationship between exposure and symptoms)

Defense experts frequently argue:

Environmental testing provides only a snapshot. A single air sample represents 5-10 minutes of collection time. It does not reflect conditions hours earlier, days later, or during the months the plaintiff lived there before testing occurred.

Air samples do not reflect historical exposure. The mold discovered in October may have started growing in July. Testing in October does not establish what exposure levels were in July, August, and September.

Spore presence does not equal harmful dose. Detection of mold spores (which are ubiquitous) does not prove that concentrations were sufficient to cause injury. "More than outdoor levels" is not the same as "toxic levels."

Courts often demand objective data rather than assumptions based on visible growth. "There was visible mold, so exposure must have been significant" is an assumption, not evidence. And assumptions fail under cross-examination.

V. Temporal Relationship and Symptom Onset

A persuasive toxic mold case typically demonstrates:

Symptom onset after exposure began. The plaintiff was healthy before moving into the property or before the water intrusion occurred. Symptoms developed during the exposure period.

Improvement upon relocation. When the plaintiff moved out temporarily or permanently, symptoms improved or resolved.

Recurrence upon re-entry. If the plaintiff returned to the property (for belongings, inspection, etc.), symptoms recurred or worsened.

This "temporal association" can strengthen causation arguments. But courts caution that temporal sequence alone does not establish causation. **Correlation is not proof.**

Post hoc ergo propter hoc ("after this, therefore because of this") is a logical fallacy. Just because B follows A does not mean A caused B.

Plaintiffs must connect timing to mechanism. Why did exposure cause symptoms? What is the biological pathway? Is the temporal sequence consistent with known latency periods for the claimed condition?

Example of Strong Temporal Correlation:

A family moves into a rental home in January. Everyone is healthy with no respiratory complaints. In March, heavy rains cause a roof leak. The landlord is notified but delays repairs. By April, the youngest child develops nighttime coughing. By May, both children are coughing regularly. By June, the mother develops nasal congestion. In July, mold is discovered behind drywall in the children's bedroom. The family moves out immediately. Within two weeks, all symptoms resolve. When the father returns to the property a month later to retrieve belongings, he experiences throat irritation and coughing within an hour.

This temporal pattern is compelling because it shows:

- Health before exposure
- Symptom onset after moisture intrusion
- Progressive worsening as contamination grew
- Rapid improvement after removal from exposure
- Recurrence upon re-entry

Example of Weak Temporal Correlation:

A tenant has a history of seasonal allergies and occasional asthma. Symptoms vary throughout the year with no clear pattern. After living in the property for three years, the tenant discovers mold in a bathroom closet. The tenant claims that symptoms experienced over the past three years were caused by the mold.

This temporal pattern is weak because:

- Symptoms preceded discovery of mold
- No clear onset corresponding to moisture intrusion
- Pre-existing conditions complicate causation
- No improvement demonstrated upon relocation
- Alternative causes (seasonal allergies) remain viable

Temporal correlation strengthens causation arguments but does not, by itself, prove that exposure caused injury. It must be combined with dose evidence, medical literature support, and exclusion of alternatives.

VI. Accepted Injuries vs. Contested Conditions

Courts have become increasingly sophisticated about distinguishing between mold-related conditions that have strong scientific support and those that remain controversial or speculative.

Widely Accepted Conditions (Generally Admissible)

Courts are generally receptive to claims involving:

Allergic Rhinitis: Nasal congestion, sneezing, runny nose, itchy eyes, postnasal drip. This is the most common and well-accepted mold-related health effect. Defense experts typically concede that mold can cause allergic symptoms in sensitized individuals.

Asthma Exacerbation: Worsening of pre-existing asthma including increased wheezing, shortness of breath, chest tightness, increased medication use, and more frequent rescue inhaler use. The Institute of Medicine (now National Academy of Medicine) found sufficient evidence linking indoor dampness and mold to asthma exacerbation.

Irritant Symptoms: Eye, nose, and throat irritation even in non-allergic individuals exposed to high mold spore concentrations. These symptoms result from physical irritation rather than immune response.

Hypersensitivity Pneumonitis: A rare inflammatory lung condition caused by repeated inhalation of specific antigens. In the mold context, it typically requires heavy exposure but can occur in residential settings with extreme contamination. This condition requires clinical diagnosis with specific findings (restrictive lung function pattern, imaging abnormalities, sometimes lung biopsy).

These conditions align with established immunologic responses to mold spores. Expert testimony supporting these diagnoses generally survives admissibility challenges when properly documented with:

- Medical records showing diagnosis and treatment
- Pulmonary function testing (for asthma claims)
- Allergy testing showing mold sensitivity (for allergic claims)
- Temporal correlation between exposure and symptoms
- Improvement upon cessation of exposure

Contested Conditions (Frequently Challenged, Often Excluded)

Courts are more skeptical of:

Cognitive Impairment: Claims of "brain fog," memory problems, difficulty concentrating, confusion, or other neurological symptoms attributed to mold exposure absent invasive fungal infection. Courts typically require evidence of fungal invasion of the central nervous system (extraordinarily rare except in severely immunocompromised individuals).

Chronic Inflammatory Response Syndrome (CIRS): A controversial diagnosis involving multiple symptoms allegedly caused by biotoxin exposure in water-damaged buildings. Proponents argue it represents a legitimate illness. Critics (and most courts) note limited peer-reviewed validation, lack of generally accepted diagnostic criteria, and reliance on laboratory tests (visual contrast sensitivity testing, certain inflammatory markers) that lack standardized interpretation.

Broad Immune Dysfunction: Claims that mold exposure caused general immune system compromise, increased susceptibility to infections, recurrent illness, or autoimmune conditions. These claims typically lack sufficient scientific support in residential exposure contexts absent specific documented immunodeficiency.

Neurological Syndromes Absent Invasive Infection: Claims of peripheral neuropathy, balance disorders, tremors, or other neurological deficits attributed to mycotoxin exposure. Absent documented invasive fungal infection reaching the nervous system, these claims face substantial admissibility challenges.

Chronic Fatigue, Fibromyalgia-like Syndromes: Claims that mold exposure caused persistent fatigue, widespread pain, or multi-system symptoms. While individuals with these conditions deserve sympathy and treatment, courts are skeptical of causally linking them to residential mold exposure absent strong scientific support.

Claims involving systemic toxicity often require substantial scientific support. Absent peer-reviewed validation and reliable exposure data, such claims face admissibility challenges.

The gap between these categories represents the difference between a $50,000 settlement and a $500,000 settlement. Or between a viable case and summary judgment dismissal.

VII. Biomarkers and Laboratory Testing

Some plaintiffs introduce laboratory testing to support systemic illness claims, including:

Urinary Mycotoxin Panels: Tests claiming to detect mycotoxins in urine. Proponents argue these demonstrate exposure and explain symptoms. Critics (and most courts) note:

- Lack of standardized reference ranges (no established "normal" vs. "toxic" levels)
- Uncertainty regarding environmental source (mycotoxins in food vs. inhalation)
- Absence of FDA approval for diagnostic use
- Limited peer-reviewed validation of testing methods
- Questions about whether urinary mycotoxin detection correlates with illness

Inflammatory Markers: Tests measuring various cytokines, C4a, TGF-beta, or other inflammatory markers. Challenges include:

- Non-specificity (many conditions cause inflammation)
- Lack of established reference ranges
- Absence of validated interpretation criteria
- Limited evidence linking markers to mold exposure specifically

Genetic Susceptibility Testing: Tests claiming to identify individuals with genetic variations (e.g., HLA types) that increase susceptibility to mold-related illness. Concerns include:

- Lack of regulatory recognition
- Limited peer-reviewed validation
- Uncertainty about predictive value

- Risk of genetic discrimination

Visual Contrast Sensitivity (VCS) Testing: A screening test sometimes used in CIRS diagnosis. Challenges include:

- Non-specificity (many conditions affect visual contrast)
- Lack of standardization
- Limited validation for mold exposure assessment
- Easy to administer incorrectly

Defense challenges typically focus on:

- Lack of standardized reference ranges
- Uncertainty regarding environmental source attribution
- Absence of regulatory recognition (FDA approval)
- Limited peer-reviewed validation

Courts frequently require proof that such tests are scientifically accepted and reliably interpreted. Many jurisdictions exclude these tests as unreliable under Daubert/Frye standards.

Practitioner Warning:

EXPERT SELECTION ALERT

Before retaining a medical expert who relies on urinary mycotoxin testing, VCS testing, or CIRS diagnosis, research whether courts in your jurisdiction have admitted such testimony. Many jurisdictions have excluded it. Retaining an expert whose methodology has been repeatedly rejected wastes resources and damages credibility. Start with mainstream allergists, pulmonologists, or occupational medicine specialists whose opinions rest on peer-reviewed literature and generally accepted diagnostic methods.

VIII. Alternative Causation Defenses

Defense counsel routinely identify alternative explanations for symptoms, including:

Seasonal Pollen: Spring and fall allergies affect millions. Symptoms (sneezing, congestion, itchy eyes) overlap substantially with mold allergy symptoms. Defense experts will compare symptom timing to pollen counts.

Dust Mites: One of the most common indoor allergens. Present in virtually all homes. Cause respiratory symptoms identical to mold allergies. Difficult to distinguish without specific allergy testing.

Pet Dander: Another extremely common allergen. If the plaintiff owns pets (or the property previously housed pets), this becomes a viable alternative cause.

Tobacco Smoke: Whether the plaintiff smokes, lives with smokers, or is exposed occupationally. Smoke causes respiratory symptoms including coughing, wheezing, and congestion.

Occupational Exposures: Does the plaintiff work in construction, healthcare, manufacturing, or other fields with respiratory exposures? Are there workplace air quality issues?

Viral Illness: Respiratory viruses cause coughing, congestion, and fatigue. Defense experts will note that symptoms attributed to mold may simply reflect seasonal viral infections.

Pre-existing Asthma or Allergies: If the plaintiff had asthma or allergies before moving into the property, defense experts will argue that symptoms represent continuation or worsening of pre-existing conditions from multiple causes, not mold exposure alone.

Anxiety and Stress: The stress of discovering mold, worry about health effects, financial strain from relocation, and litigation stress can cause or exacerbate physical symptoms including fatigue, sleep problems, and difficulty concentrating.

If plaintiffs cannot effectively rule out these alternatives, specific causation weakens dramatically. The burden ultimately rests with the plaintiff to demonstrate that mold exposure was a substantial contributing factor, not merely one of many possible explanations.

A credible differential diagnosis addresses each alternative specifically:

"I considered seasonal allergies. However, the patient's symptoms were year-round, not seasonal. Allergy testing showed mold sensitivity but negative reactions to common pollen allergens. I considered dust mites. The patient's symptoms improved dramatically when staying away from the property but not when using HEPA filtration at home, suggesting a location-specific rather than general indoor allergen cause. I considered smoking. The patient is a non-smoker with no occupational smoke exposure. I considered occupational exposures. The patient works in an office with no known air quality issues and symptoms did not correlate with work schedule..."

This level of analysis strengthens causation opinions. Vague assertions that alternatives were "considered and ruled out" without explanation do not.

IX. The Role of Epidemiology

Epidemiological studies examine disease patterns in populations. They can establish general causation (whether a substance can cause a particular health effect) but rarely resolve specific causation (whether it caused this plaintiff's injury).

Courts often require:

Consistency with published literature: Are the plaintiff's claimed injuries consistent with what epidemiological studies show mold exposure causes?

Dose-response alignment: Do the exposure levels in this case align with exposure levels in studies showing health effects?

Biological plausibility: Is there a scientifically understood mechanism by which the exposure could cause the claimed injury?

Absence of contradictory findings: Are there studies showing no association between mold exposure and the claimed condition?

Experts who extrapolate beyond epidemiological evidence risk exclusion. For example, citing a study showing asthma exacerbation in children exposed to dampness does not support testimony that mold causes cognitive impairment in adults.

Epidemiology provides context but does not substitute for individual causation analysis. Population-level associations do not prove individual injury.

The most important epidemiological resource is the 2004 Institute of Medicine report "Damp Indoor Spaces and Health," which comprehensively reviewed mold and health literature. Courts frequently reference this report. It found:

- **Sufficient evidence** linking indoor dampness/mold to: upper respiratory tract symptoms, cough, wheeze, asthma exacerbation (in sensitized individuals)
- **Limited or suggestive evidence** for: lower respiratory illness in healthy children, dyspnea
- **Inadequate or insufficient evidence** for: many other claimed health effects

This report remains influential. Plaintiffs asserting conditions outside the "sufficient evidence" category face steeper admissibility challenges.

X. Psychological and Emotional Distress Claims

Some mold cases involve claims of anxiety, insomnia, or emotional distress stemming from living in contaminated environments.

Courts vary in their treatment of such claims:

Some jurisdictions allow emotional distress damages tied to habitability violations. The distress arises not from fear of mold per se but from being forced to live in substandard, unhealthy conditions. These claims may survive even when systemic physical injury claims fail.

Others require physical injury to recover non-economic damages. In these jurisdictions, emotional distress without accompanying physical harm is not compensable.

Some recognize negligent infliction of emotional distress when the defendant's conduct was particularly egregious (e.g., deliberate concealment, ignoring repeated complaints from families with young children).

Where systemic illness claims fail, emotional distress damages may remain viable, particularly when habitability breaches are documented. A family forced to live for months in a home with visible mold growth, persistent musty odors, and ongoing water intrusion may recover emotional distress damages even if cognitive impairment or immune dysfunction claims are excluded.

These damages are typically modest compared to serious physical injury claims but can still meaningfully contribute to settlement value, especially when combined with property damage and relocation expenses.

What Effective Emotional Distress Testimony Looks Like:

Compare these approaches:

Ineffective (Vague and Conclusory): "Living in that moldy house was terrible. I was stressed out all the time worrying about my kids getting sick. I had anxiety and couldn't sleep."

Effective (Specific and Documented): "After we discovered the mold in July, I couldn't sleep in the back bedroom anymore. The smell made me nauseous. I moved to the couch but worried constantly about my children sleeping in rooms with mold. I made three doctor appointments for my daughter in August alone. I called the landlord twelve times. Each time he promised to fix it and didn't. I felt trapped because I couldn't afford to break the lease and move. My doctor prescribed anxiety medication in September, which I'd never needed before. I lost fifteen pounds because I had no appetite. My performance review at work in October noted that I seemed distracted and stressed, which had never been mentioned before."

The second testimony is specific, documented, and tied to defendant's conduct. It's far more persuasive.

XI. Strategic Implications for Litigators

To Establish Specific Medical Causation, Plaintiff's Counsel Should:

1. **Secure thorough environmental documentation early.** Don't rely on tenant photographs alone. Hire qualified industrial hygienists or certified mold inspectors who follow recognized protocols.

2. **Retain qualified medical experts with peer-reviewed grounding.** Prioritize board-certified allergists, pulmonologists, or occupational medicine physicians over practitioners offering controversial diagnoses. Check whether the expert's methodology has been previously admitted in your jurisdiction.

3. **Develop a clear exposure timeline.** Document when moisture intrusion began, when contamination was discovered, when symptoms started, and when improvement occurred after relocation.

4. **Anticipate Daubert challenges.** Before filing suit, have the medical expert review the case file and confirm that causation opinions will survive reliability scrutiny. Get this in writing.

5. **Prepare to rebut alternative causation theories.** Obtain allergy testing, review smoking history, document occupational exposures, and address pre-existing conditions explicitly in expert reports.
6. **Document medical treatment contemporaneously.** Symptoms described two years after exposure are less credible than symptoms documented in contemporaneous medical records.
7. **Limit claims to scientifically defensible injuries.** Resist the temptation to allege every possible health effect. Claims of respiratory irritation and allergic rhinitis are far more likely to survive than claims of cognitive impairment and immune dysfunction.

Defense Counsel Should:

1. **Challenge exposure assumptions.** Demand evidence of actual measured exposure levels, not assumptions based on visual observation.
2. **Scrutinize laboratory methodologies.** Challenge urinary mycotoxin tests, non-standard inflammatory marker panels, and other unvalidated testing.
3. **Emphasize absence of dose data.** Environmental sampling showing mold presence does not prove toxic dose.
4. **Retain allergists and toxicologists.** These specialists can credibly concede allergic effects while challenging systemic toxicity claims.
5. **Narrow claims to accepted respiratory effects.** Stipulate that mold can cause allergies and asthma exacerbation (which is scientifically undeniable) while vigorously contesting broader injury claims.
6. **File early Daubert motions.** Don't wait until trial approaches. Move to exclude speculative causation testimony early, potentially resolving the case on summary judgment.
7. **Document prompt response.** If remediation occurred promptly after notice, emphasize this to undermine claims of prolonged exposure.

Specific causation is not won through dramatic imagery or sympathetic plaintiffs. It is won through disciplined, defensible science presented by credible experts whose opinions withstand cross-examination.

XII. Why Specific Causation Determines Value

In toxic mold litigation, damages expand or contract based on causation strength.

Where systemic illness is excluded:

Damages may be limited to:

- Property loss (personal belongings damaged): $5,000 - $25,000
- Relocation expenses (temporary housing, moving costs): $10,000 - $50,000
- Modest medical expenses (urgent care visits, medications): $2,000 - $10,000
- Temporary respiratory symptoms treatment: $5,000 - $20,000
- Emotional distress (in permitting jurisdictions): $10,000 - $50,000

Total settlement range: $30,000 - $150,000

Where allergic rhinitis and asthma exacerbation survive admissibility:

Damages may include:

- All of the above, plus:
- Ongoing respiratory treatment and medications: $25,000 - $75,000
- Pulmonary rehabilitation: $10,000 - $30,000
- Lost wages during acute illness periods: $10,000 - $50,000
- Increased emotional distress linked to documented physical injury: $25,000 - $100,000

Total settlement range: $150,000 - $400,000

Where serious chronic respiratory disease survives admissibility:

Damages may include:

- All of the above, plus:
- Long-term medical monitoring and treatment: $50,000 - $200,000

- Permanent respiratory impairment: $100,000 - $500,000
- Lost earning capacity: $50,000 - $300,000
- Significantly increased pain and suffering: $100,000 - $500,000

Total settlement range: $400,000 - $1,500,000+

These ranges assume strong liability evidence and insurance coverage. But they illustrate that causation is the pivot point between modest settlements and multi-million-dollar outcomes.

Accordingly, causation analysis should drive case selection. An attorney evaluating a potential mold case should ask:

- Can I prove meaningful exposure with environmental data?
- Can I retain a medical expert whose opinions will survive Daubert?
- Can I document temporal correlation and eliminate alternatives?
- Are the claimed injuries within the range of scientifically accepted mold-related conditions?

If the answers are "no," the case may not justify the investment of time and resources required for mold litigation.

XIII. Conclusion

Toxic mold litigation in 2026 is defined by evidentiary rigor. Courts demand reliable science, measurable exposure, and defensible medical reasoning.

General fear of "black mold" no longer drives verdicts. Specific medical proof does.

Three takeaways:

1. **Measure exposure, don't assume it.** Environmental testing is essential, not optional.
2. **Retain experts whose opinions rest on peer-reviewed literature.** Clinical judgment alone is insufficient for contested conditions.
3. **Address alternative causes systematically.** Differential diagnosis must be comprehensive and methodologically sound.

The next chapter turns from medical causation to the statutory and regulatory frameworks that shape liability, examining federal guidance, housing regulations, and evolving state standards governing mold remediation and disclosure. Understanding these frameworks helps define what defendants "knew or should have known" and what constitutes reasonable response to moisture intrusion.

PART II: Regulatory and Legislative Frameworks

4

Federal Regulatory Framework and Housing Standards

In Toxic Mold Litigation

What the Government Says Matters (Even When It Doesn't Regulate)

In a 2024 New Jersey case, the plaintiff's attorney argued that the landlord's failure to remediate mold within 48 hours of notification violated federal standards and constituted negligence per se. The defense moved to dismiss, pointing out a fundamental problem: no federal standard requires 48-hour mold remediation.

The court granted the motion, noting that while federal agencies provide guidance on mold issues, they do not establish enforceable exposure limits, mandatory response timelines, or regulatory thresholds for residential properties.

Yet in the same courthouse, six months later, another judge allowed a plaintiff's expert to testify that the landlord's response was "unreasonable under federal EPA guidance" because remediation was delayed for six months after notification. The defense objected that EPA guidance is advisory, not mandatory. The court overruled the objection, stating that while EPA guidance does not create strict liability, it informs what constitutes reasonable conduct.

These contrasting outcomes illustrate the peculiar role federal law plays in toxic mold litigation. There is no comprehensive federal regulatory scheme. There are no enforceable exposure limits. There is no federal mold statute creating private rights of action.

Yet federal agencies shape expectations, define best practices, and influence how courts evaluate reasonableness. Understanding what federal law does (and does not) require is essential for evaluating duty, breach, and reasonable response in toxic mold cases.

I. The Regulatory Vacuum: Why Federal Law Matters (and Doesn't)

One of the defining characteristics of toxic mold litigation in the United States is the absence of a comprehensive federal regulatory scheme governing indoor mold exposure.

What doesn't exist:

- No federal statute establishing permissible indoor mold exposure limits
- No OSHA residential mold threshold or permissible exposure limit (PEL)
- No EPA-enforced numerical standards defining "toxic" spore concentrations
- No HUD regulation mandating specific remediation timelines for all housing
- No federal building code requiring mold-resistant construction methods

- No mandatory federal disclosure requirements for mold in real estate transactions

This regulatory vacuum exists for several reasons:

Scientific uncertainty. Establishing numerical exposure limits requires dose-response data that simply does not exist for most mold species in residential settings. What concentration of Aspergillus causes harm? Over what duration? In which populations? The science does not provide clear answers.

Variability in conditions. Exposure scenarios vary enormously. A family in a humid coastal climate faces different risks than one in an arid desert climate. An immunocompromised individual has different vulnerabilities than a healthy adult. One-size-fits-all federal standards are difficult to craft when conditions and susceptibilities vary so dramatically.

Jurisdictional complexity. Housing regulation traditionally falls to states and localities. Federal intervention in residential indoor air quality raises federalism concerns and political resistance.

Industry opposition. Property owners, developers, and insurers have successfully lobbied against federal mold regulations that might create strict liability or impose costly compliance mandates.

Yet federal agencies play a powerful indirect role in shaping toxic mold litigation. Their guidance documents, housing regulations, workplace standards, and military housing oversight frameworks frequently become reference points in court.

Understanding what federal law does (and does not) require is essential for litigators evaluating duty, breach, and reasonableness.

II. EPA Guidance: Advisory, Not Enforceable

The United States Environmental Protection Agency (EPA) provides extensive guidance on mold remediation and moisture control. However, EPA publications are advisory. They do not create enforceable exposure thresholds or mandatory remediation protocols.

Key EPA principles include:

Mold growth indicates moisture problems. The EPA emphasizes that mold growth is fundamentally a moisture problem. Addressing mold without correcting the water source will result in recurrence. This principle matters in litigation because it shifts focus from mold species identification to moisture source correction.

Prompt remediation is recommended when mold is visible. EPA guidance suggests addressing mold contamination promptly, typically within 24-48 hours of water intrusion. While not a regulatory mandate, this timeline influences what courts consider "reasonable response."

Small areas of contamination can often be handled by trained personnel without extensive testing. EPA guidance distinguishes between small areas (less than 10 square feet) that can be cleaned with standard precautions and large areas requiring professional remediation. This distinction affects litigation by establishing different standards based on contamination scope.

Fixing the water source is more important than measuring spore counts. EPA emphasizes that stopping water intrusion matters more than extensive testing to identify specific mold species. This undermines claims that failure to conduct comprehensive air sampling constitutes negligence.

How EPA Guidance Functions in Litigation

In litigation, EPA guidance is frequently cited to argue:

For Plaintiffs:

- Property owners had notice of remediation best practices through widely available federal guidance
- Industry standards for response time were publicly accessible and reasonable to follow
- Failure to remediate promptly (within days or weeks, not months) was unreasonable
- The defendant cannot claim ignorance of proper remediation methods when EPA published clear guidance

For Defendants:

- EPA guidance does not define toxic levels or establish per se liability
- Absence of federal numerical standards means plaintiffs cannot point to regulatory violations

- EPA's emphasis on moisture control over species identification supports focus on building repairs rather than extensive testing
- Small areas of mold do not require professional remediation under EPA guidance

Defense counsel often emphasize that EPA guidance does not define toxic levels or establish per se negligence. Plaintiffs counter that while not creating strict liability, guidance establishes the baseline for reasonable conduct.

Most courts adopt a middle position: EPA guidance is admissible evidence of industry standards and reasonable practices, but violation of guidance does not automatically establish liability, nor does compliance provide absolute defense.

Case in Focus: EPA Guidance as Evidence of Reasonableness

A 2025 Florida case involved a landlord who discovered mold in a rental unit and immediately ordered remediation. The contractor completed work within one week of discovery. The tenant sued, claiming the landlord should have conducted pre-remediation testing to document contamination levels and post-remediation testing to verify clearance.

The landlord's expert testified that EPA guidance does not require testing for small to moderate contamination areas when visible mold is addressed and moisture is corrected. The court agreed, finding that the landlord's response was reasonable under federal guidance even without comprehensive testing.

The case settled for $35,000 (covering the tenant's relocation costs and property damage), far less than the $200,000 demand. The landlord's adherence to EPA guidance (prompt response, moisture correction, professional remediation) significantly reduced exposure.

III. HUD and Federally Assisted Housing

The United States Department of Housing and Urban Development (HUD) oversees public housing and Section 8 programs. HUD has issued guidance requiring public housing authorities to address mold and moisture issues promptly to ensure safe and habitable conditions.

While HUD guidance does not impose numeric exposure limits, it reinforces:

The obligation to maintain habitable housing. HUD requires public housing authorities to maintain properties in decent, safe, and sanitary condition. Visible mold growth and persistent moisture problems violate this standard.

Timely inspection and remediation protocols. HUD expects housing authorities to respond promptly to tenant complaints, conduct inspections within reasonable timeframes, and remediate confirmed problems without undue delay.

Tenant notification procedures. HUD guidelines encourage transparency with tenants regarding mold issues, remediation plans, and any need for temporary relocation.

Maintenance documentation requirements. Public housing authorities must maintain records of complaints, inspections, work orders, and remediation efforts. This documentation becomes critical evidence in litigation.

HUD's Housing Quality Standards (HQS)

For Section 8 housing, HUD's Housing Quality Standards require properties to be free from health and safety hazards. While HQS does not mention mold specifically, severe mold contamination can constitute an HQS violation requiring correction.

Local housing authorities conduct periodic HQS inspections. Failure to maintain properties in compliance can result in loss of Section 8 funding. In litigation, HQS violations can serve as evidence of breach of duty.

Litigation Implications

In public housing litigation, plaintiffs often argue that failure to comply with HUD guidance demonstrates negligence or breach of statutory duty.

For Plaintiffs:

- HUD guidance establishes what reasonable public housing authorities do
- Failure to follow guidance shows deliberate indifference or institutional neglect
- HQS violations provide documentary evidence of substandard conditions

- Federal funding comes with federal responsibilities

For Defendants:

- HUD guidance is not regulation; it provides recommendations, not mandates
- Budget constraints affect response timelines (though this defense is often weak)
- Compliance documentation may provide defense leverage

Conversely, compliance documentation (timely inspections, prompt work orders, thorough remediation) may provide defense leverage by demonstrating reasonable institutional practices.

Public housing cases often hinge on documentation. Housing authorities with systematic maintenance tracking, prompt response protocols, and clear remediation records fare better than those with haphazard recordkeeping and delayed responses.

IV. OSHA and Workplace Mold Exposure

The Occupational Safety and Health Administration (OSHA) does not set specific mold exposure limits for general industry or residential buildings. However, OSHA's General Duty Clause (Section 5(a)(1) of the OSH Act) requires employers to provide a workplace free from recognized hazards likely to cause serious harm.

In workplace mold claims:

Employees may allege that mold constituted a recognized hazard. If mold contamination is visible, persistent, and causing health complaints, employees may argue it constitutes a recognized hazard under the General Duty Clause.

Employers may argue that no regulatory threshold was exceeded. Without specific OSHA mold exposure limits, employers can argue that presence of mold does not automatically constitute a violation.

OSHA inspections and citations can become evidentiary anchors in civil litigation. If OSHA inspects a workplace and cites the employer for mold-related hazards, that citation becomes powerful evidence in subsequent civil suits by affected employees.

OSHA's Limited Guidance

OSHA has published informational materials on mold in the workplace but has not promulgated formal standards. The agency recommends:

- Addressing water intrusion promptly (within 24-48 hours)
- Removing porous materials that cannot be adequately cleaned
- Using appropriate personal protective equipment during remediation
- Providing medical evaluation for employees with symptoms

These recommendations influence what courts consider reasonable workplace practices.

Litigation Implications

The absence of numeric OSHA standards again shifts emphasis to expert testimony regarding recognized risk and reasonable response rather than regulatory compliance or violation.

For Plaintiffs:

- General Duty Clause creates obligation to address recognized hazards
- OSHA guidance informs what reasonable employers do
- Employer knowledge of mold combined with employee health complaints can establish recognized hazard

For Defendants:

- Absence of specific standards means no per se violation
- Employer response (even if delayed) may demonstrate good faith efforts
- Alternative causes of employee symptoms remain viable defenses

In practice, workplace mold cases proceed similarly to residential cases: the focus is on reasonableness of response given knowledge of conditions, not regulatory compliance with non-existent numerical standards.

V. The Fair Housing Act and Disability Claims

The Fair Housing Act (FHA) plays a significant role in toxic mold disputes involving tenants with respiratory disabilities.

Under the FHA:

Landlords must provide reasonable accommodations for tenants with qualifying disabilities. Disabilities include conditions that substantially limit major life activities, such as breathing. Asthma qualifies as a disability under the FHA.

Failure to address mold that exacerbates asthma or other documented conditions may trigger liability. When a tenant with diagnosed asthma requests remediation of mold that aggravates their condition, failure to respond may violate the FHA's reasonable accommodation requirements.

Reasonable accommodation may include prompt remediation, relocation during remediation, or rent abatement. What constitutes "reasonable" depends on the specific circumstances, but ignoring documented medical needs is rarely defensible.

How FHA Claims Work in Practice

A typical FHA mold case might proceed as follows:

1. Tenant has documented asthma (qualifying disability)
2. Tenant notifies landlord of mold and requests remediation
3. Tenant provides medical documentation showing mold exacerbates asthma
4. Landlord delays or refuses remediation
5. Tenant files FHA complaint alleging failure to provide reasonable accommodation

FHA violations can result in:

- Compensatory damages (medical expenses, pain and suffering, emotional distress)
- Punitive damages (in cases of intentional discrimination)

- Attorney's fees (mandatory for prevailing plaintiffs)
- Injunctive relief (requiring remediation)

Plaintiffs increasingly frame mold cases as disability discrimination matters when landlords fail to respond adequately to medically documented sensitivities. This approach can expand remedies beyond traditional negligence or habitability claims.

Case in Focus: FHA Transforms Mold Case Value

A 2024 Massachusetts case involved a tenant with documented severe asthma living in a unit with chronic moisture intrusion and visible mold. The tenant requested remediation in writing, providing letters from her pulmonologist stating that mold exposure was triggering asthma attacks requiring emergency room visits.

The landlord responded that "some mold is normal" and offered to "spray with bleach" but did not address the underlying moisture problem. Over six months, the tenant had four ER visits and two hospital admissions for asthma exacerbations.

Filed as a straight negligence/habitability case, the claim might have settled for $75,000-$125,000. Filed as an FHA reasonable accommodation failure, the case settled for $285,000, including:

- Medical expenses: $45,000
- Pain and suffering: $120,000
- Emotional distress: $60,000
- Attorney's fees: $60,000

The FHA framework transformed case value by:

- Establishing federal statutory violation (not just common law breach)
- Making attorney's fees mandatory
- Allowing emotional distress damages more easily
- Creating punitive damage exposure
- Shifting burden to defendant to prove accommodation was unreasonable

Practitioner Tip:

When evaluating mold cases involving tenants with asthma, COPD, or other respiratory conditions, always consider FHA theories. Documented medical conditions + written accommodation requests + landlord refusal or delay = strong FHA claim that may dramatically increase settlement value.

VI. Military Housing and Federal Contractors

Mold litigation in military housing has grown substantially in recent years. Many installations are managed by private contractors operating under federal agreements.

Claims involving military housing often raise issues under:

The Federal Tort Claims Act (FTCA). If suing the federal government directly, plaintiffs must comply with FTCA administrative exhaustion requirements, notice provisions, and procedural rules. FTCA claims face strict filing deadlines and prohibit punitive damages.

Government contractor defenses. Private entities managing housing on federal property may invoke government contractor immunity, arguing they followed federal specifications and cannot be liable for following government directions.

Sovereign immunity doctrines. Direct claims against the United States face sovereign immunity barriers unless specifically waived by statute.

The Privatized Military Housing Model

Most modern military housing is operated under public-private partnerships:

- Federal government owns the land
- Private companies (often large residential management firms or real estate investment trusts) construct, renovate, and manage housing
- Service members' Basic Allowance for Housing (BAH) funds rent payments
- Long-term (50+ year) ground leases govern the relationship

When private entities manage housing on federal property, liability analysis becomes layered. Plaintiffs must determine:

Whether the defendant is a federal agency or private contractor. This determines which immunity doctrines apply and which procedural rules govern.

Whether immunity doctrines apply. Federal agencies enjoy sovereign immunity; private contractors may invoke government contractor defenses but do not have absolute immunity.

Whether contractual remediation obligations were breached. Private military housing contracts typically impose maintenance and remediation obligations. Breach of these contracts can create liability even when sovereign immunity might bar direct claims against the government.

Recent high-value settlements demonstrate that mold claims in military housing can survive immunity challenges when negligence is attributable to private operators.

The $10 million Fort Cavazos settlement discussed in the Introduction involved a private military housing operator, not the federal government directly. The operator's internal emails showing deliberate delay for budgetary reasons eliminated any plausible immunity defense.

Why Military Housing Cases Command Attention

Several factors make military housing mold claims particularly significant:

Captive population. Service members typically cannot choose their housing. They are assigned to installations and must accept available housing or live off-base at their own expense (often economically infeasible for junior enlisted personnel).

Power imbalance. Service members may fear retaliation (negative performance reviews, undesirable assignments) if they complain too aggressively about housing conditions.

Vulnerable populations. Military families often include young children who are more susceptible to mold-related health effects.

Public accountability. Service members serve the nation. Subjecting them and their families to substandard housing conditions generates public outrage and political pressure.

Congressional oversight. High-profile military housing cases have triggered congressional hearings, leading to increased scrutiny and legislative reforms.

These factors create leverage in litigation even when legal doctrines might favor defendants.

VII. The Regulatory Gap and Its Litigation Consequences

The absence of federally mandated exposure limits creates both opportunity and uncertainty in toxic mold litigation.

For Plaintiffs:

No safe harbor shields property owners based on numerical compliance. Defendants cannot point to staying below regulatory limits because no such limits exist. This forces evaluation based on reasonableness rather than regulatory compliance.

Visible mold and moisture amplification may support claims of unreasonable conditions. Courts understand that preventing prolonged moisture intrusion is reasonable. Even without exposure thresholds, failing to fix leaks or address visible mold growth can constitute breach.

Federal guidance can demonstrate notice of remediation obligations. EPA and HUD guidance is publicly available. Defendants cannot credibly claim ignorance of basic remediation principles when federal agencies have published clear guidance.

For Defendants:

Lack of exposure thresholds weakens claims of systemic toxicity. Without regulatory limits, plaintiffs cannot argue that specific spore concentrations exceeded safe levels. Causation becomes entirely expert-dependent.

Plaintiffs cannot rely on regulatory violations to establish per se negligence. Absence of regulations means no regulatory violations. This forces plaintiffs to prove negligence through common law principles rather than statutory violations.

Guidance is advisory, not mandatory. Following EPA or HUD guidance may demonstrate reasonable conduct, but slight deviations do not automatically constitute negligence.

In contrast to asbestos or lead-based paint litigation (where federal regulations establish clear thresholds and mandatory abatement procedures), mold claims lack a clear statutory violation framework. This makes each case more fact-intensive and dependent on expert credibility.

VIII. Federal Preemption and Environmental Law Arguments

Defendants occasionally argue that federal environmental statutes preempt state tort claims. However, mold litigation rarely triggers full federal preemption because:

Mold is not regulated as a hazardous substance under CERCLA. The Comprehensive Environmental Response, Compensation, and Liability Act (Superfund) does not classify mold as a hazardous substance requiring federal cleanup.

Indoor air quality in residential settings is not comprehensively governed by federal statute. Unlike outdoor air quality (Clean Air Act) or drinking water (Safe Drinking Water Act), indoor residential air quality remains primarily a state and local concern.

Federal housing programs do not fully preempt state tort law. HUD regulations supplement but do not displace state landlord-tenant law, habitability doctrines, or negligence principles.

As a result, toxic mold litigation remains largely governed by state tort and contract law, even when federal housing programs or military installations are involved.

Preemption arguments occasionally succeed in narrow contexts (e.g., claims alleging that federal agency employees were negligent may be preempted and channeled into FTCA procedures), but mold litigation against private parties generally proceeds under state law.

IX. Documentation and Compliance as Defensive Tools

In the absence of numeric standards, documentation becomes critical for defense.

Property owners and managers can mitigate liability by maintaining:

Inspection logs. Documenting regular property inspections shows proactive maintenance rather than reactive response only after tenant complaints.

Work orders. Recording maintenance requests, response times, and actions taken demonstrates responsiveness. Delayed work orders show negligence; prompt work orders show reasonable conduct.

Moisture response timelines. Dating when leaks were reported, when repairs began, and when they were completed establishes response timeframe. The difference between 48-hour response and 6-month response is the difference between defensible conduct and negligence.

Remediation invoices and contracts. Professional remediation contractor invoices demonstrate that work was performed by qualified personnel, not unqualified handymen with bleach spray bottles.

Clearance testing reports. Post-remediation environmental testing showing mold levels returned to normal provides objective evidence that remediation was effective.

Federal housing guidance increasingly emphasizes documentation as evidence of compliance. In litigation, such records can demonstrate reasonableness even if mold was present.

The absence of documentation often suggests something to hide. When property owners cannot produce work orders, inspection logs, or remediation records, juries (and judges) infer that problems were ignored. Documentation protects against this inference.

X. Climate Change and Federal Policy Evolution

As extreme weather events increase, federal agencies are revisiting moisture control, resilience, and building code integration.

Future developments may include:

Enhanced federal housing inspection protocols. HUD and military housing oversight may implement more rigorous mold and moisture inspection requirements.

Updated resilience standards for publicly funded construction. Federal construction projects and federally funded housing may face new moisture management requirements.

Expanded funding for moisture mitigation in aging housing stock. Federal grants may become available for moisture control improvements in public housing and affordable housing developments.

Possible coordination between EPA, HUD, and FEMA on flood-prone housing. As climate-driven flooding increases, federal agencies may develop coordinated guidance on moisture prevention and mold risk in flood zones.

While federal mold exposure thresholds remain unlikely in the near term (scientific uncertainty persists), regulatory attention to water intrusion is increasing. Future litigation may see more references to federal resilience standards and climate adaptation guidelines.

XI. Strategic Implications for Litigators

Understanding federal guidance allows attorneys to:

Frame duty of care arguments. "The EPA recommends prompt remediation within 24-48 hours. The landlord waited six months. This delay was unreasonable."

Evaluate public housing exposure. HUD guidance creates expectations for reasonable response in federally assisted housing. Violations strengthen liability arguments.

Assess military housing liability. Understanding FTCA procedures, sovereign immunity, and contractor defenses is essential for navigating military housing claims.

Analyze workplace claims. OSHA's General Duty Clause and guidance on workplace mold inform employer obligations.

Consider FHA theories when tenants have disabilities. Documented respiratory conditions + accommodation requests + landlord delay = potential FHA violation with enhanced damages and mandatory attorney's fees.

Federal agencies do not define what is "toxic mold." They define expectations for response. And in modern toxic mold litigation, the adequacy and timeliness of response often determines liability more than the species of mold detected.

Practical Litigation Checklist:

✓ Research EPA guidance relevant to the contamination scope
✓ Determine whether HUD regulations apply (public/Section 8 housing)
✓ Evaluate FHA theories if tenant has documented disability
✓ For military housing, identify whether defendant is federal agency or private contractor
✓ For workplace cases, check whether OSHA conducted inspections
✓ Review federal guidance to establish reasonable response expectations
✓ Gather documentation showing compliance or non-compliance with guidance

XII. Conclusion

Federal law does not establish what level of mold is "toxic." It does not provide numerical indoor air standards. It does not create a uniform national mold statute.

But federal guidance shapes the litigation landscape by defining:

- Habitability expectations (HUD guidance for public housing)
- Workplace safety obligations (OSHA General Duty Clause)
- Reasonable accommodation requirements (FHA for tenants with disabilities)
- Military contractor responsibilities (federal housing contracts)
- Best practices for remediation (EPA guidance)

In the absence of bright-line exposure rules, courts rely on reasonableness, documentation, and expert testimony. Federal guidance informs what "reasonable" means without mandating specific conduct.

Key Takeaways:

1. **Federal guidance is admissible evidence of industry standards** but does not create strict liability
2. **Documentation of compliance with federal guidance strengthens defense positions** without providing absolute immunity
3. **FHA claims can transform mold case value** when tenants have documented disabilities

4. **Military housing claims require careful navigation** of sovereign immunity and contractor defenses

5. **The absence of federal exposure thresholds** makes every case fact-intensive and expert-dependent

The next chapter shifts from federal frameworks to state legislative models, beginning with the most frequently cited statute in mold litigation: California's approach to mold disclosure and remediation. Understanding state-level variation is essential because mold litigation outcomes often depend more on state law than federal guidance.

5

The California Model: Statutory Disclosure, Remediation Standards

And the Evolution of Mold Liability

The State That Shaped the National Conversation

In 2001, as national media coverage of toxic mold reached fever pitch, California did something bold: it enacted comprehensive mold legislation. The California Toxic Mold Protection Act was hailed by some as groundbreaking consumer protection and criticized by others as government overreach that would bankrupt landlords and property owners.

Twenty-five years later, neither prediction proved accurate.

The Act did not create automatic liability for every mold spore. It did not establish numerical exposure limits that plaintiffs could point to as proof of toxicity. It did not transform California into a plaintiff's paradise where mold cases routinely produced multi-million-dollar verdicts.

But it did something more subtle and more lasting: it elevated mold from a maintenance annoyance to a recognized public health issue. It formalized state acknowledgment that indoor mold exposure could pose legitimate health risks. It influenced how courts interpret habitability obligations, how real estate professionals approach disclosure, and how property owners think about moisture management.

By 2026, the California framework remains one of the most cited statutory reference points in toxic mold litigation nationwide. Not because it created strict liability, but because it demonstrated how legislative recognition shapes expectations without necessarily simplifying litigation.

Understanding California's approach is essential because many other states modeled their responses after it (or deliberately chose not to follow it), and because California case law interpreting the statute influences courts nationwide.

I. California as the Blueprint for Mold Legislation

California has long served as a bellwether in environmental and housing regulation. In the realm of toxic mold litigation, it became one of the first states to respond legislatively to growing public concern over indoor mold exposure.

The centerpiece of that response is the California Toxic Mold Protection Act (TMPA), codified primarily in California Health and Safety Code Sections 26100-26156. While the Act did not create a sweeping private right of action, it significantly influenced how mold cases are evaluated in California courts and beyond.

The Act emerged from several high-profile California mold cases in the late 1990s and early 2000s, including substantial settlements and media coverage that generated public alarm. Legislators faced pressure to "do something" about toxic mold while lacking scientific consensus on what regulatory thresholds would be appropriate.

The result was legislation that:

- Directed study and potential standard-setting
- Encouraged public education
- Enhanced disclosure expectations
- Influenced professional practices

But stopped short of creating automatic liability or enforceable exposure limits.

II. Legislative Purpose and Structure

Enacted in 2001, the California Toxic Mold Protection Act directed the California Department of Public Health (then the Department of Health Services) to:

Study mold exposure and associated health effects. The Act mandated review of existing scientific literature and consultation with experts to understand mold-related health risks.

Develop permissible exposure limits (if feasible). The Act contemplated establishing numerical thresholds for indoor mold exposure. However, this provision was conditional: limits would be established only "to the extent feasible."

Establish remediation standards. The Act directed development of guidelines for identifying and remediating mold contamination in indoor environments.

Provide public education guidance. The Act called for creation of informational materials to help property owners, tenants, and the public understand mold risks and prevention strategies.

Although the Act contemplated development of exposure limits, regulators ultimately stopped short of establishing enforceable numerical indoor mold thresholds. Scientific uncertainty and variability in environmental conditions made uniform limits difficult to define.

The Department of Public Health explained its position in subsequent reports:

"Due to the current state of scientific knowledge about mold exposure and health effects, and considering the enormous variability in mold species, indoor environmental conditions, building materials, and individual susceptibilities, establishing a single permissible exposure limit for all molds is not scientifically supportable at this time."

This decision disappointed some advocates who wanted bright-line standards but reflected scientific reality.

Nevertheless, the Act accomplished several important objectives:

1. It formalized state recognition of mold as a public health issue. Before the Act, defendants could argue that mold concerns were media-driven hysteria. After the Act, California had officially acknowledged that indoor mold exposure warranted legislative attention.

2. It encouraged development of remediation guidelines. Even without mandatory standards, the Act influenced professional practices by directing development of recommended protocols.

3. It influenced disclosure obligations in real estate transactions. By elevating mold to a matter of legislative concern, the Act reinforced that mold history constitutes a material condition potentially requiring disclosure.

4. It shaped landlord response expectations in habitability disputes. Courts interpreting California's implied warranty of habitability increasingly referenced the legislative recognition of mold as a significant environmental concern.

III. The Absence of Numeric Exposure Limits: What It Means

One of the most consequential outcomes of the TMPA was what it did **not** do: it did not create enforceable spore count thresholds.

This omission has significant litigation implications.

For Plaintiffs:

Claims cannot rely on statutory exceedance of numeric limits. Plaintiffs cannot argue "the mold levels exceeded California's permissible exposure limit" because no such limit exists. This eliminates the possibility of proving negligence per se through regulatory violation.

Proof of dangerous exposure remains dependent on expert testimony. Without numerical thresholds, plaintiffs must rely entirely on expert witnesses to opine that exposure levels were unreasonable or unsafe.

This returns litigation to the battle of competing experts rather than objective regulatory compliance.

The Act provides no independent cause of action. The TMPA does not create a private right to sue for mold exposure. Plaintiffs still must rely on traditional tort theories (negligence, breach of warranty of habitability) or statutory claims under other laws (habitability statutes, consumer protection acts).

For Defendants:

Compliance cannot be measured solely by environmental testing results. Defendants cannot claim "we were below the regulatory limit" because no limit exists. But they also benefit because plaintiffs cannot point to regulatory violations.

Liability turns on reasonableness of response rather than fixed benchmarks. Without numerical standards, courts evaluate whether the defendant's response to moisture and mold was reasonable under the circumstances, not whether specific concentrations were exceeded.

The Act did not create strict liability. Presence of mold does not automatically establish liability. Plaintiffs must still prove breach of duty, causation, and damages under traditional legal frameworks.

California courts, like federal courts, therefore evaluate mold cases based on factual context and expert reliability rather than statutory violation per se.

Case in Focus: Why Absence of Standards Matters

A 2024 San Diego case illustrates how the absence of numerical standards affects litigation strategy. The plaintiff's environmental consultant documented Aspergillus and Penicillium at concentrations 15 times outdoor baseline levels. The plaintiff's attorney initially framed the case around "excessive mold exposure violating California health standards."

The defense immediately moved for summary judgment on this theory, pointing out that no such standards exist. The court granted the motion as to claims based on alleged regulatory violations.

The case continued under habitability and negligence theories but with significantly reduced settlement value. Had California established numerical thresholds (even advisory ones), the plaintiff could have argued that indoor levels exceeded state guidelines. Without thresholds, the case became a pure battle of experts over whether the measured levels were "dangerous."

The case ultimately settled for $95,000 (versus an initial $400,000 demand). The absence of regulatory thresholds fundamentally changed the litigation dynamics.

IV. Mold and the Warranty of Habitability in California

California's implied warranty of habitability doctrine has long imposed duties on landlords to maintain residential premises in safe and sanitary condition.

Under California law (California Civil Code Section 1941 and related statutes), conditions that materially affect health and safety may render a dwelling uninhabitable. Mold contamination, particularly when associated with moisture intrusion, can fall within that framework.

Courts typically assess:

Extent and visibility of mold growth. Minor surface mold in a bathroom may not render premises uninhabitable. Extensive growth throughout living areas likely does.

Duration of moisture intrusion. A brief leak that is promptly addressed differs substantially from months of chronic water intrusion.

Landlord notice and response time. Did the landlord know about the problem? How quickly did they respond? Was response adequate?

Impact on tenant health and use of premises. Are tenants experiencing symptoms? Has the contamination made rooms unusable?

In practice, mold cases in California often proceed under habitability and negligence theories rather than direct statutory claims under the TMPA. The Act provides context and recognition but does not create independent liability.

How California Courts Apply Habitability Analysis

California courts have consistently held that landlords must maintain rental properties in habitable condition. Relevant case law includes:

Green v. Superior Court, 10 Cal. 3d 616, 111 Cal. Rptr. 704 (1974): Established that the implied warranty of habitability cannot be waived by lease provisions. Even "as-is" clauses do not eliminate landlord obligations to maintain habitable conditions.

Stoiber v. Honeychuck, 101 Cal. App. 3d 903, 162 Cal. Rptr. 194 (1980): Clarified that tenants can recover damages for breach of habitability even if they continue living on the premises. Constructive eviction is not required.

Erlach v. Sierra Asset Servicing, 226 Cal. App. 4th 1281, 173 Cal. Rptr. 3d 196 (2014): Addressed the intersection of foreclosure and habitability, confirming that new property owners assume habitability obligations upon taking title.

While these cases don't specifically address mold, they establish the framework within which mold habitability claims proceed:

1. Landlord has a non-waivable duty to maintain habitable premises
2. Tenants can recover damages without moving out
3. Habitability obligations transfer with property ownership
4. Materiality depends on severity and duration of conditions

The TMPA reinforced this framework by adding legislative recognition that mold constitutes a legitimate habitability concern.

V. Disclosure Obligations in Real Estate Transactions

California has some of the most rigorous property disclosure requirements in the country. Sellers must disclose known material defects affecting property value or desirability.

The primary disclosure mechanism is the **Transfer Disclosure Statement (TDS)**, required under California Civil Code Section 1102 for most residential property sales. The TDS specifically asks sellers about water intrusion, flooding, drainage problems, and environmental hazards.

While the TDS does not explicitly list "mold" as a separate item, the Act's passage heightened awareness that mold and moisture problems constitute material conditions potentially requiring disclosure.

Failure to disclose known mold or chronic water intrusion can give rise to claims for:

Fraud. Intentional concealment of known material defects with intent to deceive.

Negligent misrepresentation. Careless or negligent failure to disclose material facts.

Concealment. Active hiding of conditions (e.g., painting over mold, replacing drywall without addressing moisture source).

Breach of contract. Violation of express representations in the purchase agreement.

The TMPA reinforced public awareness of mold as a material condition, increasing the likelihood that undisclosed mold problems would be viewed as legally significant. Even though the Act does not explicitly mandate mold disclosure, it shaped reasonable expectations about what sellers should reveal.

Real estate professionals must also comply with statutory transfer disclosure statements. Omission of known moisture damage may expose brokers to liability, particularly post-TMPA when mold is widely recognized as a significant issue.

What Constitutes "Known" Conditions

California disclosure law focuses on seller knowledge. Sellers must disclose:

- Conditions they actually know about
- Conditions they should reasonably know about through property ownership

Sellers generally are not required to conduct inspections to discover unknown conditions, but they cannot ignore obvious problems.

Red flags that create constructive knowledge:

- Visible water staining
- Musty odors
- Previous insurance claims for water damage
- Prior remediation attempts
- Neighbor or tenant complaints

If these red flags exist, sellers cannot claim ignorance. They have constructive knowledge requiring disclosure.

Case in Focus: When Non-Disclosure Costs More Than the Mold

A 2025 Los Angeles case involved sellers who painted over water-stained drywall and replaced musty carpet before listing their home. They checked "no" on the TDS question about water intrusion or drainage problems.

The buyers discovered extensive Stachybotrys growth behind the freshly painted walls within six weeks of closing. Investigation revealed:

- The sellers had filed an insurance claim for roof damage two years earlier
- Contractor invoices (found in the garage during move-in) documented "mold remediation" work
- Text messages between the sellers discussed "just painting over it"

The buyers sued for fraud and concealment. The case settled for $425,000, including:

- Remediation and reconstruction costs: $180,000
- Diminution in property value: $120,000
- Emotional distress and relocation expenses: $75,000
- Punitive damages: $50,000

Had the sellers disclosed the prior water intrusion and remediation on the TDS, the property likely would have sold for $150,000 less, and the sale might still have closed with appropriate inspections and negotiations. Instead, the attempted concealment cost them nearly three times as much.

The lesson: In California's post-TMPA environment, disclosure is almost always less expensive than concealment.

VI. Construction Defect and Building Code Integration

California's extensive building code framework intersects with mold litigation in construction defect cases. The state's building standards address moisture management, though not mold specifically.

Key recurring issues in California construction defect mold litigation include:

Improper flashing installation. Window and door flashing must be installed according to manufacturer specifications and building code. Improper installation allows water penetration that leads to mold growth in wall cavities.

Window and roofing defects. These are among the most common moisture intrusion sources in California construction defect cases, particularly in stucco-clad buildings.

Balcony and deck waterproofing failures. California's climate allows year-round outdoor use, but waterproofing failures in balconies and decks create chronic moisture problems.

Stucco and cladding moisture entrapment. The EIFS (Exterior Insulation and Finish System) and traditional stucco failures of the 1990s and early 2000s resulted in thousands of construction defect cases involving moisture and mold.

HVAC condensation problems. Improperly sized or installed HVAC systems create condensation that leads to mold growth, particularly in tightly sealed energy-efficient construction.

In multi-unit developments, systemic design defects can result in widespread moisture intrusion, amplifying litigation exposure across hundreds of units.

Although the TMPA itself does not regulate construction practices, it operates within a broader regulatory culture that emphasizes moisture prevention and building envelope integrity. Courts increasingly view chronic moisture intrusion as construction negligence rather than mere maintenance issues.

California's Right to Repair Act (SB 800)

California's construction defect litigation is significantly shaped by the Right to Repair Act (Civil Code Section 895 et seq.), which establishes standards for residential construction and procedures for resolving claims before litigation.

Under SB 800:

- Builders must be given notice and opportunity to inspect and repair defects
- Specific performance standards apply to various building components
- Water intrusion and moisture problems are covered under multiple standards
- Failure to meet standards creates actionable construction defects

Mold growth resulting from building envelope failures, plumbing defects, or design flaws falls within SB 800's framework. While SB 800 doesn't mention mold specifically, it addresses the underlying causes (water intrusion, defective waterproofing, inadequate drainage) that create mold conditions.

The combination of TMPA recognition and SB 800 standards creates a comprehensive framework for construction-related mold claims in California.

VII. Insurance Coverage in California Mold Cases

California's active insurance litigation environment has produced substantial case law interpreting mold exclusions and resulting-loss provisions.

Common disputes involve:

Whether water damage constitutes a covered peril. Most property policies cover sudden and accidental water damage (burst pipes, roof damage from storms). They typically exclude gradual water intrusion or lack of maintenance.

Whether mold is excluded as a pollutant. Some insurance policies include pollution exclusions and define "pollutant" broadly enough to encompass mold. California courts have sometimes interpreted pollution exclusions narrowly, finding they were intended for traditional environmental contamination, not residential mold.

Application of anti-concurrent causation clauses. These provisions state that if any excluded cause contributes to a loss, coverage is barred entirely. California courts scrutinize these clauses carefully and sometimes find them ambiguous or unenforceable.

Sub-limits for mold remediation. Many policies cap mold-related remediation at $5,000 to $10,000 even when other property damage is fully covered. Policyholders challenge these sub-limits as inadequate, but courts generally enforce them when clearly stated.

California courts have sometimes interpreted coverage provisions narrowly against insurers, particularly where policy language is ambiguous. The state's pro-consumer orientation influences coverage disputes.

As mold exclusions evolved after the early 2000s litigation wave, California became a testing ground for coverage disputes that later influenced national policy drafting.

Case in Focus: Resulting Loss Coverage Dispute

A 2024 Sacramento case involved a homeowner whose burst pipe caused water damage and subsequent mold growth. The insurance policy covered "sudden and accidental water damage" but included a mold exclusion with a $5,000 sub-limit.

The carrier paid:

- $75,000 for water damage repairs (replacing flooring, drywall, cabinets)
- $5,000 for mold remediation (the sub-limit maximum)

The homeowner argued that mold growth was a "resulting loss" from the covered water damage and should be fully covered despite the exclusion. The carrier argued the exclusion and sub-limit applied regardless of cause.

The dispute settled after mediation for an additional $35,000 (on top of the initial $80,000 payment). The carrier agreed to pay more to avoid potentially adverse precedent about resulting-loss interpretation.

This pattern repeats frequently: coverage disputes settle in the middle ground between full coverage and strict exclusion application, with California's pro-consumer reputation pressuring carriers toward settlement.

VIII. Enforcement and Public Health Integration

California health departments may become involved when mold conditions are severe, particularly in multi-family or public housing contexts.

Enforcement actions may include:

Notices of violation. Local health departments or code enforcement agencies issue violations for substandard housing conditions including mold and moisture problems.

Orders to remediate. Administrative orders requiring property owners to correct conditions within specified timeframes.

Civil penalties. Fines for failure to comply with remediation orders or for maintaining uninhabitable conditions.

Tenant relocation directives. In extreme cases, health departments may order temporary relocation of occupants while remediation occurs.

Such administrative records often become key evidence in civil litigation. A documented history of health department complaints can strengthen plaintiff claims of notice and failure to act.

A series of health department violations demonstrates:

- Third-party acknowledgment that conditions were substandard
- Official notice to property owner
- Failure to respond to governmental authority (not just tenant complaints)
- Pattern of neglect

Juries respond strongly to evidence that property owners ignored not only tenant complaints but also governmental enforcement actions.

IX. The California Model's Influence on Other States

Although not all states enacted mold-specific statutes, California's approach influenced national trends in several ways:

1. Elevated public awareness of indoor air quality. Media coverage of California's legislative response raised national consciousness about mold as a legitimate concern (though also sometimes exaggerated risks).

2. Encouraged development of industry remediation standards. Professional organizations (IICRC, AIHA, ACGIH) developed or refined mold remediation protocols partly in response to California's legislative attention.

3. Integrated mold considerations into real estate disclosure norms. Even states without mold-specific statutes saw increased disclosure of moisture and mold issues after California's Act heightened awareness.

4. Highlighted the complexity of establishing exposure limits. California's inability to establish numerical standards despite legislative mandate demonstrated the scientific challenges, influencing other states to avoid attempting similar standards.

States such as Texas, Nevada, and New York have adopted varying approaches to mold regulation, but few have implemented enforceable numeric exposure standards. Most followed California's lead in recognizing mold as a legitimate concern while stopping short of bright-line liability rules.

State Responses to California's Model

States that enacted mold-specific legislation:

- **Texas:** Created licensing for mold assessors/remediators
- **Maryland:** Enhanced disclosure requirements
- **New Jersey:** Strengthened landlord remediation duties

States that addressed mold through existing frameworks:

- **New York:** Increased housing code enforcement
- **Florida:** Clarified habitability standards
- **Illinois:** Enhanced tenant remedies

States that deliberately avoided mold legislation:

- Many states concluded that existing landlord-tenant laws, habitability doctrines, and negligence principles adequately addressed mold issues without need for specific legislation

California's model demonstrates that legislative recognition does not necessarily simplify litigation. It shapes expectations without creating automatic liability.

X. Practical Lessons for Litigators

From a litigation perspective, California offers several key lessons:

Mold statutes may shape expectations without creating strict liability. The TMPA elevated mold as a recognized concern but did not transform it into a strict liability regime. Courts still require proof of breach, causation, and damages.

Absence of numeric limits keeps causation battles expert-driven. Without thresholds, every case becomes a battle of competing experts over whether conditions were dangerous. This makes expert selection critical.

Disclosure failures can expand damages exposure significantly. California's robust disclosure requirements mean concealment cases can produce substantial damages including punitive awards, even when underlying mold contamination is modest.

Administrative enforcement records can influence jury perception. Health department violations and code enforcement actions create powerful evidence of notice and indifference.

Insurance disputes often parallel liability claims. California's complex coverage jurisprudence means mold cases frequently involve simultaneous liability and coverage litigation.

Attorneys practicing in or modeling arguments after California jurisprudence must integrate statutory awareness with traditional tort and contract principles. The TMPA provides context and recognition but does not replace fundamental proof requirements.

XI. The Continuing Evolution of Mold Law in California

As of 2026, California continues to refine housing standards in response to:

Climate-driven moisture events. Atmospheric rivers, increased winter rainfall, and drought-flood cycles create recurring moisture challenges.

Aging housing stock. California's older housing inventory requires ongoing maintenance, and deferred maintenance increases mold risk.

Increased tenant advocacy. Tenant rights organizations have become more sophisticated in documenting conditions and pursuing legal remedies.

Insurance market adjustments. Carriers continue refining exclusions and sub-limits in response to California's pro-consumer coverage interpretations.

While comprehensive indoor exposure standards remain unlikely (scientific uncertainty persists), enforcement mechanisms tied to habitability and disclosure are strengthening.

California remains less a model of strict mold liability and more a model of integrated housing regulation that recognizes mold as a legitimate concern without creating automatic liability.

XII. Conclusion

The California Toxic Mold Protection Act did not create automatic liability for mold exposure. It did not establish numerical toxicity thresholds. It did not transform mold litigation into a statutory tort regime.

Instead, it:

Elevated mold as a recognized public health concern. Legislative acknowledgment matters even without specific regulatory thresholds.

Influenced disclosure and remediation expectations. Property owners, landlords, and real estate professionals cannot credibly claim ignorance about mold risks in California's post-TMPA environment.

Reinforced habitability doctrines. Courts interpret habitability obligations with awareness that the legislature views mold as significant.

Shaped insurance and construction defect litigation. The Act provides context for evaluating reasonableness in coverage disputes and construction cases.

California's framework illustrates a central truth of toxic mold litigation in 2026:

Statutory recognition may guide the narrative, but liability ultimately turns on proof. Proof of moisture intrusion. Proof of notice. Proof of unreasonable response. And proof of medical causation.

The TMPA did not simplify California mold litigation. It made it more nuanced by establishing that mold matters without defining precisely when it creates liability. That determination remains fact-intensive, case-specific, and dependent on traditional proof requirements.

Key Takeaways:

1. **Legislative recognition ≠ strict liability.** California acknowledged mold risks without creating automatic liability
2. **Absence of numerical standards** makes expert credibility decisive in every case
3. **Disclosure requirements** create substantial exposure for concealment
4. **Insurance coverage disputes** are as important as underlying liability
5. **California's model influenced national approaches** without being universally adopted

The next chapter broadens the lens, examining how other states are revising building codes, rental statutes, and remediation standards in response to evolving mold litigation trends. Understanding jurisdictional variation is critical because where you litigate often matters as much as what evidence you have.

6

State-by-State Legislative Shifts

Building Codes, Rental Law Reform, and Emerging Mold Standards

---

Fifty States, Fifty Approaches

In March 2024, two nearly identical mold cases were filed on the same day, 1,200 miles apart:

Case A: Filed in Seattle, Washington

- Family discovered extensive mold in rental home
- Landlord ignored complaints for four months
- Environmental testing showed Stachybotrys at 20x outdoor levels
- Child's asthma worsened during occupancy

Case B: Filed in Birmingham, Alabama

- Family discovered extensive mold in rental home

- Landlord ignored complaints for four months
- Environmental testing showed Stachybotrys at 20x outdoor levels
- Child's asthma worsened during occupancy

Identical facts. Dramatically different outcomes.

The Seattle case settled in eight months for $285,000. Washington's strong tenant protection statutes, mandatory attorney's fees for prevailing tenants, and court-imposed repair timelines created leverage that the landlord's insurer couldn't ignore.

The Birmingham case settled eighteen months later for $47,000. Alabama's more limited tenant remedies, absence of fee-shifting provisions, and landlord-friendly procedural rules fundamentally changed the litigation economics.

Same mold. Same negligence. Same child with asthma. Different state law. Different result.

This chapter examines the patchwork nature of mold regulation in the United States and how state-level legislative choices create the frameworks within which toxic mold litigation succeeds or fails.

I. The Patchwork Nature of Mold Regulation in the United States

Unlike lead-based paint or asbestos, toxic mold is not governed by a unified national statutory regime. Instead, mold regulation in the United States is a state-driven patchwork of:

- Building code amendments addressing moisture control
- Landlord-tenant statutory revisions clarifying remediation duties
- Real estate disclosure laws requiring transparency about water intrusion history
- Health department enforcement rules establishing inspection and remediation protocols
- Insurance regulatory adjustments governing policy exclusions and sub-limits

By 2026, several states have tightened moisture-control standards and clarified remediation duties, often in response to high-profile litigation, climate-driven water intrusion events, and public housing scandals.

This chapter examines the evolving state-level landscape and how those changes influence toxic mold litigation strategy. Understanding jurisdictional differences is not academic. It determines:

- Whether cases are economically viable
- What settlement ranges are realistic
- Which legal theories will succeed
- How quickly cases resolve

Location matters as much as the mold itself.

II. California: Integrated Housing Regulation

As discussed in Chapter 5, California remains a reference point due to the California Toxic Mold Protection Act and its broader habitability framework.

Recent developments in California (2024-2026) include:

Increased enforcement of substandard housing conditions. Local code enforcement agencies have become more aggressive in citing property owners for mold and moisture violations, particularly in multi-family housing.

Greater scrutiny of multi-family moisture complaints. Housing authorities increasingly view pattern complaints (multiple units reporting similar problems) as evidence of systemic defects requiring comprehensive remediation rather than unit-by-unit patchwork.

Expanded tenant advocacy tied to indoor air quality. Tenant rights organizations have integrated indoor air quality into broader housing justice campaigns, increasing tenant awareness of legal remedies.

Post-pandemic attention to ventilation. COVID-19 heightened awareness of indoor air quality. This consciousness extends to mold issues, making tenants and property owners more alert to ventilation and moisture problems.

Although California still lacks enforceable numeric mold exposure limits, its integration of mold into housing habitability analysis makes it one of the more plaintiff-receptive jurisdictions for property-based claims.

California's Litigation Climate (2024-2026)

Strengths for Plaintiffs:

- Strong tenant protection statutes (rent abatement, repair-and-deduct remedies)
- Broad habitability doctrine interpretation
- Attorney's fees available under multiple statutes
- Emotional distress damages without requiring severe physical injury
- Pro-consumer insurance coverage interpretations

Challenges for Plaintiffs:

- High cost of litigation (expert fees, filing costs)
- Sophisticated defense bar with extensive mold experience
- Strict Daubert application for systemic injury claims
- Insurance exclusions increasingly refined to limit coverage

Typical Settlement Range (moderate case): $125,000 - $350,000

III. Texas: Licensing and Remediation Structure

Texas historically adopted a more structured regulatory approach to mold assessment and remediation, though some provisions have evolved over time.

Key features of Texas's approach include:

Licensing requirements for mold assessors and remediators. Texas created a framework requiring professional licensing, though requirements have been modified. Licensed professionals must meet training and experience standards.

Remediation protocols. Texas established guidelines for proper mold remediation, emphasizing containment, removal, and post-remediation verification.

Certificate of Mold Remediation requirements. Following remediation work, property owners receive certificates documenting that work was completed according to established protocols.

Litigation Implications

For Plaintiffs:

Failure to use licensed professionals may strengthen negligence claims. When property owners or landlords use unlicensed handymen to address mold rather than licensed remediators, this deviation from state-established norms can support negligence arguments.

Documentation of remediation certificates can serve as defensive evidence. Conversely, defendants who followed Texas protocols and obtained proper certification can demonstrate reasonable response.

Regulatory compliance does not eliminate causation challenges. Following Texas remediation protocols does not automatically defeat medical causation claims, but may reduce punitive exposure by showing good faith efforts.

For Defendants:

Texas's structured approach provides clearer guidance on reasonable conduct but does not create safe harbor from liability. Courts still require plaintiffs to prove causation, and Texas courts remain demanding regarding medical causation, particularly for systemic illness claims.

Texas's Litigation Climate (2024-2026)

Strengths for Plaintiffs:

- Licensing framework establishes professional standards
- Certificate requirements create documentation expectations
- Some plaintiff-friendly jurisdictions (Harris County, Travis County)

Challenges for Plaintiffs:

Conservative damage awards in many jurisdictions

Strict medical causation standards

Tort reform provisions limiting certain damages

Limited emotional distress recovery without physical injury

Typical Settlement Range (moderate case): $75,000 - $200,000

Case in Focus: Licensing Requirements as Evidence

A 2024 Houston case involved a landlord who discovered mold in a rental unit and hired an unlicensed contractor to "spray it with bleach and paint over it." The work cost $500.

Three months later, the mold returned more extensively. The tenant sued, and the plaintiff's expert testified that:

- The remediation failed to address moisture source
- Painting over mold without proper removal is ineffective
- Texas licensing requirements exist precisely to prevent this type of inadequate response
- Proper remediation by licensed professionals would have cost approximately $8,000

The jury awarded $165,000, including $50,000 in punitive damages. The landlord's decision to save $7,500 by avoiding licensed professionals cost him $165,000. The licensing framework provided clear evidence of what reasonable conduct required.

IV. Nevada: Habitability and Disclosure Emphasis

Nevada has experienced significant mold-related litigation, including multi-million-dollar residential settlements. The state's approach focuses on clarifying landlord maintenance obligations and strengthening tenant remedies.

Recent legislative attention has focused on:

Clarifying landlord maintenance obligations. Nevada statutes specify landlord duties to maintain premises in habitable condition, including addressing moisture intrusion.

Strengthening tenant remedies for uninhabitable conditions. Tenants have clearer paths to rent abatement, repair-and-deduct remedies, and constructive eviction claims.

Enhancing disclosure expectations in residential sales. Sellers must disclose known material defects, and post-litigation awareness has made mold and moisture history recognized as material conditions.

In Nevada, mold cases often proceed under:

- **Breach of warranty of habitability** (the most common theory)
- **Negligence** (when landlord knew or should have known of moisture problems)
- **Failure to disclose** (in purchase transactions)

While statutory reform has reinforced tenant protections, courts still require reliable scientific proof for substantial personal injury damages. Nevada's approach recognizes mold as a habitability issue without creating automatic liability.

Nevada's Litigation Climate (2024-2026)

Strengths for Plaintiffs:

- Strong habitability protections
- Successful high-value settlements (Las Vegas $6.6M case demonstrates viability)
- Growing tenant advocacy infrastructure
- Attorney's fees available in some contexts

Challenges for Plaintiffs:

- Medical causation still requires strong expert testimony
- Some rural jurisdictions are defense-oriented
- Insurance exclusions limit available settlement funds

Typical Settlement Range (moderate case): $90,000 - $275,000

V. New York: Housing Code Enforcement and Public Housing Litigation

New York's mold litigation landscape is shaped heavily by municipal housing codes, particularly in dense urban environments like New York City.

Recent trends include:

Increased inspection protocols for public housing. New York City Housing Authority (NYCHA) faces ongoing scrutiny over mold conditions in public housing, leading to enhanced inspection requirements.

Administrative violation tracking systems. Digital systems now track code violations, creating detailed records of landlord non-compliance that become powerful litigation evidence.

Heightened public scrutiny of delayed remediation. Media coverage of mold conditions in public housing and rent-stabilized apartments has increased political pressure for enforcement.

HPD (Housing Preservation and Development) enforcement. NYC's HPD issues violations for mold and moisture problems, and accumulated violations create strong evidence of notice.

In multi-family and public housing contexts, documented housing code violations frequently become foundational evidence in civil suits. A series of HPD violations demonstrates:

- Official acknowledgment that conditions were substandard
- Notice to property owner
- Failure to comply with governmental authority
- Pattern of neglect rather than isolated incident

However, as in other jurisdictions, plaintiffs must bridge the gap between code violations and specific medical injury. New York courts may be receptive to habitability and emotional distress claims even when systemic illness theories fail.

New York's Litigation Climate (2024-2026)

Strengths for Plaintiffs:

- Extensive housing code framework creates clear standards
- HPD violations provide documentary evidence
- Strong tenant protection culture in NYC
- Emotional distress damages available in some circumstances
- Warranty of habitability well-established

Challenges for Plaintiffs:

- High litigation costs in NYC
- Sophisticated institutional defendants (large property management companies)
- Medical causation remains challenging
- Some upstate jurisdictions less plaintiff-friendly

Typical Settlement Range (moderate case): $100,000 - $300,000 (NYC); $50,000 - $150,000 (upstate)

Case in Focus: HPD Violations as Leverage

A 2025 Bronx case involved a tenant in a rent-stabilized apartment who complained about water intrusion and mold for fourteen months. The landlord repeatedly promised repairs but failed to act.

HPD issued violations including:

- Water penetration (issued month 3)
- Mold/mildew conditions (issued month 6)
- Failure to maintain premises (issued month 9)
- Emergency repair order (issued month 12)

The landlord ignored all violations. By month 14, the tenant had accumulated four HPD violations, an emergency repair order, and medical records documenting three urgent care visits for respiratory symptoms.

The case settled for $215,000 before trial. The landlord's attorney candidly acknowledged that the HPD violation history made trial untenable: "A Bronx jury seeing fourteen months of governmental violations with zero landlord response would award far more than $215,000."

The HPD violations transformed what might have been a $75,000 case into a $215,000 settlement.

VI. Building Code Revisions and Moisture Control

Several states are updating building codes in response to:

- Flooding events and climate-driven precipitation increases
- Increased humidity patterns affecting regions previously considered dry
- Energy-efficient but tightly sealed construction creating condensation issues
- Condensation-related failures in high-performance buildings

Emerging trends in building code reform include:

Enhanced flashing requirements. Updated specifications for window and door flashing installation, recognizing that improper flashing is a leading cause of moisture intrusion.

Drainage plane clarifications. Codes increasingly require clear drainage planes behind exterior cladding to channel water away from structural components.

HVAC ventilation standards. Recognition that tightly sealed energy-efficient construction requires enhanced mechanical ventilation to control humidity and prevent condensation.

Vapor barrier specifications. Climate-zone-specific requirements for vapor barrier placement, acknowledging that what works in Arizona doesn't work in Washington.

Mold-resistant material recommendations in flood-prone areas. Some jurisdictions now recommend or require mold-resistant drywall, treated lumber, or other materials in areas with high flood risk.

Although building codes do not create automatic tort liability, violations can serve as persuasive evidence of negligence. Construction defect litigation increasingly incorporates moisture-management code analysis as a central theme.

How Code Violations Function in Litigation

Negligence Per Se Arguments:

Some jurisdictions treat building code violations as negligence per se (automatic breach of duty). Others treat them merely as evidence of negligence. The distinction matters:

Negligence Per Se Jurisdiction:

- Plaintiff proves code violation
- Burden shifts to defendant to prove violation didn't cause harm
- Significantly strengthens plaintiff's position

Evidence of Negligence Jurisdiction:

- Code violation is admissible but not conclusive
- Plaintiff still must prove breach and causation
- Defendant can argue compliance with code at time of construction or that violation didn't cause the mold

Attorneys must understand their jurisdiction's approach to code violations when evaluating construction defect mold cases.

VII. Rental Law Modernization and Tenant Remedies

Between 2024 and 2026, several states have revisited landlord-tenant statutes to address:

- Repair timelines (how quickly must landlords respond to moisture complaints?)
- Withholding and abatement procedures (when can tenants withhold rent for uninhabitable conditions?)
- Relocation requirements during remediation (must landlords pay for temporary housing?)

- Notice documentation obligations (what constitutes adequate notice to landlord?)

Modern rental statutes increasingly emphasize:

Prompt investigation upon written complaint. Landlords must investigate tenant complaints within reasonable timeframes (often 24-72 hours for emergency conditions, 7-14 days for non-emergency issues).

Clear communication with tenants. Landlords must inform tenants of inspection findings, remediation plans, and expected timelines.

Safe remediation protocols. If remediation requires occupant relocation, landlords must provide alternative housing or rent abatement.

Written documentation. Both tenant complaints and landlord responses should be in writing to establish notice and response timeline.

Failure to respond promptly may expose landlords to statutory damages, attorney fees, or administrative penalties even when medical causation is disputed.

State-by-State Comparison: Tenant Remedies

Tenant Remedies – Visual Comparison Matrix

✓ = Yes ◓ = Limited / Case-by-case ⊗ = No ⊗ = Except specific statutory provisions

State	Repair Timeline	Rent Withholding	Relocation Required	Attorney's Fees
California	Reasonable (~30 days per courts)	✓ Yes *(procedural required)*	◓ Case-by-case	✓ Prevailing tenant
Washington	10 days (written notice required)	✓ Yes (strict procedures)	✓ Major remediation	✓ Prevailing tenant
Texas	Reasonable *(no statutory deadline)*	◓ Limited	⊗ No statutory requirement	✗ No*
Florida	7 days (*written notice required*)	✓ Yes *(procedural required)*	⊗ No statutory *requirement*	◓ Limited
New York	Reasonable (HPD timelines vary)	✓ Yes *(procedural required)*	◓ Case-by-case	◓ Limited
New York	Reasonable (HPD timelines vary)	✓ Yes *(procedural required)*	◓ Case-by-case	◓ Limited

Tenant Remedies - Visual Comparison

This chart illustrates why identical mold cases settle for dramatically different amounts in different states. Washington's 10-day repair timeline, mandatory relocation for major work, and attorney's fees create leverage that Texas's more landlord-friendly framework doesn't provide.

VIII. Climate Change as a Legislative Driver

Extreme weather events are accelerating moisture-related claims nationwide and driving legislative responses.

States experiencing frequent climate-driven moisture events are more likely to update:

Resilience standards. Building codes incorporating climate adaptation and resilience principles.

Drainage requirements. Enhanced stormwater management and property drainage specifications.

Flood remediation protocols. Clear guidance on post-flood moisture control and mold prevention.

Disclosure requirements for flood-prone properties. Enhanced disclosure obligations for properties in flood zones or with flooding history.

Regional Climate Patterns Affecting Legislation

Atlantic Coast (Hurricanes):

North Carolina, South Carolina, Florida, Georgia updating flood resilience codes

Enhanced requirements for elevated construction

Mold-resistant material specifications for flood-prone areas

Gulf Coast (Hurricanes, Humidity):

Texas, Louisiana, Mississippi, Alabama addressing chronic humidity

HVAC sizing requirements to manage moisture

Enhanced ventilation standards

West Coast (Atmospheric Rivers):

- California, Oregon, Washington addressing intense precipitation events
- Drainage plane requirements
- Enhanced flashing and waterproofing standards

Midwest (Severe Storms, Flooding):

- Multiple states updating stormwater management
- Foundation drainage requirements
- Basement waterproofing standards

As climate-related building stress increases, legislative focus is shifting toward prevention rather than post-loss litigation. However, this shift is gradual, and many existing buildings predate modern codes.

IX. The Insurance Regulatory Response

State insurance regulators are also shaping mold litigation indirectly through policy approval processes.

Key trends include:

Approval of stricter mold exclusion endorsements. Insurance departments in most states have approved increasingly restrictive mold exclusions, sub-limits, and anti-concurrent causation clauses.

Sub-limits on mold remediation coverage. Typical sub-limits range from $5,000 to $10,000, far below actual remediation costs in many cases.

Anti-concurrent causation clause enforcement. Courts increasingly uphold these provisions, which bar coverage if any excluded cause contributes to loss.

Increased underwriting scrutiny in high-moisture regions. Insurers are declining coverage or charging premium surcharges for properties in flood zones or with moisture history.

In some jurisdictions, consumer advocates are challenging broad exclusions as contrary to public policy, arguing that effectively eliminating mold coverage leaves property owners without protection for preventable risks.

Insurance policy interpretation remains a state-law issue, creating significant jurisdictional variation in coverage outcomes. A mold exclusion enforced strictly in Texas might be interpreted more narrowly in California, affecting settlement dynamics.

X. Comparative Litigation Climate by State

While every case turns on facts, certain general patterns have emerged by 2026:

More Plaintiff-Receptive Jurisdictions:

Characteristics:

- Strong habitability doctrines
- Robust tenant protection statutes
- Active housing code enforcement
- Liberal expert admissibility standards (or less strict Daubert application)
- Attorney's fees available for prevailing plaintiffs
- Emotional distress damages without severe physical injury requirement

Examples: California (urban areas), Washington, Oregon, Massachusetts, New York (NYC), Illinois (Chicago), Maryland

Typical Settlement Range (moderate case): $150,000 - $400,000

More Defense-Oriented Jurisdictions:

Characteristics:

- Limited tenant statutory protections
- Narrow habitability interpretation
- Strict Daubert application
- Conservative damage expectations
- Attorney's fees generally not recoverable

- Physical injury required for emotional distress
- Strong enforcement of insurance exclusions

Examples: Alabama, Mississippi, Wyoming, South Dakota, portions of Texas (rural areas)

Typical Settlement Range (moderate case): $40,000 - $125,000

Middle-Ground Jurisdictions:

Most states fall somewhere in between, with outcomes depending heavily on:

- Specific county or judicial district
- Quality of evidence
- Expert credibility
- Severity of conduct

Forum selection (where permissible) can significantly impact valuation. For defendants, understanding jurisdictional differences helps calibrate settlement authority and litigation strategy.

XI. The Emerging Trend: Codifying "Reasonableness"

Across jurisdictions, a unifying theme has emerged by 2026:

States are not defining toxic mold numerically. They are defining reasonable response procedurally.

Legislation increasingly focuses on:

Inspection timing: How quickly must landlords investigate complaints?

Remediation protocol adherence: Must licensed professionals be used? What standards apply?

Disclosure transparency: What must sellers reveal about moisture history?

Documentation maintenance: What records must property owners keep?

The shift is away from scientific threshold-setting and toward behavioral standards. This shift aligns with courts' emphasis on reasonableness rather than rigid exposure metrics.

Rather than saying "mold levels above X spores/m^3 are dangerous," legislation says "landlords must investigate written moisture complaints within 72 hours and commence remediation within 14 days."

This procedural approach:

- Avoids scientific uncertainty about exposure thresholds
- Creates clear expectations for property owners
- Provides objective benchmarks for evaluating conduct
- Focuses on prevention rather than post-damage litigation

XII. Strategic Implications for Litigators

Attorneys handling toxic mold litigation must:

1. Analyze jurisdiction-specific landlord-tenant statutes.

Before accepting a case, research:

- Repair timelines required by statute
- Rent withholding procedures
- Attorney's fee provisions
- Damage limitations
- Notice requirements

2. Examine building code provisions related to moisture control.

Determine whether:

- Code violations can support negligence per se claims
- Construction occurred under current or older codes
- Defendant can raise compliance defenses

3. Evaluate licensing requirements for remediation professionals.

In states with licensing frameworks, investigate:

- Whether defendant used licensed professionals
- Whether remediation certificates were obtained
- Whether protocols were followed

4. Review insurance regulatory guidance.

Understand:

- How courts in your jurisdiction interpret mold exclusions
- Whether resulting-loss provisions provide coverage avenues
- Whether bad faith claims are viable

5. Consider forum selection impacts.

Where venue is discretionary:

- Evaluate plaintiff-receptive vs. defense-oriented jurisdictions
- Consider urban vs. rural differences within states
- Analyze local jury verdict trends

State statutory nuance often determines leverage before medical causation is ever litigated.

Practical Litigation Checklist:

✓ Research state-specific habitability statutes
✓ Determine repair timeline requirements
✓ Identify attorney's fee provisions
✓ Review building code moisture-control provisions
✓ Check for professional licensing requirements
✓ Analyze insurance regulatory environment
✓ Evaluate local jury verdict data
✓ Consider venue options if multiple forums available

XIII. Conclusion

By 2026, toxic mold regulation in the United States remains decentralized but increasingly structured.

States are:

- **Tightening moisture-control building codes** in response to climate-driven precipitation changes
- **Clarifying landlord remediation duties** through statutory reform
- **Expanding tenant remedies** including rent abatement, repair-and-deduct, and attorney's fees
- **Refining insurance oversight** as carriers and policyholders battle over coverage

Yet no state has solved the central challenge of mold litigation: establishing clear exposure thresholds for medical causation. Scientific uncertainty persists, and establishing one-size-fits-all numerical standards remains elusive.

As legislative reforms continue to focus on prevention, transparency, and procedural response standards, the courtroom battle remains rooted in proof:

- Proof of moisture intrusion
- Proof of notice
- Proof of unreasonable response
- Proof of causation

But the definition of "unreasonable response" increasingly comes from state statutes rather than common law evolution. A landlord who responds in 60 days might be reasonable in Alabama but unreasonable in Washington.

Key Takeaways:

1. **Jurisdiction determines viability** as much as underlying facts
2. **State statutes increasingly define reasonable response** procedurally rather than scientifically
3. **Climate change is driving legislative updates** to building codes and remediation standards
4. **Insurance regulation varies dramatically** by state

5. **Forum selection matters** - same case, different state, different outcome

The next chapter turns to one of the most frequently invoked causes of action in mold litigation: **Breach of the Warranty of Habitability.** Understanding this doctrine is essential because it provides the foundation for most residential mold claims, regardless of which state's law governs.

PART III: Core Legal Theories and Expanding Liability

7

Breach of the Warranty of Habitability

The Core Claim in Toxic Mold Litigation

The Claim That Survives When Others Fail

In June 2024, a Massachusetts tenant filed a mold lawsuit alleging:

- Negligence
- Breach of warranty of habitability
- Negligent infliction of emotional distress
- Violation of state consumer protection statutes
- Failure to maintain premises in compliance with state sanitary code

The tenant's medical expert claimed that mold exposure caused "chronic inflammatory response syndrome with cognitive impairment and immune dysregulation." The landlord moved to exclude the expert testimony under Daubert. The court granted the motion, finding the CIRS diagnosis lacked sufficient peer-reviewed support and the causation methodology was unreliable.

With the medical expert excluded, four of the five claims collapsed:

- **Negligence:** Without medical causation, no recoverable personal injury damages
- **Negligent infliction of emotional distress:** Requires physical injury under Massachusetts law
- **Consumer protection violation:** Required proof of actual harm beyond property damage
- **Sanitary code violation:** Administrative remedy, not private cause of action for medical damages

One claim survived: **Breach of warranty of habitability.**

The case proceeded to trial on habitability alone. The jury never heard about CIRS, immune dysregulation, or mycotoxins. They heard about:

- A roof leak that persisted for eleven months
- Fourteen documented tenant complaints
- Visible mold growth in three rooms
- The landlord's repeated promises to fix it followed by inaction
- The family's forced relocation to temporary housing
- The child's inability to sleep in her own bedroom for six months

The jury awarded $165,000:

- Past rent abatement: $18,000
- Property damage (ruined belongings): $12,000
- Temporary housing costs: $15,000
- Emotional distress (habitability-based): $45,000
- Loss of use of premises: $35,000
- Attorney's fees: $40,000

The landlord paid more after losing on habitability alone than the case would likely have settled for if the medical expert had been admitted. Why? Because habitability claims shift focus from contested medical causation to undeniable landlord conduct.

While toxic mold litigation may involve negligence, product liability, construction defect, and insurance bad faith claims, the most common and durable cause of action remains **breach of the warranty of habitability**.

In residential landlord-tenant disputes, mold claims rarely begin with toxicology. They begin with habitability.

I. The Foundation of Most Residential Mold Cases

The implied warranty of habitability, recognized in virtually every U.S. jurisdiction, requires landlords to maintain rental premises in a condition fit for human habitation. When moisture intrusion and mold growth materially affect health or safety, that duty may be breached.

By 2026, habitability claims form the backbone of most toxic mold lawsuits involving residential property because:

They survive even when medical causation fails. Habitability focuses on whether premises were fit for habitation, not whether they caused specific medical injuries.

They don't require expert testimony. Juries can evaluate whether conditions were uninhabitable using common sense. Visible mold, persistent musty odors, and water intrusion speak for themselves.

They provide meaningful damages. Rent abatement, relocation costs, emotional distress, and loss of use can generate substantial awards even without medical damages.

They often include attorney's fees. Many state habitability statutes make attorney's fees mandatory for prevailing tenants, fundamentally changing litigation economics.

They focus on landlord conduct. Rather than debating mycotoxin science, habitability cases ask: "Did the landlord maintain habitable premises?" This shifts the battle to more favorable terrain.

II. The Legal Origins of Habitability

The modern warranty of habitability emerged in the 20th century as courts shifted away from the doctrine of **caveat lessee** ("let the tenant beware"), which treated residential leases like property conveyances with no implied landlord obligations.

The landmark case *Javins v. First National Realty Corp.*, 428 F.2d 1071 (D.C. Cir. 1970) revolutionized landlord-tenant law by holding that residential leases contain an implied warranty that premises are habitable. The court reasoned that:

- Modern tenants rent for shelter, not land
- Tenants lack ability to inspect and repair
- Housing codes establish minimum standards
- Consumer protection principles apply to residential leases

Since Javins, virtually all states recognize some form of implied warranty of habitability, though specifics vary by jurisdiction.

Today, landlords generally must provide and maintain:

Weatherproofing and waterproofing. Roofs, walls, windows, and foundations must keep water out.

Plumbing in good working order. No leaks, adequate water pressure, functional drainage.

Safe electrical systems. Wiring that meets code and doesn't create fire hazards.

Adequate ventilation. Sufficient air circulation to prevent moisture accumulation and maintain healthy air quality.

Structural integrity. Sound floors, walls, ceilings, and stairs.

Compliance with applicable housing codes. Meeting minimum standards established by local ordinances.

Mold cases typically arise when moisture conditions undermine one or more of these elements.

III. When Mold Becomes a Habitability Violation

Not every instance of mold constitutes a breach. Courts must determine whether conditions materially affected habitability.

Courts typically consider:

1. Severity of contamination: Is the mold extensive or isolated? Minor surface mold on bathroom grout differs from black staining covering entire walls.

2. Duration: How long did the condition persist? A brief appearance quickly addressed differs from months of chronic growth.

3. Health impact: Were occupants affected? Did anyone experience respiratory symptoms, allergic reactions, or other health problems? (Note: health impact supports habitability claims even without proving medical causation.)

4. Landlord notice: Did the landlord know or should they have known? Written complaints establish actual notice. Visible conditions during routine inspections establish constructive notice.

5. Response time: Was remediation prompt and reasonable? Response within days looks different from months of inaction.

Minor surface mold in a bathroom due to tenant cleaning issues may not qualify. Chronic moisture intrusion from roof failure causing extensive visible growth likely does.

Habitability claims focus less on species identification and more on livability.

The question is not "Was this Stachybotrys or Aspergillus?" but rather "Could a reasonable tenant live safely and comfortably in these conditions?"

Case in Focus: When Modest Contamination Supports Habitability Claims

A 2024 Oregon case involved a rental house with mold in a single bedroom closet, measuring approximately 8 square feet of visible growth. Environmental testing showed Penicillium and Cladosporium at levels only moderately above outdoor baseline.

Defense counsel argued the contamination was minor and didn't render the entire premises uninhabitable. The court disagreed, finding habitability breach based on:

- The affected closet was in the child's bedroom
- The child slept in that room nightly for seven months
- Parents documented the musty odor throughout the bedroom
- The landlord delayed remediation for seven months despite three written complaints
- The closet was unusable during this period
- The bedroom's habitability was materially affected even if other rooms were fine

The case settled for $78,000. The lesson: habitability doesn't require the entire premises to be uninhabitable. Material impairment of significant living spaces can suffice, especially when children's rooms are affected.

IV. Notice and Opportunity to Cure

A central element in habitability cases is notice. Landlords cannot breach duties they don't know about.

Tenants typically must show:

Written or documented complaints. Oral complaints may suffice, but written notice (emails, texts, certified letters) provides indisputable proof.

Maintenance requests. Formal work orders or maintenance request forms document notice and create tracking records.

Inspection reports. If the landlord conducted inspections, their own reports may document knowledge.

Visible conditions obvious to management. Extensive visible mold during routine property visits establishes constructive notice even without formal complaints.

Once notified, landlords must act within a reasonable time. What's "reasonable" varies by jurisdiction and circumstances:

- **Emergency conditions** (burst pipes, flooding): 24-48 hours
- **Serious conditions** (roof leaks, extensive mold): 7-14 days to begin response

- **Non-emergency repairs:** 30 days is common threshold for "reasonable"

Failure to investigate or remediate after notice frequently transforms a maintenance issue into a legal violation.

Documentation is decisive. Emails, work orders, inspection logs, and complaint histories often determine outcomes. The difference between a tenant who says "I complained many times" and one who produces fourteen timestamped emails is the difference between settlement and dismissal.

The 72-Hour Rule

PRACTITIONER WARNING

In jurisdictions with strong tenant protections, landlord response within 72 hours of written moisture complaint often provides near-complete defense to habitability claims. After 72 hours, exposure escalates. After two weeks, exposure multiplies. After 30 days, punitive damages become viable.

The timeline matters more than the species of mold. A landlord who responds to Stachybotrys within 48 hours faces minimal exposure. A landlord who ignores Cladosporium for six months faces substantial liability.

V. Remedies Available to Tenants

Habitability breaches can support a range of remedies:

Rent abatement. Tenants may recover the difference between rent paid and the reasonable rental value of premises in their uninhabitable condition. If premises were 40% uninhabitable for six months, tenants may recover 40% of rent paid during that period.

Repair-and-deduct remedies. Some states allow tenants to arrange repairs themselves and deduct costs from rent, following specific statutory procedures.

Constructive eviction. If conditions become so severe that premises are essentially uninhabitable, tenants may vacate and terminate the lease without penalty.

Relocation costs. Tenants forced to move may recover moving expenses, temporary housing costs, and related expenses.

Emotional distress damages. In some jurisdictions, tenants can recover for anxiety, sleep disruption, and distress caused by living in uninhabitable conditions, even without physical injury.

Attorney's fees. Where authorized by statute, prevailing tenants can recover attorney's fees, dramatically altering litigation economics.

Punitive damages. In egregious cases involving willful disregard of tenant rights, punitive damages may be available.

In some states, tenants may withhold rent if conditions materially affect health and safety, though improper withholding can expose tenants to eviction. Strategic guidance is essential.

Strategically, mold cases often begin as defensive eviction matters before expanding into affirmative damage claims. A tenant who withholds rent due to mold conditions faces eviction. The tenant defends by asserting habitability breach as justification. The defense becomes an affirmative counterclaim for damages.

VI. Constructive Eviction and Relocation

Where mold conditions are severe, tenants may claim **constructive eviction**, arguing that premises became so uninhabitable they were forced to vacate.

To succeed on constructive eviction, tenants generally must show:

Substantial interference with use and enjoyment. Conditions must be severe enough that a reasonable tenant would feel compelled to leave. Inconvenience isn't enough; uninhabitability is required.

Timely notice to the landlord. Tenants must notify the landlord and provide reasonable opportunity to cure before vacating.

Departure within a reasonable period after failure to cure. Tenants who continue living in conditions for months after they become severe may undermine constructive eviction claims.

Actual vacation of the premises. Constructive eviction requires the tenant to move out. Tenants who remain can claim breach of habitability but not constructive eviction.

Constructive eviction claims can significantly increase damages exposure by adding:

Moving costs. Expenses for hiring movers, truck rentals, packing materials.

Temporary housing expenses. Hotel costs, short-term rentals, increased rent at new premises.

Security deposit disputes. Tenants who vacate mid-lease often forfeit security deposits, which they can recover if constructive eviction is proven.

Lost time and inconvenience. Time off work for moving, disruption to family life.

Case in Focus: Constructive Eviction Transforms Case Value

A 2025 Washington case involved a family living with mold conditions for eight months while repeatedly requesting remediation. When their two-year-old was hospitalized for pneumonia (arguably related to mold but with contested causation), they immediately vacated and moved into temporary housing.

Filed as a habitability breach without constructive eviction, estimated settlement: $95,000 Filed with constructive eviction, actual settlement: $187,000

The difference included:

- $15,000 temporary housing (3 months)
- $8,000 moving costs
- $12,000 lease-breaking penalty (recovered)
- $22,000 increased emotional distress (forced sudden relocation with sick child)
- $35,000 additional attorney's fees

Constructive eviction nearly doubled settlement value by expanding recoverable damages categories.

VII. Emotional Distress and Habitability

Some jurisdictions permit emotional distress damages tied to habitability violations, even when medical causation for systemic illness is weak.

Courts may allow recovery for:

Anxiety about living conditions. Fear of health effects, worry about children's safety, stress from living in substandard conditions.

Sleep disruption. Inability to sleep due to musty odors, concerns about mold exposure, or stress about conditions.

Embarrassment. Shame about inviting guests to moldy premises, social isolation resulting from conditions.

Loss of enjoyment of the premises. Inability to use rooms fully, disruption of family life, loss of home as a sanctuary.

However, jurisdictions vary widely. Some require physical injury to recover non-economic damages. Others allow emotional distress damages based solely on habitability violations without physical manifestations.

Key distinction: Habitability-based emotional distress focuses on living conditions, not toxic exposure. The distress arises from being forced to live in substandard housing, not from fear of mycotoxin poisoning.

When systemic toxic injury claims fail under scientific scrutiny, habitability-based emotional distress claims often remain viable because they don't depend on contested medical causation.

Jurisdiction-by-Jurisdiction: Emotional Distress Recovery

Jurisdiction-by-Jurisdiction: Emotional Distress Recovery

Jurisdiction	Physical Injury Required?	Typical Award Range
California	No (habitability violation sufficient)	$15,000 – $75,000
Washington	No (severe conditions sufficient)	$20,000 – $60,000
Massachusetts	Case-by-case	$10,000 – $50,000
Texas	Generally yes	$5,000 – $25,000 (if allowed)
New York	Case-by-case (more liberal in NYC)	$15,000 – $65,000
Florida	Generally yes	Limited if physical injury absent

Jurisdiction-by-Jurisdiction: Emotional Distress Recovery

This variability means identical emotional distress in California might recover $50,000 while the same distress in Texas recovers nothing without physical injury.

VIII. Tenant-Contributed Conditions

Landlords frequently defend habitability claims by asserting tenant contribution to mold growth.

Common defenses include:

Failure to ventilate bathrooms. Not running exhaust fans after showers, keeping windows closed in humid conditions.

Blocking airflow. Pushing furniture against exterior walls, preventing air circulation.

Ignoring minor leaks. Failing to report small leaks promptly, allowing them to worsen.

Poor housekeeping. Leaving wet towels on floors, allowing spills to remain, creating conditions conducive to mold.

Overcrowding. Excessive occupancy creating humidity from cooking, bathing, and respiration.

Unauthorized alterations. Installing impermeable wall coverings, blocking ventilation systems.

Comparative fault principles may reduce or bar recovery if tenant negligence contributed substantially to mold growth. In some jurisdictions, any tenant contribution defeats the claim. In others, damages are reduced proportionally.

Expert testimony regarding moisture causation can be decisive in allocating responsibility. Building science experts who can distinguish between tenant-caused surface mold (bathroom condensation) and landlord-caused structural mold (roof leaks) provide critical testimony.

Case in Focus: When Tenant Conduct Defeats Claims

A 2024 Minnesota case involved extensive mold in a basement bedroom. The tenant sued for habitability breach.

Discovery revealed:

- Tenant blocked basement window with furniture
- Tenant never ran dehumidifier provided by landlord
- Tenant dried laundry by hanging wet clothes on basement walls
- Tenant kept bedroom door closed continuously
- Basement had adequate ventilation if used properly

Expert testimony established that tenant behavior created the high-humidity conditions that caused mold growth. The landlord had provided adequate ventilation; the tenant defeated it through conduct.

The case was dismissed on summary judgment. The lesson: landlords can defeat habitability claims by proving tenant conduct was the primary cause of conditions.

IX. Housing Code Violations as Evidence

Municipal housing code citations often strengthen habitability claims dramatically.

Violations documenting:

Water intrusion. Code violations for roof leaks, plumbing failures, or drainage problems.

Structural defects. Violations for deteriorated building components allowing moisture penetration.

Plumbing failures. Citations for defective plumbing causing water damage.

Visible mold. Direct code violations for mold growth exceeding acceptable levels.

These violations serve as persuasive evidence of breach. Courts and juries give substantial weight to governmental determinations that conditions violated minimum housing standards.

However, code violations alone do not establish medical causation. They establish defective conditions. This distinction is critical: habitability claims may succeed even when toxic exposure claims fail.

The power of code violations in litigation:

- **Third-party validation:** Not just tenant complaints but governmental acknowledgment
- **Objective standards:** Code enforcement applies defined criteria
- **Notice:** Violations prove landlord received official notice
- **Pattern evidence:** Multiple violations show systemic neglect
- **Penalty enhancement:** Ignored violations may support punitive damages

Case in Focus: Code Violations Transform Settlement Dynamics

A Philadelphia case involved a tenant complaining about basement water intrusion and mold. The landlord disputed whether conditions were severe enough to warrant expensive remediation.

The city's Department of Licenses and Inspections (L&I) inspected and issued violations for:

1. Water penetration through foundation
2. Inadequate basement drainage
3. Mold exceeding acceptable levels
4. Failure to maintain property in safe condition

The landlord received the violations but delayed remediation for 90 days while disputing the findings. During this period, the tenant's respiratory symptoms worsened.

Without the L&I violations, estimated settlement: $60,000-$90,000 With the L&I violations showing 90-day delay despite official orders, actual settlement: $175,000

The violations eliminated the landlord's ability to argue conditions were debatable or tenant perception was unreasonable. The city had officially determined conditions violated minimum standards, and the landlord ignored the determination for three months.

X. Multi-Family and Institutional Housing

In apartment complexes, public housing, and student housing, mold claims may involve:

Systemic maintenance failures. Building-wide deferred maintenance affecting multiple units.

Deferred capital improvements. Delayed roof replacements, aging HVAC systems, deteriorating building envelopes.

Inadequate staffing. Insufficient maintenance personnel to respond promptly to moisture complaints.

Repeated tenant complaints. Pattern evidence showing management awareness of recurring problems.

In these contexts, plaintiffs often argue that management had constructive notice of recurring moisture problems affecting not just one unit but entire buildings.

Large-scale housing cases may lead to:

Coordinated tenant litigation. Multiple tenants filing together or consecutively.

Class action attempts. Though individualized issues often defeat certification, pattern evidence strengthens individual claims.

Regulatory enforcement proceedings. Health departments or housing authorities intervening.

Systematic remediation orders. Courts ordering building-wide remediation rather than unit-by-unit patchwork.

The advantage of pattern evidence:

When ten tenants in the same building report similar mold problems over two years, management cannot credibly claim:

- They didn't know problems were recurring
- Conditions were isolated incidents
- Tenant behavior was the cause
- Response was adequate

Pattern evidence transforms habitability cases from "he said, she said" disputes into systemic failure cases.

XI. The Intersection with State Statutes

While habitability is largely common-law based, many states have codified elements of the doctrine within landlord-tenant statutes.

For example, statutes may:

Define required repair timelines. Specific deadlines for responding to different categories of complaints.

Authorize rent withholding. Procedures tenants must follow to withhold rent legally.

Mandate relocation assistance. Requirements for landlords to provide alternative housing during major repairs.

Provide statutory damages. Fixed damage amounts (e.g., one month's rent per violation) in addition to actual damages.

In California, habitability analysis frequently intersects with the framework influenced by the California Toxic Mold Protection Act (discussed in Chapter 5), though mold claims themselves proceed primarily under warranty and negligence theories.

Understanding statutory overlays is essential for evaluating exposure and available remedies.

State-by-State Statutory Enhancements

California (Civil Code § 1941):

- Defines uninhabitable conditions
- Allows rent withholding with procedures
- Permits repair-and-deduct (up to one month's rent)
- Attorney's fees for prevailing tenants

Massachusetts (G.L. c. 239, § 8A):

- Strong tenant protection culture

- Rent withholding with escrow
- Mandatory code compliance
- Attorney's fees and treble damages for retaliation

New York (Multiple Dwelling Law, Real Property Law):

- NYC-specific protections
- HPD violation framework
- Rent abatement procedures
- Emergency repair provisions

Washington (RCW 59.18):

- 10-day notice requirement
- Specific repair obligations
- Relocation assistance mandates
- Mandatory attorney's fees

These statutory enhancements often determine whether cases are economically viable. States with attorney's fee provisions create incentives for representation even when damages are modest.

XII. Strategic Considerations for Plaintiffs

To strengthen a habitability-based mold claim, plaintiffs should:

1. Provide written notice promptly. Email or text immediately upon discovering moisture or mold. Follow up in writing at regular intervals.

2. Document conditions with photographs and inspection reports. Timestamped photos showing progression of mold growth. Professional environmental reports documenting extent.

3. Maintain medical records if symptoms arise. Even if medical causation is contested, records showing temporal correlation support habitability claims.

4. Avoid withholding rent without legal guidance. Improper withholding can result in eviction. Consult attorneys before withholding.

5. Preserve correspondence showing landlord delay. Every email exchange, text message, and phone log documenting complaints and landlord responses (or lack thereof).

6. Report to housing authorities if conditions persist. Code violations strengthen claims substantially.

7. Keep receipts for all expenses. Relocation costs, hotel stays, property damage, cleaning supplies.

Habitability cases are often won through documentation rather than dramatic expert testimony. A tenant with fourteen timestamped emails over six months defeats a landlord with no maintenance records.

XIII. Strategic Considerations for Landlords

Landlords and property managers can reduce exposure by:

1. Responding promptly to complaints. Investigate within 24-72 hours. Begin remediation within days, not weeks.

2. Investigating moisture sources immediately. Don't just address visible mold; identify and correct the water intrusion source.

3. Retaining qualified remediation professionals. Use licensed contractors who follow industry protocols, not handymen with bleach.

4. Maintaining thorough maintenance logs. Document every complaint, inspection, work order, and remediation effort.

5. Communicating transparently with tenants. Keep tenants informed of investigation findings, remediation plans, and timelines.

6. Providing temporary relocation if necessary. When major remediation is required, offer alternative housing or rent abatement.

7. Obtaining post-remediation clearance testing. Document that work was effective and conditions returned to normal.

Reasonableness and documentation are the primary defenses. A landlord who responds within 48 hours, hires licensed remediators, corrects the moisture source, and obtains clearance testing faces minimal exposure even if mold was initially extensive.

Conversely, a landlord who delays for months, ignores complaints, uses unqualified personnel, and fails to document efforts faces substantial liability even if contamination was modest.

XIV. Why Habitability Drives Valuation

In many toxic mold cases, systemic medical claims fail under strict causation standards. Yet habitability claims may still produce substantial settlements because they involve:

Rent abatement calculations. Six months at 50% uninhabitable = three months' rent. At $3,000/month, that's $9,000 in rent abatement alone.

Relocation costs. Temporary housing for a family can easily exceed $10,000-$20,000.

Emotional distress. Even without physical injury, anxiety from living in moldy conditions may recover $25,000-$75,000 in plaintiff-friendly jurisdictions.

Attorney's fees. Mandatory fees in many states can equal or exceed underlying damages.

Potential punitive exposure in egregious cases. Willful disregard of tenant complaints after formal notice can trigger punitive damages of $25,000-$100,000+.

Thus, even when toxic injury is scientifically contested, habitability may sustain substantial liability.

Comparison: Toxic Injury vs. Habitability Case Values

Scenario 1: Toxic Injury Focus

- Medical expert excluded (CIRS, immune dysfunction claims fail)
- Property damage: $10,000
- Modest respiratory symptoms: $15,000
- **Settlement: $25,000-$40,000**

Scenario 2: Habitability Focus (same facts)

- Rent abatement (6 months, 40%): $7,200

- Temporary housing: $12,000
- Property damage: $10,000
- Emotional distress (habitability-based): $35,000
- Loss of use: $15,000
- Attorney's fees: $30,000
- **Settlement: $109,200**

Habitability more than doubled recovery by shifting focus from contested medical causation to undeniable landlord misconduct.

XV. Conclusion

Breach of the warranty of habitability remains the most reliable and frequently invoked claim in toxic mold litigation.

It shifts the focus:

- From mycotoxins to moisture
- From systemic illness to livability
- From speculative toxicity to documented response failure

In 2026, successful toxic mold litigation often begins not with proving toxins but with proving that a landlord failed to maintain a safe and habitable dwelling.

Key Takeaways:

1. **Habitability survives when medical causation fails** - focus on conditions, not toxins
2. **Documentation is decisive** - written complaints and response timelines determine outcomes
3. **Notice and response time are critical** - 72 hours vs. 6 months makes millions in difference
4. **Code violations provide powerful leverage** - governmental determinations validate claims

5. **Attorney's fees transform economics** - mandatory fees make modest cases viable
6. **Emotional distress doesn't require physical injury** in many jurisdictions
7. **Pattern evidence in multi-family housing** creates systemic failure narratives

The next chapter examines negligence and construction defect theories, where mold becomes evidence of broader professional failure rather than solely a landlord-tenant dispute. Understanding when to expand the defendant roster beyond landlords is essential for maximizing recovery and identifying all potentially liable parties.

8

Negligence and Construction Defect Litigation

When Mold Signals Professional Failure

Beyond the Landlord-Tenant Framework

In September 2024, a homeowner in Phoenix discovered extensive mold growth behind kitchen cabinets in her three-year-old townhome. Her initial instinct was to blame poor maintenance. Then her contractor opened the wall.

The investigation revealed:

- Window flashing installed backwards, directing water into the wall cavity instead of away from it
- No drainage plane behind the exterior stucco
- House wrap installed upside down, trapping moisture rather than shedding it

- Missing sealant at critical wall-to-window transitions
- Evidence of chronic water intrusion since original construction

This wasn't a maintenance problem. It was a construction defect problem.

The homeowner's initial target was the homeowners' association (HOA) for failing to maintain common areas. Within three months, the defendant list expanded to include:

1. The original developer
2. The general contractor
3. The window installation subcontractor
4. The stucco subcontractor
5. The architect who designed the building envelope
6. The window manufacturer (for allegedly inadequate installation instructions)
7. The construction superintendent who signed off on the work

Each defendant had insurance coverage. Each had documentation showing knowledge of proper installation methods. Each pointed fingers at the others. The resulting settlement ($680,000) reflected aggregate exposure across multiple parties, not just one negligent property owner.

This chapter examines how toxic mold litigation expands beyond landlord-tenant disputes into negligence and construction defect claims, where mold becomes evidence of deeper systemic failure.

I. Moving Beyond Landlord-Tenant Claims

While breach of warranty of habitability dominates residential rental disputes, toxic mold litigation frequently expands into **negligence and construction defect claims** involving multiple professional parties.

In these cases, mold is not merely a maintenance issue. It is evidence of deeper systemic failure:

- Improper building design that fails to manage water
- Defective construction practices violating industry standards

- Faulty material selection or installation
- Inadequate waterproofing systems
- Substandard remediation creating new problems

By 2026, mold litigation increasingly intersects with construction law, professional malpractice, and product liability. Understanding when and how to expand the defendant roster is essential for:

- Identifying all sources of recovery
- Maximizing insurance coverage availability
- Properly allocating fault among multiple parties
- Ensuring complete remediation (not just surface-level repairs)

II. The Elements of Negligence in Mold Cases

To establish negligence, plaintiffs must prove:

1. **Duty:** The defendant owed a duty of reasonable care to the plaintiff.

2. **Breach:** The defendant failed to meet the applicable standard of care.

3. **Causation:** The breach caused property damage or personal injury.

4. **Damages:** The plaintiff suffered compensable harm.

In construction-related mold claims, the duty typically arises from:

Contractual obligations. Express or implied promises in construction contracts to build in a workmanlike manner according to plans and specifications.

Building code compliance. Duty to meet minimum standards established by applicable building codes.

Industry standards. Obligation to follow generally accepted construction practices even when not specifically required by code.

Professional licensure responsibilities. Licensed architects, engineers, and contractors owe professional standards of care to those foreseeably affected by their work.

Unlike habitability claims (which often succeed based on lay testimony), negligence cases typically hinge on expert testimony regarding building science and construction practices.

III. Common Construction Failures Leading to Mold

1. Building Envelope Defects

The "building envelope" refers to the physical barrier between interior conditioned space and the exterior environment. When this barrier fails, water intrusion follows, and mold growth becomes inevitable.

Water intrusion often originates from:

Improperly installed flashing. Flashing is metal or membrane material that directs water away from vulnerable transitions (window-to-wall, roof-to-wall, deck-to-wall). Improper installation is one of the most common construction defects leading to mold.

Common flashing errors:

- Installing flashing backwards (directing water inward)
- Omitting flashing entirely at critical transitions
- Using insufficient overlap between flashing pieces
- Failing to integrate flashing with drainage planes
- Not following manufacturer specifications

Defective window systems. Windows are complex assemblies requiring precise installation. Failures include:

- Missing or improperly installed window pan flashing
- Inadequate sealant at window perimeter
- Installing windows without proper slope for drainage
- Failing to integrate window with weather-resistant barrier
- Using windows not rated for local climate conditions

Roof membrane failures. Both flat and sloped roofs can fail through:

- Improper membrane installation
- Inadequate roof slope causing water ponding
- Missing or deteriorated roof-to-wall flashing
- Penetrations (vents, chimneys) improperly sealed
- Ice dam formation in cold climates

Balcony waterproofing errors. Balconies and decks present complex waterproofing challenges:

- Failed waterproof membrane beneath tile or pavers
- Improper slope allowing water accumulation
- Missing or inadequate deck-to-wall flashing
- Deteriorated sealants at penetrations
- Drainage systems that fail or become clogged

Stucco cladding moisture entrapment. The EIFS (Exterior Insulation and Finish System) and traditional stucco failures of the 1990s-2000s created thousands of construction defect mold cases. Common problems:

- No drainage plane behind cladding
- Improper flashing at penetrations
- Missing weep screeds at wall base
- Foam insulation absorbing water
- Stucco applied directly to substrate without moisture barrier

Building envelope failures can allow slow, chronic intrusion that goes undetected for years, causing extensive hidden damage before mold becomes visible.

2. HVAC and Ventilation Deficiencies

Improperly sized or maintained HVAC systems can contribute to:

Condensation buildup. When HVAC systems are oversized (a common error), they cool spaces too quickly without adequate dehumidification, leaving excess moisture that condenses on cold surfaces.

Excess humidity. Undersized or poorly maintained systems may fail to control indoor humidity, particularly in humid climates.

Inadequate air exchange. Modern energy-efficient construction creates tightly sealed buildings. Without adequate mechanical ventilation, moisture from cooking, bathing, and breathing accumulates.

Ductwork condensation. Poorly insulated ductwork in unconditioned spaces (attics, crawlspaces) can develop condensation that drips onto insulation or ceiling materials.

Energy-efficient construction that tightly seals buildings without proper ventilation has amplified condensation-related mold issues. The building science principle is clear: tighter buildings require better ventilation systems.

3. Plumbing and Drainage Errors

Common issues include:

Improperly sloped drain lines. Drain lines must slope adequately for gravity drainage. Insufficient slope causes water to stand in pipes, potentially leading to leaks or backups.

Hidden pipe leaks. Slow leaks within wall cavities or under slabs can persist for years undetected, creating ideal conditions for concealed mold growth.

Poor site grading. Ground should slope away from foundations. Improper grading directs water toward buildings rather than away, causing foundation leaks.

Foundation drainage failures. Missing or clogged foundation drains allow groundwater to penetrate basements and crawlspaces.

In multi-family construction, plumbing defects can affect multiple units vertically (through plumbing stacks) or horizontally (through shared walls), increasing litigation exposure exponentially.

Case in Focus: Building Science Reveals Systemic Defect

A 2025 Seattle case involved 47 townhome units in a development where multiple owners discovered mold. Initial investigations suggested isolated maintenance issues.

A building envelope expert retained by one owner traced the pattern and discovered:

- All affected units shared common architectural details
- Window head flashing was consistently installed incorrectly throughout the development
- The error appeared in construction documents (design defect)
- The error was perpetuated during construction (installation defect)
- Water intrusion pathways were identical in all affected units

What began as individual homeowner complaints became coordinated litigation involving all 47 units. The settlement ($8.2 million) included:

- Complete building envelope remediation for all units
- Interior reconstruction for affected homes
- Temporary relocation for residents during work
- Diminution in property values
- Engineering fees and testing costs

The key insight: recognizing pattern defects early allows strategic coordination that increases recovery for all affected parties.

IV. Professional Standard of Care

Architects, engineers, and contractors are held to professional standards of care defined by:

Industry practice. What do competent professionals customarily do in similar circumstances?

Building codes. Minimum standards established by law that define baseline acceptable practice.

Contract specifications. Specific requirements agreed to in construction contracts.

Custom and usage. Recognized practices within the construction industry.

To prevail, plaintiffs typically retain experts to testify that:

The design deviated from accepted standards. Architects who design building envelopes must consider water management, vapor control, and drainage. Failure to design adequate water management systems may breach professional standards.

Installation was improper. Even good designs fail when improperly executed. Contractors must follow plans, specifications, and industry standards for installation.

Moisture management principles were ignored. Building science principles regarding water management are well-established. Ignoring these principles (e.g., failing to provide drainage planes, omitting flashing) may constitute negligence.

Preventable intrusion occurred. Experts must establish that the water intrusion was foreseeable and preventable through proper design or construction.

Defense experts counter by asserting:

Compliance with code at the time of construction. Building codes evolve. Compliance with then-applicable codes may provide defense (though codes establish minimum standards, and professional practice may exceed them).

Proper installation procedures. Defendants will produce documentation showing work was performed according to specifications and industry standards.

Lack of foreseeability. Some water intrusion events (unprecedented storms, earthquakes) may be unforeseeable.

Improper maintenance by property owners. Defendants often argue that proper maintenance would have prevented or mitigated problems, shifting responsibility to owners.

The battle over "standard of care" often defines liability in construction defect mold cases.

How Experts Establish Professional Standards

Expert testimony regarding standard of care typically includes:

Industry publications and guidelines:

- ASTM standards (American Society for Testing and Materials)
- Building Science Corporation research
- IRC/IBC (International Residential/Building Code) requirements
- Manufacturer installation instructions
- Trade association best practices (NAHB, AIA, etc.)

Professional training and education:

- What is taught in architecture and engineering programs?
- What training do contractors receive?
- What do industry certifications require?

Common practice evidence:

- How do competent professionals typically handle similar situations?
- What do peer professionals consider minimum acceptable practice?

Technical literature:

- Building science research on moisture management
- Journal articles on building envelope design
- Case studies of successful moisture control strategies

Strong expert testimony combines these sources to establish a clear professional standard against which defendant conduct is measured.

V. Building Codes as Evidence of Breach

Although building codes do not automatically create civil liability, violations may serve as persuasive evidence of negligence.

Codes governing:

- Waterproofing requirements
- Drainage plane specifications
- Vapor barrier installation
- Roofing assemblies and underlayment
- Window installation procedures
- Ventilation requirements for habitable spaces

are frequently introduced in construction defect mold cases.

Some jurisdictions treat code violations as **negligence per se** (violation automatically establishes breach of duty). Others treat them as **evidence of negligence** (admissible but not conclusive). The distinction significantly affects plaintiff's burden of proof.

Negligence Per Se Jurisdiction:

- Plaintiff proves code violation existed at substantial completion
- Burden shifts to defendant to prove violation didn't cause harm
- Plaintiff's proof burden substantially reduced

Evidence of Negligence Jurisdiction:

- Code violation is admissible but not dispositive
- Plaintiff still must prove breach through expert testimony
- Defendant can argue compliance with code at time of construction
- More balanced burden between parties

Understanding the evidentiary treatment of code violations in the relevant jurisdiction is critical for case evaluation and strategy.

The "Code Compliance" Defense and Its Limitations

Defendants often assert: "We complied with all applicable building codes at the time of construction."

This defense has limitations:

Codes establish minimum standards. Professional standard of care may exceed code requirements. Compliance with code doesn't immunize from negligence if professional practice requires more.

Codes are often outdated. By the time codes are adopted, building science may have advanced beyond code requirements. Professionals are expected to stay current with industry knowledge.

Codes vary by jurisdiction. Some jurisdictions have more stringent moisture management codes than others. Building in a jurisdiction with minimal codes doesn't excuse ignoring known moisture management principles.

Some defects violate any version of the code. Certain errors (installing flashing backwards, omitting it entirely) violate even the most minimal codes.

However, code compliance provides significant defensive value by establishing that defendant met legal minimum requirements, even if professional practice might have exceeded them.

VI. Multi-Unit and Large-Scale Developments

Mold claims in condominiums, apartment complexes, and mixed-use developments often involve:

Systemic design flaws affecting multiple units. When design defects exist, they typically affect many units similarly, creating pattern evidence.

Mass joinder litigation. Multiple unit owners or tenants filing coordinated claims.

Homeowners' association (HOA) involvement. HOAs may pursue claims on behalf of all owners for common area defects or may be defendants if they controlled maintenance.

Allocation of responsibility among developers and subcontractors. Complex projects involve numerous parties, each potentially bearing partial responsibility.

In such cases, plaintiffs may assert:

Breach of implied warranty of workmanship. Even without express warranties, contractors impliedly warrant that work will be performed in a workmanlike manner.

Breach of contract. Violation of specific contract provisions regarding quality, materials, or methods.

Negligence. Failure to meet professional standards of care.

Strict liability for defective construction. Some jurisdictions recognize strict liability for construction defects causing property damage.

Large-scale construction defect cases can involve millions in remediation costs even absent substantial personal injury claims because:

- Remediation must address all affected units
- Building envelope repairs are expensive (often $50,000-$150,000 per unit)
- Temporary relocation of occupants is required
- Property values decline due to defect history
- Engineering and testing costs are substantial

Case in Focus: Multi-Unit Pattern Litigation

A 2024 Portland case involved a 128-unit condominium development with systemic balcony waterproofing failures. Initial discovery showed:

Affected units: 89 of 128 units had documented moisture intrusion **Cause:** Waterproof membrane beneath balcony tile was improperly installed in all affected units **Pattern:** Same installation error throughout the project **Responsible parties:** General contractor failed to supervise; subcontractor performed work improperly; developer failed to conduct adequate quality control

The HOA filed suit on behalf of all owners. Settlement included:

- $14.2 million for complete balcony reconstruction (all 128 units, whether currently affected or not, to prevent future failures)
- $3.8 million for interior repairs in affected units
- $2.1 million for temporary relocation during construction
- $1.9 million for engineering, testing, and project management
- $2.4 million for diminution in property values

- **Total: $24.4 million**

Individual unit owners would never have achieved this recovery. Coordinated action through the HOA maximized leverage and ensured comprehensive remediation.

VII. Statutes of Limitation and Repose

Construction-related mold claims frequently implicate statutes of limitation and statutes of repose, creating timing challenges.

Statute of Limitations: Time limit for filing suit after the cause of action accrues (typically when damage is discovered or should have been discovered).

Statute of Repose: Absolute time limit for filing suit after a specific event (typically substantial completion of construction), regardless of when damage is discovered.

Key timing issues include:

Discovery rule application. When was mold discovered or reasonably discoverable? Hidden mold in wall cavities may toll the statute until discovery.

Latent defect analysis. Defects not apparent during reasonable inspection may extend limitation periods.

State-specific repose periods. Repose statutes vary dramatically:

- Some states: 6 years from substantial completion
- Other states: 10-12 years
- Some states: No repose statute

The Discovery Rule Trap

The discovery rule helps plaintiffs by starting the limitations clock when damage is discovered rather than when it occurred. However, it creates a trap:

Courts often find mold "should have been discovered" earlier than actual discovery based on:

- Musty odors that were ignored
- Minor water staining that wasn't investigated
- Previous repairs that should have prompted comprehensive inspection
- Visible conditions that suggested hidden problems

Defense counsel routinely argue that plaintiffs unreasonably delayed investigation of obvious warning signs, barring claims under the discovery rule.

Statute of Repose: The Absolute Bar

Statutes of repose create absolute bars to claims after a defined period from substantial completion, regardless of discovery.

Example timeline:

- Construction completed: January 2015
- Statute of repose: 10 years
- Mold discovered behind walls: March 2026
- Claim filed: May 2026

Result: Barred by repose statute (expired January 2025)

Even though mold was undiscoverable until 2026, the repose statute bars claims. This harsh rule reflects legislative policy balancing plaintiff rights against the need to give contractors closure.

In some jurisdictions, statutes of repose can extinguish claims regardless of when mold is discovered. Strategic early investigation is essential to avoid repose bars.

STATUTE OF REPOSE TRAP

In construction defect mold cases, the clock may start running years before mold is discovered. Check your jurisdiction's statute of repose immediately. Missing this deadline is malpractice. Many states have 6-10 year repose periods from substantial completion. Hidden mold discovered in year 11 may be completely barred regardless of how serious the defect.

VIII. Comparative Fault and Allocation of Liability

Construction defect mold cases often involve multiple defendants:

- Developer (overall responsibility for project)
- General contractor (construction oversight and coordination)
- Subcontractors (specific trades: framing, roofing, windows, stucco, plumbing)
- Architects (design of building envelope and systems)
- Engineers (structural, mechanical, civil engineering)
- Material manufacturers (if products failed or were misrepresented)

Courts may allocate fault proportionally among defendants based on:

Percentage of responsibility for causing the defect. Did design or installation contribute more to the problem?

Ability to discover and correct the problem. Who had opportunity to identify and fix the defect?

Contractual duties and responsibilities. What did contracts require each party to do?

Common allocation disputes involve:

Whether design or installation caused intrusion. Architect designed inadequate flashing vs. contractor installed proper design incorrectly.

Whether maintenance failures exacerbated the condition. Owner failed to maintain vs. defect was so severe maintenance couldn't prevent damage.

Whether remediation was improperly performed. Initial defect was minor but remediation contractor made it worse.

Apportionment can significantly affect recovery and settlement leverage. A plaintiff who can prove several defendants share liability increases total available recovery and creates pressure for settlement as defendants point fingers at each other.

Strategic Use of Cross-Claims

In multi-defendant construction cases, cross-claims and third-party claims proliferate:

- General contractor sues subcontractors for indemnity
- Subcontractors sue material suppliers
- Architect sues contractor for deviating from plans
- Contractor sues architect for inadequate design
- Developer sues everyone

This finger-pointing creates settlement pressure. No defendant wants to be the lone remaining defendant at trial, facing 100% liability. Coordinated mediation with all parties often produces global settlements.

IX. Remediation Negligence and Secondary Contamination

Not all mold negligence arises from original construction. Improper remediation may itself constitute negligence, creating secondary claims.

Common remediation failures include:

Lack of containment. Failing to isolate work areas allows spores to spread throughout buildings during demolition and removal.

Failure to use negative air pressure. Without negative pressure in work areas, disturbed spores migrate to clean areas.

Inadequate removal of porous materials. Surface cleaning of porous materials (drywall, insulation) is insufficient. These materials must be removed and replaced.

Failure to correct moisture source. Remediating mold without fixing the leak guarantees recurrence.

Inadequate post-remediation clearance testing. Without testing, there's no verification that work was effective.

Using unqualified personnel. In states with licensing requirements, using unlicensed remediators may constitute negligence per se.

When remediation spreads contamination or fails to solve the problem, plaintiffs may assert independent negligence claims against remediation contractors.

Documentation of remediation protocols becomes pivotal:

- Was containment established before demolition?
- Were negative air machines used?
- Were HEPA filters employed?
- Was moisture source corrected before addressing mold?
- Was clearance testing performed?
- Were industry standards (IICRC S520, ANSI/IICRC S520) followed?

Case in Focus: When the Cure Is Worse Than the Disease

A 2025 Michigan case involved a homeowner who discovered mold in a bathroom. She hired a contractor who advertised "mold remediation services" for $2,500.

The contractor:

- Used no containment
- Operated without negative pressure
- Spread spores throughout the home via HVAC system
- Failed to address plumbing leak causing the mold
- Provided no post-remediation testing

Three months later, mold appeared in previously unaffected rooms. Proper remediation ultimately cost $45,000.

The homeowner sued the contractor for negligent remediation. The contractor's defenses:

- "I'm not licensed because the state doesn't require it" (Michigan doesn't license remediators)
- "I followed YouTube tutorials"

- "The homeowner should have hired someone more expensive"

The jury awarded $127,000:

- $45,000 proper remediation costs
- $15,000 property damage from spread contamination
- $10,000 additional temporary housing
- $22,000 emotional distress
- $35,000 punitive damages (gross negligence)

The lesson: improper remediation creates independent liability and often costs more than proper initial response would have.

X. Economic Loss vs. Personal Injury

Construction defect mold cases frequently focus on **economic loss** (property damage) rather than bodily injury.

Damages may include:

Demolition and reconstruction costs. Removing and replacing contaminated building components.

Diminution in property value. Permanent reduction in value even after remediation due to defect history.

Relocation expenses. Temporary housing during remediation.

Loss of use. Inability to occupy or rent property during remediation period.

Repair of structural components. Addressing underlying defects (not just mold symptoms).

Engineering and testing costs. Investigation, destructive testing, and post-remediation verification.

Where personal injury is alleged, plaintiffs must satisfy the medical causation standards discussed in Chapter 3. However, many construction defect cases resolve based on economic loss alone because:

- Property damage is objectively measurable

- Personal injury causation is contested
- Economic loss alone can generate substantial damages
- Avoiding medical causation battles simplifies litigation

The Economic Loss Doctrine

The economic loss doctrine (recognized in many jurisdictions) provides that purely economic losses (property damage, lost profits, repair costs) cannot be recovered in tort absent physical injury to person or property beyond the defective product itself.

In construction defect mold cases, courts analyze:

Is mold damage "other property" damage? If mold contamination extends beyond the defective component (e.g., defective windows caused wall cavity mold affecting entire rooms), it may constitute damage to "other property" and be recoverable in tort.

Or is it damage to "the product itself"? If only the defectively installed component is damaged, recovery may be limited to contract remedies.

Application varies significantly by jurisdiction and fact pattern. In practice, mold damage extending beyond the immediate defective component usually qualifies as "other property" damage, allowing tort recovery.

XI. Insurance Coverage in Construction Mold Cases

Construction defect mold claims often trigger complex insurance coverage disputes involving:

Commercial General Liability (CGL) policies. These provide coverage for property damage and bodily injury caused by contractor work.

Completed operations coverage. CGL policies cover damages arising from work after project completion (as opposed to during construction).

Mold exclusions. Modern CGL policies include fungi/bacteria exclusions limiting mold coverage.

"Your work" exclusions. CGL policies typically exclude damage to the contractor's own work (but may cover damage to other property caused by faulty work).

Resulting loss provisions. Even with mold exclusions, coverage may exist for property damage "resulting from" covered causes.

Coverage analysis may determine whether remediation funds are available. Common coverage disputes include:

Whether mold damage constitutes "property damage" under the policy. This should be straightforward, but insurers sometimes argue mold is excluded entirely.

Whether exclusions apply. Insurers invoke mold/fungi exclusions; policyholders argue resulting loss provisions preserve coverage.

Whether "your work" exclusion bars coverage. Contractors argue they're not seeking coverage for their own work but for damage their work caused to other property.

Allocation among multiple insurers. Long-tail claims spanning multiple policy periods require allocation among carriers.

Insurance disputes can influence settlement timing and strategy. Cases with clear coverage settle faster. Cases with disputed coverage may require coverage litigation before underlying claims resolve.

XII. Defense Strategies in Construction Mold Litigation

Defense counsel often focus on:

1. **Code compliance at time of construction.** Arguing that work met applicable standards when performed, even if standards have since evolved.

2. **Proper maintenance obligations of owners.** Shifting responsibility to owners who failed to maintain systems or address problems promptly.

3. **Intervening causes.** Arguing that subsequent events (severe storms, earthquakes, owner modifications) caused damage, not original construction.

4. **Failure to mitigate damages.** Claiming owners unreasonably delayed addressing problems, allowing damage to worsen.

5. **Statutes of limitation or repose.** Asserting claims are time-barred.

6. Economic loss doctrine. Limiting recovery to contract remedies rather than tort damages.

7. Comparative fault. Allocating substantial percentage of fault to other defendants or to plaintiff's own conduct.

Engineering testimony frequently becomes more important than medical testimony in property-focused construction cases. Establishing that installation met professional standards at the time of construction can defeat claims even when mold damage is extensive.

XIII. Plaintiff Strategies in Construction Mold Litigation

Plaintiffs should:

1. Retain qualified building envelope experts early. Don't wait until litigation begins. Early investigation preserves evidence and identifies all responsible parties.

2. Document intrusion pathways thoroughly. Destructive testing showing how water entered and migrated establishes causation.

3. Analyze construction drawings and change orders. Plans may show design complied with standards; as-built conditions may show deviation.

4. Preserve evidence of moisture mapping and destructive testing. Photograph everything before, during, and after testing. Video document invasive investigations.

5. Evaluate class or coordinated litigation options where systemic defects exist. Pattern defects affecting multiple units warrant coordinated action.

6. Identify all insurance policies. Developers, contractors, subcontractors, and material suppliers may all have coverage. Maximum recovery requires identifying all policies.

7. Investigate prior similar complaints. Have other units or projects by the same defendants experienced similar problems? Pattern evidence strengthens claims.

8. Consider timing carefully. Repose statutes and insurance policy triggers make timing critical. Don't delay investigation.

Strong technical analysis often drives early settlement discussions because defendants recognize that comprehensive building science investigation will reveal systemic problems.

XIV. Why Mold Signals Systemic Failure

In construction defect litigation, mold is rarely the root problem. It is the visible symptom.

Mold reveals:

- Water management failures in design
- Installation deviations from specifications
- Quality control failures during construction
- Material selection errors
- Professional oversight breakdowns

Jurors often understand water intrusion intuitively. When plaintiffs demonstrate preventable design or construction errors allowing chronic water intrusion, liability may attach even if medical damages are limited or excluded.

The narrative is simple and persuasive:

"Water got into the walls because these professionals didn't do their jobs properly. The law requires professionals to meet basic standards. They didn't. Now my home is damaged and requires extensive repairs. They should pay to fix what they broke."

This narrative succeeds whether or not mycotoxin causation can be proven.

XV. Conclusion

Negligence and construction defect claims expand toxic mold litigation beyond landlord-tenant disputes into the realm of professional accountability.

The central question is not whether mold exists but whether preventable design, construction, or remediation failures allowed moisture intrusion to occur and persist.

By 2026, toxic mold litigation routinely encompasses architects, engineers, contractors, subcontractors, and manufacturers. Mold is the visible manifestation of deeper design and construction decisions.

As plaintiffs increasingly trace moisture intrusion upstream, litigation becomes more technically complex and financially significant. But it also becomes more objective: building codes, industry standards, and professional practices provide clear benchmarks against which conduct is measured.

Key Takeaways:

1. **Mold in newer construction suggests design or installation defects** requiring investigation beyond maintenance
2. **Building envelope failures are the most common cause** of construction-related mold
3. **Multiple defendants increase recovery potential** through aggregate insurance coverage
4. **Building codes provide objective standards** but compliance doesn't guarantee immunity
5. **Pattern defects warrant coordinated litigation** to maximize recovery
6. **Statutes of repose create absolute bars** requiring early investigation
7. **Remediation negligence creates independent claims** when improperly performed
8. **Economic loss alone justifies substantial recovery** even without personal injury

The next chapter examines another expanding area of liability: **Failure to disclose mold and moisture defects in real estate transactions**, where honesty matters more than toxicity and concealment often costs more than the underlying problem.

9

Failure to Disclose

Mold, Moisture Intrusion, and Real Estate Transaction Liability

When Honesty Would Have Been Cheaper

In May 2024, a couple in suburban Atlanta purchased their dream home for $575,000. The seller's disclosure statement checked "No" for water intrusion, drainage problems, and environmental hazards. The home inspector found no visible mold. The sale closed smoothly.

Six weeks later, the buyers noticed a musty smell in the master bedroom. Investigation revealed:

- Extensive Stachybotrys growth behind drywall in three rooms
- Evidence of chronic roof leak dating back at least three years
- Water-stained attic sheathing showing repeated intrusion
- Previous remediation attempts (visible from paint texture differences)
- Contractor invoices discovered in the garage during unpacking, dated 18 months before closing, for "mold removal and painting"

The sellers had known. They had paid for remediation. Then they painted over it, replaced carpet, and checked "No" on the disclosure form.

The buyers sued for fraud, concealment, and negligent misrepresentation. During discovery, text messages between the sellers emerged:

Seller 1: "Should we disclose the mold thing on the form?"
Seller 2: "It's fixed. And if we mention it, we'll never sell this place."
Seller 1: "But what if they find out?"
Seller 2: "They won't. We painted over everything. Just check no."

The case settled eight months later for $487,000, including:

- Proper remediation and reconstruction: $185,000
- Diminution in property value: $150,000
- Relocation expenses: $42,000
- Emotional distress: $60,000
- Punitive damages: $50,000

Had the sellers disclosed the prior water intrusion and remediation on the disclosure form, the property might have sold for $525,000 instead of $575,000 (a $50,000 reduction). Buyers might have negotiated additional inspection or repair credits totaling $20,000.

Cost of honesty: $70,000 reduction in net proceeds
Cost of dishonesty: $487,000 plus litigation stress and reputational damage

Toxic mold litigation no longer begins and ends with tenants and landlords. An increasingly significant category of claims arises **after a property changes hands,** when buyers discover concealed water intrusion, hidden remediation, or chronic mold contamination that sellers knew about but failed to disclose.

I. The Expanding Front of Mold Litigation

Buyers who discover concealed moisture problems frequently pursue claims for:

Fraud. Intentional misrepresentation or concealment of known material facts with intent to deceive.

Negligent misrepresentation. Careless or negligent failure to disclose material facts in circumstances where disclosure was required.

Concealment. Active hiding of conditions through cosmetic repairs, painting, or other efforts to obscure problems.

Breach of contract. Violation of express representations in purchase agreements or disclosure statements.

Violation of statutory disclosure duties. Failure to complete mandated disclosure forms truthfully.

In these cases, the central issue is not simply the presence of mold. It is whether the condition was **known and not disclosed**. The question shifts from "Is this toxic?" to "Did you hide it?"

By 2026, failure-to-disclose claims represent one of the most financially consequential branches of toxic mold litigation because:

- They avoid complex medical causation battles
- They focus on objective documentary evidence (what did seller know?)
- They allow punitive damages when concealment is proven
- They involve significant property repair costs
- Juries respond strongly to dishonesty

II. The Duty to Disclose Material Defects

Most states impose statutory and/or common law duties requiring sellers to disclose known material defects that affect the value or desirability of residential property.

A defect is generally considered **"material"** if:

- A reasonable buyer would consider it important in deciding whether to purchase
- A reasonable buyer would consider it important in determining what price to pay
- It affects the property's value, desirability, or habitability

Chronic water intrusion and mold contamination frequently qualify as material under all three tests.

Disclosure duties may arise from:

Statutory transfer disclosure forms. Most states require sellers to complete standardized disclosure statements listing known defects.

Common law fraud principles. Even without statutes, sellers have common law duties not to conceal material facts.

Real estate licensing regulations. Licensed agents have independent duties to disclose known material facts, separate from seller obligations.

Contractual representations and warranties. Purchase agreements often include representations that seller has disclosed all known defects.

Failure to disclose known mold conditions can expose sellers (and sometimes agents) to substantial liability.

What Makes a Condition "Material"?

Courts evaluate materiality by asking:

Would a reasonable buyer care? Mold visible on surfaces that can be cleaned might not be material. Hidden mold requiring $50,000 in remediation clearly is.

Does it affect property value? Even if not currently dangerous, a history of moisture problems and mold contamination reduces property value and is material.

Does it affect habitability or use? Conditions making rooms unusable or requiring occupants to relocate are material.

Does it require costly repairs? Defects requiring expensive remediation are material regardless of current severity.

Courts generally find chronic moisture intrusion and significant mold contamination material even if sellers believe they've addressed the problem. The history itself affects value.

III. Elements of a Fraud or Concealment Claim

To prevail on a fraud-based nondisclosure claim, a buyer typically must prove:

1. The seller knew of a material defect. Actual knowledge is typically required for fraud (as opposed to negligence). Evidence includes prior repair invoices, insurance claims, contractor reports, or seller admissions.

2. The defect was not disclosed. Seller either affirmatively misrepresented conditions (checking "No" on disclosure form) or failed to disclose when duty required it.

3. The seller intended to induce the buyer's reliance. Fraud requires intent to deceive or knowledge that misrepresentation would induce reliance. This is often inferred from circumstances.

4. The buyer reasonably relied on the nondisclosure. Buyer relied on disclosure statements or seller's silence about conditions.

5. The buyer suffered damages. Buyer incurred costs for remediation, property value loss, or other quantifiable harm.

The **knowledge element** is often the most contested. Sellers frequently claim ignorance: "I didn't know about the mold."

Evidence establishing knowledge includes:

Prior repair invoices. Documents showing seller paid for mold remediation, roof repairs, plumbing fixes, or waterproofing work.

Insurance claims. Claims filed for water damage establish knowledge of moisture problems.

Contractor communications. Emails, texts, or reports from contractors describing mold or moisture issues.

Home inspection reports from prior transactions. If seller purchased the property, their purchase inspection may have documented moisture problems.

Tenant complaints. If property was previously rented, tenant maintenance requests establish knowledge.

Obvious visible conditions. Extensive water staining, musty odors, or visible mold growth establish constructive knowledge even without documentation.

The Text Message/Email Gold Mine

In the digital age, electronic communications provide powerful evidence of knowledge and intent. Discovery frequently reveals:

- Text messages between spouses discussing "the mold issue"
- Emails with contractors negotiating remediation scope and cost
- Photos taken on sellers' phones showing conditions before cosmetic repairs
- Social media posts mentioning water leaks or damage
- Online searches for "how to sell house with mold" or "do I have to disclose mold"

These communications are often more damaging than formal documents because they're candid and unguarded.

PRACTITIONER TIP

Always request text messages, emails, and digital photos as part of initial discovery. Many cases settle quickly once sellers realize their electronic communications establish knowledge and intent to conceal. Cloud backups and metadata can recover "deleted" messages.

IV. "As-Is" Clauses and Their Limits

Sellers often rely on **"as-is"** clauses in purchase agreements to limit liability. These clauses state that buyer accepts property in present condition without warranties or representations.

However, courts generally hold that:

"As-is" does not shield intentional concealment. Clauses disclaiming warranties don't eliminate fraud liability. Sellers cannot contract around their duty not to lie.

A seller cannot contract away fraud. As-is clauses are effective for unknown defects or conditions apparent upon inspection, but not for active concealment.

Active concealment nullifies disclaimers. Painting over mold, replacing stained drywall without addressing moisture sources, or cosmetically hiding problems constitutes active concealment that as-is clauses don't protect.

While "as-is" clauses may limit claims based on unknown defects, they rarely protect sellers who had actual knowledge and concealed material problems.

Case in Focus: When "As-Is" Doesn't Matter

A 2024 Colorado case involved sale of a property "as-is, where-is, with all faults." The seller checked "No" on the disclosure form for water intrusion but included an as-is clause in the purchase agreement.

Post-closing, the buyer discovered extensive mold and evidence of previous remediation attempts. The seller moved to dismiss fraud claims based on the as-is clause.

The court denied the motion, stating:

"As-is clauses protect sellers from buyer disappointment about property conditions. They do not shield sellers from liability for affirmative misrepresentations or active concealment. The seller's completion of the disclosure form stating 'No' water intrusion, when evidence suggests prior knowledge of chronic moisture problems and remediation attempts, potentially constitutes fraud regardless of any as-is language."

The case settled shortly after the ruling for $235,000. The as-is clause provided no protection against documented concealment.

V. Real Estate Agents and Broker Liability

Licensed real estate professionals may face independent liability if they:

Knew of mold issues and failed to disclose them. Agents who have actual knowledge of material defects must disclose them to prospective buyers, even if sellers instruct them not to.

Ignored visible signs of water damage. Licensed professionals are expected to recognize obvious warning signs (water staining, musty odors, paint texture suggesting recent repairs) and either disclose them or recommend inspection.

Advised sellers to minimize or omit disclosure. Agents who counsel sellers to conceal defects or complete disclosure forms dishonestly may be personally liable.

Failed to conduct reasonable investigation. While agents aren't inspectors, they're expected to exercise reasonable diligence in examining properties they list.

Many states impose statutory duties on agents to disclose known material facts through real estate licensing laws. These duties exist independent of seller disclosure obligations.

Agents may argue they relied on seller representations and had no independent knowledge. But courts increasingly expect licensed professionals to exercise independent judgment when red flags are visible:

- Fresh paint in isolated areas suggesting concealment
- Texture differences in drywall indicating recent repairs
- Musty odors not explained by normal conditions
- Water staining around windows, ceilings, or foundations
- Evidence of dehumidifiers or fans suggesting ongoing moisture management

Professional liability insurance (E&O coverage) frequently becomes implicated in agent liability disputes.

Dual Agency and Disclosure Complications

When an agent represents both buyer and seller (dual agency), disclosure obligations become particularly important. Dual agents must:

- Disclose their dual agency status
- Remain neutral between parties
- Disclose all material facts known to them to both parties
- Not favor one party's interests over the other

Dual agents who withhold material information from buyers to protect sellers' interests face substantial liability exposure.

VI. Moisture History as a Litigation Trigger

The most dangerous evidence in mold nondisclosure cases is often not the mold itself, but the **history of water intrusion**.

Documents that may establish prior knowledge include:

Roof repair invoices. Even if seller had a roof "repaired," the fact that leaks occurred is material and should be disclosed.

Plumbing repair records. Prior plumbing leaks, especially those requiring wall or ceiling opening, suggest potential hidden moisture damage.

Insurance claims for water damage. These are discoverable through CLUE reports (Comprehensive Loss Underwriting Exchange) and establish knowledge of moisture events.

Mold remediation contracts. Any prior remediation attempts, even if successful, are material because they indicate moisture problems existed.

Home inspection reports from prior transactions. If seller purchased the property, their inspection report may document moisture issues that persisted.

HOA maintenance records. In condominiums, association records may document complaints, inspections, or common-area repairs affecting the unit.

Property insurance applications. Applications asking about prior water damage or claims history may contain seller admissions.

Buyers who discover hidden mold shortly after closing often obtain these documents through discovery, revealing pre-sale awareness.

The CLUE Report: Insurance History Exposed

CLUE (Comprehensive Loss Underwriting Exchange) reports maintained by LexisNexis contain seven years of insurance claim history. They're available to:

- Property owners (about their own property)
- Prospective buyers (with seller authorization, though often not provided)
- Litigants (through discovery)

In litigation, CLUE reports frequently reveal:

- Prior water damage claims seller "forgot" to disclose

- Multiple claims suggesting recurring problems
- Claim descriptions providing details about extent of damage
- Dates establishing when seller became aware of problems

Many nondisclosure cases settle quickly once CLUE reports reveal undisclosed claims.

VII. Inspection Controversies and Buyer Due Diligence

Defendants frequently argue that buyers failed to conduct adequate inspections. Common defenses include:

The buyer waived inspection contingencies. In hot markets, buyers sometimes waive inspections to make offers more competitive. Sellers argue this waiver absolves them of disclosure duties.

The condition was discoverable upon reasonable inspection. If a competent home inspector should have found the problem, sellers argue non-disclosure was not material.

The buyer had notice of water staining or musty odor. If conditions were apparent, sellers argue buyer assumed the risk.

The buyer conducted a limited inspection. Some buyers obtain "walk-through" inspections rather than comprehensive ones, which may limit recourse.

However, courts distinguish between defects that are readily observable and those that are actively concealed.

Key principles include:

Active concealment defeats inspection defenses. If sellers painted over mold, replaced stained materials, or took steps to hide problems, buyers are not charged with discovering what was intentionally hidden.

Inspection contingencies don't eliminate disclosure duties. Even if buyer conducted inspections, seller still must disclose known material defects. Inspections supplement disclosure; they don't replace it.

Latent defects aren't discoverable. If mold is hidden behind walls or beneath flooring where inspection wouldn't reveal it, buyers are not charged with constructive knowledge.

Home inspectors have limitations. Standard home inspections are visual and non-invasive. Inspectors don't open walls, remove flooring, or conduct destructive testing. Hidden mold beyond visual inspection scope doesn't defeat disclosure claims.

Case in Focus: When Inspection Doesn't Save Seller

A 2025 Minnesota case involved buyers who conducted a thorough home inspection before closing. The inspection revealed no mold. Post-closing, the buyers opened walls during remodeling and discovered extensive mold behind fresh drywall.

The seller argued: "The buyers had a professional inspection. The inspector found no problems. I had no duty to disclose what even an inspector couldn't find."

Discovery revealed:

- Seller had paid a contractor to replace moldy drywall six months before listing
- Contractor recommended addressing moisture source (roof valley defect) before closing walls
- Seller declined, instructed contractor to "just close it up"
- Seller painted entire room to hide texture differences from new drywall

The court rejected seller's inspection defense, finding active concealment defeated any argument that buyers should have discovered the problem. Settlement: $198,000.

The lesson: Home inspections don't protect sellers who actively conceal defects. Courts distinguish between buyers missing visible conditions and buyers unable to discover conditions sellers deliberately hid.

VIII. Damages in Mold Nondisclosure Cases

Failure-to-disclose cases can produce significant damage awards, including:

Remediation costs. Cost to properly address mold, correct moisture sources, and restore property to habitable condition.

Reconstruction expenses. Replacing materials, repairing structures, restoring finishes damaged during remediation.

Diminution in property value. Permanent reduction in value even after repairs due to disclosure requirements in future sales, property history, and market stigma.

Relocation expenses. If occupancy during remediation is unsafe or impossible, temporary housing costs.

Lost rental income. For investment properties, lost rents during remediation period.

Emotional distress. In some jurisdictions, anxiety, stress, and disappointment from purchasing defective property.

Punitive damages for intentional fraud. When concealment was deliberate and egregious, punitive damages multiply exposure.

Attorney's fees. Some states allow fee recovery in fraud cases; others require specific statutory authorization.

- Punitive damages become a real possibility when concealment is proven through:
- Documentary evidence showing knowledge (repair invoices, claims history)
- Communications showing intent to conceal (texts, emails)
- Active steps to hide problems (cosmetic repairs over mold)
- Affirmative misrepresentations on disclosure forms

High-value settlements often arise from egregious nondisclosure rather than contested medical injury.

Damage Valuation in Nondisclosure Cases

Example Calculation (Mid-Range Case):

Purchase price: $425,000

Proper remediation and repair: $85,000
Diminution in value (15% reduction): $63,750
Temporary housing (3 months): $9,000
Moving/storage costs: $4,500
Property damage (furniture, belongings): $8,000
Emotional distress: $25,000
Subtotal compensatory damages: $195,250

Punitive damages (1.5x compensatory, moderate case): $97,625
Attorney's fees (if recoverable): $65,000
Total potential exposure: $357,875

Had the seller disclosed the prior moisture problems and remediation on the disclosure form, the property might have sold for $385,000 (a $40,000 reduction), or the buyer might have negotiated a $15,000 credit for further investigation/repairs.

Disclosure cost: $40,000-$55,000 reduction in net proceeds
Concealment cost: $357,875 plus litigation stress

IX. Commercial Property Transactions

In commercial real estate, disclosure obligations may be governed more heavily by contract and negotiated due diligence rather than statutory disclosure forms.

Sophisticated buyers are often expected to conduct:

Environmental assessments (Phase I, Phase II). Investigating potential environmental contamination including mold.

Engineering inspections. Comprehensive evaluation of building systems, envelope, and structures.

Moisture evaluations. Specific testing for water intrusion and mold.

Document review. Examining maintenance records, tenant complaints, prior remediation efforts.

However, even in commercial transactions, intentional concealment of known defects can support fraud claims. The difference is that commercial buyers typically have greater resources and sophistication to conduct independent investigations.

Allocation of risk depends heavily on contract language:

"As-is, where-is" provisions. Common in commercial deals, but still don't protect against fraud.

Representation and warranty sections. Sellers may warrant no knowledge of environmental problems; breach supports claims.

Indemnification provisions. Detailed indemnity clauses may allocate environmental risks contractually.

Due diligence contingencies. Buyers often have extended periods to investigate, reducing reliance on seller disclosure.

Commercial disputes often turn on:

- What specific representations seller made
- What buyer's investigation revealed or should have revealed
- Whether seller actively concealed problems or simply failed to volunteer information
- Contractual allocation of environmental risks

X. Statutes of Limitation and the Discovery Rule

Failure-to-disclose claims frequently hinge on timing. Statutes of limitation begin running when:

The buyer discovers the defect. Actual discovery of mold, moisture intrusion, or concealed remediation history.

The defect reasonably should have been discovered. Constructive discovery when reasonable investigation would have revealed problems.

In mold cases, discovery may occur months or even years after closing, particularly when hidden intrusion gradually manifests. Courts apply the "discovery rule" to determine when the limitations clock started.

Arguments over "reasonable discovery":

Defendants argue: Visible water staining, musty odors, or paint texture differences should have prompted earlier investigation. Buyers who ignore warning signs face bars on delayed claims.

Plaintiffs argue: Hidden mold in wall cavities, beneath flooring, or in attics isn't discoverable through ordinary occupancy. Discovery occurs when problems become visible or when investigation reveals concealment.

Typical limitation periods:

- **Fraud:** 2-4 years from discovery in most states
- **Negligent misrepresentation:** 2-3 years from discovery
- **Breach of contract:** 4-6 years from closing (varies by state)

Strategic timing matters:

- File promptly once concealment is discovered and documented
- Don't delay while negotiating informally with seller
- Preserve evidence immediately (photos, samples, reports)
- Conduct comprehensive investigation quickly to establish full extent

When the Clock Starts: Discovery Rule Disputes

Case Example: Early vs. Late Discovery

Buyers closed on property in January 2020. In March 2020, they noticed a musty smell in one bedroom. They opened windows, assumed it was "old house smell," and took no further action.

In November 2022, they hired a contractor to remodel the bedroom. The contractor opened walls and discovered extensive mold and evidence of prior remediation.

Buyers filed suit in February 2023 (three years from closing, four months from actual discovery of mold).

Seller's defense: The musty smell in March 2020 should have prompted investigation. Reasonable inquiry would have revealed the mold. The claim accrued in March 2020 and is barred by the three-year statute of limitations.

Court's analysis: The court found that musty odors alone, in an older home, don't necessarily put buyers on inquiry notice requiring invasive investigation. Discovery occurred when the contractor found mold in November 2022. The claim filed in February 2023 was timely.

The lesson: Courts are often forgiving regarding when buyers "should have known." But prolonged delay after clear warning signs can bar claims.

XI. The Role of Mold Testing After Purchase

Buyers often discover mold through:

Indoor air quality testing. Testing prompted by odors, health complaints, or general due diligence.

Visible growth during renovation. Remodeling projects that open walls, ceilings, or floors reveal hidden contamination.

Contractor discovery during repair work. Contractors addressing unrelated issues (updating electrical, plumbing repairs) find mold.

Insurance claims. After water damage events (storms, pipe leaks), remediation contractors discover pre-existing mold.

Tenant complaints. In investment properties, tenant reports of mold or moisture problems.

Environmental reports generated post-closing can establish the extent of contamination but do not automatically prove pre-sale knowledge. The litigation battle centers on **what the seller knew before the transaction**.

Evidence establishing pre-sale knowledge despite post-closing testing:

- Growth patterns suggesting years of development
- Forensic analysis of water staining (age of staining)
- Discovery of repair attempts (paint layers, texture differences)
- Documents showing prior awareness (invoices, insurance claims)
- Seller admissions or inconsistent statements about knowledge

Expert testimony from environmental consultants and building scientists can date moisture intrusion and mold growth, establishing problems existed at closing even if not discovered until later.

XII. The Influence of State Statutes

States with robust disclosure frameworks (such as California with its Transfer Disclosure Statement requirement) have heightened awareness of mold as a material condition.

Even where mold-specific statutes do not create private rights of action (like California's Toxic Mold Protection Act), they reinforce the view that mold contamination is a significant defect requiring transparency.

State-by-state disclosure variations:

California: Extensive statutory disclosure requirements; seller must complete detailed TDS addressing water intrusion, drainage, environmental hazards.

Texas: Seller's Disclosure Notice required; must disclose material defects including moisture problems.

Florida: Seller must disclose known facts materially affecting property value.

New York: Property Condition Disclosure Statement required (though sellers can opt out by providing $500 credit).

Colorado: Seller disclosure of all known material defects; broad interpretation of materiality.

In jurisdictions with less prescriptive disclosure laws, common law fraud principles remain the primary remedy. But trend is toward increased statutory disclosure requirements.

States Where Sellers Can "Opt Out" of Disclosure

Some states (New York, for example) allow sellers to avoid completing disclosure forms by providing a credit to buyers (typically $500). This "opt-out" provisions prevents sellers from being bound by disclosure statements.

However, opting out:

- Doesn't eliminate common law fraud liability for active concealment
- May signal to buyers that seller is hiding something, affecting marketability
- Doesn't protect against fraud claims based on oral misrepresentations

- May trigger more aggressive buyer due diligence

Strategic considerations: Sellers with problem properties sometimes opt out to avoid disclosure liability. But sophisticated buyers view opt-outs as red flags requiring enhanced investigation.

XIII. Strategic Considerations for Plaintiffs

Buyers pursuing nondisclosure claims should:

1. Obtain prior insurance and repair records immediately. Request CLUE reports, subpoena insurance claim files, identify contractors who worked on property before sale.

2. Subpoena contractor invoices. Contractors who performed work for sellers before closing may have records documenting moisture or mold issues.

3. Review prior MLS listings for mention of repairs. Sometimes listing descriptions reference "recent repairs" or "newly painted" that suggest concealment efforts.

4. Analyze seller disclosure forms carefully. Compare what was disclosed (or not disclosed) with post-closing discoveries.

5. Preserve environmental and remediation evidence. Photograph extensively before remediation. Collect samples for age-dating analysis.

6. Obtain forensic analysis. Building scientists can often date moisture intrusion and mold growth, establishing problems predated closing.

7. Request electronic communications. Text messages, emails, and photos may reveal seller knowledge and intent.

8. Interview prior occupants. If property was rented before sale, former tenants may have complained about moisture or mold.

Establishing knowledge is paramount. Cases with documentary proof of seller knowledge settle quickly. Cases relying solely on inference or circumstantial evidence face greater challenges.

XIV. Strategic Considerations for Defendants

Sellers and agents can reduce risk by:

1. **Fully disclosing prior water intrusion events.** Even if repaired, disclose the history. Let buyers decide if they're comfortable with repairs.

2. **Retaining documentation of completed remediation.** If mold was professionally remediated, provide buyers with:

- Contractor invoices and scope of work
- Post-remediation clearance testing
- Warranties on remediation work
- Documentation that moisture source was corrected

3. **Avoiding cosmetic concealment of prior damage.** Don't paint over staining, replace materials without addressing underlying problems, or hide evidence of repairs.

4. **Maintaining written records of repairs.** Document dates, contractors, work performed, costs.

5. **Encouraging buyer inspections.** Make property fully accessible for comprehensive inspection. Provide buyers with repair records to review.

6. **Being truthful on disclosure forms.** When in doubt, disclose. The risk of non-disclosure far exceeds any benefit from incomplete disclosure.

7. **Consulting attorneys before listing properties with known issues.** Legal guidance on disclosure obligations specific to jurisdiction.

8. **Obtaining releases if buyers accept property with known defects.** If disclosure prompts negotiation of reduced price or repair credit, document buyer acknowledgment and acceptance of conditions.

Transparency is the most effective defense. Sellers who fully disclose past problems rarely face fraud claims. Sellers who conceal problems always remain exposed.

XV. Why Nondisclosure Cases Often Outperform Toxic Injury Claims

Failure-to-disclose cases frequently produce larger recoveries than toxic exposure claims because:

They avoid complex medical causation battles. No need to prove mold caused specific illness. Damages focus on property repair and value loss.

They focus on documentary evidence of knowledge. Paper trail of invoices, claims, and communications establishes liability more objectively than contested expert opinions.

They allow punitive damages in fraud scenarios. Intent to deceive supports punitive awards that multiply exposure.

They involve significant property repair costs. Remediation and reconstruction expenses are objectively measurable and often substantial.

Jurors respond strongly to concealment. "The seller lied" is a powerful narrative. Jurors understand dishonesty viscerally and punish it accordingly.

While proving systemic mold illness may be difficult, proving dishonesty is often more straightforward. Documentary evidence of knowledge combined with false disclosure statements creates liability that's hard to defend.

Settlement Value Comparison

Toxic Injury Case (Contested Medical Causation):

- Medical expert excluded or impeached
- Property damage: $75,000
- Emotional distress: Limited or excluded
- **Settlement Range: $50,000 - $120,000**

Nondisclosure Case (Same Property, Clear Concealment):

- Remediation costs: $75,000
- Diminution in value: $85,000
- Relocation expenses: $12,000
- Emotional distress: $40,000
- Punitive damages: $80,000
- **Settlement Range: $250,000 - $350,000**

The nondisclosure frame consistently outperforms contested medical causation because it shifts the battle to more favorable terrain where documentary evidence and jury attitudes favor plaintiffs.

XVI. Conclusion

Failure-to-disclose claims represent a powerful and expanding component of toxic mold litigation.

The central issue is not mycotoxins or exposure thresholds. It is honesty.

Did the seller know?
Did the agent disclose?
Was the buyer misled?

When mold is concealed rather than remediated and disclosed, liability exposure can exceed that of the underlying environmental condition itself.

Key Takeaways:

1. **Disclosure is cheaper than concealment** - savings from non-disclosure are illusory and temporary
2. **"As-is" clauses don't protect against fraud** - active concealment defeats contractual disclaimers
3. **Electronic communications reveal intent** - texts and emails provide powerful evidence of knowledge
4. **Insurance history is discoverable** - CLUE reports expose prior claims sellers "forgot"
5. **Agents have independent duties** - licensed professionals must disclose known material facts
6. **Punitive damages transform exposure** - intentional fraud supports awards multiplying compensatory damages
7. **Property damage alone justifies substantial recovery** - no medical causation required
8. **Documentary evidence defeats defenses** - paper trails are more powerful than testimony

The next chapter turns to another increasingly critical front in mold litigation: **insurance coverage disputes and the evolving landscape of mold exclusions**. Understanding how insurance shapes, and often determines, litigation outcomes is essential because coverage frequently drives settlement possibilities more than underlying liability strength.

10

Insurance Coverage and Mold Exclusions

Navigating the Modern Battlefield

When the Real Fight Is About Coverage

In March 2024, a Chicago landlord received notice of a mold lawsuit from a former tenant. The claim alleged chronic water intrusion, extensive mold growth, and respiratory injuries. The demand was $450,000.

The landlord immediately submitted the claim to his commercial general liability (CGL) insurer, confident his $2 million policy would provide coverage. Three weeks later, he received the carrier's response:

"Coverage is denied pursuant to the Fungi or Bacteria Exclusion, Section IV, Paragraph g. The loss alleged falls within the absolute exclusion for damage caused by, arising out of, or resulting from fungi, wet rot, dry rot, or bacteria. As such, we have no duty to defend or indemnify this claim."

The landlord was shocked. He'd paid premiums for years. He faced a lawsuit demanding nearly half a million dollars. And his insurance company was walking away based on a single paragraph buried on page 17 of his policy.

He hired coverage counsel who spent six months litigating whether:

- The water damage that caused the mold was a covered occurrence
- Mold was a "resulting loss" from covered water damage
- The anti-concurrent causation clause barred coverage entirely
- The carrier had a duty to defend even if indemnity might be denied
- The denial was made in bad faith

The coverage dispute settled for $185,000 (insurer's contribution) after the landlord agreed to contribute $50,000 from personal funds. The underlying tenant claim settled for $235,000. The landlord spent $65,000 on coverage counsel fees that his policy didn't reimburse.

Total out-of-pocket cost: $115,000, despite having $2 million in "coverage."

By 2026, this experience is no longer unusual. **No area of toxic mold litigation has evolved more aggressively than insurance coverage.**

I. The Insurance Dimension of Toxic Mold Litigation

In the early 2000s, insurers reacted to high-profile mold verdicts by rewriting policies to limit exposure. By 2026, mold-related coverage disputes are often as complex (and financially significant) as the underlying liability claims.

In many cases, the true battle is not whether mold exists, but whether the insurance policy will pay for:

- Remediation costs
- Structural repairs
- Temporary relocation expenses
- Defense costs against liability claims
- Indemnity payments to injured parties

- Consequential property damage

Understanding mold exclusions and coverage triggers is essential for both plaintiff and defense counsel because:

Coverage determines settlement feasibility. Defendants without insurance coverage have limited ability to pay substantial settlements. Knowing coverage status early affects case evaluation.

Coverage disputes delay resolution. When carriers deny coverage or reserve rights, litigation bifurcates into liability and coverage tracks, extending timelines.

Bad faith exposure changes dynamics. Carriers who unreasonably deny coverage face their own liability exposure, creating settlement pressure.

Multiple policies may apply. Property, liability, umbrella, and excess policies may all potentially respond, requiring coordination.

II. First-Party vs. Third-Party Coverage

Mold claims typically arise under two types of policies:

1. First-Party Property Policies

These policies cover damage to the insured's own property. Common in:

- Homeowners insurance
- Condominium association master policies
- Commercial property policies
- Landlord property coverage

Common issues include:

Whether water intrusion was caused by a covered peril. Most policies cover "sudden and accidental" water damage (burst pipes, storm damage) but exclude gradual seepage, wear and tear, or neglect.

Whether mold is a covered "resulting loss." Many policies exclude mold directly but cover damage "resulting from" covered water events. Courts struggle with where to draw the line.

Application of mold-specific exclusions or sub-limits. Modern policies cap mold remediation at $5,000 to $10,000 regardless of other coverage limits.

Coverage for additional living expenses (ALE). When properties become uninhabitable, ALE provisions may cover temporary housing, but carriers dispute whether mold conditions justify relocation.

2. Third-Party Liability Policies

These policies (often Commercial General Liability or CGL policies) cover claims made against the insured by third parties. Common in:

- Landlord liability policies
- Contractor general liability
- Property manager E&O coverage
- Builder's risk and completed operations

Issues include:

Whether mold constitutes "property damage" or "bodily injury." CGL policies cover these defined terms. Insurers sometimes argue mold doesn't fit either definition (though this defense rarely succeeds).

Whether exclusions apply. Fungi or bacteria exclusions, pollution exclusions, and "expected or intended" exclusions may bar coverage.

Whether the insurer has a duty to defend. Defense obligations are often broader than indemnity obligations. Even if ultimate coverage is denied, carriers may owe defense costs.

Allocation among multiple policy periods. Long-tail claims (chronic water intrusion over years) may trigger multiple annual policies, requiring allocation.

In construction defect mold cases, CGL coverage frequently determines whether settlement funds are available. Without insurance, contractors and developers may lack resources to pay substantial settlements.

III. The Evolution of Mold Exclusions

After early 2000s litigation produced substantial mold verdicts, insurers introduced increasingly restrictive language to limit exposure.

Common exclusion types now include:

Absolute Mold Exclusions

Language barring all mold-related coverage regardless of cause:

"*We will not pay for loss or damage caused by, resulting from, contributed to, or made worse by any of the following: ... fungi, wet rot, dry rot, or bacteria.*"

These exclusions aim to eliminate coverage entirely, even when mold results from covered water damage.

Fungi or Bacteria Endorsements

Specific policy endorsements added to standard forms:

"*The following exclusion is added: We do not cover loss or damage caused directly or indirectly by any of the following: fungi, mold, mildew, or bacteria.*"

These endorsements modify base policy language to narrow or eliminate mold coverage.

Pollution Exclusions Referencing Mold

Some insurers classify mold as a "pollutant" and invoke existing pollution exclusions:

"*This insurance does not apply to bodily injury or property damage arising out of the actual, alleged, or threatened discharge, dispersal, release, or escape of pollutants, including but not limited to fungi, mold, or bacteria.*"

Pollution exclusions were originally intended for traditional environmental contamination (chemical spills, hazardous waste) but have been extended to mold.

Anti-Concurrent Causation Clauses

Provisions stating that if any excluded cause contributes to a loss, coverage is barred entirely:

"*We will not pay for loss or damage caused directly or indirectly by any of the following, regardless of any other cause or event contributing concurrently or in any sequence to the loss: ... fungi or bacteria.*"

This language prevents policyholders from arguing that covered causes (water damage) should trigger coverage despite mold involvement.

Sub-Limits

Rather than absolute exclusions, some policies cap mold coverage:

"The most we will pay for all loss or damage arising out of fungi or bacteria is $10,000, regardless of the number of claims, locations, or policy years involved."

Sub-limits allow minimal coverage while protecting carriers from catastrophic exposure.

By 2026, policy language varies widely by carrier, state, property type, and policy year. Coverage analysis requires close examination of:

- Base policy definitions
- Exclusion language and scope
- Endorsements modifying coverage
- Resulting-loss provisions
- State-specific regulatory requirements

Even small wording differences can dramatically alter coverage outcomes.

Case in Focus: How a Single Word Changed Everything

Two landlords in adjacent states faced nearly identical mold claims. Both had CGL policies from different carriers.

Policy A (Illinois landlord): *"We do not cover damage caused by or resulting from fungi."*

Policy B (Wisconsin landlord): *"We do not cover damage caused by, resulting from, or arising out of fungi."*

Both claims involved mold growth following burst pipes. Both landlords argued the covered water damage should trigger coverage despite mold involvement.

Illinois result: Court found "caused by or resulting from" ambiguous regarding whether mold must be the sole cause or merely a contributing cause. Applying contra proferentem (ambiguities construed against insurer), court found coverage.

Wisconsin result: Court found "arising out of" is broader than "caused by" and includes any causal connection, however remote. Coverage denied.

The addition of two words ("arising out of") changed the outcome entirely. Illinois landlord received $285,000 in coverage. Wisconsin landlord received zero.

IV. The Resulting-Loss Doctrine

Many property policies exclude mold but preserve coverage for damage "resulting from" covered perils.

Typical scenario:

1. A burst pipe (covered peril) causes water damage
2. Water leads to mold growth
3. Policy excludes mold but covers water damage

Litigation centers on:

Whether mold is independent damage. If mold is a separate, excluded cause of loss, no coverage exists.

Whether mold is inseparable from covered water damage. If mold damage is inherently part of the water damage loss, coverage may exist.

Whether the exclusion applies to both remediation and resulting structural damage. Some courts distinguish between covering removal of the mold itself (excluded) and damage to property caused by the underlying water intrusion (covered).

Courts differ significantly in interpreting resulting-loss provisions.

Policyholder-friendly interpretations:

- Water damage caused mold growth as a natural consequence
- The initial covered cause (burst pipe) set the loss in motion
- Mold remediation is part of restoring property from covered water damage

- Exclusions should be narrowly construed

Insurer-friendly interpretations:

- Mold is a separate, intervening cause
- Exclusions apply once mold becomes involved
- Anti-concurrent causation language bars coverage when any excluded cause contributes
- Policyholders should have purchased separate mold coverage if they wanted protection

State law variations mean identical policy language produces different outcomes in different jurisdictions.

V. Anti-Concurrent Causation Clauses

Modern policies often include anti-concurrent causation language, stating that if an excluded peril contributes in any way to the loss, coverage is barred.

Standard language:

"We will not pay for loss or damage caused directly or indirectly by excluded causes, regardless of any other cause or event contributing concurrently or in any sequence to the loss."

Insurer arguments:

- Even if water damage was covered, mold contributed concurrently
- Therefore, the entire loss is excluded
- The clause eliminates "efficient proximate cause" analysis that might otherwise favor coverage

Policyholder counters:

- The primary cause was covered
- Mold was secondary or consequential
- Anti-concurrent causation clauses are ambiguous or unfair
- State law prohibits such broad exclusions

Jurisdictional interpretation of anti-concurrent causation clauses significantly affects outcomes. Some states enforce them strictly. Others find them contrary to public policy or construe them narrowly.

State-by-State Enforcement:

States enforcing anti-concurrent causation strictly:

- Texas (generally enforces as written)
- Florida (typically upholds clauses)
- Arizona (enforces in most circumstances)

States questioning or limiting enforcement:

- California (scrutinizes closely, sometimes finds ambiguous)
- Washington (examines reasonableness)
- New Jersey (applies consumer protection analysis)

Understanding your jurisdiction's approach is critical to evaluating coverage.

VI. Pollution Exclusions and Mold

Some insurers invoke pollution exclusions to deny mold claims, arguing that mold constitutes a "pollutant."

Courts vary in response:

Courts rejecting pollution exclusion for residential mold:

Reasoning:

- Pollution exclusions were intended for traditional environmental contamination
- Mold in homes doesn't constitute "pollution" in ordinary usage
- Applying pollution exclusions to residential mold exceeds reasonable interpretation
- Contra proferentem requires narrow construction favoring coverage

Courts upholding pollution exclusion for mold:

Reasoning:

- Policy explicitly defines "pollutants" to include fungi or mold
- Modern exclusions clearly encompass mold
- Sophisticated parties understood scope of exclusion
- Clear language should be enforced as written

Policy drafting has evolved to address judicial resistance. Modern policies explicitly include mold, fungi, and bacteria in pollutant definitions, reducing ambiguity.

Example of clear drafting:

"Pollutants means any solid, liquid, gaseous, or thermal irritant or contaminant, including but not limited to smoke, vapor, soot, fumes, acids, alkalis, chemicals, fungi, mold, mildew, bacteria, and waste."

This language leaves little room for arguing mold isn't covered by the pollution exclusion.

VII. Construction Defect and CGL Coverage

In construction defect cases, CGL policies frequently provide defense and indemnity coverage for property damage caused by defective work.

Coverage issues include:

Whether mold damage constitutes an "occurrence." CGL policies cover occurrences (accidents), not intentional or expected damage. Courts analyze whether mold growth was fortuitous or expected.

Whether damage is to "property." Mold contamination clearly damages property, supporting coverage.

Whether "your work" exclusion bars coverage. CGL policies exclude damage to the contractor's own work but may cover damage to other property. Courts analyze whether mold damage extends beyond the defective work itself.

Whether fungi/bacteria endorsements apply. Construction defect policies increasingly include fungi exclusions limiting or eliminating mold coverage.

Trigger of coverage. Determining which policy year applies when defects span multiple years.

Allocation among insurers. Long-tail construction defect claims may implicate multiple annual policies requiring allocation of defense and indemnity costs.

Coverage disputes can be as complex as the underlying defect case, involving:

- Multiple insurance carriers across multiple policy years
- Disputes over allocation methodology (pro rata vs. all sums)
- Reservation of rights creating conflicts requiring independent counsel
- Competing claims of primary vs. excess coverage
- Subrogation and contribution claims among carriers

These disputes often require coverage specialists separate from litigation counsel.

VIII. Duty to Defend vs. Duty to Indemnify

In many jurisdictions, the duty to defend is broader than the duty to indemnify.

Key principles:

Duty to defend triggered by allegations in complaint. If the complaint alleges potentially covered claims, insurers must defend, even if ultimate coverage is uncertain.

Defense obligations exist until coverage is definitively excluded. Ambiguities favor defense obligations.

Duty to indemnify determined by actual facts. What really caused the loss determines whether indemnity is owed.

Strategic implications:

For plaintiffs: Draft complaints to include covered water intrusion allegations to trigger defense obligations. This brings carrier resources to the table and creates settlement pressure.

For insurers: Issue reservation of rights letters preserving ability to deny indemnity later while providing defense. File declaratory judgment actions to resolve coverage disputes early.

For policyholders: Defend using carrier-provided counsel but preserve rights to independent counsel if conflicts arise.

Insurers frequently file declaratory judgment actions to clarify coverage before underlying claims resolve. These parallel proceedings add complexity and cost.

Case in Focus: Defense Obligation Drives Settlement

A 2024 Washington case involved a mold claim against a property manager. The complaint alleged:

- Negligent maintenance causing water intrusion
- Failure to repair leaking roof
- Resulting mold growth causing property damage and personal injury

The CGL carrier issued a reservation of rights, citing the fungi exclusion, but agreed to defend under reservation.

During litigation, the carrier spent:

- $85,000 defending the underlying claim
- $40,000 on coverage counsel analyzing indemnity obligations

Settlement negotiations occurred 18 months into litigation. The carrier faced a choice:

- Continue defending to verdict (estimated additional $150,000 in defense costs)
- Settle the underlying claim and resolve coverage dispute

The carrier settled the underlying claim for $175,000 (within policy limits) and resolved the coverage dispute. Total carrier cost: $300,000.

Had the carrier denied defense obligations at the outset, the policyholder might have settled for less (lacking resources for protracted litigation). But denying defense risked bad faith exposure if coverage was later determined to exist.

The duty to defend often determines settlement dynamics more than ultimate indemnity obligations.

IX. Bad Faith Exposure

When insurers deny mold claims, policyholders may assert bad faith.

Bad faith claims typically require proof that:

The insurer unreasonably denied or delayed payment. Denial must lack reasonable basis or ignore policy language.

The insurer failed to conduct a proper investigation. Cursory review without adequate analysis may constitute bad faith.

The insurer misapplied policy provisions. Incorrectly interpreting clear policy language or ignoring applicable law.

The insurer prioritized its interests over policyholder's interests. Refusing settlement within limits when liability is clear, exposing policyholder to excess judgment.

In jurisdictions permitting punitive damages for bad faith, exposure can exceed the underlying policy limits dramatically.

What constitutes bad faith in mold cases:

Automatically denying claims based on exclusions without investigating causation. If the claim involves both covered water damage and excluded mold, reasonable investigation is required to determine whether resulting-loss provisions apply.

Unreasonable delay in coverage determinations. Taking months to issue denials while tenants remain in contaminated conditions may constitute bad faith.

Selective reliance on policy language. Emphasizing exclusions while ignoring provisions favoring coverage.

Failure to explain coverage decisions clearly. Denial letters must articulate specific policy bases for denial with reasonable specificity.

Insurers often defend by asserting:

Clear exclusion language supported denial. If policy unambiguously excludes mold, denial is reasonable.

Ambiguity resolved in good faith. Where coverage is genuinely uncertain, reasonable interpretation supports defense.

Reasonable reliance on expert opinion. Carriers who consult coverage counsel and follow advice establish good faith.

Prompt, thorough investigation conducted. Documentation of investigative steps supports reasonableness.

Documentation of claim handling is critical. Carriers who maintain detailed files showing investigation, analysis, and reasoning fare better than those with sparse documentation suggesting cursory review.

X. Additional Living Expenses (ALE)

Mold contamination frequently forces occupants to vacate premises during remediation.

Coverage disputes arise over:

Whether relocation was necessary. Carriers sometimes argue tenants could remain during work, avoiding ALE costs.

Duration of ALE payments. How long remediation "should" take vs. how long it actually takes creates disputes.

Reasonableness of temporary housing costs. Carriers may dispute whether tenants' temporary housing was comparable to their original premises or excessive.

Whether delay was justified. If remediation takes months due to contractor scheduling, carriers may refuse to pay ALE for periods they deem unreasonable.

Delays in approving remediation can increase ALE exposure and fuel bad faith claims. Carriers who delay authorizing work while ALE costs accumulate face arguments that their conduct exacerbated damages.

Case in Focus: ALE Dispute Exceeds Remediation Cost

A family discovered mold in their home requiring remediation estimated at $35,000. Their homeowners policy had a $10,000 mold sub-limit but covered ALE up to 12 months.

The carrier approved the $10,000 remediation (its maximum mold obligation) but disputed whether relocation was necessary. The family moved out anyway, incurring $4,500 per month in temporary housing.

Remediation took seven months due to:

- Two months waiting for carrier approval (disputed)
- Three months for actual work
- Two months waiting for post-remediation clearance and reinstatement

ALE claimed: $31,500 (7 months × $4,500)

Carrier paid: $13,500 (3 months × $4,500, arguing family could have remained during work and that delays were unjustified)

Policyholder sued for bad faith, arguing:

- Relocation was necessary per remediation contractor and physician recommendation
- Carrier's two-month delay in approving work was unreasonable
- Delays in clearance were due to carrier-required additional testing

Settlement: $48,000 (including unpaid ALE, emotional distress, and attorney's fees)

The ALE dispute exceeded the original remediation cost, demonstrating how coverage disputes over secondary expenses create substantial exposure.

XI. Allocation and Long-Term Intrusion

Chronic water intrusion cases may span multiple policy periods, raising allocation issues.

Key questions include:

When did damage begin? Determining the inception date triggers the first policy.

Was it continuous? Continuous damage implicates all policies in effect during the damage period.

How should liability be allocated among insurers? Multiple methodologies exist.

Allocation methodologies:

Pro rata allocation by time: Each carrier pays proportionally based on time on risk. Example: Three annual policies, equal limits, each pays one-third.

Pro rata allocation by limits: Each carrier pays proportionally based on policy limits. Example: Policy A ($500K), Policy B ($1M), Policy C ($500K). Total: $2M. Policy B pays 50%, others 25% each.

All sums allocation: Each carrier potentially liable for entire loss up to its limits, with contribution rights against other carriers. Policyholder chooses which carrier to seek payment from.

Different jurisdictions apply different methods. Understanding applicable law affects settlement strategy with multiple carriers.

These technical allocation disputes can delay resolution for years as carriers litigate among themselves regarding responsibility shares.

XII. Strategic Considerations for Policyholders

Policyholders should:

1. **Provide prompt notice of claims.** Delayed notice can void coverage. Notice when you discover conditions that might become claims.

2. **Document all water-related events.** Photograph damage, preserve emails with contractors, maintain repair invoices.

3. **Preserve remediation invoices and reports.** Document costs and work performed to establish coverage claims.

4. **Request written coverage explanations.** If carrier denies or limits coverage, demand written explanation citing specific policy provisions.

5. **Consult coverage counsel early.** Coverage lawyers specialize in insurance disputes and can evaluate carrier positions.

6. Don't admit policy violations. Statements that you "knew about the problem for years" or "didn't maintain the property" can provide coverage defenses.

7. Cooperate with carrier investigations. Failure to cooperate can void coverage.

8. Consider bad faith claims carefully. Bad faith adds complexity but may be necessary when denials are unreasonable.

Early missteps can jeopardize coverage permanently.

XIII. Strategic Considerations for Insurers

Insurers must:

1. Conduct thorough investigations. Document investigations showing reasonable inquiry into cause, extent, and coverage.

2. Evaluate water intrusion independently of mold growth. Don't automatically deny based on mold presence without analyzing whether covered water damage exists.

3. Avoid blanket denial without policy analysis. Generic denial letters suggesting "mold is always excluded" without policy-specific analysis risk bad faith.

4. Document claim handling decisions. Maintain detailed files showing analysis, consultations, and reasoning.

5. Anticipate bad faith exposure. When coverage is debatable, denial creates bad faith risk requiring careful evaluation.

6. Issue clear reservation of rights letters. If defending under reservation, clearly explain coverage uncertainties.

7. Consider independent counsel for policyholders. When conflicts exist between carrier's interests and policyholder's interests, provide independent counsel.

8. Settle reasonably within limits. Refusing reasonable settlements within policy limits exposes carriers to excess judgments.

Modern mold litigation often scrutinizes claims handling as closely as policy language.

XIV. Why Insurance Often Determines Case Value

In toxic mold litigation, the existence of coverage frequently dictates:

Whether defendants can fund remediation. Defendants without coverage may lack resources to pay substantial settlements.

Whether settlements are feasible. Carriers with coverage provide settlement funds; their involvement (or absence) shapes negotiations.

Whether plaintiffs pursue systemic injury claims. Larger policy limits justify investment in expert testimony and extended litigation.

Whether construction defect cases proceed to trial. Multiple insured defendants with substantial coverage create settlement pressure.

A viable insurance policy may transform a marginal case into a meaningful settlement opportunity. Conversely, absence of coverage may limit recovery regardless of liability strength.

Settlement leverage equation:

Liability strength + Medical causation + Coverage availability = Settlement value

Remove any one element and value drops significantly. Remove coverage entirely and even strong liability cases may settle for minimal amounts.

XV. Conclusion

Insurance coverage disputes are no longer peripheral to toxic mold litigation. They are central.

Modern policies reflect two decades of drafting refinement aimed at limiting mold exposure. Yet ambiguities remain, and courts continue to interpret exclusions in varied ways.

By 2026, toxic mold litigation frequently unfolds on parallel tracks:

Track 1: Liability for moisture intrusion and contamination
Track 2: Coverage for the financial consequences of remediation and injury

Understanding both tracks is essential for realistic case evaluation and effective representation.

Key Takeaways:

1. **Policy language varies dramatically** by carrier, year, and state
2. **Mold exclusions are ubiquitous** but interpretation differs by jurisdiction
3. **Resulting-loss provisions** create coverage opportunities despite exclusions
4. **Anti-concurrent causation clauses** can bar coverage when any excluded cause contributes
5. **Duty to defend is broader than duty to indemnify** creating defense obligations even when ultimate coverage is uncertain
6. **Bad faith exposure** multiplies carrier risk when denials are unreasonable
7. **Coverage determines settlement feasibility** more than liability strength alone

The next chapter examines an increasingly powerful companion claim in mold disputes: **Insurance Bad Faith and the expanding liability of carriers who mishandle mold-related claims.** Understanding when coverage disputes become bad faith claims is essential because bad faith exposure often drives settlement more effectively than underlying liability.

11

Insurance Bad Faith in Toxic Mold Claims

Expanding Carrier Liability

When the Coverage Denial Becomes the Bigger Case

In August 2023, a Seattle landlord discovered extensive mold in a rental property after a tenant complained about water intrusion. The landlord immediately:

- Relocated the tenant to temporary housing at landlord's expense ($2,800/month)
- Hired a licensed remediation contractor ($42,000 estimate)
- Submitted a claim to his CGL carrier within 48 hours
- Cooperated fully with the carrier's investigation

Three months later, after the tenant filed a lawsuit demanding $275,000, the carrier issued its coverage determination:

"Claim denied. Fungi Exclusion bars coverage. The loss arises from mold growth, which is specifically excluded under endorsement CG 04 57. We have no duty to defend or indemnify."

The landlord's coverage attorney reviewed the file and discovered:

- The carrier never inspected the property
- The denial letter cited only the fungi exclusion without analyzing whether covered water damage existed
- The carrier's file contained a single-page "coverage analysis" completed in 15 minutes
- The carrier ignored the landlord's engineering report showing roof defect (covered peril) caused water intrusion leading to mold
- The policy's resulting-loss provision was never mentioned in the denial

The landlord sued for bad faith. Discovery revealed internal carrier emails:

Claims adjuster to supervisor: "This is a mold claim. Standard deny under fungi exclusion."
Supervisor response: "Approved. Use standard mold denial letter."

No analysis of whether the roof leak constituted covered water damage. No consideration of resulting-loss provisions. No property inspection despite landlord's request. Just automatic denial based on the word "mold" appearing in the claim.

The bad faith case settled 14 months later for $890,000:

- Defense costs the carrier refused to pay: $125,000
- Settlement of underlying tenant claim: $185,000
- Carrier's own defense costs in bad faith case: $180,000
- Bad faith damages (emotional distress, lost business opportunities): $275,000
- Punitive damages: $125,000

Had the carrier spent two hours properly investigating and analyzing coverage, they likely would have concluded:

- Roof defect constituted covered property damage
- Resulting-loss provision might apply
- Duty to defend was triggered by complaint allegations
- Settlement within policy limits was appropriate

Cost of proper claims handling: $185,000 (settling underlying claim)
Cost of bad faith claims handling: $890,000 plus reputational damage

As mold exclusions tightened and policy language grew more restrictive, insurance disputes became inevitable. But in many toxic mold cases, the litigation does not end with a denial of coverage. It escalates into bad faith claims against insurers who allegedly deny coverage unreasonably, delay remediation approvals, underpay water damage claims, or misapply exclusions.

I. When Coverage Disputes Become Independent Causes of Action

By 2026, insurance bad faith claims represent one of the most financially dangerous components of toxic mold litigation. In some jurisdictions, punitive damages for bad faith can exceed the value of the underlying property claim.

The evolution occurred because:

Carriers adopted aggressive denial strategies. Early 2000s litigation prompted reflexive denials of mold-related claims without adequate investigation.

Policyholders pushed back legally. Courts recognized that insurers owe duties beyond contract performance, including good faith and fair dealing.

State legislatures enhanced protections. Unfair claims practices acts and consumer protection statutes created statutory bad faith remedies.

Juries punish insurer overreach. When carriers are perceived as prioritizing profits over policyholder protection, juries award substantial damages.

II. The Elements of Insurance Bad Faith

Although standards vary by state, bad faith claims generally require proof that:

1. A policy existed and benefits were due. Without coverage, no bad faith liability arises. Policyholders must establish that coverage existed or was at least debatable.

2. The insurer unreasonably denied or delayed payment. The denial or delay must lack reasonable basis. Mere disagreement about coverage isn't bad faith if the insurer's position was reasonable.

3. The insurer knew or recklessly disregarded the lack of reasonable basis. Bad faith requires more than negligence. It requires knowledge that the denial was unreasonable or reckless disregard of policyholder rights.

4. The policyholder suffered damages. Beyond the unpaid policy benefits, policyholders must show additional harm (emotional distress, consequential damages, lost opportunities).

Some jurisdictions require proof of **"unreasonable conduct."** Others require a showing of **conscious disregard** or **reckless indifference.** The distinction affects burden of proof and damage recovery.

In mold litigation, the central dispute often revolves around whether the denial was based on legitimate policy interpretation or improper claims handling designed to avoid payment.

III. The Reasonable Investigation Requirement

Insurers have a duty to conduct a reasonable investigation before denying a claim. What constitutes "reasonable" depends on claim complexity, but minimum standards exist.

In mold-related cases, reasonable investigation may include:

Inspecting the property promptly. Desktop reviews without site visits may be inadequate when causation is disputed. Visual inspection can distinguish roof leaks (covered) from tenant negligence (excluded).

Retaining qualified experts. Complex mold cases may require environmental consultants, building scientists, or engineers to determine causation.

Distinguishing between covered water damage and excluded mold. Carriers must analyze whether mold resulted from covered perils or excluded causes. Automatic denial based on mold presence alone may be unreasonable.

Evaluating resulting-loss provisions. If policies contain resulting-loss language, carriers must analyze whether damage "resulted from" covered causes despite mold involvement.

Considering alternative causes. If multiple potential causes exist, investigation must reasonably explore causation rather than simply accepting the explanation most favorable to denial.

Responding to policyholder evidence. When policyholders provide engineering reports, contractor assessments, or other evidence supporting coverage, carriers must consider and address that evidence.

Bad faith exposure increases when insurers:

Rely solely on desk review without inspection. Particularly when policyholders request inspection, refusal may indicate bad faith.

Ignore contradictory expert findings. When policyholder experts conclude covered perils caused damage, carriers cannot simply ignore contrary opinions without reasoned analysis.

Delay testing or remediation approvals. Mold cases are time-sensitive. Delays allowing contamination to worsen may constitute bad faith, particularly when delays serve carrier interests over policyholder protection.

Fail to explain denial rationale clearly. Generic denial letters citing exclusions without explaining application to specific facts may indicate inadequate investigation.

Documentation of investigative steps is critical in defending against bad faith allegations. Carriers who maintain detailed files showing inspection, expert consultation, analysis, and reasoning demonstrate reasonableness.

Case in Focus: Investigation Failures Create Bad Faith

A 2024 California case involved a homeowner whose property sustained water damage from a storm. The homeowner submitted a claim including $65,000 in remediation costs for mold that developed during the carrier's 45-day delay in approving emergency drying.

The carrier approved $28,000 in water damage repairs but denied mold remediation, citing the fungi exclusion.

The homeowner's bad faith case established:

Inadequate investigation:

- Carrier never inspected property despite homeowner's three requests
- Carrier's adjuster relied entirely on phone conversation with homeowner
- No expert retained to assess causation or extent of damage
- Denial issued seven weeks after claim submission

Ignored evidence:

- Homeowner provided contractor report showing storm damage caused moisture intrusion
- Contractor documented that mold developed due to carrier's delay in approving drying
- Carrier file contained no analysis of contractor report

Delayed response:

- Carrier took 45 days to approve emergency drying (industry standard: 24-48 hours)
- During delay, moisture created ideal conditions for mold growth
- Carrier's delay directly contributed to mold development

Inadequate denial rationale:

- Denial letter cited fungi exclusion without explaining why resulting-loss provision didn't apply
- No analysis of whether storm damage (covered) caused mold growth
- Generic form letter with blanks filled in

Jury verdict: $485,000

- Policy benefits wrongfully denied: $65,000

- Consequential damages (property value loss, temporary housing): $85,000
- Emotional distress: $60,000
- Punitive damages: $275,000

The carrier's attempt to save $65,000 cost $485,000 plus $220,000 in defense costs and attorney's fees.

IV. Delay as a Catalyst for Bad Faith

Mold cases are time-sensitive. Delayed response can worsen contamination, expand remediation scope, and increase displacement costs.

Common delay-related allegations include:

Slow approval of emergency water mitigation. Industry standards call for mitigation within 24-48 hours of water intrusion. Carriers who delay approval allowing moisture to persist may be liable for resulting mold growth.

Prolonged reservation-of-rights letters. Issuing reservation of rights is appropriate when coverage is uncertain. But using reservation as pretext for indefinite delay while determining coverage may constitute bad faith.

Failure to respond to communications. When policyholders call repeatedly seeking claim status and receive no response, delay may be unreasonable.

Repeated requests for redundant documentation. Requesting the same documents multiple times or demanding documentation not reasonably necessary prolongs claims handling.

Scheduling delays for inspections. Taking weeks to schedule inspections that should occur within days suggests prioritizing carrier convenience over policyholder needs.

Where delay exacerbates damage, plaintiffs may argue that the insurer's conduct caused additional loss beyond the original claim. This compounds bad faith exposure because carriers become liable not just for benefits owed but also for damages their delay caused.

The 48-Hour Emergency Response Standard

In water damage cases, industry best practices call for emergency mitigation within 24-48 hours to prevent mold growth. Carriers who delay emergency authorizations beyond this window may face bad faith claims for:

- Mold growth that could have been prevented
- Increased remediation costs due to delayed response
- Extended displacement due to worsened conditions
- Property damage exacerbated by carrier delay

Courts increasingly recognize that unreasonable delay in time-sensitive situations constitutes bad faith even if ultimate coverage decision was debatable.

V. The Water vs. Mold Framing Strategy

A recurring bad faith issue involves how insurers characterize the loss.

Policyholders often argue:

- The initial cause was covered water damage (roof leak, pipe burst, storm intrusion)
- Mold was a secondary consequence of that covered damage
- Remediation should be covered as loss "resulting from" covered perils
- The policy's resulting-loss provision preserves coverage despite mold exclusion

Insurers may respond:

- Mold is excluded regardless of origin
- Anti-concurrent causation language bars coverage when any excluded cause contributes
- The claim is fundamentally about mold (excluded), not water damage (covered)
- Policyholders are trying to circumvent clear exclusion language

Bad faith claims arise when policyholders contend that insurers deliberately frame losses as mold-dominant to invoke exclusions, even when covered water intrusion was the primary driver.

Evidence of bad faith framing:

Internal emails showing strategic characterization. Carrier communications instructing adjusters to "frame as mold claim" rather than water damage claim.

Inconsistent treatment of similar claims. Covering water damage claims without mold but denying identical claims where mold developed.

Ignoring temporal sequence. When water damage clearly preceded mold growth, denying based solely on mold presence suggests bad faith.

Refusing to segregate covered from excluded damage. Even if some damage is excluded, carriers must pay for covered portions. Blanket denial of all damage may be unreasonable.

Case in Focus: Framing the Loss

A 2025 Oregon case involved water damage from a burst pipe that went undetected for three weeks (policyholder was traveling). By discovery, significant mold had developed.

Carrier framed the claim as: "Mold damage claim, denied per fungi exclusion."

Policyholder framed the claim as: "Water damage from burst pipe (covered peril) that resulted in mold growth during time reasonably necessary for discovery and response."

The court found the carrier's framing unreasonable:

"The undisputed evidence establishes that a covered peril (burst pipe) caused the initial loss. While mold subsequently developed, it arose from the covered water intrusion. The carrier cannot deny all coverage simply because mold eventually appeared. The policy's resulting-loss provision requires analyzing what damage resulted from the covered pipe burst. The carrier's failure to conduct that analysis suggests bad faith rather than reasonable coverage interpretation."

Settlement: $215,000 (including bad faith damages)

VI. Reservation of Rights and Declaratory Actions

Insurers frequently issue reservation-of-rights letters while investigating mold claims. These letters preserve the insurer's ability to later deny coverage while providing defense or investigation services.

Reservation of rights is appropriate when:

- Coverage is genuinely uncertain
- Facts are still being developed
- Legal interpretation is unsettled
- Multiple claims exist with different coverage implications

Problems arise when:

Reservations are overly vague. Generic language preserving "all rights" without specifying coverage concerns fails to inform policyholders of issues.

Insurers fail to clarify coverage positions. Issuing reservation but never following up with coverage determination leaves policyholders in limbo.

Defense counsel appointed by the insurer faces conflicts. When carrier's coverage interests conflict with policyholder's defense interests, ethical issues arise requiring independent counsel.

Reservation becomes pretext for indefinite delay. Using reservation to defer coverage decisions while pursuing discovery serving carrier's interests rather than policyholder's defense.

In high-value mold litigation, insurers may file declaratory judgment actions to resolve coverage disputes proactively. These actions ask courts to declare whether coverage exists before underlying claims resolve.

Strategic considerations:

For carriers: Declaratory actions provide coverage certainty and may eliminate bad faith exposure if court rules no coverage exists.

For policyholders: Declaratory actions can delay underlying claim resolution and create additional litigation costs. Policyholders may argue carriers should defend under reservation while coverage is resolved.

Bad faith claims may accompany or follow declaratory judgment proceedings, particularly if carriers prosecute coverage disputes in ways that prejudice underlying defense.

VII. Failure to Pay Additional Living Expenses (ALE)

Displacement is common in mold claims. When properties become uninhabitable due to contamination or remediation, ALE provisions may cover temporary housing.

Insurers often dispute:

Whether relocation was medically necessary. Carriers question whether conditions truly required evacuation or whether occupants could remain during remediation.

Duration of alternative housing. Disagreements about how long remediation "should" take vs. actual duration.

Reasonableness of costs. Whether temporary housing was comparable to original premises or excessive.

Causation of extended displacement. Whether delays were necessary for proper remediation or unnecessarily prolonged.

Failure to approve ALE promptly may support allegations that the insurer placed financial pressure on policyholders to accept inadequate settlements.

In jurisdictions recognizing emotional distress damages in bad faith cases, denial of relocation benefits can increase exposure.

When families (particularly those with children or vulnerable members) are forced to remain in contaminated conditions while carriers deliberate over ALE coverage, bad faith exposure escalates dramatically.

Case in Focus: ALE Denial Bad Faith

A 2024 New York case involved a family with a severely asthmatic child living in a home with extensive mold. The child's pulmonologist wrote a letter stating that continued occupancy posed serious health risks and immediate relocation was medically necessary.

The carrier:

- Received the physician's letter
- Acknowledged it in the file
- Took six weeks to respond
- Denied ALE, stating "relocation not necessary; remediation can occur while occupied"
- Did not consult medical experts about necessity
- Did not inspect property to assess habitability during work

During the six-week delay and subsequent denial period:

- The child was hospitalized twice for asthma attacks
- The family incurred $8,400 in hotel costs
- The parents missed work caring for the child
- Family stress escalated dramatically

Bad faith settlement: $385,000

- ALE benefits wrongfully denied: $8,400
- Medical expenses: $12,000
- Lost wages: $6,500
- Emotional distress: $125,000
- Punitive damages: $233,100

The carrier's refusal to pay $8,400 in ALE cost $385,000. The jury was particularly influenced by evidence showing:

- Carrier ignored physician's medical opinion without obtaining contrary medical evidence
- Carrier prioritized claims cost over child's health
- Internal emails discussed "making them pay their own way" to pressure settlement

VIII. Expert Selection and Bias Allegations

Insurance bad faith cases frequently examine the experts retained by carriers.

Plaintiffs may allege:

Repeated use of defense-oriented consultants. Carriers who consistently retain the same experts who always find coverage inapplicable create appearance of bias.

Biased interpretation of results. When environmental testing shows borderline conditions, experts who always interpret data in carrier's favor suggest predetermined conclusions.

Selective reliance on literature. Experts who cite only studies minimizing mold risks while ignoring consensus scientific literature.

Financial incentives. Experts who derive substantial income from carrier repeat business may be motivated to provide carrier-favorable opinions.

While insurers are entitled to defend claims vigorously, courts may scrutinize patterns suggesting predetermined outcomes rather than objective evaluation.

Transparent expert selection and balanced evaluation reduce bad faith risk.

Best practices for insurers:

- Retain experts with recognized credentials and independence
- Provide experts with complete facts, not just information supporting denial
- Document that expert selection was based on qualifications, not expected opinions
- Consider second opinions when initial expert conclusions are contradicted by policyholder experts
- Avoid financial arrangements creating appearance of expert dependence on repeat business

IX. Statutory Bad Faith and Unfair Claims Practices

Many states have enacted statutes prohibiting unfair insurance practices. These statutes often provide additional remedies beyond common law bad faith.

Common statutory violations include:

Misrepresenting policy provisions. Telling policyholders that coverage doesn't exist when policy language suggests it might.

Failing to adopt reasonable standards for investigation. Systematically denying claims without adequate investigation violates unfair practices acts.

Not attempting good-faith settlement when liability is clear. Refusing settlement within policy limits when liability and damages are reasonably clear.

Compelling litigation through lowball offers. Making settlement offers so inadequate they force litigation when reasonable settlement is possible.

Failing to promptly pay undisputed portions. Even if coverage amount is disputed, carriers must pay amounts clearly owed without delay.

Violations may support independent statutory causes of action or enhance damages under common law bad faith.

Attorneys must analyze both common law and statutory frameworks because:

- Statutory claims may have different elements than common law
- Statutory remedies may include attorney's fees where common law doesn't
- Statutory claims may allow punitive damages where common law limits them
- Burden of proof may differ
- Some statutes provide administrative remedies through insurance commissioners

State-by-State Variations:

California: Unfair competition law, unfair practices act, implied covenant of good faith and fair dealing

Washington: Consumer Protection Act applies to insurance, unfair claims settlement practices statute

Texas: Prompt Payment of Claims statute, unfair settlement practices provisions

Florida: Unfair Insurance Trade Practices Act, specific bad faith statute

New York: Insurance law provisions on unfair claims settlement

Each state's framework creates different strategic considerations.

X. Punitive Damages Exposure

In egregious cases, bad faith may support punitive damages designed to punish insurers and deter future misconduct.

Courts consider:

Intentional misconduct. Deliberate denial of coverage known to exist or deliberately inadequate investigation.

Reckless disregard for policyholder rights. Conscious disregard of obvious coverage or policyholder interests.

Systemic claim-handling deficiencies. Company-wide policies or practices designed to minimize payouts regardless of coverage.

Internal communications reflecting improper motive. Emails or documents showing profit prioritization over policyholder protection.

Financial condition of insurer. Punitive damages must be sufficient to impact large insurers meaningfully.

Internal emails and claims manuals often become central evidence in bad faith litigation.

Discovery frequently reveals:

- Performance metrics rewarding adjusters for denial rates or low payout amounts
- Training materials encouraging aggressive denial strategies
- Communications characterizing policyholders as adversaries rather than customers

- Corporate policies prioritizing claims cost reduction over fair evaluation

Such evidence dramatically increases punitive damage risk.

Punitive exposure significantly increases settlement pressure because:

- Punitive damages can exceed policy limits by multiples
- Punitive awards are often not covered by carrier's own insurance
- Publicity from punitive verdicts damages carrier reputation
- Appeals rarely eliminate punitive awards entirely, only reduce them

XI. Defense Strategies for Insurers

To reduce bad faith exposure, insurers should:

1. Investigate promptly and thoroughly. Document inspection, expert retention, analysis, and reasoning. Detailed files showing comprehensive investigation provide strong defense.

2. Distinguish clearly between covered and excluded damage. When claims involve both covered and excluded elements, analyze and pay for covered portions while explaining exclusion of other portions.

3. Provide detailed written explanations for coverage decisions. Denial letters should cite specific policy provisions, explain application to specific facts, and address policyholder arguments.

4. Avoid delay in emergency mitigation approval. For time-sensitive situations (water intrusion, habitability issues), authorize emergency response promptly even while broader coverage is analyzed.

5. Maintain consistent and transparent communication. Return calls, respond to emails, provide status updates. Communication lapses suggest indifference.

6. Document disagreement as legitimate coverage dispute. When denying debatable coverage, articulate reasonable basis showing good-faith interpretation rather than pretext.

7. Consider independent defense counsel when conflicts exist. When carrier's coverage interests conflict with policyholder's defense strategy, provide independent counsel to avoid ethical issues.

8. Review claims handling for compliance with unfair practices statutes. Ensure practices meet statutory requirements for investigation, communication, and payment.

Good documentation is the strongest defense. Carriers who maintain comprehensive files showing reasonable investigation, analysis, and decision-making fare far better than those with sparse documentation suggesting cursory review.

XII. Plaintiff Strategies in Bad Faith Mold Cases

Policyholders pursuing bad faith claims should:

1. Preserve all communications with the insurer. Save emails, letters, phone logs, text messages. Document every interaction showing delay, inadequate response, or unreasonable positions.

2. Document timelines of delay. Create chronologies showing when carrier was notified, when responses occurred, when delays happened. Timelines make delay patterns visible.

3. Retain independent environmental experts. Obtain objective analysis of causation and extent. Expert reports contradicting carrier positions strengthen bad faith arguments.

4. Identify inconsistencies in coverage positions. When carriers change rationales for denial or apply policies inconsistently, document contradictions.

5. Evaluate statutory remedies in the jurisdiction. Research unfair practices statutes, consumer protection laws, and prompt payment requirements that may apply.

6. Gather evidence of similar denials. Pattern evidence showing carrier systematically denies certain claim types supports allegations of unfair practices.

7. Request complete claim file. Many states require carriers to provide complete files upon request. Review for inadequate investigation, bias, or improper motivations.

8. Document consequential damages. Track costs incurred due to carrier delay or denial: additional property damage, health impacts, emotional distress, lost opportunities.

Bad faith claims often provide leverage when underlying coverage is disputed but plausible. The threat of bad faith exposure (particularly punitive damages) creates settlement pressure even when carriers believe coverage defenses exist.

XIII. The Economic Reality of Bad Faith Claims

In many toxic mold disputes, the insurance policy limit defines the ceiling of direct coverage. A $500,000 policy limits indemnity to $500,000 (absent bad faith).

Bad faith claims, however, may:

Remove policy limits as a cap. Bad faith damages are separate from policy benefits. Total exposure can exceed limits significantly.

Permit recovery of consequential damages. Damages flowing from unreasonable denial (property value loss, business interruption, health impacts) become recoverable.

Support punitive awards. Punitive damages can equal or exceed compensatory damages, multiplying exposure.

Expand discovery into insurer operations. Bad faith litigation allows discovery of carrier practices, training, policies, and similar claim handling, revealing systemic issues.

As a result, insurers often seek early resolution when bad faith exposure becomes credible.

Example exposure calculation:

Policy limits: $500,000

Underlying claim value: $350,000
Additional damages from carrier delay: $75,000
Emotional distress from unreasonable handling: $100,000
Attorney's fees (if recoverable): $125,000
Punitive damages (2x compensatory): $650,000
Total bad faith exposure: $1,300,000

Insurer's calculation:

- Settle underlying claim for $350,000 and avoid bad faith: Total cost $350,000
- Litigate, lose on bad faith: Total cost $1,300,000+ plus defense costs and reputational damage
- **Rational choice:** Settle for $425,000, resolving both underlying claim and bad faith exposure

Bad faith exposure creates economic incentives for settlement exceeding underlying claim value.

XIV. The 2026 Trend: Narrower Policies, Higher Scrutiny

As insurers continue tightening mold exclusions and sub-limits, policyholders increasingly challenge claims handling rather than just policy language.

The modern mold case often proceeds in phases:

Phase 1: Coverage denial or limitation based on mold exclusion

Phase 2: Negotiation over water damage vs. mold causation, resulting-loss provisions

Phase 3: Allegations of unreasonable investigation, delay, or misapplication of policy

Phase 4: Assertion of bad faith based on claims handling conduct

The sophistication of these claims reflects the maturation of mold litigation as a specialized field. Insurers can no longer rely on blanket denials based on mold presence. Policyholders and their counsel increasingly understand:

- Investigation requirements
- Resulting-loss provisions
- Duties owed by carriers
- Evidence establishing bad faith
- Statutory remedies available

This evolution forces carriers to handle mold claims more carefully and makes bad faith exposure a routine consideration in mold coverage disputes.

XV. Conclusion

Insurance bad faith has become a powerful companion claim in toxic mold litigation, transforming coverage disputes into substantial independent causes of action.

Where coverage disputes are debatable and carrier conduct was reasonable, bad faith may fail.

Where investigation is careless, delay is unjustified, or denials ignore obvious coverage, exposure escalates rapidly.

By 2026, mold litigation is rarely limited to environmental contamination alone. It often becomes a case study in claims handling conduct, where how carriers respond matters as much as what policies cover.

Key Takeaways:

1. **Reasonable investigation is mandatory** before denying coverage
2. **Delay in time-sensitive situations** creates bad faith exposure
3. **Blanket denials without analysis** of covered vs. excluded damage suggest bad faith
4. **Ignoring policyholder evidence** without reasoned response indicates unreasonable handling
5. **Punitive damages can exceed policy limits** dramatically
6. **Documentation of claims handling** is the strongest defense
7. **Bad faith exposure drives settlement** often more than underlying claim value
8. **Statutory remedies supplement common law** creating multiple pathways to recovery

The next chapter examines the expanding roster of defendants in toxic mold litigation, including architects, engineers, manufacturers, and product suppliers. Understanding when construction professionals and product manufacturers share liability is essential for maximizing recovery and ensuring comprehensive remediation funding.

12

The Expanding Roster of Defendants

Architects, Engineers, Manufacturers, and Product Liability in Toxic Mold Litigation

Following the Moisture Trail Upstream

In January 2024, a Phoenix homeowner discovered mold behind kitchen cabinets in her four-year-old townhome. Her initial reaction was frustration with herself for not maintaining the property better. Then her contractor opened the wall.

What he found changed everything:

- Window flashing installed completely backwards, directing water into the wall cavity instead of away from it
- No drainage plane whatsoever behind the exterior stucco cladding

- House wrap installed upside down, creating a moisture trap rather than a moisture barrier
- Missing sealant at every window-to-wall transition
- Evidence of water intrusion since original construction based on wood rot patterns

The contractor, a 30-year construction veteran, photographed everything and told the homeowner: "This isn't your fault. This is construction negligence. Multiple professionals failed here."

Within 90 days, the homeowner's attorney had identified eight potentially liable parties:

1. **The developer** (overall project responsibility)
2. **The general contractor** (construction supervision failure)
3. **The window installation subcontractor** (backwards flashing installation)
4. **The stucco subcontractor** (no drainage plane, improper installation)
5. **The framing subcontractor** (upside-down house wrap)
6. **The architect** (inadequate construction documents and details)
7. **The construction superintendent** (failed quality control inspections)
8. **The window manufacturer** (allegedly inadequate installation instructions)

Each defendant had commercial general liability insurance. Each had documentation in their files showing they knew proper installation methods. Each began pointing fingers at the others during initial settlement discussions.

The case settled 18 months later for $725,000:

- Complete building envelope remediation: $485,000
- Interior reconstruction: $125,000
- Temporary relocation during repairs: $42,000
- Diminution in property value: $73,000

Had the homeowner sued only the HOA (her initial plan), recovery would likely have been limited to the HOA's inadequate reserves (approximately $50,000) with no comprehensive fix. By identifying all responsible parties, she obtained full remediation funding and appropriate compensation.

This chapter examines how toxic mold litigation has expanded from simple landlord-tenant disputes to complex multi-party construction and product liability cases.

I. From Landlords to the Entire Construction Chain

Toxic mold litigation in its early years focused primarily on landlords and property managers. By 2026, that narrow focus has expanded dramatically.

Today's mold lawsuit may name:

Design professionals:

- Architects who designed building envelope systems
- Structural engineers who specified waterproofing
- Mechanical engineers who designed HVAC and ventilation systems
- Civil engineers who designed site drainage

Construction professionals:

- General contractors who supervised construction
- Construction managers who oversaw quality control
- Subcontractors who installed specific building components
- Developers who bore ultimate project responsibility

Material suppliers and manufacturers:

- Lumber and engineered wood product manufacturers
- Window and door manufacturers
- Roofing material suppliers
- Waterproofing membrane manufacturers
- Paint and coating companies claiming mold-resistant properties

- Stucco and cladding system manufacturers

Mold is rarely the root cause. It is the visible symptom of design decisions, material performance failures, construction practice violations, or remediation errors that occurred months or years earlier.

As litigation strategies have evolved, plaintiffs increasingly follow the moisture pathway backward until they identify every entity that may have contributed to conditions allowing chronic water intrusion.

II. Architects and Design Professionals

Design Duty and Standard of Care

Architects owe professional duties to design buildings that meet applicable codes and conform to industry standards. The duty extends not just to aesthetic and functional design, but to building science fundamentals including water management.

In mold-related cases, alleged design failures may include:

Inadequate flashing details. Construction documents that omit flashing specifications, provide insufficient detail for proper installation, or show flashing details that violate manufacturer requirements or building science principles.

Improper roof slope specifications. Flat or low-slope roofs designed without adequate pitch for drainage, creating water ponding that leads to membrane failure and intrusion.

Insufficient drainage plane design. Wall assemblies designed without proper drainage planes between cladding and substrate, allowing moisture to become trapped rather than drain away.

Poorly ventilated wall assemblies. Designs that create vapor-impermeable assemblies without adequate ventilation, causing condensation and moisture accumulation.

Inadequate vapor barrier placement. Vapor barriers specified on wrong side of insulation for the climate zone, or omitted entirely when required.

Improper HVAC sizing. Mechanical systems specified that are inadequate for humidity control in the climate and building type.

Plaintiffs must typically prove that the architect's design deviated from the accepted standard of care at the time of design.

What constitutes the standard of care:

Building codes. Minimum requirements established by applicable codes (International Building Code, International Residential Code, state amendments).

Manufacturer specifications. Installation requirements published by material manufacturers that architects must consider when specifying products.

Industry publications. Guidelines from organizations like ASHRAE (American Society of Heating, Refrigerating and Air-Conditioning Engineers), Building Science Corporation, ASTM International.

Professional practice standards. What competent architects customarily do in similar circumstances, established through expert testimony.

Published building science research. Peer-reviewed research on moisture management, building envelope design, and mold prevention available at time of design.

Defense arguments often emphasize:

Compliance with then-existing codes. Arguing design met all code requirements in effect at the time, even if best practices or later codes would require more.

Owner budget constraints. Claiming design limitations resulted from owner's budget restrictions rather than professional failures.

Value engineering decisions. Asserting that cost-reduction measures were owner-directed changes to original design.

Proper delegation of installation to contractors. Arguing that design was adequate but contractors failed to follow specifications or substituted inferior methods.

Professional liability (errors and omissions) insurance policies often govern defense and indemnity for architects, creating additional coverage issues.

Case in Focus: Design Defect Liability

A 2024 Washington state case involved a 64-unit condominium building with systemic water intrusion affecting 41 units. Investigation revealed that the architect had designed the building envelope with:

- Insufficient overhang to protect upper-story windows from wind-driven rain
- Window head flashing details that violated manufacturer installation instructions
- No weep screeds at the base of stucco cladding to allow moisture drainage
- Balcony-to-wall transitions with inadequate flashing specifications

The architect defended by arguing:

- Design met building code minimum requirements
- Contractor was responsible for proper installation
- Owner had reduced budget, limiting design options

Expert testimony established:

- Building code requirements establish minimums; professional standard of care requires consideration of climate, exposure, and building science
- Architect's details were inconsistent with manufacturer instructions, which professional architects must review and follow
- Budget constraints don't excuse fundamental building science failures
- Design documents lacked sufficient detail for contractors to install properly

Settlement: $4.2 million (architect's E&O carrier contributed $1.8 million)

The architect's failure to provide adequate building envelope details cost his carrier nearly $2 million and damaged his professional reputation.

III. Engineers and Building Systems Failures

Mechanical, structural, and civil engineers may be implicated where mold arises from systems within their professional responsibility.

Mechanical engineers may face liability for:

HVAC condensation issues. Systems improperly sized or configured, creating condensation on ductwork, air handlers, or building surfaces.

Inadequate dehumidification. Mechanical systems insufficient for climate conditions, failing to control indoor humidity below mold-growth thresholds.

Poor ventilation design. Insufficient air exchange in tightly sealed buildings, causing moisture accumulation from occupant activities.

Ductwork design failures. Duct routing through unconditioned spaces without adequate insulation, causing condensation.

Structural engineers may face liability for:

Inadequate waterproofing specifications. Foundation and below-grade waterproofing systems that fail to prevent groundwater intrusion.

Improper structural slope. Roof or deck structures designed without adequate slope for drainage.

Balcony and deck design failures. Cantilevered structures without proper waterproofing, allowing water to penetrate back into building envelope.

Civil engineers may face liability for:

Site grading failures. Grading plans that direct water toward buildings rather than away, causing foundation leaks.

Inadequate drainage system design. Storm drainage, French drains, or foundation drains improperly designed or specified.

Retaining wall failures. Walls designed without adequate waterproofing or drainage, causing moisture migration into adjacent structures.

HVAC-related mold cases are particularly common in tightly sealed, energy-efficient buildings where humidity control requires active mechanical systems rather than infiltration-based air exchange.

Expert testimony typically focuses on whether design specifications anticipated moisture loads, whether ventilation rates met recognized standards (ASHRAE 62.1, 62.2), and whether system commissioning was properly specified.

IV. General Contractors and Subcontractors

Construction-phase errors frequently trigger mold claims where installation deviated from plans, specifications, or industry standards.

Common installation failures include:

Improper flashing installation. Installing flashing backwards, upside down, with insufficient overlap, or omitting it entirely at critical transitions.

Failure to seal window assemblies. Missing sealants, improper sealant application, or failure to integrate windows with weather-resistant barriers.

Inadequate waterproof membrane application. Improper membrane installation on decks, balconies, or below-grade foundations.

Delayed weatherproofing during construction. Leaving buildings open to weather during construction, allowing materials to become saturated before envelope is sealed.

Failure to protect materials from rain exposure. Storing lumber, drywall, and other moisture-sensitive materials in weather, then installing wet or contaminated materials.

Quality control failures. Superintendent sign-off on work that visibly violated specifications or standards.

Subcontractors often bear responsibility for specific systems or components:

Roofing subcontractors: Membrane installation, flashing, penetration sealing
Stucco subcontractors: Drainage planes, weep screeds, proper installation sequence
Plumbing subcontractors: Proper pipe installation, leak testing, protection during construction
Window installation subcontractors: Flashing integration, sealant application, proper anchoring
Waterproofing subcontractors: Below-grade waterproofing, deck membranes, foundation drainage

Allocation disputes among contractors are common. General contractors typically argue subcontractors performed work improperly. Subcontractors argue they weren't properly supervised, plans were inadequate, or other trades damaged their work.

Contribution and indemnity claims frequently expand litigation complexity as defendants seek reimbursement from each other.

Case in Focus: Subcontractor Allocation Dispute

A 2025 Colorado case involved mold in 23 townhomes traced to window installation failures. The general contractor, window subcontractor, and stucco subcontractor all faced claims.

General contractor argued:

- Window subcontractor installed windows without proper flashing
- Stucco subcontractor failed to properly integrate cladding with window assemblies
- Both subcontractors deviated from specifications

Window subcontractor argued:

- Plans didn't clearly show flashing details
- General contractor failed to provide adequate supervision
- Stucco work covered windows before inspection could occur

Stucco subcontractor argued:

- Windows were already improperly installed when stucco work began
- Cannot integrate stucco properly with defectively installed windows
- General contractor rushed schedule, preventing proper sequencing

Expert testimony established:

- Plans contained adequate flashing details (architectural liability minimal)
- Window subcontractor installed flashing incorrectly (primary liability)

- Stucco subcontractor should have identified window issues before proceeding (secondary liability)
- General contractor failed to inspect window installation before allowing stucco to proceed (supervisory liability)

Settlement allocation:

- Window subcontractor: 50% ($1.2 million)
- General contractor: 35% ($840,000)
- Stucco subcontractor: 15% ($360,000)

Total: $2.4 million

The allocation disputes took 14 months to resolve, with each defendant spending $80,000-$150,000 on coverage counsel and experts analyzing contribution percentages.

V. Developers and Large-Scale Projects

In multi-unit developments, plaintiffs may pursue claims against developers for systemic issues affecting entire projects.

Developer liability theories include:

Systemic design flaws. Developers who approved inadequate building envelope designs to reduce costs.

Cost-cutting decisions affecting moisture control. Value engineering that eliminated critical waterproofing elements.

Failure to supervise construction. Developers who failed to oversee general contractors adequately.

Use of inappropriate materials in high-moisture environments. Specifying materials unsuitable for climate or exposure conditions to save money.

Large developments may result in:

Mass joinder lawsuits. Dozens or hundreds of unit owners joining in coordinated litigation.

HOA-led litigation. Homeowners associations filing on behalf of all owners for common interest defects.

Coordinated proceedings. Courts consolidating related cases for efficiency.

Developers often face exposure for both economic loss (repair costs) and remediation costs, even when personal injury claims are limited. In 200-unit developments with $75,000 average remediation per unit, exposure can reach $15 million before considering individual owner damages.

VI. Lumber and Building Material Manufacturers

Mold cases increasingly target product manufacturers where materials allegedly contributed to moisture retention or susceptibility to fungal growth.

Common allegations include:

Use of moisture-sensitive engineered wood products. Oriented strand board (OSB), engineered lumber, or composite materials that degrade rapidly when exposed to moisture.

Failure of exterior sheathing systems. Sheathing products that absorb water, lose structural integrity, or fail to perform as represented.

Inadequate product instructions. Manufacturer literature that fails to specify proper installation methods or moisture protection requirements.

Lack of mold-resistant treatment. Products marketed for exterior use without adequate protection against moisture and fungal growth.

Plaintiffs may assert:

Strict product liability. Product was defective in design or manufacture, causing harm.

Failure to warn. Manufacturer failed to provide adequate warnings about moisture sensitivity or installation requirements.

Design defect. Product designed in a way that makes it unreasonably dangerous when exposed to foreseeable moisture conditions.

Manufacturing defect. Particular batch or production run was defective, even if design was adequate.

Manufacturers typically defend by arguing:

Materials performed as designed. Products function properly when installed and maintained according to specifications.

Installation errors caused intrusion. Contractor failure, not product failure, allowed moisture intrusion.

Maintenance failures led to deterioration. Property owners failed to maintain drainage, gutters, or other systems protecting materials.

Products were misapplied. Materials used in applications they weren't designed or warranted for.

Product liability adds another layer of expert-intensive litigation requiring materials science, engineering, and construction expertise.

Case in Focus: OSB Sheathing Failure

A 2024 California case involved widespread moisture intrusion in a 180-unit development. Investigation revealed extensive OSB sheathing deterioration behind stucco cladding.

Plaintiffs alleged:

- OSB manufacturer marketed product for exterior use
- Product absorbed moisture through stucco cladding
- OSB swelled, delaminated, and lost structural integrity
- Manufacturer knew product was moisture-sensitive but failed to warn
- Alternative products (exterior-grade plywood, foam sheathing) would have performed better

Manufacturer defended:

- OSB was code-compliant sheathing material
- Proper installation includes drainage planes preventing moisture contact
- Failure was installation defect (no drainage plane), not product defect
- Warnings in literature specified proper moisture protection

Expert testimony established:

- OSB is more moisture-sensitive than traditional plywood
- Manufacturer literature contained moisture protection requirements
- Construction failed to include drainage plane (installation defect)
- But manufacturer knew stucco installers frequently omitted drainage planes and should have provided stronger warnings

Settlement: $6.8 million (manufacturer contributed $2.4 million of $6.8 million total)

The manufacturer's contribution reflected shared responsibility: installation was deficient, but stronger product warnings might have prevented widespread use without proper moisture protection.

VII. Window, Roofing, and Waterproofing Systems

Window and roofing assemblies are frequent focal points in mold litigation because they represent primary building envelope penetrations.

Window system allegations include:

Defective sealants. Sealant products that fail prematurely, allowing water intrusion.

Improper drainage channel design. Windows without adequate weep holes or drainage channels, trapping water.

Inadequate water diversion systems. Missing or defective drip caps, sill pans, or head flashing.

Known design vulnerabilities. Manufacturers who knew specific window models were prone to leakage but continued marketing them.

Roofing system allegations include:

Membrane failures. Waterproof membranes that deteriorate prematurely or are inadequate for climate.

Flashing component failures. Metal flashings that corrode or degrade, pre-formed components that don't fit properly.

System incompatibilities. Roof assemblies where components from different manufacturers prove incompatible.

When systemic product failure affects multiple properties, litigation may expand beyond individual cases into coordinated product liability actions involving hundreds or thousands of affected installations.

Internal manufacturer documents often become critical:

- Prior complaints about product performance
- Testing data showing failure rates
- Internal communications about known defects
- Decisions to continue marketing despite known issues

Case in Focus: Window Manufacturer Pattern Liability

A 2025 Oregon case involved a specific window model installed in over 300 homes in the Pacific Northwest between 2017-2020. By 2023, water intrusion problems had been documented in 127 homes.

Discovery revealed:

- Manufacturer's internal testing showed sill pan design was inadequate for wind-driven rain
- Engineering department recommended design modification in 2016
- Marketing department overruled change, citing retooling costs
- Windows continued to be sold with known deficiency through 2020
- Manufacturer received 87 complaints from homeowners and builders before discontinuing model

Coordinated litigation involved:

- 127 individual homeowners
- 14 builders who had installed windows
- 8 window distributors
- Multiple insurance carriers

Settlement: $18.4 million

- Window manufacturer: $12.2 million (primary liability)
- Installation errors by some builders: $3.8 million (improper flashing integration)
- Inadequate maintenance by some homeowners: $2.4 million (clogged weep holes)

The manufacturer's decision to continue marketing a known defective product for four years after internal testing identified the problem dramatically increased liability compared to a design defect discovered only after market release.

VIII. Paint, Coating, and Mold-Resistant Product Claims

An emerging category involves allegations that coatings or products marketed as "mold-resistant" failed to perform as represented.

Claims may assert:

Misrepresentation of mold resistance. Products marketed as preventing mold that actually provide little or no protection.

Inadequate labeling. Failure to disclose that products only resist mold under specific conditions (low humidity, no water contact, etc.).

Failure to disclose limitations. Marketing materials suggesting comprehensive mold prevention when products only inhibit surface growth, not growth from moisture intrusion.

Lack of efficacy in high-humidity environments. Products that work in laboratory conditions but fail in real-world high-moisture environments.

These cases often center on advertising claims and consumer protection statutes rather than traditional negligence theories.

Courts typically require proof that:

Product was used as intended. Plaintiff followed application instructions and used product in recommended applications.

Failure was product-based rather than moisture-driven. Even mold-resistant products cannot prevent growth when subject to chronic water intrusion.

Representations were materially misleading. Marketing claims created reasonable expectations the product didn't meet.

Damages flowed from reasonable reliance. Plaintiff relied on claims and suffered harm as result.

IX. Apportionment and Comparative Fault

With multiple defendants, allocation of liability becomes central to settlement negotiations and trial strategy.

Courts may apportion fault among:

- Designers (architects and engineers)
- Contractors (general contractors and subs)
- Manufacturers (material and system suppliers)
- Property owners (maintenance failures)
- Maintenance providers (HOAs, property managers)

Some jurisdictions apply **joint and several liability:** each defendant potentially liable for entire judgment, with contribution rights against co-defendants. This benefits plaintiffs by ensuring recovery even if some defendants lack resources.

Other jurisdictions apply **several liability only:** each defendant liable only for their percentage of fault. This protects defendants but risks leaving plaintiffs unable to collect full judgment if some defendants are insolvent.

Complex expert analysis is often required to determine whether design, installation, product failure, or maintenance played the primary role in causing moisture intrusion.

Factors courts consider in allocation:

Temporal sequence. Which failures occurred first chronologically?

Causative significance. Which failures were most significant in causing moisture intrusion?

Foreseeability. Which parties should have foreseen their conduct would lead to moisture problems?

Ability to prevent. Which parties had the best opportunity to prevent or discover problems?

Contractual responsibilities. What did contracts require each party to do?

Comparative degrees of fault. Whose conduct was most culpable (intentional vs. negligent vs. inadvertent)?

X. Indemnity and Cross-Claims

Multi-defendant mold cases frequently generate extensive cross-claims as defendants seek reimbursement from each other.

Common cross-claim theories:

Contractual indemnity. Construction contracts often contain indemnification clauses requiring subcontractors to indemnify general contractors, or requiring general contractors to indemnify owners.

Equitable indemnity. Common law principles allowing defendants to seek contribution from co-defendants based on relative fault.

Contribution actions. Statutory or common law rights to seek proportional reimbursement from other responsible parties.

Breach of contract. Claims that co-defendants violated construction contracts, warranties, or other agreements.

Insurance coverage disputes among carriers. When multiple defendants have insurance, carriers often dispute which policy is primary, how costs should be allocated, and whether other carriers should contribute.

Construction contracts often contain indemnification clauses that shift liability downstream:

"Subcontractor shall indemnify, defend, and hold harmless Owner and General Contractor from all claims arising out of Subcontractor's work, including but not limited to defective workmanship, material failures, or code violations."

Such clauses can dramatically affect ultimate allocation, but courts scrutinize them for:

- Compliance with state anti-indemnity statutes (many states limit or prohibit certain indemnity provisions)
- Whether language is sufficiently clear and specific
- Whether indemnity extends to indemnitee's own negligence
- Insurance implications and coverage for indemnity obligations

The procedural complexity of cross-claims can significantly extend litigation timelines. Cases with 6-8 defendants often take 24-36 months to resolve as allocation disputes are litigated alongside underlying liability.

XI. Economic Loss Doctrine Considerations

In product-related mold cases, defendants may invoke the **economic loss doctrine**, arguing that purely economic damages (repair costs, property value loss) are not recoverable in tort absent personal injury or property damage beyond the product itself.

The doctrine generally provides:

Tort remedies (negligence, strict liability) are not available for purely economic losses. Buyers must pursue contract remedies (warranty claims, breach of contract) for defective products that damage only themselves.

Plaintiffs counter that:

Mold contamination constitutes property damage beyond the defective component. When defective windows cause wall cavity mold affecting the entire home, damage extends far beyond the windows themselves.

Personal injury claims overcome economic loss limitations. When occupants suffer respiratory injuries, tort remedies are appropriate regardless of property damage characterization.

Building components are not "products" subject to the doctrine. Some courts find integrated building components (windows installed in walls, roofing systems) differ from consumer products, making the doctrine inapplicable.

Application of the economic loss doctrine varies significantly by jurisdiction:

States applying doctrine strictly to bar recovery:

- Texas (generally bars tort recovery for economic loss)
- Illinois (strictly enforces against integrated components)
- Pennsylvania (applies broadly to construction cases)

States limiting or rejecting doctrine in construction cases:

- California (allows tort claims for construction defects)
- New Jersey (permits tort recovery when safety is implicated)
- Washington (limits doctrine application in residential construction)

Understanding your jurisdiction's approach is critical for evaluating which defendants to pursue and which legal theories to advance.

XII. Strategic Implications for Plaintiffs

When expanding the defendant roster, plaintiffs must:

1. Conduct thorough building envelope analysis early. Retain qualified building scientists and engineers who can trace moisture pathways to their source and identify all responsible parties.

2. Review architectural plans and specifications. Compare design documents to as-built conditions, identifying deviations that suggest installation failures vs. design defects.

3. Identify product manufacturers and installation subcontractors. Determine what products were used, who installed them, and whether product literature was followed.

4. Analyze warranty documents. Review express warranties from manufacturers, builders, and contractors for remaining coverage periods.

5. Consider statutes of repose. Calculate limitation periods for each potential defendant, recognizing that different defendants may have different time bars.

6. Evaluate insurance coverage for each defendant. Identify which parties have CGL coverage, E&O coverage, or product liability coverage that might respond.

7. Assess contractual indemnity provisions. Review construction contracts to understand how liability might ultimately be allocated through indemnification.

8. Balance complexity against recovery. More defendants increases potential recovery but also increases complexity, cost, and time to resolution.

Adding defendants increases potential recovery sources and creates pressure for settlement as defendants point fingers at each other. But it also increases litigation complexity and costs.

XIII. Strategic Implications for Defendants

Design professionals, contractors, and manufacturers should:

1. Preserve project documentation comprehensively. Maintain complete files including plans, specifications, change orders, RFIs, submittals, and as-built documents.

2. Review contractual indemnity provisions immediately. Understand indemnification obligations and rights before responding to claims.

3. Retain independent engineering experts early. Don't wait for formal litigation. Early technical evaluation identifies defenses and allocation opportunities.

4. Evaluate insurance coverage triggers promptly. Notify carriers immediately, analyze policy applicability, and understand defense and indemnity coverage.

5. Monitor statute-of-repose defenses. Determine whether claims are time-barred under applicable repose statutes.

6. Document allocation arguments. Gather evidence showing other parties' comparative fault to support contribution or indemnity claims.

7. Consider early mediation with all parties. Global mediations with all defendants and carriers often produce more efficient resolutions than sequential negotiations.

Early technical evaluation often narrows exposure by identifying primary responsible parties and supporting allocation defenses.

XIV. The Trend Toward Systemic Accountability

The expansion of defendants reflects a broader trend in how courts and juries view mold litigation:

Mold is no longer treated solely as a maintenance problem.
It is viewed as a systems failure involving design, construction, materials, and maintenance.

Modern toxic mold litigation examines:

- Design assumptions about water management
- Construction sequencing and quality control
- Product performance in real-world conditions
- Climate resilience and adaptation
- Cost-driven material substitution and value engineering

Accountability extends beyond landlords to the entire building lifecycle, from initial design through construction and occupancy.

This evolution benefits plaintiffs by expanding recovery sources and creating settlement pressure through multi-party finger-pointing. It challenges defendants by requiring comprehensive technical defense and careful allocation strategies.

XV. Conclusion

By 2026, toxic mold litigation routinely encompasses architects, engineers, contractors, subcontractors, and manufacturers. Mold is the visible manifestation of deeper design and construction decisions that preceded occupancy by years.

As plaintiffs increasingly trace moisture intrusion upstream to its source, litigation becomes more technically complex, financially significant, and dependent on sophisticated expert analysis.

Key Takeaways:

1. **Follow moisture upstream** to identify all responsible parties

2. **Design professionals owe duties** beyond code compliance to building science principles
3. **Multiple defendants increase recovery** through aggregate insurance coverage
4. **Installation failures are more common** than design failures
5. **Product manufacturers face liability** for inadequate warnings and known defects
6. **Allocation disputes are inevitable** and often take longer to resolve than underlying liability
7. **Cross-claims and indemnity** reshape ultimate financial responsibility
8. **Economic loss doctrine** limits tort recovery in some jurisdictions
9. **Early coordination creates settlement pressure** as defendants point fingers at each other

The next chapter examines commercial and multi-family housing mold claims, where scale changes everything. Understanding how institutional ownership, regulatory oversight, and pattern evidence reshape litigation dynamics is essential for handling large-scale residential and commercial property cases.

PART IV: Institutional and Large-Scale Litigation

13

Commercial and Multi-Family Housing Mold Claims

Scale, Regulation, and Institutional Exposure

When One Problem Becomes Two Hundred

In April 2024, a single tenant in a 240-unit apartment complex in Atlanta complained about a musty smell and visible mold in her bathroom. The property manager investigated, found minor surface growth, and had maintenance spray it with bleach. Problem solved, or so they thought.

Three weeks later, four more tenants in the same building reported similar issues. Then seven more. Then fifteen.

By month three, 47 tenants had filed formal complaints. The property management company hired an environmental consultant who discovered that all affected units shared common characteristics:

- Bathroom exhaust fans that vented into attic spaces rather than outside
- Inadequate attic ventilation causing condensation
- HVAC systems sized improperly for Georgia's humidity
- A recurring roof leak in one section affecting multiple units vertically
- Plumbing stack issues allowing moisture migration through wall cavities

This wasn't 47 separate maintenance problems. It was five systemic defects affecting nearly 20% of the building.

The litigation that followed involved:

Defendants:

- Property management company (operating entity)
- Property owner (institutional investor owning 18,000 units nationally)
- Original developer (building completed 2019)
- General contractor (systemic construction defects)
- HVAC subcontractor (improper system design and installation)
- Roofing subcontractor (recurring leak issues)
- Architect (inadequate ventilation design)

Claims:

- 47 individual tenant habitability claims
- Class action attempt (denied due to individualized damages)
- Coordinated litigation through single master complaint
- Building code violations (city housing authority)
- Fair Housing Act claims (three tenants with asthma)

Settlement (22 months later): $8.9 million

- Building-wide HVAC replacement: $2.8 million

- Roof repairs and replacement (affected sections): $1.4 million
- Interior remediation (47 units): $1.9 million
- Tenant relocation during repairs: $780,000
- Individual tenant damages: $1.2 million
- City code violation penalties: $180,000
- Attorney's fees: $640,000

The property manager's initial response (spray with bleach) cost $45. The ultimate resolution cost $8.9 million. The difference? Recognition that scale changes everything.

This chapter examines how mold litigation transforms when it moves from single-family homes to large multi-family and commercial properties.

I. When Mold Litigation Scales Up

Toxic mold litigation changes fundamentally when it moves from individual residences to:

Large residential properties:

- Apartment complexes (50+ units)
- Condominium developments
- Student housing facilities
- Senior living communities
- Public housing projects

Commercial properties:

- Office buildings
- Retail centers
- Hotels and hospitality
- Mixed-use developments
- Industrial facilities

In these contexts, mold is rarely an isolated defect. It reflects systemic moisture intrusion, deferred maintenance, or design flaws affecting dozens or hundreds of units/spaces.

By 2026, multi-family and commercial mold cases represent some of the highest financial exposure scenarios in the field because:

Pattern evidence creates leverage. When 20 tenants report identical problems, individual maintenance failure arguments collapse.

Regulatory oversight intensifies. Health departments, building inspectors, and housing authorities become involved, creating public records and governmental pressure.

Institutional defendants have deeper pockets. Large property owners and management companies have substantial assets and insurance coverage.

Media attention escalates. Large-scale mold problems generate news coverage, increasing reputational pressure for settlement.

Aggregate damages multiply quickly. Even modest per-unit damages ($15,000-$25,000) times 100 affected units create seven-figure exposure.

II. Multi-Family Housing: Repetition and Pattern Evidence

In apartment complexes and large rental communities, plaintiffs often argue that mold conditions are not incidental but systemic.

Common allegations include:

Chronic roof leaks affecting multiple units. When water intrusion affects units on multiple floors in the same vertical line, it suggests roof system failure rather than isolated damage.

Repeated plumbing stack failures. Plumbing serving multiple units vertically can affect numerous units when leaks occur within wall cavities.

Balcony and façade water intrusion. Building envelope failures at balconies often affect all units with similar balcony designs.

HVAC condensation issues building-wide. Undersized or improperly maintained systems create condensation problems across entire buildings.

Delayed remediation policies. Corporate policies that defer repairs or minimize response create pattern evidence of institutional indifference.

When multiple tenants report similar conditions in similar timeframes, pattern evidence becomes powerful litigation leverage.

What pattern evidence establishes:

Notice. Multiple complaints demonstrate management knew or should have known about recurring problems.

Systemic nature. Repetition across units suggests design or construction defects rather than tenant-caused issues.

Inadequate response. When similar complaints receive similar inadequate responses, it shows policy rather than isolated error.

Corporate knowledge. Pattern problems reported through work order systems create institutional knowledge traceable to management.

Foreseeability. Recurring problems establish that continued occurrences were foreseeable and preventable.

Internal maintenance logs, complaint histories, and deferred capital expenditure records frequently become central exhibits demonstrating that management recognized systemic problems but failed to address root causes.

Case in Focus: Pattern Evidence Defeats Individual Maintenance Defense

A 2024 Chicago case involved a 156-unit complex where management defended individual tenant claims by arguing each represented separate maintenance issues caused by different factors.

Discovery revealed:

Building-wide patterns:

- 38 units reported bathroom ceiling mold over 18 months
- All 38 units were on floors 2-5 (none on ground floor)
- All affected bathrooms were in same location within unit floor plans

- All units shared common plumbing stacks

Documentary evidence:

- Work orders showed 127 bathroom exhaust fan repair requests over three years
- Maintenance logs noted "recurring moisture issues upper floors"
- Engineering report from two years earlier recommended bathroom ventilation system replacement (cost: $180,000, deferred due to budget)
- Email from regional manager: "We're seeing pattern bathroom issues. Hold off on major fixes until we decide whether to sell property."

The pattern evidence transformed individual maintenance disputes into systemic failure case. Settlement: $2.4 million (vs. initial offers totaling $180,000 for all claims individually).

III. Public Housing Authorities and Governmental Entities

Public housing mold litigation presents unique challenges due to governmental defendant status.

Claims may involve:

Local housing authorities. Municipal or county agencies operating public housing projects.

Federally subsidized housing. Section 8 housing, HUD-assisted developments, low-income housing tax credit properties.

Housing voucher programs. Properties accepting housing choice vouchers where government oversight applies.

Aging building infrastructure. Public housing often involves older buildings with deferred maintenance due to funding constraints.

Plaintiffs may assert:

Breach of habitability. Standard landlord-tenant habitability claims.

Negligence. Failure to maintain safe conditions despite knowledge of problems.

Violation of housing codes. Non-compliance with municipal, state, or federal housing quality standards.

Disability discrimination under Fair Housing Act. Failure to accommodate tenants with respiratory disabilities exacerbated by mold.

Constitutional claims (in some jurisdictions). Deprivation of property or liberty interests through uninhabitable housing.

Public housing defendants may raise:

Governmental immunity defenses. Sovereign or qualified immunity limiting or barring certain claims.

Statutory notice requirements. Specific procedural requirements for claims against governmental entities (notice deadlines, administrative exhaustion).

Funding limitations. Arguments that budget constraints prevented immediate remediation (though courts are often skeptical).

Regulatory compliance. Evidence of inspections, HUD compliance, and regulatory oversight suggesting reasonable conduct.

Administrative violation records and inspection reports often play decisive roles in these cases. A series of housing authority violations, HUD inspection failures, or health department citations creates powerful evidence.

What makes public housing cases different:

Political pressure. Media coverage of mold in public housing generates political attention and settlement pressure.

Tenant advocacy organizations. Legal aid societies, housing rights groups, and community organizations often coordinate tenant representation.

Pattern affecting vulnerable populations. Children, elderly, disabled, and low-income residents create sympathetic plaintiff classes.

Governmental accountability standards. Courts may hold governmental landlords to higher standards than private landlords.

Systemic reform potential. Settlements may include injunctive relief requiring building-wide improvements, not just individual compensation.

IV. HOA and Condominium Litigation

Condominium mold cases typically involve disputes among multiple parties with overlapping responsibilities.

Key parties include:

Unit owners. Individuals claiming property damage, health effects, and property value loss.

Homeowners associations (HOAs). Entities responsible for common area maintenance and sometimes building envelope elements.

Property management companies. Firms hired by HOAs to manage day-to-day operations and maintenance.

Developers. Original builders who may bear responsibility for construction defects.

Subcontractors. Various trades who installed building components.

Key issues include:

Responsibility for common-area maintenance. HOAs typically maintain building exteriors, roofs, and common elements. Determining whether mold originated in common areas or individual units affects responsibility allocation.

Allocation of repair costs between HOA and individual owners. Who pays for remediation when moisture intrusion affects both common elements and individual units?

Adequacy of reserve funding. HOAs must maintain reserves for major repairs. Inadequate reserves may indicate improper financial management.

Board decision-making regarding remediation. HOA boards have fiduciary duties to owners. Delaying necessary repairs to avoid special assessments may breach those duties.

HOAs may face claims for:

Negligent maintenance. Failure to maintain common areas allowing moisture intrusion into units.

Breach of fiduciary duty. Board decisions prioritizing short-term cost avoidance over necessary repairs.

Failure to enforce building standards. Not requiring owners to maintain individual components affecting common elements.

Improper remediation oversight. Hiring unqualified contractors or accepting substandard remediation.

Insurance coverage disputes often arise simultaneously. HOA master policies, individual unit owner policies, and D&O (directors and officers) policies may all potentially respond, creating complex coverage allocation issues.

Case in Focus: HOA Fiduciary Breach

A 2025 Florida case involved a 72-unit condominium development with systemic balcony waterproofing failures. The HOA board knew about problems for three years but delayed comprehensive repairs to avoid special assessments before board elections.

Evidence showed:

Board knowledge:

- Engineering report in year 1 recommended $1.2 million balcony reconstruction
- Board voted to defer decision "until after elections"
- In year 2, second report showed deterioration worsening, estimated costs increased to $1.6 million
- Board authorized $85,000 in "temporary patches" to address worst areas
- In year 3, mold appeared in 23 units, costs estimated at $2.4 million

Discovery revealed:

- Email from board president: "We can't hit owners with $16,000 assessment right before election"
- Minutes showing board knew temporary patches were inadequate
- Reserve study showing adequate funds existed but board chose not

to use them

Owners sued HOA and individual board members. Settlement: $3.1 million

- HOA liability (covered by D&O insurance): $2.6 million
- Individual board member contribution: $275,000
- Increased insurance premiums going forward: $850/year per unit

Board members' attempt to avoid $16,000 one-time assessment cost them personally $275,000 and cost the HOA $2.6 million in damages plus ongoing insurance cost increases.

V. Commercial Property and Business Interruption

In office buildings, retail centers, and industrial properties, mold litigation frequently centers on economic loss rather than personal injury.

Claims may include:

Business interruption. Lost income from closed businesses during remediation.

Loss of rental income. Landlords unable to rent contaminated spaces.

Lease termination disputes. Tenants seeking to terminate leases based on uninhabitable conditions.

Tenant relocation costs. Expenses incurred by businesses relocating during remediation.

Damage to inventory or equipment. Mold contamination of stored goods, merchandise, or business equipment.

Commercial tenants may allege:

Breach of quiet enjoyment. Landlord's failure to address mold interfered with tenant's use of premises.

Constructive eviction. Conditions became so poor tenant was forced to vacate.

Failure to maintain building systems. Landlord breached obligations to maintain HVAC, roofing, or other systems.

Breach of lease provisions. Specific lease terms regarding habitability, maintenance, or environmental conditions.

Landlords often defend by pointing to:

Maintenance provisions in commercial leases. Many commercial leases allocate repair responsibility to tenants for certain items.

Tenant-caused conditions. Arguing tenant's operations or modifications created moisture problems.

Reasonable response. Documenting prompt investigation and remediation efforts.

Business interruption insurance. Arguing tenant's own insurance should cover business losses.

Contract interpretation becomes central in commercial cases. Unlike residential leases (where implied habitability applies broadly), commercial leases often allocate risks contractually.

Commercial lease provisions affecting mold claims:

"As-is" clauses. Tenant accepts premises in current condition.

Maintenance allocation. Who is responsible for HVAC, roof, plumbing, etc.

Environmental provisions. Specific terms addressing mold, indoor air quality, or environmental conditions.

Remediation procedures. Contractual processes for addressing problems when discovered.

Insurance requirements. Which party must maintain what coverage.

VI. Hotels and Hospitality Properties

Hospitality mold claims can be particularly sensitive due to reputational concerns.

Allegations may involve:

Guest exposure. Visitors staying in contaminated rooms claiming health effects.

Event cancellations. Conferences, weddings, or other events cancelled due to mold remediation.

Conference facility closures. Meeting spaces closed for extended periods affecting bookings.

Negative publicity. Online reviews, media coverage, and social media attention damaging reputation.

Lost business opportunities. Customers choosing competitors due to mold-related reputation damage.

While many claims resolve quietly to avoid publicity, large-scale mold contamination can lead to significant remediation costs and insurance disputes.

Guest personal injury claims must still satisfy specific medical causation standards discussed in Chapter 3. Brief exposure during hotel stays rarely supports substantial medical damages.

However, business interruption and property damage claims can be substantial:

Typical hotel/hospitality mold scenario:

1. Roof leak or HVAC failure affects multiple rooms
2. Problem goes undetected for weeks or months
3. Guests begin complaining about musty odors or visible growth
4. Online reviews mention mold problems
5. Investigation reveals contamination in 15-30 rooms
6. Remediation requires taking rooms out of service for 2-4 months
7. During remediation, booking rates drop due to reputation concerns

Damages calculation:

- Room revenue loss (30 rooms × $150/night × 90 days): $405,000
- Remediation costs: $180,000
- Reputation damage (reduced bookings for 6 months): $250,000
- Event cancellation penalties: $85,000

- **Total: $920,000**

For hotels operating on thin margins, losses approaching $1 million can be catastrophic. Insurance becomes critical, and coverage disputes over business interruption are common.

VII. Class Actions and Mass Joinder Attempts

Where multiple tenants or occupants experience similar mold conditions, plaintiffs may attempt class certification or coordinated mass actions.

Certification challenges often hinge on:

Individualized medical causation. Different tenants have different health conditions, exposure durations, and pre-existing sensitivities. Courts find individual causation issues predominate over common questions.

Variations in exposure levels. Units on different floors, in different buildings, or with different orientations may have varying contamination levels.

Differences in remediation history. If management addressed some units but not others, individual histories vary.

Damages variability. Property damage, relocation expenses, and health effects differ substantially among tenants.

Courts frequently deny certification of personal injury mold claims due to individualized causation issues. Uniform exposure and injury don't exist when mold affects large populations with different health statuses.

However, property damage or rent abatement claims may present more viable class theories because:

Common questions predominate. Whether landlord breached habitability duties is common to all tenants.

Damages can be calculated formulaically. Rent abatement based on duration of conditions can be determined systematically.

Common remediation remedy. All class members benefit from building-wide fixes.

Even when class certification is denied, coordinated litigation offers benefits:

Efficiency. Single master complaint, coordinated discovery, joint experts.

Cost sharing. Litigation expenses spread across multiple plaintiffs.

Pattern evidence. Multiple similar claims strengthen individual cases.

Settlement leverage. Aggregate exposure creates pressure for comprehensive resolution.

Defendants prefer global settlements. Resolving all claims simultaneously eliminates ongoing exposure and allows comprehensive remediation.

VIII. Institutional Landlords and Private Equity Ownership

An emerging trend in multi-family housing involves institutional ownership by:

Real estate investment trusts (REITs). Publicly traded entities owning thousands of rental units.

Private equity firms. Investment funds acquiring apartment complexes as assets.

National property management companies. Firms managing tens of thousands of units across multiple markets.

Corporate landlords. Large companies with extensive residential portfolios.

Plaintiffs increasingly scrutinize:

Corporate maintenance policies. Systematic approaches to repair requests, work order processing, and capital improvement decisions.

Budget allocations. Whether adequate funds were allocated to maintenance and repairs or diverted to investor returns.

Response timelines. Corporate policies regarding time to investigate complaints, approve repairs, and complete remediation.

Centralized decision-making structures. Whether local managers had authority to address problems or required corporate approval creating delays.

Internal communications regarding cost-saving measures may become critical evidence:

- Emails discussing deferring repairs to improve quarterly financial performance
- Directives to minimize repair costs to maximize returns
- Performance metrics rewarding property managers for keeping maintenance expenses below budget
- Corporate policies requiring multiple approval levels for expenditures above certain amounts

Large institutional owners often have greater financial exposure due to:

Deeper pockets and substantial insurance. Ability to pay substantial settlements.

Reputational concerns. Negative publicity affecting entire portfolio, not just single property.

Pattern evidence across portfolio. Plaintiffs may discover similar problems at other properties owned by same entity.

Investor pressure. Publicly traded companies face shareholder and regulatory scrutiny of large liabilities.

But they also have more structured documentation systems, which can cut both ways:

Helpful to defense: Documented maintenance procedures, work order tracking, and regular inspections show systematic approach.

Harmful to defense: Paper trails revealing knowledge, delay, or cost-cutting decisions create powerful evidence.

IX. Remediation Protocols at Scale

Remediating mold in a single-family residence differs fundamentally from remediating contamination across dozens of units.

Large-scale remediation may require:

Temporary relocation of multiple tenants. Finding alternative housing for 20, 50, or 100 families simultaneously.

Staged containment. Isolating work in phases to minimize disruption while maintaining occupied areas.

Coordinated contractor teams. Multiple remediation crews working simultaneously across different buildings or floors.

Environmental clearance testing. Post-remediation verification for each unit before re-occupancy.

Ongoing monitoring. Follow-up testing to ensure remediation was effective and recurrence doesn't occur.

Comprehensive moisture source correction. Addressing building-wide systems (roofing, HVAC, drainage) causing problems.

Failure to manage remediation effectively can:

Multiply tenant claims. Inadequate containment spreading contamination to previously unaffected units.

Increase business interruption losses. Extended timelines increasing displacement costs.

Expand insurance disputes. Carriers questioning necessity and reasonableness of building-wide work.

Generate regulatory violations. Health departments or housing authorities citing improper remediation methods.

Institutional response planning becomes essential. Properties with documented remediation protocols, qualified contractor relationships, and established relocation procedures fare better than those improvising responses to large-scale problems.

X. Regulatory Oversight and Inspection Regimes

Multi-family and public housing properties are often subject to:

Municipal housing inspections. Regular code compliance inspections by local building or housing departments.

Health department oversight. Environmental health inspections focusing on habitability and safety.

HUD compliance reviews. For federally assisted housing, periodic inspections ensuring compliance with housing quality standards.

State building authority enforcement. State-level oversight of building code compliance and safety.

Fire marshal inspections. Safety inspections that may identify moisture and mold issues.

Repeated inspection failures serve as compelling evidence of notice and systemic neglect. When governmental agencies have documented problems through formal inspections and violations, defendants cannot credibly argue ignorance.

What regulatory violations establish:

Official notice. Governmental inspection reports provide indisputable notice of conditions.

Third-party validation. Not just tenant complaints but official determination that conditions violated standards.

Timeline documentation. Inspection reports date when problems were identified and orders were issued.

Pattern evidence. Multiple violations across different inspections show recurring problems.

Failure to comply with authority. Ignoring governmental orders demonstrates deliberate disregard.

Conversely, documented compliance efforts can strengthen defense positions:

- Records showing prompt response to inspection citations
- Evidence of systematic inspection programs
- Documentation of repairs following governmental orders
- Proof of reinspections and clearances

XI. Damages in Large-Scale Mold Litigation

Exposure in multi-family and commercial cases may include:

Aggregate rent abatement. When 50 tenants each receive $8,000 in rent abatement (40% of $20,000 annual rent for 12 months), aggregate exposure is $400,000.

Large remediation contracts. Building-wide remediation can cost $50,000-$150,000 per unit in severe cases. For 100 units, total costs can reach $5-$15 million.

Structural reconstruction. Addressing underlying building envelope failures may require façade work, roof replacement, or balcony reconstruction across entire developments.

Business interruption. Commercial properties may lose months of rental income during remediation.

Relocation expenses. Temporary housing for displaced tenants during remediation (50 families × $2,500/month × 3 months = $375,000).

Attorney's fees. In jurisdictions with mandatory fee-shifting, plaintiff attorney's fees can reach $500,000-$1,000,000 in complex multi-party cases.

Potential punitive damages. When conduct was egregious, punitive awards can multiply exposure substantially.

While individual medical damages may be modest (limited to respiratory effects), aggregate property-related losses can be substantial.

Insurance coverage frequently determines whether global settlement is feasible. Without adequate coverage, even institutional owners may lack liquidity to fund eight-figure settlements.

XII. Strategic Considerations for Plaintiffs

Plaintiffs in large-scale mold cases should:

1. Identify systemic patterns through maintenance records. Request complete work order histories, identifying recurring problems in similar units or locations.

2. Preserve tenant complaint documentation. Collect written complaints, emails, texts, and photos from all affected tenants to establish pattern and timeline.

3. Retain building envelope experts early. Comprehensive investigation identifying systemic defects strengthens claims and identifies all responsible parties.

4. Evaluate class or coordinated action viability. Analyze whether certification is possible or whether coordinated individual actions provide better path.

5. Assess institutional decision-making structures. Trace decision-making to corporate level, identifying policies and practices creating systemic problems.

6. Obtain regulatory inspection records. FOIA requests to housing authorities, health departments, and building departments often reveal valuable governmental inspection histories.

7. Coordinate with tenant advocacy organizations. Legal aid societies and housing rights groups may assist with tenant organizing and litigation support.

8. Consider media strategy carefully. Public attention can increase settlement pressure but may also complicate negotiations and harden positions.

Scale enhances leverage when systemic failures are evident. Aggregate exposure creates powerful incentives for comprehensive resolution.

XIII. Strategic Considerations for Institutional Defendants

Institutional landlords and property managers should:

1. Implement standardized moisture-response protocols. Establish clear procedures for investigating moisture complaints, approving emergency repairs, and conducting root cause analysis.

2. Maintain centralized documentation systems. Track work orders, complaints, inspections, and remediation efforts in searchable databases accessible to all management levels.

3. Conduct periodic building envelope inspections. Proactive third-party inspections identifying problems before tenant complaints or regulatory citations.

4. Budget proactively for deferred maintenance. Allocate adequate capital improvement budgets addressing building systems before failures create widespread problems.

5. Coordinate closely with insurers during large remediation projects. Early carrier involvement in significant projects ensures coverage understanding and claims handling.

6. Train property managers on appropriate response. Ensure local managers understand corporate policies, response timelines, and escalation procedures.

7. Document response efforts comprehensively. Maintain detailed records showing investigation, analysis, decision-making, and remediation efforts.

8. Consider voluntary remediation before litigation. When systemic problems are identified, comprehensive voluntary remediation may cost less than defending widespread tenant claims.

Proactive compliance reduces litigation risk substantially. The cost of preventing problems is invariably less than the cost of defending and resolving widespread tenant claims.

XIV. Why Scale Changes Leverage

In single-unit mold cases, disputes often revolve around individual health claims and specific landlord-tenant interactions.

In multi-family and commercial contexts, litigation shifts toward:

Pattern evidence. Repetition demonstrates systemic failure rather than isolated error.

Institutional decision-making. Corporate policies and budget priorities become central issues.

Budgetary priorities. Whether maintenance was adequately funded or sacrificed for financial performance.

Risk management failures. Whether institutional systems for identifying and addressing problems functioned properly.

Regulatory compliance. Whether properties met governmental inspection and habitability standards.

Even where medical causation claims are limited (respiratory effects only), systemic maintenance failures can generate significant economic liability through:

- Aggregate rent abatement across dozens of tenants
- Building-wide remediation costs
- Regulatory fines and penalties
- Reputational damage affecting entire portfolios

XV. Conclusion

Commercial and multi-family mold litigation represents the intersection of environmental conditions, institutional management, and regulatory oversight.

When mold affects entire buildings rather than individual rooms, exposure expands dramatically. Not only financially, but also:

Reputationally. Negative publicity affects property values and marketability.

Operationally. Remediation disrupts normal operations for extended periods.

Strategically. Corporate priorities and decision-making face scrutiny.

Politically. Public housing cases generate media attention and governmental pressure.

By 2026, large-scale mold claims are among the most complex and consequential in this evolving field. They require:

- Sophisticated coordination of multiple plaintiffs
- Comprehensive building science investigation
- Understanding of institutional structures and policies

- Navigation of regulatory compliance requirements
- Strategic use of pattern evidence
- Coordination with public agencies and advocacy groups

Key Takeaways:

1. **Pattern evidence transforms individual disputes** into systemic failure cases
2. **Institutional defendants have deeper pockets** and greater settlement capacity
3. **Regulatory violations provide powerful evidence** of notice and neglect
4. **Scale multiplies damages** through aggregate tenant claims
5. **Coordinated litigation creates leverage** even without class certification
6. **Corporate policies and budget decisions** become central litigation issues
7. **Proactive building-wide remediation** costs less than defending widespread claims
8. **Documentation systems cut both ways** depending on what records reveal

The next chapter examines military housing and government contractor liability, where sovereign immunity doctrines, federal oversight, and unique power dynamics add additional layers of complexity to toxic mold litigation. Understanding how governmental involvement reshapes claims is essential for navigating this specialized litigation area.

14

Military Housing and Government Contractor Liability

Sovereign Immunity, Federal Oversight, and High-Stakes Mold Claims

When Service Members Can't Choose Their Housing

In June 2023, a military family stationed at Fort Cavazos, Texas, reported a musty smell in their on-base housing unit. The property manager logged the complaint and scheduled an inspection for "within 30 days per standard protocol."

Three weeks later, the family's three-year-old daughter was hospitalized for pneumonia. After discharge, respiratory symptoms persisted. The family reported worsening conditions. The manager scheduled "follow-up inspection within 45 days."

Two months after the initial complaint (and one month after the second), a maintenance worker visited. He opened a hallway closet the family rarely used. Behind stored boxes, black staining covered the wall from floor to ceiling. The smell was overwhelming.

Environmental testing revealed Stachybotrys concentrations forty times outdoor baseline levels. Further investigation showed:

- Roof leak persisting for at least thirteen months
- Prior work orders for "water staining" in the attic above the unit
- Contractor's written warning to management nine months earlier that moisture intrusion was "creating conditions for significant mold amplification"
- Email from regional supervisor: "Remediation budget is tapped out this quarter. Can we push to Q3?"
- No action taken for six additional months

The family's attorney faced a complex jurisdictional landscape:

Was this a claim against:

- The federal government (requiring Federal Tort Claims Act procedures)?
- A private contractor (subject to standard tort law but potentially immune under government contractor defense)?
- Both (requiring coordination of different legal frameworks)?

Which law applied:

- Federal law (if federal property and federal defendant)?
- State law (if private contractor defendant)?
- A hybrid (depending on claim theories)?

What immunities might bar claims:

- Sovereign immunity (if suing federal government)?
- Contractor immunity (if contractor followed federal specifications)?
- Discretionary function exception (if decisions involved policy

choices)?

The case eventually settled for $10 million after 18 months of litigation navigating these complexities. But the path was far more complicated than a standard landlord-tenant mold case.

This chapter examines the unique legal landscape of military housing mold litigation, where federal property, private contractors, sovereign immunity, and governmental oversight create layered complexity.

I. Mold on Federal Installations: A Distinct Litigation Environment

Toxic mold litigation involving military housing occupies a unique and highly complex legal space unlike private residential disputes.

Key distinguishing features:

Hybrid public-private structure. Most modern military housing is federally owned but privately operated under long-term contracts.

Sovereign immunity concerns. Claims against the federal government face immunity barriers that private landlord claims don't.

Federal vs. state law questions. Determining which law applies affects available remedies and procedural requirements.

Specialized federal statutes. Federal Tort Claims Act (FTCA), Military Housing Privatization Initiative authorities, and other federal frameworks govern claims.

Congressional oversight. Military housing controversies generate congressional attention creating political pressures alongside legal ones.

Captive tenant population. Service members typically cannot choose housing freely, creating power imbalances.

By 2026, mold claims involving military installations have drawn national attention, driven in part by:

- High-value settlements (Fort Cavazos $10 million, others in similar ranges)
- Congressional hearings investigating housing conditions

- Media investigations documenting widespread problems
- Service member advocacy creating public pressure
- GAO and Inspector General reports identifying systemic issues

II. The Public-Private Military Housing Model

In the late 1990s and early 2000s, the federal government shifted toward privatized military housing under the Military Housing Privatization Initiative (MHPI).

The model works as follows:

The federal government:

- Retains ownership of land
- Provides long-term ground leases (typically 50+ years)
- Guarantees basic allowance for housing (BAH) payments from service members as rent

Private companies:

- Finance, construct, renovate, and manage housing units
- Collect BAH directly as rent payments
- Bear responsibility for maintenance and operations
- Profit from efficient management and long-term property appreciation

This hybrid structure creates complex questions regarding liability:

When mold contamination occurs, plaintiffs must determine:

Whether the proper defendant is a federal agency or private contractor. This determines which immunities apply and which procedural rules govern.

Whether sovereign immunity bars claims. Direct claims against the United States face immunity unless explicitly waived.

Whether federal or state law governs substantive claims. The answer affects available causes of action and remedies.

Whether contractor immunities apply. Government contractor defenses may shield private operators from liability.

Whether administrative exhaustion is required. Some claims require exhausting administrative remedies before filing suit.

III. Sovereign Immunity and the Federal Tort Claims Act

The doctrine of sovereign immunity generally shields the federal government from suit unless immunity has been waived by statute.

The primary waiver mechanism is the Federal Tort Claims Act (FTCA), which permits certain negligence claims against the United States.

FTCA claims face important limitations:

Administrative exhaustion requirements. Plaintiffs must first file administrative claims with the appropriate federal agency. Suit can only be filed after denial or six months without response.

Strict filing deadlines. Administrative claims must be filed within two years of claim accrual. After denial, suit must be filed within six months.

Discretionary function exception. FTCA does not waive immunity for claims based on discretionary governmental functions involving policy judgment.

Prohibition of punitive damages. FTCA claims cannot seek punitive damages regardless of defendant conduct.

No jury trial. FTCA cases are tried to judges, not juries.

Limited to negligence claims. FTCA generally covers negligence but not intentional torts or constitutional violations.

In many military housing mold cases, plaintiffs focus on private contractors to avoid sovereign immunity barriers. Private companies operating military housing are typically subject to state tort law without sovereign immunity protection.

FTCA procedural requirements:

Step 1: File Standard Form 95 (SF-95) administrative claim with appropriate agency within two years of incident.

Step 2: Agency investigates (typically 6-12 months).

Step 3: Agency issues final denial or six months passes without response.

Step 4: File lawsuit in federal district court within six months of denial.

Failure to comply strictly with these procedures bars claims. Many military housing mold claims are dismissed for procedural failures rather than merits.

IV. Liability of Private Military Housing Operators

Private companies managing military housing are typically subject to state tort law, including:

Negligence. Failure to exercise reasonable care in maintaining safe housing conditions.

Breach of warranty of habitability. Maintaining premises in uninhabitable condition.

Failure to remediate. Ignoring known mold conditions or responding inadequately.

Misrepresentation. Providing false information about housing conditions during move-in.

Breach of contract. Violating lease obligations regarding maintenance and safety.

Unlike federal agencies, these entities **do not enjoy sovereign immunity.** They can be sued like any private landlord, subject to standard tort law.

Recent mold litigation has alleged:

Delayed response to moisture complaints. Property managers taking weeks or months to investigate serious moisture problems.

Cosmetic concealment of mold. Painting over mold or replacing drywall without addressing moisture sources.

Inadequate remediation. Using unqualified personnel, failing to correct root causes, or performing superficial cleaning.

Poor maintenance documentation. Failing to track complaints, work orders, or remediation efforts systematically.

Budget-driven decision-making. Deferring necessary repairs to meet quarterly financial targets.

High-profile settlements in military housing cases have increased public and legislative scrutiny. The $10 million Fort Cavazos settlement mentioned in this chapter's opening became a catalyst for congressional oversight.

V. The Government Contractor Defense

Private contractors may invoke the **government contractor defense**, arguing they should not be liable for following federal specifications or directives.

The defense typically requires proving:

1. The government approved reasonably precise specifications. The government provided specific requirements the contractor followed.

2. The contractor conformed to those specifications. The contractor's performance met governmental requirements.

3. The contractor warned the government of known dangers. If the contractor discovered risks, they notified appropriate governmental authorities.

This defense is more common in product liability cases (military equipment, aircraft) but may arise in housing cases if contractors argue they followed specific governmental design or maintenance requirements.

The defense faces challenges in housing cases because:

Housing maintenance involves contractor discretion. Unlike manufacturing products to government specs, housing maintenance involves ongoing discretionary decisions.

Government contracts typically establish performance standards, not detailed specifications. Contracts may require "safe, habitable housing" without specifying exact maintenance procedures.

Contractors typically have greater expertise than government overseers. Courts expect professional property managers to exercise independent judgment about maintenance needs.

Warning requirements create documentation issues. Contractors claiming they warned the government must produce evidence of specific warnings about specific dangers.

In practice, government contractor defenses rarely succeed in military housing mold cases unless contractors can demonstrate they identified problems, reported them to the government, and were specifically directed not to remediate.

VI. Duty to Inspect and Remediate

Military housing contracts typically impose inspection and maintenance obligations on private operators.

Litigation frequently examines:

1. **Work order response times.** How quickly contractors investigated and addressed tenant complaints.
2. **Maintenance staffing levels.** Whether contractors maintained adequate personnel for property size and tenant population.
3. **Inspection protocols.** Whether systematic inspection programs existed to identify problems proactively.
4. **Recordkeeping practices.** Whether complaints, inspections, and remediation efforts were documented adequately.
5. **Remediation procedures.** Whether industry-standard protocols were followed when addressing mold.

Failure to follow contractual remediation standards can form the basis for negligence claims independent of federal involvement.

Typical military housing contract maintenance requirements:

Response time standards:

- Emergency (no heat, water, sewer): 24 hours
- Urgent (leaks, HVAC failure): 48-72 hours
- Routine (non-urgent repairs): 7-14 days

Inspection requirements:

- Move-in/move-out inspections (100% of units)
- Periodic property condition inspections (sample of units quarterly)
- Common area inspections (monthly)
- Building system inspections (annually or per manufacturer recommendations)

Remediation protocols:

- Licensed contractors for specialized work
- Industry standard methods (IICRC S520 for mold)
- Post-remediation verification testing
- Documentation of all work performed

Documentation becomes decisive. Contractors who can demonstrate:

- Prompt response to complaints
- Thorough investigations
- Qualified personnel performing work
- Proper remediation protocols
- Post-work verification testing

face substantially less exposure than those with sparse or missing documentation.

VII. Unique Damages Considerations

Military families alleging mold exposure may seek damages for:

Property damage. Personal belongings contaminated or damaged during exposure or remediation.

Relocation costs. Temporary housing expenses during remediation or after constructive eviction.

Medical expenses. Treatment for respiratory symptoms, allergic reactions, or asthma exacerbation.

Emotional distress. Anxiety, stress, and fear arising from living in contaminated conditions.

Lost personal property. Items that must be discarded due to mold contamination.

Diminished quality of life. Impact on family wellbeing during exposure and remediation periods.

FTCA claims against the government do not allow punitive damages. This limitation significantly reduces potential exposure compared to private landlord cases where punitive damages may be available.

Claims against private contractors may include punitive damages when conduct was sufficiently egregious (deliberate concealment, willful disregard of known dangers).

Additionally, frequent relocations inherent to military life can complicate proof:

Duration and exposure challenges:

- Families typically stationed at installations for 2-4 years
- Shorter exposure periods than long-term civilian residents
- Difficulty establishing chronic exposure when assignments rotate

Causation complications:

- Service members may have lived in multiple housing units during military careers
- Prior exposures at other installations may affect current symptoms
- Occupational exposures (deployment to dusty/moldy environments) may contribute to symptoms

Despite these challenges, successful military housing mold cases demonstrate that serious exposure during 1-3 year assignments can support substantial recoveries.

VIII. Medical Causation in Military Cases

As with civilian mold litigation, plaintiffs must establish specific medical causation under standards discussed in Chapter 3.

Challenges unique to military housing cases include:

Transient housing assignments. Families typically occupy military housing for 2-4 years, creating shorter exposure windows than long-term civilian occupancy.

Exposure in multiple residences. Service members may have lived in several installations, complicating attribution of symptoms to specific housing.

Limited environmental testing records. Military housing operators may not have conducted testing during occupancy, requiring retrospective exposure reconstruction.

Pre-existing medical conditions. Service members may have respiratory conditions from prior deployments or occupational exposures.

Deployment-related exposures. Burn pits, desert dust, shipboard environments, or other deployment exposures may contribute to respiratory symptoms.

Defense experts often argue that symptoms are attributable to:

- Multiple prior housing assignments
- Deployment-related occupational exposures
- Common allergens (pollen, dust mites, pet dander)
- Smoking or environmental tobacco smoke exposure
- Pre-existing asthma or allergies

Plaintiffs must bridge the same scientific hurdles as civilian cases, establishing:

- Meaningful mold exposure occurred at the specific installation
- Temporal correlation between exposure and symptom onset
- Medical diagnosis consistent with mold-related conditions
- Differential diagnosis ruling out alternative causes
- Expert testimony surviving Daubert/Frye scrutiny

Despite challenges, the Fort Cavazos case and similar settlements demonstrate that strong evidence of:

- Extensive contamination (testing showing high spore concentrations)
- Prolonged exposure (months or years in contaminated housing)
- Documented health impacts (medical records during occupancy)
- Temporal correlation (symptoms during occupancy, improvement after relocation)

can support substantial medical causation findings.

IX. Congressional Oversight and Regulatory Reform

Military housing mold controversies have prompted increased congressional oversight and policy reform efforts.

Legislative responses have included:

Enhanced tenant complaint systems. Requirements for confidential reporting mechanisms allowing service members to report problems without fear of retaliation.

Strengthened reporting requirements. Contractors must report health and safety issues to military installation commanders and higher authorities.

Increased funding for inspection and remediation. Congressional appropriations for military housing quality improvements.

Greater transparency mandates. Public disclosure of housing conditions, inspection results, and contractor performance metrics.

Tenant bill of rights. Formal recognition of service member housing rights including safe, habitable conditions and effective complaint processes.

Third-party oversight. Independent inspections and audits of privatized military housing conditions.

While such reforms may not directly create private causes of action, they shape expectations of reasonable response and establish governmental standards for housing quality.

Internal compliance audits often become relevant evidence in litigation:

- Installation commander inspection reports

- Third-party audit findings
- Contractor performance evaluations
- GAO or Inspector General investigative reports
- Congressional hearing testimony and exhibits

These governmental documents provide independent validation of problems and often reveal:

- How long problems existed
- Whether contractors met performance standards
- What government officials knew and when
- Whether corrective actions were taken

X. Jurisdictional Complexity

Military housing cases may raise complex jurisdictional questions:

Federal enclave doctrine. Some military installations are considered federal enclaves where federal law exclusively applies, potentially limiting application of state landlord-tenant statutes.

Choice of law. Determining whether federal law, state law of installation location, or other law governs substantive claims.

Venue selection. Whether cases must be filed in the district where installation is located or where plaintiffs currently reside (after reassignment).

Applicability of state landlord-tenant statutes. Whether state habitability laws apply to federally owned property operated by private contractors under federal contracts.

Supremacy clause preemption. Whether federal interests preempt state law claims in some circumstances.

Federal question jurisdiction. Whether claims arise under federal law (supporting federal court jurisdiction) or state law (potentially requiring state court).

Attorneys must analyze jurisdiction carefully at the outset to determine:

- Proper court (federal or state)
- Applicable law (federal or state)
- Available remedies (which may differ under federal vs. state law)
- Procedural requirements (FTCA exhaustion, service of process, etc.)

Case in Focus: Jurisdictional Complexity

A 2024 case involved military housing at Fort Hood (now Fort Cavazos), Texas. The plaintiff family filed suit in Texas state court asserting:

- Breach of Texas warranty of habitability
- Negligence under Texas common law
- Texas Deceptive Trade Practices Act violations

Defendants (private contractor and federal government) removed to federal court arguing:

- Federal question jurisdiction (federal property, federal contracts)
- Federal enclave jurisdiction (Fort Hood is federal enclave)
- FTCA claims must be in federal court

Plaintiffs moved to remand arguing:

- Claims were against private contractor, not federal government
- State law applies to private contractor landlord-tenant relationship
- Federal enclave doctrine doesn't displace state landlord-tenant law

The court found:

- Private contractor claims remanded to state court (no federal question)
- Federal government claims remained in federal court (FTCA)
- Case bifurcated into parallel state and federal proceedings

This jurisdictional complexity added 14 months to litigation timeline and $85,000 in additional attorney's fees before reaching merits.

XI. Insurance and Indemnity in Military Housing

Private housing operators typically carry:

Commercial general liability coverage. Covering bodily injury and property damage claims by third parties (tenants).

Professional liability policies. Covering errors and omissions in property management services.

Environmental impairment policies. Specific coverage for pollution and mold-related claims (though often with significant exclusions).

Coverage disputes may arise over:

Mold exclusions. As discussed in Chapter 10, CGL policies typically contain fungi/bacteria exclusions limiting or eliminating mold coverage.

Allocation among insurers. Long-tail claims spanning multiple policy years requiring allocation of defense and indemnity costs.

Duty to defend under federal contracts. Whether carrier obligations differ for claims arising from federal contract performance.

Subrogation and contribution claims among carriers. Multiple insurance layers (primary, excess, umbrella) creating complex allocation disputes.

Indemnification provisions between contractors and the federal government may also become relevant:

Military housing contracts often contain indemnification clauses requiring contractors to:

- Indemnify the government for claims arising from contractor negligence
- Maintain specified insurance coverage
- Provide government as additional insured

These provisions can shift ultimate financial responsibility even when the government is named as defendant.

Insurance availability often influences settlement dynamics:

- Cases with clear contractor liability coverage settle faster

- Coverage disputes delay resolution while carriers litigate
- Uninsured or underinsured contractors create collection challenges
- Government indemnification may provide recovery even if contractor coverage is disputed

XII. Strategic Considerations for Plaintiffs

Plaintiffs pursuing military housing mold claims should:

1. **Determine the correct defendant early.** Identify whether claims are against federal government (requiring FTCA procedures), private contractor (standard tort law), or both.

2. **Evaluate sovereign immunity implications.** Understand FTCA requirements and limitations before filing.

3. **Preserve maintenance and work order records.** Request complete files from housing office including all complaints, inspections, and work orders.

4. **Identify systemic complaint patterns across units.** Research whether other families at same installation reported similar problems.

5. **Analyze contractual remediation obligations.** Review public contracts between government and private operators to understand performance standards.

6. **Obtain governmental inspection reports.** FOIA requests to installation commanders, GAO, or Inspectors General may reveal independent audits.

7. **Consider timing relative to reassignment.** File before permanent change of station (PCS) moves if possible to maintain connection to jurisdiction.

8. **Document all communication with housing office.** Emails, texts, work orders, and inspection reports establish notice and response timeline.

Government structure does not eliminate liability, but it complicates procedural paths to recovery.

XIII. Strategic Considerations for Contractors and Agencies

Defendants in military housing cases should:

1. **Maintain robust documentation systems.** Track every complaint, inspection, work order, and remediation effort in searchable databases.

2. **Implement transparent complaint tracking.** Ensure tenants can verify complaint status and understand timelines.

3. **Respond promptly to moisture reports.** Moisture complaints require immediate investigation given rapid mold growth potential.

4. **Preserve communications regarding remediation decisions.** Document decision-making processes, budget approvals, and contractor selection.

5. **Coordinate early with coverage counsel.** Notify insurers immediately and analyze coverage while claims are developing.

6. **Follow contract performance standards scrupulously.** Document compliance with contractual maintenance requirements.

7. **Conduct proactive inspections.** Don't wait for complaints; systematic inspections identify problems early.

8. **Consider voluntary remediation.** When widespread problems are identified, comprehensive voluntary remediation may cost less than defending numerous tenant claims.

Given public scrutiny and congressional oversight, reputational risk often parallels legal exposure in military housing cases.

XIV. The Broader Significance of Military Mold Litigation

Military housing cases highlight broader themes in toxic mold litigation:

Institutional management challenges. Large-scale housing operations require systematic approaches to maintenance, not ad hoc responses.

Systemic maintenance failures. Pattern problems reveal institutional priorities and decision-making processes.

The importance of documentation. Comprehensive records protect defendants; missing documentation suggests problems.

The centrality of reasonable response. How quickly and effectively management responds matters more than perfection.

Vulnerable populations deserve protection. Families serving national interests should not endure substandard housing.

They also underscore the human dimension of mold disputes. Service members cannot freely choose housing. They move frequently on military orders. They may fear retaliation if they complain too aggressively. Power imbalances are pronounced.

Public perception significantly influences settlement dynamics. Cases involving military families generate:

- Media attention and public sympathy
- Congressional interest and oversight
- Political pressure for accountability
- Reputational concerns for contractors

These factors often create settlement pressure exceeding pure legal liability analysis.

XV. Conclusion

Military housing mold litigation sits at the intersection of federal law, private contracting, and traditional tort principles.

Sovereign immunity complicates some claims while private contractor liability expands others.

Documentation and contractual compliance often determine outcomes more than legal theories.

By 2026, these cases illustrate how toxic mold litigation extends beyond residential disputes into matters of public accountability, federal oversight, and service member welfare.

Key Takeaways:

1. **Hybrid public-private structure creates jurisdictional complexity** requiring careful analysis of proper defendants and applicable law
2. **Sovereign immunity bars direct federal government claims** unless

FTCA procedures are followed

3. **Private contractors face standard tort liability** without sovereign immunity protection
4. **Government contractor defense rarely succeeds** in housing maintenance contexts
5. **Contractual performance standards define duty** more clearly than general negligence principles
6. **Congressional oversight creates political pressure** alongside legal liability
7. **Documentation is critical** for both plaintiffs (proving notice) and defendants (proving response)
8. **Public accountability standards may exceed private sector** creating higher expectations
9. **Captive tenant populations deserve protection** given inability to choose housing freely

The next chapter turns to damages, examining how courts calculate medical, property, emotional distress, and punitive damages in toxic mold litigation. Understanding valuation strategies shapes settlement negotiations and determines whether cases justify litigation investment.

PART V: Trial Practice and Valuation

15

Damages in Toxic Mold Litigation

Valuation, Proof, and Strategic Leverage

When the Evidence Changes Everything

In October 2024, two nearly identical mold cases went to mediation on the same day in different cities:

Case A: Chicago

- Family discovered mold after six months in rental home
- Landlord ignored four written complaints over three months
- Environmental testing showed Stachybotrys at 25x outdoor levels
- Two children experienced respiratory symptoms
- Medical records documented urgent care visits
- Plaintiff's expert: board-certified allergist limiting testimony to respiratory irritation and asthma exacerbation

Plaintiff's demand: $285,000
Actual settlement: $242,000

Breakdown:

- Medical expenses: $8,400
- Property damage (belongings): $12,000
- Temporary housing: $18,500
- Rent abatement: $15,600
- Emotional distress: $65,000
- Loss of use: $42,500
- Attorney's fees: $80,000

Case B: Phoenix

- Family discovered mold after six months in rental home
- Landlord ignored four written complaints over three months
- Environmental testing showed Stachybotrys at 25x outdoor levels
- Two children experienced respiratory symptoms
- Medical records documented urgent care visits
- Plaintiff's expert: clinical ecologist testifying to "chronic inflammatory response syndrome, immune dysregulation, and neurological impairment"

Plaintiff's demand: $875,000
Settlement offer before mediation: $35,000
Mediation result: Impasse
Motion to exclude expert: Granted
Settlement three weeks later: $48,000

Breakdown:

- Medical expenses: $8,400
- Property damage (belongings): $12,000
- Temporary housing: $18,500

- Rent abatement: $9,100
- Total: $48,000

Same facts. Same contamination. Same health complaints. Different expert approach. Nearly $200,000 difference in outcome.

The Chicago case succeeded because damages were grounded in scientifically defensible claims, thoroughly documented, and strategically presented. The Phoenix case collapsed because inflated medical claims led to expert exclusion, eliminating leverage and forcing settlement for property damages alone.

This chapter examines how damages drive mold litigation outcomes and how strategic valuation shapes settlements from first demand through final resolution.

I. Why Damages Drive Mold Litigation

In toxic mold litigation, **liability without damages has little practical consequence**. Conversely, modest liability findings paired with substantial, well-documented damages can produce significant settlements or verdicts.

By 2026, valuation strategy has become as important as causation strategy. Mold cases may involve:

Medical damages (when causation is established and survives scrutiny)
Property remediation costs (objectively measurable)
Diminution in value (requiring expert valuation)
Relocation expenses (documented through receipts)
Emotional distress (jurisdiction-dependent availability)
Lost income (when exposure prevented work)
Punitive damages (for egregious conduct)
Attorney's fees (when statutorily authorized)

Understanding how courts assess and limit damages is essential for realistic case evaluation and effective negotiation.

II. Medical Damages: Narrowed but Not Eliminated

Medical damages depend on satisfying the specific causation requirements discussed in Chapter 3. The scope of recoverable medical damages has narrowed significantly as courts apply stricter evidentiary standards.

A. Accepted Respiratory Claims

Courts are most receptive to damages involving:

Allergic rhinitis. Nasal congestion, sneezing, runny nose, itchy/watery eyes. Common, well-documented allergic response to mold spores.

Asthma exacerbation. Worsening of pre-existing asthma or development of new asthma symptoms including wheezing, shortness of breath, chest tightness, increased inhaler use.

Irritant symptoms. Eye, nose, and throat irritation from exposure to high spore concentrations, even without allergic sensitization.

Hypersensitivity pneumonitis (in rare, well-documented cases). Inflammatory lung condition requiring clinical diagnosis with specific findings including restrictive lung function patterns, imaging abnormalities, sometimes lung biopsy confirmation.

Medical expenses for these conditions may include:

- Physician consultations (primary care, allergists, pulmonologists)
- Diagnostic testing (pulmonary function tests, allergy testing, imaging)
- Prescription medications (antihistamines, nasal steroids, inhalers, controllers)
- Pulmonary therapy or rehabilitation
- Follow-up care and monitoring

These claims are typically modest in value unless symptoms are chronic, severe, or require ongoing treatment. Well-documented respiratory claims with clear temporal correlation typically support medical damages of:

Minor symptoms (brief duration, full recovery): $2,000 to $8,000
Moderate symptoms (3-6 months, partial ongoing treatment): $10,000 to $35,000
Severe symptoms (chronic condition, ongoing treatment): $40,000 to $150,000+

B. Contested Systemic Injury Claims

Claims alleging broader systemic injuries face higher evidentiary hurdles and frequent exclusion:

Neurological impairment. "Brain fog," memory problems, difficulty concentrating, cognitive dysfunction attributed to mold exposure.

Immune dysfunction. Claims of compromised immune system, increased susceptibility to infections, autoimmune responses.

Chronic inflammatory conditions. Chronic inflammatory response syndrome (CIRS), multi-system inflammatory disorders.

Chronic fatigue or fibromyalgia-like syndromes. Persistent fatigue, widespread pain, multi-system complaints.

Where systemic injury testimony survives admissibility challenges (increasingly rare), damages exposure increases significantly, potentially including:

- Long-term medical monitoring and treatment
- Specialized testing and evaluations
- Future medical care costs
- Lost earning capacity
- Reduced quality of life
- Permanent impairment or disability

However, **most courts limit recovery to respiratory and allergy-based conditions** absent strong scientific support that passes Daubert/Frye scrutiny.

Practical reality: Cases asserting systemic injury often result in expert exclusion, eliminating medical damages entirely and forcing settlement based on property damages alone.

III. Property Damage and Remediation Costs

Property damage often represents the most tangible and measurable component of mold litigation. Unlike contested medical causation, property damage is objectively verifiable.

Recoverable costs typically include:

Demolition of contaminated materials. Removal of mold-affected drywall, insulation, flooring, ceiling tiles, cabinetry, or other porous materials that cannot be adequately cleaned.

Typical costs:

- Drywall removal and disposal: $2-$4 per square foot
- Insulation removal: $1-$3 per square foot
- Flooring removal (carpet, hardwood): $2-$6 per square foot
- Cabinet removal and disposal: $500-$2,000 per unit

Replacement of building components. Installing new materials to replace those removed during remediation.

Typical costs:

- Drywall installation and finishing: $3-$7 per square foot
- Insulation replacement: $1.50-$4 per square foot
- Flooring replacement: $5-$15 per square foot (depending on material)
- Painting: $2-$5 per square foot
- Cabinet replacement: $3,000-$15,000 per kitchen

HVAC system cleaning or replacement. When mold spores contaminate ductwork, air handlers, or entire systems.

Typical costs:

- Duct cleaning: $500-$1,500
- Air handler cleaning/sanitization: $800-$2,000
- Complete HVAC replacement: $5,000-$15,000

Mold remediation contractor fees. Professional remediation following industry protocols (IICRC S520).

Typical costs:

- Small job (under 100 sq ft): $1,500-$4,000

- Medium job (100-500 sq ft): $4,000-$12,000
- Large job (over 500 sq ft): $12,000-$50,000+
- Complex multi-room remediation: $50,000-$200,000+

Environmental testing and clearance. Pre-remediation assessment, post-remediation clearance testing, and ongoing monitoring.

Typical costs:

- Initial assessment (air and surface samples): $800-$2,000
- Post-remediation clearance: $600-$1,200
- Multiple rounds of testing: $2,000-$5,000

In construction defect cases, remediation costs can reach millions of dollars, particularly in multi-unit developments where systemic building envelope failures affect dozens or hundreds of units.

Expert testimony regarding scope and reasonableness of remediation is critical. Defendants routinely challenge:

- Whether all work performed was necessary
- Whether less expensive alternatives existed
- Whether contractors charged reasonable rates
- Whether plaintiff mitigated damages appropriately

Well-documented remediation with:

- Licensed contractor invoices
- Detailed scope of work descriptions
- Before/after photographs
- Industry-standard protocol compliance
- Post-remediation clearance testing

substantially strengthens property damage claims.

IV. Diminution in Value

Even after remediation, plaintiffs may claim that mold history reduces property value through market stigma.

Diminution claims require:

Real estate appraisal testimony. Licensed appraiser comparing property value before and after mold history became known.

Market comparison analysis. Evidence of how similar properties with mold history sold compared to comparable properties without such history.

Evidence of stigma. Market data demonstrating actual value loss attributable to mold disclosure requirements and buyer perception.

Courts vary in willingness to award stigma damages. Some require proof that:

Remediation was incomplete. Ongoing contamination justifies value reduction.

Market data demonstrates actual value loss. Comparable sales showing price impacts from disclosed mold history.

Disclosure requirements affect marketability. Future buyers must be informed of mold history, affecting pricing.

Speculative stigma claims lacking objective market support often fail.

Typical diminution ranges:

No diminution (proper remediation, clearance testing, transferable warranty): 0%
Minor diminution (brief exposure, comprehensive remediation): 3-8%
Moderate diminution (extended exposure, disclosed history): 8-15%
Significant diminution (recurring problems, incomplete fix): 15-25%+

On a $400,000 property:

- 5% diminution: $20,000
- 10% diminution: $40,000
- 15% diminution: $60,000

Appraisers must provide market-based justification, not mere opinion that "mold stigma" exists generally.

V. Loss of Use and Relocation Expenses

Temporary displacement frequently accompanies mold remediation, generating measurable economic losses.

Recoverable expenses may include:

Temporary housing costs. Hotel stays, short-term rentals, extended-stay accommodations during remediation period.

Typical costs:

- Hotel (family of 4): $150-$300 per night
- Short-term furnished rental: $2,500-$5,000 per month
- Extended stay hotel: $100-$200 per night

Storage fees. Costs for storing furniture and belongings during remediation.

Typical costs: $100-$400 per month depending on storage unit size

Moving costs. Expenses for relocating out of and back into property.

Typical costs: $1,500-$5,000 for professional movers (depending on distance and volume)

Increased commuting expenses. Additional transportation costs when temporary housing is farther from work or school.

Meals and incidentals. Increased food costs when living in hotels without kitchen facilities.

Pet boarding. If remediation requires temporary pet relocation.

Typical costs: $30-$75 per day per pet

Insurance coverage for additional living expenses (ALE) often intersects with these claims. When insurance pays ALE, plaintiffs cannot double-recover, but disputes over adequacy of insurance payments may create additional claims.

Documentation requirements:

Courts require receipts, invoices, and detailed records. Speculative or estimated relocation costs receive little weight. Plaintiffs should preserve:

- Hotel/rental receipts
- Moving company invoices
- Storage facility contracts and payment records
- Mileage logs for increased commuting
- Pet boarding receipts

Duration challenges:

Defendants often argue relocation duration was excessive. Courts consider:

- Industry-standard remediation timelines
- Reasonableness of contractor schedules
- Whether delays were plaintiff-caused or defendant-caused
- Whether clearance testing justified extended displacement

Three-month displacement for comprehensive multi-room remediation: reasonable
Nine-month displacement for single-bathroom remediation: likely excessive

VI. Emotional Distress Damages

Mold cases often involve claims of anxiety, sleep disruption, fear, embarrassment, and stress arising from living in contaminated conditions or dealing with remediation disruption.

Jurisdictional rules vary significantly:

Jurisdictions Permitting Emotional Distress Without Physical Injury

Some states allow emotional distress damages based on habitability violations, property damage, or other recognized harms without requiring physical manifestations.

California: Emotional distress recoverable for habitability breaches, fraud, and other recognized torts without physical injury requirement.

Washington: Allows emotional distress damages when conditions were severe enough to justify them.

New York: Case-by-case analysis; more liberal in contexts involving housing violations.

Typical awards: $10,000 to $75,000 depending on:

- Severity of conditions
- Duration of exposure
- Presence of children or vulnerable family members
- Defendant's conduct (knowledge, delay, concealment)
- Documentation of distress (medical treatment, therapy)

Jurisdictions Requiring Physical Injury

Other states require some physical manifestation before allowing emotional distress recovery.

Texas: Generally requires physical injury to recover emotional distress damages.

Florida: Typically limits emotional distress recovery without accompanying physical injury.

Arizona: Physical injury usually required except in narrow circumstances.

In these jurisdictions, respiratory symptoms (coughing, congestion, breathing difficulty) may satisfy the "physical injury" requirement, allowing emotional distress recovery.

What effective emotional distress testimony looks like:

Compare these approaches:

Ineffective (vague and conclusory): "Living in that house was terrible. I was stressed constantly. I couldn't sleep. I worried about my kids all the time."

Effective (specific, documented, tied to conditions): "After discovering the mold in March, I developed insomnia. I would wake up at 2 a.m. checking on my daughter because she'd been hospitalized the month before with pneumonia. I started seeing a therapist in April (Dr. Smith, records provided).

She diagnosed anxiety related to housing conditions. I lost 18 pounds over three months because I had no appetite. My work performance review in May noted I seemed distracted and stressed, which had never been mentioned in 8 years of employment. When we finally moved out in June, my symptoms improved within two weeks."

The second testimony is specific, documented with medical records and employment records, and tied directly to housing conditions.

VII. Lost Income and Earning Capacity

Plaintiffs may seek recovery for:

Missed work due to illness. Time off for medical appointments, illness, or caring for sick family members.

Reduced productivity. Inability to perform job duties at normal levels due to symptoms.

Job loss. Termination or forced resignation due to performance issues arising from health problems.

Lost earning capacity. Permanent reduction in ability to earn income due to chronic health conditions.

Such claims require:

Medical documentation. Physician statements connecting absence or limitations to mold-related illness.

Employment records. Pay stubs, termination notices, performance reviews showing work impact.

Expert economic analysis. Economist or vocational expert calculating past and future lost earnings.

Lost income claims are more viable when systemic injury with ongoing limitations is proven. Where medical causation is weak or limited to temporary respiratory symptoms, courts may limit or exclude lost income claims.

Calculation methods:

Past lost wages:

- Actual days missed × daily wage rate
- Documentation: employer letters, pay stubs, tax returns

Future earning capacity:

- Present value of reduced earning capacity over working life
- Requires medical testimony establishing permanent limitations
- Economist testimony regarding calculation methodology

For temporary respiratory symptoms causing 10 days missed work: $2,000-$5,000
For chronic condition reducing earning capacity 20% over 20 years: $200,000-$500,000+

The gap illustrates why proving permanent injury dramatically increases damages exposure.

VIII. Punitive Damages

Punitive damages arise in cases involving egregious conduct designed to punish defendants and deter similar behavior.

Conduct supporting punitive damages:

Intentional concealment. Seller or landlord deliberately hiding known mold conditions through cosmetic repairs or false disclosure statements.

Fraudulent nondisclosure. Knowingly providing false information about property conditions with intent to deceive.

Willful failure to remediate. Landlord ignoring known dangerous conditions for extended periods despite tenant complaints and available resources.

Egregious insurance bad faith. Carrier unreasonably denying coverage in reckless disregard of policyholder rights.

Punitive awards are designed to:

- Punish reprehensible conduct
- Deter defendant and others from similar conduct
- Express societal condemnation

Factors courts consider:

Reprehensibility of conduct. How egregious was the behavior? Deliberate concealment vs. negligent oversight.

Ratio to compensatory damages. Constitutional limits generally require reasonable ratio between punitive and compensatory awards (often 1:1 to 9:1, though some jurisdictions allow higher ratios for particularly egregious conduct).

Defendant's financial condition. Awards must be sufficient to impact defendant meaningfully without being financially devastating beyond punitive purpose.

Statutory caps. Some states cap punitive damages at multiples of compensatory damages or fixed dollar amounts.

Examples of conduct supporting punitive damages:

- Internal emails showing deliberate decision to conceal rather than disclose
- Budget documents showing remediation deferred to maximize profits
- Pattern of similar conduct with other properties or tenants
- Falsification of inspection reports or testing results
- Retaliation against tenants who complained

Documentary evidence showing conscious wrongdoing is critical. Mere negligence, even gross negligence, typically does not support punitive damages.

Typical punitive damage awards in mold cases:

Moderate case (clear concealment, no prior pattern): 1x to 2x compensatory
Serious case (deliberate fraud, some pattern evidence): 2x to 4x compensatory
Egregious case (systemic fraud, extensive pattern): 4x to 9x compensatory

On compensatory damages of $200,000:

- 1.5x punitive: $300,000 total
- 3x punitive: $600,000 total

- 5x punitive: $1,000,000 total

IX. Attorney's Fees and Statutory Enhancements

Certain statutes permit recovery of attorney's fees, fundamentally changing litigation economics.

Statutes commonly allowing fee recovery include:

Landlord-tenant statutes. Many states make attorney's fees mandatory for prevailing tenants in habitability cases.

Consumer protection laws. Deceptive trade practices acts often authorize fee recovery.

Insurance bad faith statutes. Some states allow fee recovery in successful bad faith claims.

Fair Housing Act. Federal civil rights statute makes fees mandatory for prevailing plaintiffs.

Fee-shifting provisions significantly influence litigation strategy because:

Economic viability changes. Cases with modest damages become viable when defendants must pay plaintiff's fees.

Settlement leverage increases. Defendants facing fee liability may settle for amounts exceeding damages alone to avoid accumulating fee exposure.

Attorney willingness to litigate increases. Contingent fee attorneys accept cases knowing fees are recoverable beyond contingent percentage.

Example of fee impact:

Without fee-shifting:

- Compensatory damages: $65,000
- Attorney's fees (contingent 33%): $21,450 (from recovery)
- Net to plaintiff: $43,550

With fee-shifting:

- Compensatory damages: $65,000 (to plaintiff)

- Attorney's fees: $45,000 (paid separately by defendant)
- Net to plaintiff: $65,000 (100% of compensatory damages)
- Defendant's total payment: $110,000

Fee-shifting can increase total defendant exposure by 50-100% while increasing plaintiff's net recovery substantially.

X. Aggregate Damages in Multi-Unit Cases

In large-scale housing cases involving multiple tenants or units, aggregate damages may include:

Rent abatement across dozens of tenants. When 50 tenants each receive $12,000 in rent abatement, aggregate exposure is $600,000.

Systemic remediation costs. Building-wide repairs addressing root causes may cost millions when affecting entire developments.

Relocation of multiple families. Temporary housing for 30 families for 4 months at $3,000/month each totals $360,000.

Civil penalties. Administrative fines, code violation penalties, or statutory damages multiply across violations.

Administrative fines. Housing authority citations may impose $500-$5,000 per violation, multiplied by number of affected units.

While individual damages may be modest, cumulative exposure can be substantial:

Example calculation (100-unit building, 40 affected units):

Individual damages per unit (average):

- Rent abatement: $8,000
- Property damage: $3,000
- Relocation: $6,000
- Emotional distress: $12,000
- Subtotal per unit: $29,000

Aggregate tenant damages (40 units × $29,000): $1,160,000

Building-wide remediation:

- HVAC system replacement: $850,000
- Roof repairs: $425,000
- Interior remediation (40 units × $15,000): $600,000
- Subtotal building work: $1,875,000

Other:

- Attorney's fees: $350,000
- Code violation penalties: $85,000
- Subtotal other: $435,000

Total exposure: $3,470,000

Institutional defendants must assess total risk across all affected parties rather than isolated individual claims.

XI. Mitigation and Reasonableness

Defendants frequently argue that plaintiffs failed to mitigate damages, seeking reductions for:

Delaying notice to landlord. Waiting weeks or months to report problems, allowing contamination to worsen.

Refusing access for remediation. Denying landlord entry to perform repairs, extending problem duration.

Ignoring cleaning or ventilation recommendations. Failing to follow reasonable suggestions that might have limited growth.

Continuing to occupy premises unnecessarily. Remaining in severe conditions when relocation was medically recommended and financially feasible.

Courts may reduce damages where plaintiffs fail to act reasonably in protecting their interests.

Defendants must prove:

Plaintiff unreasonably failed to mitigate. Conduct fell below what reasonable person would do in similar circumstances.

Damages would have been reduced. Defendant must show specific damages that mitigation would have prevented.

Plaintiff's conduct caused increased damages. Causal connection between failure to mitigate and additional harm.

What constitutes failure to mitigate:

- Tenant aware of small leak but not reporting it for 6 months, allowing extensive mold growth
- Tenant refusing landlord's offer to remediate, continuing to live in conditions while damages accumulate
- Tenant staying in hotel costing $250/night when comparable extended-stay options available for $100/night

What does NOT constitute failure to mitigate:

- Tenant reporting problem promptly even if mold growth occurred before reporting
- Tenant refusing inadequate remediation attempt (bleach spray without addressing moisture source)
- Tenant choosing quality temporary housing comparable to original residence

Documentation of cooperation or reasonable resistance is critical. Contemporaneous communications showing plaintiff's attempts to facilitate repairs or reasonable objections to inadequate efforts protect against mitigation defenses.

XII. The Role of Experts in Damage Valuation

Damage claims often require specialized experts beyond medical causation experts:

Environmental consultants. Quantify contamination extent, remediation scope, and post-remediation verification.

General contractors or remediation contractors. Provide cost estimates for demolition, remediation, and reconstruction.

Real estate appraisers. Value property before and after mold disclosure, establishing diminution.

Economists. Calculate lost wages, lost earning capacity, present value of future losses.

Vocational rehabilitation specialists. Assess work limitations and reduced earning capacity from permanent injuries.

Credible, well-supported expert testimony enhances valuation credibility. Conversely, inflated or speculative damage claims may undermine overall case credibility, leading to:

- Skepticism about all damage categories
- Reduced settlement offers
- Unfavorable jury verdicts
- Sanctions for frivolous claims

Best practices for damage presentation:

✓ Support every category with documentary evidence
✓ Use qualified, credible experts with relevant experience
✓ Provide detailed cost breakdowns, not lump sums
✓ Acknowledge and address weaknesses proactively
✓ Distinguish between certain damages and speculative claims
✓ Scale demands to evidence strength

XIII. Settlement Valuation in 2026

Modern toxic mold settlements often reflect:

Strength of habitability or negligence evidence. Documented delay, repeated complaints, and governmental violations increase value.

Viability of medical causation claims. Whether expert testimony will survive Daubert determines whether medical damages are recoverable.

Availability of insurance coverage. Defendants with substantial coverage can fund larger settlements than uninsured parties.

Potential punitive exposure. Evidence of deliberate concealment or egregious conduct multiplies settlement pressure.

Jurisdictional tendencies. Plaintiff-friendly vs. defense-oriented venues affect realistic valuation.

High-value settlements frequently involve:

Clear documentation of long-term neglect. Email trails, work orders, and internal communications showing knowledge and inaction.

Vulnerable occupants. Children with asthma, elderly residents with respiratory conditions, immunocompromised individuals.

Systemic maintenance failures. Pattern evidence across multiple units or properties showing institutional indifference.

Insurance bad faith exposure. Carrier mishandling creating additional liability beyond underlying claim.

Cases limited to minor respiratory symptoms and isolated moisture events typically resolve for far less:

Minor case (brief exposure, modest symptoms, prompt response): $15,000 to $45,000
Moderate case (several months exposure, documented symptoms, delayed response): $75,000 to $200,000
Serious case (extended exposure, vulnerable plaintiffs, egregious conduct): $250,000 to $750,000
Major case (systemic problems, severe documented harm, punitive exposure): $1,000,000+

XIV. The Psychological Dimension of Mold Damages

Mold carries emotional weight beyond objective harm. Jurors may associate it with:

Hidden danger. Invisible threat lurking behind walls creating fear.

Neglect. Property owners who allowed conditions to persist suggesting indifference.

Risk to children. Particular sympathy when children's health is affected.

Institutional indifference. Large landlords or corporations prioritizing profits over tenant safety.

Effective presentation balances emotional resonance with scientific credibility.

Overstating medical harm can backfire. When experts claim catastrophic injuries unsupported by evidence, credibility collapses and entire cases may fail.

Understating documented neglect minimizes impact. Presenting months of ignored complaints as mere "dispute over repair timeline" fails to capture jury's sense of injustice.

Strategic framing is essential.

The most successful damage presentations:

- Lead with objectively measurable harms (property damage, relocation costs, documented medical expenses)
- Support each category with documentary evidence (receipts, invoices, medical records)
- Present emotional distress as natural consequence of living in substandard conditions, not speculative fear of toxic exposure
- Connect damages directly to defendant's documented conduct (delay, concealment, indifference)
- Scale demands realistically to evidence strength

XV. Conclusion

Damages in toxic mold litigation range from modest respiratory treatment costs to multi-million-dollar remediation and punitive awards.

The central determinants of valuation include:

Strength of causation evidence. Can plaintiff prove medical injuries through admissible expert testimony?

Severity and duration of moisture intrusion. Chronic long-term exposure commands higher damages than brief isolated events.

Quality of documentation. Receipts, invoices, medical records, and contemporary communications establish damages objectively.

Conduct of defendants. Egregious behavior (concealment, deliberate delay, retaliation) multiplies exposure.

Insurance availability. Coverage provides settlement funds; its absence limits recovery regardless of liability strength.

In 2026, toxic mold cases are rarely about mold alone. They are about responsibility, response, and the financial consequences of preventable water intrusion.

Key Takeaways:

1. **Medical damages require admissible causation testimony** surviving Daubert/Frye scrutiny
2. **Property damages are objectively measurable** and often anchor settlements
3. **Emotional distress availability varies dramatically** by jurisdiction
4. **Punitive damages require egregious conduct** with documentary evidence
5. **Attorney's fees transform economics** making modest cases viable
6. **Documentation is decisive** for all damage categories
7. **Mitigation failures can reduce recovery** when plaintiffs act unreasonably
8. **Expert credibility matters** as much as expert opinions
9. **Strategic valuation shapes outcomes** from first demand through final settlement

The next chapter examines the pivotal role of expert testimony and evidentiary battles where admissibility decisions often determine whether damages expand or collapse before trial. Understanding how to select, prepare, and present experts is essential because gatekeeping rulings frequently decide cases before juries ever hear evidence.

16

Expert Battles and Evidentiary Strategy

Winning the Admissibility War in Toxic Mold Litigation

The Most Important Trial Happens Before the Jury

In March 2024, two toxic mold cases approached trial in adjacent federal courthouses, both involving families exposed to Stachybotrys in rental properties for approximately one year.

Case A: Northern District of Illinois

Plaintiff's medical expert: Board-certified allergist and immunologist, 25 years clinical experience, affiliated with major medical center, published 40+ peer-reviewed articles on indoor allergens.

Expert's opinion (limited and defensible):

- Exposure to elevated Stachybotrys levels can cause allergic rhinitis and asthma exacerbation

- Plaintiff's symptoms (nasal congestion, coughing, wheezing) consistent with mold-induced allergic response
- Temporal correlation: symptoms began after occupancy, worsened during exposure, improved after relocation
- Differential diagnosis: ruled out seasonal allergies (year-round symptoms), dust mites (improved away from property), smoking (non-smoker)
- Medical literature supporting causation (cited 12 peer-reviewed studies)

Defendant's Daubert motion: Denied

Trial result: Jury verdict $185,000

Case B: Northern District of Texas

Plaintiff's medical expert: Clinical ecologist, 15 years experience, operates private "environmental medicine" clinic, authored two self-published books on "toxic mold syndrome."

Expert's opinion (expansive and speculative):

- Exposure caused "chronic inflammatory response syndrome with multi-system dysfunction"
- Cognitive impairment, immune dysregulation, chronic fatigue, fibromyalgia-like symptoms
- Based on: clinical observation, patient reports, urinary mycotoxin testing, visual contrast sensitivity testing
- Methodology: "I diagnose CIRS in 80% of my mold-exposed patients using Dr. Shoemaker's protocol"
- Literature cited: 3 articles, none peer-reviewed, all published in journals not recognized by mainstream medicine

Defendant's Daubert motion: Granted (expert excluded)

Result: Case dismissed on summary judgment (no admissible medical causation evidence)

Settlement (after appeal failed): $22,000 (property damage and relocation costs only)

Same exposure duration. Same mold species. Similar documented symptoms. But Case A settled for $185,000 while Case B collapsed to $22,000 because **one expert passed the admissibility gate and the other didn't**.

In toxic mold litigation, the most important trial often occurs before the jury is ever seated. It happens at the admissibility stage, where motions to exclude expert testimony under Daubert, Frye, or comparable standards determine whether cases proceed to trial, settle favorably, or collapse entirely.

I. The Case Within the Case

In toxic mold litigation, evidentiary rulings on expert testimony frequently determine outcomes more than any other factor.

By 2026, toxic mold litigation is defined less by dramatic photographs of contamination and more by pretrial evidentiary rulings on:

Environmental testing methodology. Whether sampling protocols, laboratory analysis, and interpretation meet reliability standards.

Medical causation opinions. Whether physicians can testify that mold exposure caused plaintiff's specific injuries using scientifically valid methodology.

Dose-response analysis. Whether experts can connect measured exposure levels to claimed health effects through peer-reviewed science.

Building science conclusions. Whether engineers and architects can reliably identify design or construction defects causing moisture intrusion.

Damages projections. Whether economists, appraisers, and vocational experts use accepted methodologies for calculating losses.

Expert credibility is leverage. Admissibility is survival.

When medical experts are excluded, personal injury damages evaporate, transforming potential six-figure settlements into modest property damage recoveries. When environmental consultants' methodologies are discredited, causation chains break, eliminating liability foundations.

II. Categories of Experts in Mold Litigation

Toxic mold cases typically involve multiple expert disciplines, each subject to distinct admissibility challenges.

1. Environmental Hygienists and Industrial Hygienists

What they evaluate:

- Air sampling results (spore trap analysis, viable culture plates)
- Surface sampling (tape lifts, swabs, bulk samples)
- Moisture mapping (moisture meters, infrared thermography)
- Source identification (tracing water intrusion pathways)
- Remediation scope (what work is necessary to address contamination)
- Post-remediation verification (clearance testing confirming work effectiveness)

Common challenges to methodology:

Sampling timing and conditions. Was testing conducted under representative conditions or during atypical circumstances (windows open, dehumidifiers running, after partial cleaning)?

Protocol adherence. Did consultant follow recognized standards (ASTM, AIHA, ACGIH) or use ad hoc methods?

Chain of custody. Can samples be traced from collection through laboratory analysis without breaks suggesting contamination or tampering?

Laboratory accreditation. Is the testing laboratory AIHA-LAP, LLC accredited or otherwise recognized for quality?

Interpretation standards. Are conclusions based on established guidelines or personal opinion unsupported by literature?

Outdoor comparison validity. Were outdoor samples collected simultaneously under similar conditions to provide meaningful baselines?

Defendants attack environmental testimony by highlighting:

- Single-point-in-time sampling not reflecting historical exposure
- Absence of universally accepted "toxic" thresholds
- Failure to account for seasonal variations in outdoor mold levels
- Sampling conducted after remediation attempts, not reflecting peak conditions
- Consultant's financial interest in finding problems (hired by plaintiff's attorney)

Plaintiffs strengthen environmental testimony by:

- Using certified industrial hygienists (CIH credential)
- Following published sampling protocols (ASTM D7391, etc.)
- Documenting methodology comprehensively
- Comparing results to peer-reviewed reference data
- Providing multiple sampling events showing consistency
- Using accredited laboratories with quality control documentation

2. Building Envelope and Construction Experts

What they assess:

- Flashing installation compliance with specifications and codes
- Waterproofing systems adequacy and proper installation
- HVAC design appropriateness for climate and building type
- Building code compliance at time of construction
- Construction sequencing and quality control
- Deviation from plans, specifications, or industry standards

Common challenges:

Qualifications disputes. Is expert a licensed architect/engineer with relevant experience in building envelope design?

Standards identification. What specific code provisions or industry standards allegedly were violated?

Causation linkage. Can expert connect design/construction defect to specific moisture intrusion that caused mold?

Hindsight bias. Is expert applying current standards to older construction governed by different codes?

Alternative explanations. Can expert eliminate maintenance failures, tenant conduct, or other causes as moisture sources?

Building science experts often prove more durable than medical experts because their testimony rests on:

- Objective code requirements
- Manufacturer installation instructions
- Published industry standards (ASHRAE, ASTM, etc.)
- Physical evidence (actual building conditions)
- Engineering principles with mathematical foundations

Courts generally find building science testimony more straightforward and grounded in measurable data than contested medical causation theories.

3. Medical Experts

Typically allergists, pulmonologists, toxicologists, or occupational medicine physicians testifying about health effects.

What they must address:

General causation. Can mold exposure cause the type of condition alleged?

Specific causation. Did mold exposure in this case cause this plaintiff's specific injury?

Differential diagnosis. Systematic process ruling out alternative causes.

Dose-response. Was exposure level sufficient to cause the claimed injury?

Temporal relationship. Do timing of exposure and symptom onset support causation?

Alternative causes. Have other explanations been adequately considered and excluded?

Common grounds for exclusion:

Lack of dose measurement. Expert assumes exposure without quantitative data linking measured concentrations to injury.

Reliance on unvalidated tests. Urinary mycotoxin panels, non-standard inflammatory markers, or other tests lacking peer-review validation.

Unsupported extrapolation. Extending findings from agricultural or industrial exposures to residential scenarios without scientific basis.

Inadequate differential diagnosis. Failing to consider or rule out seasonal allergies, dust mites, smoking, occupational exposures, viral illness.

Theory lacks general acceptance. CIRS, broad immune dysfunction, or neurological syndromes without peer-reviewed support in residential mold context.

Medical testimony is the most vulnerable to admissibility challenges, particularly when systemic injury beyond respiratory effects is claimed.

4. Damages Experts

Including appraisers (property valuation), economists (lost wages, earning capacity), life-care planners (future medical needs), and contractors (repair costs).

What they calculate:

Real estate appraisers:

- Pre-mold fair market value
- Post-disclosure value with mold history
- Diminution in value attributable to mold stigma

Economists:

- Past lost wages (documented work absences)
- Future earning capacity (present value of reduced earnings)

- Household services (value of services plaintiff can no longer perform)

Contractors/remediation specialists:

- Scope of necessary demolition and remediation
- Cost of materials and labor
- Reasonableness of prices charged

Life-care planners:

- Future medical treatment needs
- Cost of ongoing care and monitoring
- Present value of lifetime medical expenses

Damages experts' opinions must rest on admissible liability and causation findings. If medical expert is excluded, life-care planner and economist opinions regarding medical damages become moot.

III. Daubert and Reliability Challenges

In federal courts and most states, expert testimony must satisfy reliability standards under *Daubert v. Merrell Dow Pharmaceuticals*, 509 U.S. 579 (1993). Some jurisdictions apply the older **Frye "general acceptance"** standard.

Daubert factors courts consider:

1. **Whether the theory or technique can be (and has been) tested.** Is methodology based on testable hypotheses or unfalsifiable assertions?

2. **Whether it has been subjected to peer review and publication.** Has the scientific community examined and critiqued the methodology?

3. **The known or potential error rate.** How often does the technique produce false results?

4. **Whether standards controlling the technique's operation exist.** Are there professional protocols governing the methodology?

5. **Whether the theory has gained general acceptance in the relevant scientific community.** Do mainstream practitioners recognize this approach as valid?

Courts serve as "gatekeepers" to exclude unreliable expert testimony before it reaches juries.

Common judicial concerns in mold cases:

Reliance on peer-reviewed literature. Does expert base opinions on published, peer-reviewed research or personal beliefs?

Measurement of exposure. Was exposure quantified or merely assumed based on visible mold presence?

Methodology testability. Can the expert's approach be replicated by other scientists?

Differential diagnosis rigor. Were alternative causes systematically evaluated or summarily dismissed?

Extrapolation beyond established science. Does expert extend findings beyond what research actually supports?

Experts who rely on anecdotal reports, unvalidated laboratory tests, or speculative toxin theories often face exclusion.

When exclusion occurs, consequences are severe:

Medical expert excluded: Personal injury damages eliminated, case value collapses to property damages
Environmental expert excluded: Causation chain breaks, difficulty proving mold exposure occurred
Building science expert excluded: Harder to prove construction defect or landlord negligence
Damages expert excluded: Difficulty establishing economic losses, diminution, or future costs

IV. Differential Diagnosis: Necessary but Not Sufficient

Plaintiffs often rely on differential diagnosis, a clinical method where physicians identify possible causes and systematically rule out alternatives.

Courts accept differential diagnosis when:

The underlying causal theory is scientifically valid. Mold causing allergic rhinitis: valid. Mold causing cognitive impairment: contested.

Exposure is documented. Visual observation, environmental testing, or other objective evidence confirms exposure occurred.

Alternative causes are meaningfully addressed. Each alternative is considered individually with explanation for exclusion.

Methodology follows accepted clinical practice. Process mirrors how competent physicians actually diagnose patients.

Courts reject differential diagnosis when:

Expert assumes exposure without measurement. "Patient lived in moldy house, so exposure must have occurred" without quantitative data.

Alternative causes are ignored or inadequately analyzed. Seasonal allergies, dust mites, smoking, pets, occupational exposures dismissed without explanation.

Underlying theory lacks scientific support. Even perfect differential diagnosis cannot salvage causation theory that mainstream science rejects.

Expert cherry-picks alternatives. Only considering unlikely explanations while ignoring obvious ones.

Example of inadequate differential diagnosis:

Doctor testifies: "I considered chronic fatigue syndrome, fibromyalgia, and Lyme disease. Tests for those were negative. Therefore, mold exposure caused the symptoms."

Problems:

- Didn't consider depression, anxiety, sleep disorders, thyroid disorders, vitamin deficiencies, medication effects
- Didn't explain why mold is more likely than unconsidered alternatives
- Temporal relationship weak (symptoms preceded mold discovery)
- No objective medical findings supporting claimed mold-related syndrome

Example of stronger differential diagnosis:

Doctor testifies: "Patient developed nasal congestion, sneezing, and itchy eyes after moving into apartment. Symptoms were year-round, not seasonal, ruling out pollen allergies. Allergy testing showed sensitivity to mold antigens but not to dust mites, trees, or grasses. Symptoms improved dramatically when patient stayed at parents' home on weekends but recurred upon returning to apartment. This pattern is inconsistent with systemic allergies or viral illness. Smoking was ruled out (patient is non-smoker). Occupational exposures ruled out (symptoms worse at home than work). Symptom pattern, timing, allergy testing, and improvement away from property all support mold-induced allergic rhinitis."

The second approach systematically addresses alternatives with specific reasoning for each exclusion.

V. Establishing Exposure: The Dose Problem

Causation requires more than identifying mold species. Plaintiffs must demonstrate meaningful exposure levels capable of causing injury.

What plaintiffs must show:

Duration of exposure. How long was plaintiff exposed? Days, weeks, months, years?

Intensity of exposure. What were spore concentrations? How do they compare to outdoor baseline levels?

Route of exposure. Inhalation (breathing airborne spores)? Dermal contact? Ingestion?

Biologically plausible dose-response relationship. Does scientific literature support that measured exposure levels can cause claimed injuries?

The absence of defined indoor exposure thresholds creates evidentiary challenges. Without regulatory limits, experts must rely on:

Comparative analysis. Indoor spore counts compared to outdoor baseline or reference data.

Professional guidelines. Though advisory (not regulatory), AIHA, ACGIH, or similar organization recommendations.

Peer-reviewed research. Studies showing health effects at various exposure levels.

Moisture history reconstruction. Duration and severity of water intrusion establishing opportunity for growth.

Defense experts frequently argue:

Environmental testing provides only snapshots. Single air sample represents 5-10 minutes of collection, not months of occupancy.

Samples don't reflect historical exposure. Mold discovered in October doesn't establish what exposure was in June, July, August.

Spore presence doesn't equal harmful dose. Detection of mold (which is ubiquitous) differs from concentrations sufficient to cause injury.

"More than outdoor levels" isn't same as "toxic levels." Indoor amplification may indicate moisture problem without proving health danger.

Courts increasingly demand objective data rather than assumptions. "There was visible mold, so exposure must have been significant" is an assumption, not evidence.

How to strengthen exposure evidence:

✓ Conduct multiple sampling events showing consistency
✓ Sample during normal occupancy conditions (not after cleaning or with windows open)
✓ Include outdoor comparison samples collected simultaneously
✓ Document moisture conditions allowing mold amplification
✓ Reconstruct exposure timeline using moisture history and growth rates
✓ Retain industrial hygienists (CIH) who can defend methodology under cross-examination

VI. Temporal Relationship and Symptom Onset

Persuasive mold cases demonstrate clear temporal correlation:

Symptom onset after exposure began. Plaintiff was healthy before occupancy or before water intrusion occurred.

Improvement upon relocation. When plaintiff moved out (temporarily or permanently), symptoms improved or resolved.

Recurrence upon re-entry. If plaintiff returned to property, symptoms recurred or worsened.

This temporal association strengthens causation but **correlation alone doesn't establish causation**.

Post hoc ergo propter hoc ("after this, therefore because of this") is a logical fallacy. Courts require more than temporal sequence.

Plaintiffs must connect timing to biological mechanism:

Why did exposure cause symptoms?
What is the biological pathway?
Is temporal sequence consistent with known latency periods?
Have alternative explanations for timing been ruled out?

Example of strong temporal correlation:

"Family moved into rental January 2023. All healthy with no respiratory complaints documented in prior medical records. Heavy rains in March caused roof leak. Landlord notified but repair delayed. By May, youngest child developed nighttime coughing. By June, both children coughing regularly. By July, mother developed nasal congestion. August: mold discovered behind bedroom drywall. Family relocated immediately. Within 10 days, all symptoms resolved. Father returned to property 6 weeks later to retrieve belongings. Within one hour, experienced throat irritation and coughing he hadn't had since relocation."

Why this is compelling:

- Clear health before exposure
- Symptom onset after moisture intrusion (not before)
- Progressive worsening as contamination grew
- Rapid improvement after removal from exposure
- Recurrence upon re-entry (even brief)
- Documented in contemporaneous medical records

Example of weak temporal correlation:

"Tenant has history of seasonal allergies documented over 10 years. Symptoms vary throughout year with no clear pattern. After living in property three years, tenant discovered mold in bathroom closet. Tenant claims symptoms experienced during prior three years were caused by mold."

Why this is weak:

- Symptoms preceded mold discovery by years
- No clear onset after moving in
- Pre-existing allergic condition complicates attribution
- No improvement demonstrated upon discovering mold or attempting remediation
- Alternative causes (seasonal pollen) remain viable

VII. Accepted Injuries vs. Contested Conditions

Courts have become increasingly sophisticated about distinguishing between mold-related conditions with strong scientific support and those that remain controversial.

Widely Accepted Conditions (Generally Admissible)

Allergic rhinitis. Nasal congestion, sneezing, runny nose, itchy eyes. Well-documented allergic response to mold spores with extensive peer-reviewed literature.

Asthma exacerbation. Worsening of pre-existing asthma or development of new asthma symptoms. Institute of Medicine found sufficient evidence linking dampness/mold to asthma exacerbation.

Respiratory irritation. Coughing, wheezing, throat irritation from high spore concentrations, even without allergic sensitization. Recognized as irritant effect independent of immune response.

Hypersensitivity pneumonitis. Rare inflammatory lung condition requiring clinical diagnosis with specific findings (restrictive pattern on PFTs, ground-glass opacities on imaging, sometimes biopsy). Requires heavy exposure, usually occupational.

Defense experts typically concede these conditions while disputing broader systemic claims. This strategic concession establishes reasonableness while limiting damages.

Contested Conditions (Frequently Challenged, Often Excluded)

Cognitive impairment. "Brain fog," memory problems, difficulty concentrating attributed to mold exposure absent documented invasive infection.

Chronic inflammatory response syndrome (CIRS). Multi-symptom diagnosis based on Shoemaker protocol involving visual contrast sensitivity testing, inflammatory markers, and symptom clusters. Limited peer-review validation and general acceptance concerns.

Broad immune dysfunction. Claims of compromised immune system, increased infections, autoimmune responses. Typically lack sufficient scientific support in residential exposure contexts.

Neurological syndromes. Peripheral neuropathy, balance disorders, tremors attributed to mycotoxin exposure without documented invasive fungal infection.

Chronic fatigue, fibromyalgia-like syndromes. Persistent fatigue, widespread pain, multi-system symptoms attributed to mold. Courts skeptical of causal connection in residential settings.

The gap between accepted and contested conditions represents the difference between settlement and dismissal, between $50,000 and $500,000 in damages.

VIII. Biomarkers and Laboratory Testing

Some plaintiffs introduce laboratory testing to support systemic illness claims.

Common tests challenged in litigation:

Urinary mycotoxin panels. Tests claiming to detect mycotoxins in urine samples.

Challenges:

- Lack of standardized reference ranges (no established "normal" vs. "toxic" levels)
- Source attribution uncertainty (mycotoxins in food vs. inhalation)
- Absence of FDA approval for diagnostic use
- Limited peer-reviewed validation of testing methodology

- Questions about whether urinary detection correlates with illness

Inflammatory markers. Tests measuring cytokines, C4a, TGF-beta, or other markers.

Challenges:

- Non-specificity (many conditions cause inflammation)
- Lack of established mold-specific reference ranges
- Absence of validated interpretation criteria
- Limited evidence linking markers specifically to mold exposure

Visual contrast sensitivity (VCS) testing. Screening test sometimes used in CIRS diagnosis.

Challenges:

- Non-specific (many conditions affect visual contrast)
- Lack of standardization across testing methods
- Limited validation for mold exposure assessment
- Easy to administer incorrectly, affecting results

Genetic susceptibility testing. HLA typing allegedly showing increased mold susceptibility.

Challenges:

- Lack of regulatory recognition for diagnostic use
- Limited peer-reviewed validation
- Uncertainty about predictive value
- Risk of genetic discrimination

Courts frequently exclude these tests as unreliable under Daubert, finding:

- Insufficient peer-review validation
- Lack of accepted reference standards
- Uncertainty about what results mean clinically

- Tests not generally accepted in mainstream medical community

IX. Cross-Examination Strategy

Effective cross-examination focuses on methodology, bias, and overreach rather than attacking expert credentials.

Cross-Examining Plaintiff Experts

Focus areas:

Lack of dose measurement. "You never measured actual mycotoxin concentrations in the air my client breathed, correct? You're assuming toxic exposure based on the presence of mold you saw in photographs?"

Alternative causes not ruled out. "You're aware the plaintiff has seasonal allergies documented for 15 years before this exposure? Did you review pollen counts for the relevant time period? No? Did you consider whether symptoms might be seasonal rather than mold-related?"

Selective literature citation. "You cited three studies supporting your opinion. Are you aware of the 2016 meta-analysis of 47 studies finding insufficient evidence for cognitive effects from residential mold exposure? Why didn't you cite that?"

Financial bias. "How much of your practice income comes from plaintiff mold litigation? What percentage of cases do you testify that mold caused the alleged injury?"

Inconsistent prior testimony. "In the Johnson case in 2022, you testified that Stachybotrys concentrations needed to be 50 times outdoor baseline to cause symptoms. Here, concentrations were only 12 times baseline. What changed?"

Cross-Examining Defense Experts

Focus areas:

Financial incentives. "Insurance companies pay you $15,000 per case to review mold claims and testify, correct? How many times have you testified that mold DID cause a plaintiff's injuries? Never? In 127 cases, you've never once found mold exposure caused injury?"

Downplaying known effects. "You acknowledge mold can cause allergic reactions, correct? And you acknowledge allergic reactions can be serious, requiring medication and sometimes hospitalization? Yet you minimize my client's three ER visits as 'minor allergy symptoms'?"

Ignoring duration evidence. "You're aware moisture intrusion persisted for 13 months based on work order history? Your opinion assumes brief, limited exposure. That assumption is wrong, isn't it?"

Selective reliance on absence of standards. "You say there are no federal exposure limits for mold. But there are professional guidelines from AIHA recommending indoor levels not substantially exceed outdoor levels, correct? And in this case, indoor levels were 40 times outdoor levels? That substantially exceeds outdoor levels, doesn't it?"

Credibility matters more than credentials. Juries respond to honesty, reasonableness, and consistency. Experts who acknowledge limitations while maintaining opinions appear more credible than those who claim certainty about everything.

X. Coordinating Multi-Expert Testimony

In complex cases involving design defects, construction failures, environmental contamination, and medical injuries, coordinating multiple experts is essential.

Inconsistent opinions between experts undermine credibility:

Example of harmful inconsistency:

Environmental expert: "Moisture intrusion was ongoing for at least 18 months based on water staining patterns and wood rot severity."

Building science expert: "The roof leak occurred approximately 3 months before discovery based on shingle deterioration."

Medical expert: "Patient experienced chronic exposure over 2 years based on symptom progression."

Defense counsel will highlight these inconsistencies: "Even plaintiff's own experts can't agree how long exposure lasted. Was it 3 months, 18 months, or 2 years? How can you believe any of them when they contradict each other?"

Example of coordinated testimony:

Building science expert: "The roof defect existed from original construction in 2019. Based on flashing installation errors, water intrusion would have occurred during any significant rain event."

Environmental expert: "Moisture mapping and infrared thermography show chronic water intrusion over extended period. Wood moisture content and rot patterns consistent with 12-18 months minimum exposure."

Medical expert: "Patient moved in January 2023. Symptoms began April 2023 (3 months after occupancy), consistent with allergic sensitization period. Symptoms progressed through August 2024 (16 months exposure). This timeline aligns with environmental evidence of chronic moisture."

Coordinated testimony reinforces unified theory of the case.

Best practices:

✓ Experts should review each other's reports before finalizing opinions
✓ Counsel should identify potential inconsistencies early and resolve them
✓ Develop unified timeline all experts reference
✓ Ensure terminology is consistent across disciplines
✓ Anticipate and address apparent conflicts proactively

XI. Defense Trends in 2026

Defense strategies increasingly emphasize narrowing claims through rigorous scientific challenges:

1. Concede allergies, challenge systemic injury. Acknowledge mold can cause allergic reactions while vigorously contesting broader harm claims.

2. Attack dose-response gaps. Emphasize absence of measured exposure data showing toxic concentrations.

3. Emphasize lack of federal standards. Argue that absence of regulatory thresholds shows scientific uncertainty.

4. Highlight alternative causes systematically. Present comprehensive list of other explanations for plaintiff's symptoms.

5. Retain highly credentialed experts. Board-certified specialists from academic medical centers carry weight juries respect.

6. Move for exclusion early. File Daubert motions before discovery closes, potentially resolving case before trial.

This disciplined approach has proven effective in many jurisdictions, reducing high-value personal injury exposure by limiting recoverable injuries to well-documented respiratory effects.

XII. Plaintiff Adaptation: Evidence-Based Framing

Plaintiffs are responding by narrowing claims strategically:

Focus on documented respiratory conditions. Emphasize allergic rhinitis, asthma exacerbation, and irritant symptoms with peer-reviewed support.

Strengthen exposure documentation. Multiple sampling events, outdoor comparisons, moisture history reconstruction.

Emphasize prolonged moisture neglect. Shift focus from speculative toxicity to documented landlord failure.

Present clear exposure timelines. Detailed chronologies showing when moisture began, when mold grew, when symptoms developed.

Integrate building science with medical theory. Connect construction defects to moisture intrusion to mold growth to allergic response in coherent narrative.

By narrowing medical claims to scientifically defensible conditions, plaintiffs improve admissibility outcomes while maintaining substantial damage potential through property damages, emotional distress, and punitive exposure.

XIII. The Settlement Leverage Effect

Admissibility rulings frequently trigger settlement discussions because they fundamentally alter case value.

If systemic medical testimony survives Daubert:

- Exposure escalates significantly
- Potential for six-figure medical damages
- Emotional distress, lost wages, and future care costs become viable

- Settlement range: $250,000 to $750,000+

If medical testimony is excluded:

- Case value shifts toward property and emotional distress
- Medical damages limited to documented treatment costs
- Settlement range: $40,000 to $150,000

The difference between admissibility and exclusion often represents $200,000 to $500,000 in settlement value. Early assessment of evidentiary strength informs realistic negotiation.

Strategic timing considerations:

For plaintiffs: Retain unimpeachable experts before filing suit. Vet opinions thoroughly. File only when confident expert testimony will survive scrutiny.

For defendants: Move for exclusion early. If successful, settlement leverage shifts dramatically. If unsuccessful, reassess settlement authority before investing in trial preparation.

XIV. The Cost Factor

Expert-intensive mold litigation is expensive, creating economic feasibility challenges.

Typical expert costs:

Environmental consultant: $5,000 to $15,000 (investigation, testing, report, deposition, trial)
Building science expert: $8,000 to $20,000 (inspection, analysis, report, testimony)
Medical expert: $10,000 to $30,000 (records review, examination, report, deposition, trial)
Appraiser: $3,000 to $8,000 (property valuation, report, testimony)
Economist: $5,000 to $15,000 (lost wage calculations, life care planning)
Additional testing/investigation: $5,000 to $15,000

Total expert costs: $36,000 to $103,000

Economic feasibility must be considered relative to potential recovery. In cases with $50,000 maximum exposure, spending $80,000 on experts is economically irrational.

This creates strategic imperatives:

For plaintiffs: Screen cases carefully. Ensure potential recovery justifies expert investment. Consider limiting expert retention to essential witnesses.

For defendants: Early expert retention may identify technical defenses justifying aggressive motion practice rather than protracted litigation.

In smaller cases, expert costs can exceed anticipated damages, making some legitimate claims economically unfeasible to pursue.

XV. Conclusion

In toxic mold litigation, the expert battle is the case. Scientific rigor determines admissibility. Admissibility determines leverage. Leverage determines settlement or verdict potential.

By 2026, mold litigation has evolved into technically demanding field where disciplined expert strategy separates viable claims from speculative ones.

Key Takeaways:

- **Admissibility rulings often decide cases** before juries hear evidence
- **Medical experts must limit opinions** to scientifically defensible conditions
- **Dose evidence is essential** for causation, not just presence of mold
- **Differential diagnosis must be comprehensive** addressing all reasonable alternatives
- **Temporal correlation supports but doesn't prove** causation
- **Accepted conditions survive scrutiny** while contested theories face exclusion
- **Coordination among experts matters** avoiding contradictions that undermine credibility
- **Defense strategy emphasizes narrowing** through scientific challenges
- **Plaintiff strategy emphasizes documentation** and limiting claims to defensible injuries

- **Economic feasibility requires assessment** before expert investment

The next chapter examines settlement trends and valuation strategy, analyzing why some mold cases resolve for eight figures while others settle modestly or are dismissed outright. Understanding how evidentiary strength translates to settlement value is essential for realistic case evaluation and effective negotiation.

17

Settlement Trends and Negotiation Strategy

Valuation in an Evolving Landscape

Three Cases, Three Outcomes

In September 2024, three toxic mold settlements were finalized on the same day, illustrating the dramatic variation in outcomes based on evidentiary strength and strategic positioning:

Settlement A: Portland, Oregon

- Single-family rental, four-person family, 14-month exposure
- Landlord ignored eight written complaints over 11 months
- Environmental testing: Stachybotrys 38x outdoor baseline

- Visible mold behind kitchen cabinets, bathroom walls, bedroom closet
- Two children hospitalized for asthma attacks during exposure
- Email evidence: landlord to property manager: "Just keep putting them off. They'll eventually move out and we can deal with it then."
- Board-certified allergist limiting testimony to allergic rhinitis and asthma exacerbation
- Documented $12,400 in medical expenses
- $47,000 in remediation and reconstruction costs
- Clear temporal correlation: symptoms during occupancy, improvement after relocation

Settlement: $485,000

Breakdown:

- Medical expenses: $12,400
- Future medical monitoring: $8,000
- Property damage (belongings): $18,500
- Remediation costs: $47,000
- Emotional distress: $125,000
- Punitive damages: $200,000
- Attorney's fees (state statute allows recovery): $74,100

Why it settled high: Documentary evidence of deliberate delay, vulnerable plaintiffs (children), admissible medical testimony, punitive exposure, fee-shifting statute.

Settlement B: Dallas, Texas

- Single-family rental, three-person family, 7-month exposure
- Landlord responded to initial complaint within 14 days, attempted remediation

- Second complaint led to environmental testing (landlord-initiated)
- Testing showed elevated levels, landlord paid for relocation during professional remediation
- Dispute centered on adequacy of initial response and whether remediation was complete
- Medical treatment: urgent care visits, inhaler prescriptions
- No hospitalizations, symptoms resolved after remediation
- Plaintiff expert: clinical ecologist prepared to testify to immune dysfunction and cognitive impairment
- Defendant filed successful Daubert motion excluding systemic injury claims
- Case value shifted after expert exclusion

Settlement: $78,000

Breakdown:

- Medical expenses: $4,200
- Property damage: $8,500
- Temporary housing (already paid by landlord, credit given): $6,800
- Additional rent abatement: $12,000
- Emotional distress: $35,000
- Remediation completion costs: $11,500

Why it settled lower: Landlord demonstrated good-faith response, expert exclusion eliminated systemic injury claims, no punitive exposure, shorter exposure duration, prompt remediation efforts.

Settlement C: Phoenix, Arizona

- Condominium unit, single occupant, 5-month exposure
- Owner-occupied property (plaintiff sued HOA for common-area water intrusion)

- HOA initially denied responsibility, claimed unit owner maintenance failure
- Investigation revealed balcony flashing defect affecting multiple units
- Plaintiff had pre-existing allergies documented over 15 years
- Medical records showed symptoms pre-dated mold discovery
- Environmental testing conducted after partial remediation (lower concentrations)
- No hospitalization, no significant medication changes
- Expert testimony focused on property damage and diminution in value
- HOA raised comparative fault (plaintiff delayed reporting water intrusion visible on balcony)

Settlement: $43,000

Breakdown:

- Remediation costs (HOA responsibility for common elements): $28,000
- Interior unit restoration (plaintiff responsibility, HOA contributed): $8,000
- Lost rental income during repairs: $7,000

Why it settled lowest: Limited medical causation evidence, pre-existing conditions complicated attribution, comparative fault issues, owner-occupied property (no landlord-tenant leverage), HOA showed responsive investigation after initial denial.

Three cases. Same general fact pattern (mold exposure in residential property). Settlement values varying by more than 10x. The difference: evidentiary strength, defendant conduct, expert admissibility, and strategic leverage.

This chapter examines how toxic mold settlements are actually valued in 2026, moving beyond theoretical damages to the practical realities that drive negotiation outcomes.

I. The Settlement Landscape in 2026

By 2026, toxic mold litigation settlement patterns have stabilized around several distinct tiers based on:

- **Evidentiary strength** (admissible expert testimony, documented exposure, clear causation)
- **Defendant conduct** (deliberate concealment vs. good-faith response)
- **Plaintiff vulnerability** (children, elderly, immunocompromised individuals)
- **Jurisdiction** (plaintiff-friendly vs. defense-oriented venues)
- **Insurance availability** (coverage providing settlement funds)
- **Strategic leverage** (punitive exposure, fee-shifting, bad faith claims)

Understanding these factors allows realistic case valuation from initial consultation through final resolution.

II. Settlement Tiers: A Working Framework

While every case is unique, mold settlements tend to cluster around predictable ranges based on case characteristics.

Tier 1: Minimal Settlement ($5,000 to $25,000)

Typical characteristics:

- **Limited exposure duration:** Brief occupancy (under 3 months) or isolated moisture event quickly remediated.
- **Minor symptoms:** Temporary irritation, congestion, or cough with full recovery and no ongoing treatment.
- **Responsive landlord:** Prompt investigation and remediation after notice, even if initial response was imperfect.
- **Weak causation evidence:** Pre-existing conditions, alternative explanations, limited temporal correlation.

- **No egregious conduct:** Absence of concealment, delay, or bad-faith behavior.
- **Property damage only:** Minimal personal property loss, no significant remediation costs.

Example: Tenant reports bathroom mold. Landlord investigates within one week, hires professional remediation within two weeks, pays for tenant hotel during work. Tenant experiences temporary cough, sees doctor once, symptoms resolve. Testing shows moderate elevation above outdoor baseline. Settlement covers medical co-pays, dry cleaning of affected clothing, and token compensation for inconvenience.

Settlement range: $8,000 to $18,000

Tier 2: Moderate Settlement ($30,000 to $100,000)

Typical characteristics:

- **Moderate exposure duration:** 3 to 9 months of documented exposure before remediation.
- **Documented respiratory symptoms:** Allergic rhinitis or asthma exacerbation requiring ongoing treatment but not hospitalization.
- **Delayed but eventual response:** Landlord took weeks or months to investigate/remediate after initial complaints but eventually acted.
- **Measurable property damage:** Contaminated belongings, remediation costs, temporary relocation expenses.
- **Reasonable medical causation:** Board-certified physician limiting testimony to accepted respiratory conditions with adequate differential diagnosis.
- **Some comparative fault issues:** Tenant may have delayed reporting or failed to mitigate in some respects.

Example: Family reports water staining and musty odor. Landlord schedules inspection three weeks later, contractor arrives four weeks after that, proposes remediation timeline six weeks out. Moisture persists for total of six months from initial report to completion. Children develop nasal congestion and nighttime coughing, require antihistamines and nasal steroids. Family relocates to hotel for three weeks during remediation at own expense. Environmental testing shows Stachybotrys at 15x outdoor levels.

Settlement range: $45,000 to $85,000

Tier 3: Substantial Settlement ($125,000 to $350,000)

Typical characteristics:

- **Extended exposure duration:** 9 to 18 months or longer of documented contamination.
- **Serious respiratory conditions:** Asthma requiring emergency treatment, multiple doctor visits, prescription medications, potential hospitalization.
- **Clear landlord neglect:** Multiple ignored complaints, documented delays, inadequate or cosmetic responses.
- **Vulnerable plaintiffs:** Young children, elderly occupants, immunocompromised individuals with documented sensitivity.
- **Strong temporal correlation:** Clear health before exposure, symptom onset during occupancy, improvement after relocation.
- **Significant property damage:** Substantial remediation costs, contaminated belongings, extended relocation period.
- **Documentary evidence of knowledge:** Work orders, emails, prior complaints establishing landlord awareness.

Example: Family with asthmatic child occupies rental. Roof leak reported in month 2. Landlord acknowledges but delays repair "until we can get it on the schedule." Leak persists through rainy season (8 months). Mold discovered behind bedroom walls. Child hospitalized twice for asthma attacks. Family relocates, child's condition improves dramatically. Environmental testing shows extensive contamination, 40x outdoor baseline. Medical records document increased emergency inhaler use during occupancy. Email evidence shows landlord prioritized cost containment over timely repairs.

Settlement range: $175,000 to $285,000

Tier 4: Major Settlement ($400,000 to $1,500,000+)

Typical characteristics:

- **Egregious defendant conduct:** Deliberate concealment, fraudulent nondisclosure, retaliation against complainants, systematic neglect.
- **Multiple affected parties:** Large-scale housing affecting dozens of families, creating pattern evidence and aggregate exposure.
- **Punitive damages exposure:** Documentary evidence (emails, texts, internal memos) showing knowing disregard of tenant safety.
- **Catastrophic health consequences:** Rare severe outcomes (invasive fungal infection in immunocompromised individual, severe hypersensitivity pneumonitis requiring long-term treatment).
- **Insurance bad faith component:** Carrier unreasonably denying coverage, creating independent bad-faith liability.
- **Construction defect with systemic implications:** Multi-unit development with building envelope failures affecting entire property.
- **Fee-shifting statutes:** Attorney's fees multiplying total exposure beyond compensatory damages.

Example: Apartment complex with 40 units affected by roof system failure. Management received engineering report 18 months before tenants complained, recommending immediate repairs. Email from regional manager: "Defer until next budget cycle. Monitor complaints and address individually as needed." Multiple families report mold over 12-month period. Management response: cosmetic cleaning without addressing roof. Health department inspection finds code violations. Three children hospitalized. Pattern evidence shows systematic cost-cutting prioritized over tenant safety. Insurance carrier initially denies coverage, later reverses after bad-faith allegations.

Settlement range: $750,000 to $3,500,000 (aggregate, potentially higher)

III. Variables That Increase Settlement Value

Certain factors consistently drive settlement values upward beyond base case characteristics.

1. Documentary Evidence of Deliberate Conduct

Electronic communications showing knowledge and intentional delay are litigation gold.

High-value communications include:

Explicit admissions of knowledge:

- "We know there's mold, but if we disclose it they'll demand we fix everything immediately."
- "The inspection report showed moisture problems, but we're not telling buyers about it."
- "Yeah, we've had complaints from three other tenants about mold in that building. Just keep handling them case-by-case."

Budget-driven decisions:

- "Remediation estimate is $85K. That blows our Q3 budget. Can we push to next year?"
- "Let's patch it temporarily and see if we can get through the selling season before dealing with it comprehensively."

Concealment strategies:

- "Paint over the staining before the showing tomorrow."
- "Replace the drywall but don't worry about fixing the actual leak. New tenants won't know the difference."

Dismissive attitudes:

- "Mold complaints are just tenants looking for free rent. Ignore unless they lawyer up."
- "These people complain about everything. It's probably not even real mold."

Each of these communications supports punitive damages, dramatically increasing settlement value.

2. Vulnerable Plaintiffs

Defendants settle higher when plaintiffs include:

- **Young children** (particularly infants and toddlers with developing respiratory systems)
- **Elderly individuals** (with reduced physiological resilience)
- **Immunocompromised persons** (cancer patients, organ transplant recipients, HIV/AIDS patients)
- **Pregnant women** (raising concerns about fetal exposure)
- **Individuals with documented respiratory conditions** (pre-existing asthma exacerbated by exposure)

Juries are sympathetic to vulnerable populations. Defense attorneys recognize this and adjust settlement authority accordingly.

Settlement premium for vulnerable plaintiffs: 30% to 75% above comparable cases without vulnerability factors

3. Hospitalization or Emergency Treatment

Medical treatment requiring emergency intervention dramatically strengthens causation and increases settlement value.

- **Single emergency room visit:** Adds $15,000 to $35,000 to settlement value
- **Multiple ER visits:** Adds $40,000 to $75,000
- **Hospitalization (1-2 days):** Adds $60,000 to $150,000
- **Extended hospitalization or ICU:** Adds $200,000+

Emergency treatment provides:

- Objective medical documentation (not just patient complaints)
- Temporal correlation (treatment during exposure period)
- Severity validation (condition serious enough to require urgent care)
- Economic damages (measurable medical expenses)

4. Fee-Shifting Statutes

Jurisdictions permitting attorney's fee recovery transform settlement economics.

Without fee-shifting: Plaintiff receives 60-70% of settlement (after contingent fee)

With fee-shifting: Plaintiff receives 100% of compensatory damages, plus defendant pays attorney's fees separately

Example:

Case value: $100,000 compensatory damages

Without fee-shifting:

- Settlement: $100,000
- Attorney's fee (33%): $33,000
- Net to plaintiff: $67,000

With fee-shifting:

- Compensatory settlement: $100,000 (to plaintiff)
- Attorney's fees (defendant pays separately): $85,000 (600 hours × $200/hour + costs)
- Total defendant payment: $185,000
- Net to plaintiff: $100,000

Fee-shifting increases defendant's exposure by 50% to 100% while maximizing plaintiff recovery. Defendants recognize this leverage and adjust offers accordingly.

5. Insurance Bad Faith Exposure

When insurance coverage exists but carriers deny unreasonably, bad-faith claims create independent liability.

Bad faith transforms settlement dynamics:

- Adds emotional distress damages beyond underlying claim
- Creates punitive damages exposure

- Brings carrier to settlement table as party (not just funding source)
- Multiplies total exposure beyond policy limits

Example settlement structure with bad faith:

- Underlying habitability claim: $120,000
- Insurance policy limit: $500,000
- Carrier denied coverage, forcing policyholder to settle personally
- Policyholder sued carrier for bad faith

Bad faith settlement:

- Underlying claim amount: $120,000 (what should have been paid)
- Consequential damages (policyholder borrowed against property): $35,000
- Emotional distress (stress of personal exposure): $75,000
- Punitive damages: $150,000
- Attorney's fees (bad faith case): $95,000
- **Total carrier exposure: $475,000**

Carrier's unreasonable denial of $120,000 claim cost nearly $500,000.

IV. Variables That Decrease Settlement Value

Certain factors consistently reduce settlement values or eliminate claims entirely.

1. Pre-Existing Medical Conditions

When plaintiffs have documented histories of respiratory conditions identical to those allegedly caused by mold, causation becomes difficult.

Problematic pre-existing conditions:

- **Chronic allergic rhinitis** (documented for years before exposure)
- **Pre-existing asthma** (without clear exacerbation pattern during mold exposure)

- **COPD or emphysema** (from smoking or occupational exposures)
- **Seasonal allergies** (symptoms may not be mold-related)

Pre-existing conditions don't eliminate claims but complicate differential diagnosis and reduce settlement value.

Settlement discount for significant pre-existing conditions: 40% to 70%

Plaintiffs can overcome this by demonstrating:

- Clear exacerbation beyond baseline (measured by medication use, ER visits, pulmonary function tests)
- Temporal correlation with exposure period
- Improvement to baseline after relocation
- Medical expert testimony distinguishing pre-existing condition from mold-induced worsening

2. Delayed Reporting

When tenants delay reporting obvious problems for months, defendants argue:

- Tenant assumed risk by continuing to occupy
- Delay suggests symptoms weren't actually serious
- Tenant failed to mitigate damages
- Delay allowed contamination to worsen (tenant's fault)

Timeline matters:

- **Reported within 2 weeks of discovery:** Minimal impact on settlement
- **Reported within 1-2 months:** Slight reduction (10-15%)
- **Reported after 3-6 months:** Moderate reduction (25-40%)
- **Reported after 6+ months:** Substantial reduction (50%+) or comparative fault finding

Plaintiffs should document reasons for any delay:

- Didn't recognize problem initially
- Attempted to address through cleaning/ventilation before complaining
- Feared retaliation or lease termination
- Landlord informally acknowledged and promised to address

3. Weak Environmental Documentation

Cases lacking objective environmental testing face significant evidentiary challenges.

Impact of limited testing:

No testing at all: Settlement value reduced 30-50% (reliance on visual observations, photographs, and medical symptoms)

Testing after remediation attempts: Reduced 20-30% (doesn't capture peak exposure levels)

Testing only by plaintiff's consultant: Reduced 10-20% (concerns about bias or methodology)

Single sampling event: Reduced 15-25% (questions about representativeness)

Strong environmental evidence includes:

- Multiple sampling events showing consistency
- Testing during normal occupancy conditions
- Independent laboratory analysis
- Outdoor comparison samples
- Moisture mapping documenting water intrusion sources

4. Comparative Fault

When plaintiffs contributed to conditions creating mold growth, defendants raise comparative fault defenses.

Tenant actions potentially reducing recovery:

- **Excessive moisture generation** (drying laundry indoors without ventilation, running humidifiers excessively)
- **Blocking ventilation** (covering air vents, not using exhaust fans)
- **Unreported leaks** (not reporting plumbing problems promptly)
- **Denial of access** (refusing landlord entry for inspections or repairs)
- **Housekeeping failures** (though courts generally reject this unless extreme)

Allocation example:

- Total damages: $100,000
- Court finds landlord 70% at fault (delayed roof repair)
- Court finds tenant 30% at fault (didn't report bathroom leak for 4 months)
- Tenant recovery: $70,000

Plaintiffs minimize comparative fault by documenting:

- Prompt reporting of all problems
- Cooperation with inspection and repair access
- Reasonable occupancy and maintenance practices
- Landlord's primary responsibility for structural maintenance

5. Short Exposure Duration

Brief exposure periods complicate causation and reduce settlement value.

Exposure duration impact:

Under 1 month: Difficult to establish allergic sensitization or chronic effects. Limited to acute irritation symptoms. Settlement severely reduced.

1-3 months: Sufficient for allergic response in sensitized individuals. Moderate settlement potential if temporal correlation is clear.

3-6 months: Standard exposure window supporting documented respiratory conditions. Settlement potential increases with clear causation evidence.

6-12 months: Extended exposure supporting more serious conditions and higher damages.

12+ months: Chronic long-term exposure. Maximum settlement potential when combined with documented health effects and landlord neglect.

Medical causation experts generally require minimum exposure durations to opine on causation. Brief exposures make expert testimony more vulnerable to exclusion.

V. Jurisdictional Variations

Settlement values vary significantly by jurisdiction based on:

Jury verdict histories (plaintiff-friendly vs. conservative venues)
Evidentiary standards (Daubert vs. Frye, application rigor)
Damage availability (emotional distress, punitive damages, attorney's fees)
Procedural rules (discovery scope, expert disclosure requirements)
Cultural attitudes (urban vs. rural, regional differences)

Plaintiff-Favorable Jurisdictions

California: Robust landlord-tenant protections, consumer-friendly statutes, fee-shifting provisions, liberal emotional distress damages.

New York: Strong habitability laws, tenant advocacy traditions, high property values supporting substantial diminution claims.

Washington: Consumer protection statutes, treble damages for certain violations, sympathetic juries.

New Jersey: Strong tenant rights, liberal damage awards, aggressive discovery rules.

Typical settlement premium in plaintiff-favorable venues: 25-50% above defense-oriented jurisdictions

Defense-Favorable Jurisdictions

Texas: Tort reform limitations, caps on certain damages, more conservative juries, strict expert standards.

Florida: Comparative fault rules, damage caps in some contexts, defense-oriented appellate decisions.

Arizona: Conservative jury pools in some counties, limited emotional distress recovery without physical injury.

Typical settlement discount in defense-favorable venues: 20-40% below plaintiff-favorable jurisdictions

Strategic venue selection (when available through diversity jurisdiction or multi-district litigation) can significantly affect settlement outcomes.

VI. The Insurance Variable

Insurance availability may be the single most important factor determining whether cases settle and for how much.

Scenarios:

Defendant has substantial CGL coverage with no mold exclusion or high sub-limit: Settlement feasible up to policy limits. Carrier brings funds to table. Negotiations focus on liability and damages valuation.

Defendant has policy with $10,000 mold sub-limit: Settlement constrained by sub-limit regardless of actual damages. Plaintiff may pursue defendant's personal assets, but collection challenges arise. Often settles for sub-limit amount plus nominal contribution from defendant personally.

Defendant has no insurance (lapsed, cancelled, or never obtained): Settlement limited by defendant's personal assets and willingness to pay. May settle for substantially less than case value due to collection concerns. Judgment may be uncollectable if defendant has limited assets.

Insurance coverage is disputed: Settlement delayed during coverage litigation. May require three-party negotiation (plaintiff, defendant, carrier). Coverage disputes often resolved simultaneously with underlying claim through structured settlements allocating payments between carrier (covered amounts) and defendant (uncovered amounts).

Example of coverage-driven settlement:

- Case value if fully litigated: $350,000
- Defendant's insurance: $100,000 policy limit, carrier accepting coverage
- Defendant's personal assets: Modest (home with equity, limited liquid assets)

Realistic settlement: $115,000

- Carrier pays: $100,000 (policy limits)
- Defendant contributes: $15,000 (avoiding litigation costs and personal exposure)

The $235,000 gap between case value and settlement reflects insurance constraints and collection realities.

VII. The Timing Factor

Settlement values evolve throughout litigation lifecycle based on:

Pre-suit demand: Often inflated, testing defendant's willingness to resolve early.

Post-complaint, pre-discovery: Defendant lacks information to evaluate fully, may lowball or refuse to engage.

Mid-discovery: Parties have evidence to evaluate case realistically. Dispositive motions looming. Settlement discussions often most productive.

Post-expert disclosure, pre-Daubert ruling: High uncertainty. Plaintiff's value depends on expert admissibility. Settlement range very wide.

Post-Daubert ruling: Settlement range narrows dramatically. If experts survive, plaintiff leverage increases. If experts excluded, case value collapses.

Pretrial: Trial proximity creates pressure. Litigation costs about to escalate. Last opportunity for settlement before verdict uncertainty.

Typical Settlement Timeline Patterns

Immediate (within 60 days of claim):

Often low settlements. Defendants testing plaintiff's commitment. Plaintiffs accepting quick resolution to avoid litigation costs.

Typical settlements: 40-60% of full case value

Mid-litigation (6-12 months after filing):

Parties have exchanged discovery. Expert reports disclosed. Realistic evaluation possible. Most settlements occur in this window.

Typical settlements: 65-85% of full case value

Post-Daubert (if experts survive):

Plaintiff leverage maximized. Trial looming. Defense risk assessment increases.

Typical settlements: 75-95% of full case value

Post-Daubert (if experts excluded):

Plaintiff leverage collapses. Case value shifts to property damages alone.

Typical settlements: 20-40% of original demand

Eve of trial:

Highest settlement values (if case hasn't already settled). Litigation costs sunk. Verdict uncertainty highest. Both sides motivated.

Typical settlements: 80-100% of realistic case value

VIII. Mediation Dynamics

Most toxic mold cases that settle do so through mediation, either voluntary or court-ordered.

Effective mediation strategies:

For Plaintiffs:

- **Present organized case summary.** Timeline, medical records, environmental testing, damages calculation, expert qualifications. Professionalism enhances credibility.
- **Lead with strongest evidence.** Don't bury compelling facts in

lengthy briefs. Emails showing deliberate delay, hospitalization records, dramatic before/after photographs.

- **Acknowledge weaknesses candidly (in private caucus).** Mediators appreciate realistic assessments. Helps them evaluate appropriate settlement range.
- **Bring flexible authority.** If demand is $300,000, have authority to settle for $200,000+ if negotiation justifies. Inflexible positions waste mediation opportunity.
- **Focus on risk, not righteousness.** Defense cares about exposure and litigation costs, not moral culpability. Frame settlement as risk management.

For Defendants:

- **Bring sufficient settlement authority.** Mediations fail when defense authority is substantially below realistic case value. Obtain carrier approval for meaningful range before mediation.
- **Present affirmative defenses credibly.** Comparative fault, pre-existing conditions, alternative causation theories. But acknowledge when evidence is strong.
- **Articulate trial risks realistically.** Juries are unpredictable. Litigation is expensive. Settlement provides certainty. Appeal to economic rationality.
- **Don't minimize plaintiff's suffering.** Even if liability is disputed, acknowledge that family experienced difficult situation. Empathy facilitates resolution.
- **Consider structured settlements.** Periodic payments, medical monitoring trusts, or other creative structures may bridge valuation gaps.

Successful mediations often involve:

- Multiple caucuses allowing parties to adjust positions incrementally
- Mediator reality-testing extreme positions
- Bracketing (if plaintiff reduces demand to $X, will defendant increase offer to $Y?)
- Creative problem-solving (injunctive relief, confidentiality

agreements, remediation oversight)

- Separation of economic interests from emotional needs

Mediations fail when:

- Parties' ranges don't overlap (plaintiff's bottom exceeds defendant's top)
- Insufficient settlement authority provided
- Unrealistic expectations based on best-case trial outcomes
- Personality conflicts preventing constructive dialogue
- Insufficient preparation or evidence presentation

IX. The Attorney's Fee Multiplier

In jurisdictions with fee-shifting statutes, attorney's fees often equal or exceed compensatory damages.

Calculation methods vary:

Lodestar method: Reasonable hours × reasonable hourly rate, sometimes enhanced by multiplier for risk and results.

Percentage of recovery: Fee calculated as percentage of total recovery (typically prohibited under fee-shifting statutes but may inform reasonableness analysis).

Example lodestar calculation:

Attorney time:

- Pre-suit investigation and demand: 40 hours
- Pleadings and initial discovery: 85 hours
- Expert retention and coordination: 60 hours
- Depositions: 95 hours
- Motion practice: 70 hours
- Mediation preparation and attendance: 35 hours

- Trial preparation: 120 hours
- Trial: 65 hours
- Post-trial motions: 30 hours

Total: 600 hours × $250/hour = $150,000

Paralegal and law clerk time: 280 hours × $95/hour = $26,600

Costs:

- Court filing fees: $1,800
- Service of process: $650
- Deposition transcripts: $4,200
- Expert fees: $42,000
- Trial exhibits and technology: $3,800

Total costs: $52,450

Total attorney's fees and costs: $229,050

If compensatory damages are $185,000, total defendant exposure with fees is $414,050.

Fee exposure creates powerful settlement incentive for defendants: settling early for $225,000 avoids $414,050 post-trial exposure.

X. Valuation Tools and Frameworks

Experienced practitioners develop systematic approaches to case valuation.

Expected Value Analysis

Formula: (Probability of plaintiff verdict × Likely award if plaintiff prevails) + (Probability of defense verdict × $0) = Expected value

Example:

- Assume if plaintiff prevails, likely award is $300,000
- Plaintiff has 60% chance of favorable verdict

- Defense has 40% chance of favorable verdict

Expected value: (0.60 × \$300,000) + (0.40 × \$0) = \$180,000

Rational settlement range: \$140,000 to \$220,000 (adjusting for litigation costs and risk aversion)

This mathematical approach provides objective baseline, though subjective factors (emotional investment, precedent concerns, reputational considerations) also influence negotiations.

Range-Based Valuation

Rather than single number, establish ranges based on outcome scenarios:

Best case for plaintiff:

- All experts admitted
- Jury finds deliberate concealment
- Punitive damages awarded
- Fee-shifting applied
- **Value: \$650,000 to \$800,000**

Most likely case:

- Experts admitted but testimony limited to respiratory effects
- Negligence found but not intentional misconduct
- Compensatory damages only
- **Value: \$175,000 to \$275,000**

Worst case for plaintiff:

- Medical expert excluded
- Property damages only
- Comparative fault found
- **Value: \$35,000 to \$65,000**

Settlement negotiations focus on which scenario is most realistic and how to hedge against downside risk.

XI. Non-Economic Considerations

Settlement decisions involve more than pure economic analysis:

For Plaintiffs:

- **Emotional closure.** Some plaintiffs need trial to feel heard. Others want to move on quickly.
- **Privacy concerns.** Trials are public. Settlements can include confidentiality provisions.
- **Time investment.** Litigation extends 18-36 months through trial. Settlement may occur within 6-12 months.
- **Psychological toll.** Depositions, document production, and trial preparation are stressful for families with young children or work obligations.
- **Certainty vs. uncertainty.** Settlement guarantees recovery. Trial outcome is unpredictable.

For Defendants:

- **Precedent concerns.** High-profile settlements may encourage additional claims against institutional landlords.
- **Reputational impact.** Public verdicts generate negative publicity. Confidential settlements contain reputational damage.
- **Business continuity.** Protracted litigation distracts management from operations.
- **Insurance implications.** Verdicts affect future premiums and coverage availability more than settlements.
- **Structural relief.** Trials may result in injunctive orders requiring building-wide remediation. Settlements allow negotiated remediation scope.

Sometimes cases settle above economic value because defendants value certainty, privacy, and avoidance of precedent. Sometimes plaintiffs accept less than case value to obtain guaranteed recovery without trial risk.

XII. Structured Settlements and Creative Solutions

When parties' valuations diverge significantly, creative settlement structures may bridge gaps:

- **Periodic payments:** Defendant pays over time rather than lump sum, reducing immediate cash flow impact.
- **Contingent payments:** Additional payments triggered by specific events (property sale, refinancing, future health developments).
- **Remediation agreements:** Defendant performs comprehensive building-wide repairs rather than paying cash damages. Value to plaintiff may exceed cost to defendant.
- **Medical monitoring trusts:** Funds set aside for plaintiff's future medical surveillance, providing long-term security.
- **Waiver of lease obligations:** Tenants released from remaining lease term without penalty (valuable when lease has substantial remaining duration).
- **Relocation assistance:** Defendant pays moving costs, deposits for new housing, temporary housing during transition.
- **Injunctive components:** Defendant agrees to remediation protocols, third-party inspections, or ongoing monitoring benefiting other tenants.

Example structured settlement:

- Plaintiff's demand: $350,000 cash
- Defendant's authority: $175,000 cash

Structured resolution:

- Immediate payment: $150,000
- Remediation of plaintiff's unit plus five adjacent units: $95,000 (cost to defendant, valued by plaintiff at $75,000 per unit given benefit to community)
- Medical monitoring fund: $25,000 (placed in interest-bearing account for plaintiff's future respiratory care)
- Release from lease with waiver of remaining 14 months rent: $21,000 value

- Moving expenses and new housing deposit: $8,000

Total value to plaintiff: $299,000 (close to demand)

Total cost to defendant: $299,000 (but cash portion only $183,000, with remainder in services and waivers)

Creative structures convert non-cash items into settlement value, bridging valuation gaps.

XIII. Current Market Trends (2026)

Several trends characterize toxic mold settlements in 2026:

Narrowing medical damages: Courts increasingly limit recovery to documented respiratory effects, rejecting systemic injury claims without strong scientific support.

Property damage anchoring: Even when medical causation is weak, substantial property remediation costs anchor settlements at meaningful levels.

Insurance-driven outcomes: Coverage availability determines settlement feasibility more than liability strength alone.

Evidentiary gatekeeping: Daubert/Frye rulings on expert admissibility decide more cases than ever before.

Polarized results: Cases with strong evidence and egregious conduct settle high. Cases with modest evidence and good-faith defendant response settle low. Middle tier shrinking.

Increased defense sophistication: Repeat institutional defendants have developed systematic approaches to evaluation, reducing settlement variability.

Attorney's fees leverage: Fee-shifting jurisdictions produce higher settlements because defendants face multiplied exposure.

Pattern evidence premium: Multi-plaintiff cases with systemic problems settle for aggregate amounts substantially exceeding individual case sums.

XIV. Conclusion

Toxic mold settlements in 2026 reflect complex interaction of:

- **Evidentiary strength** (admissible experts, documented exposure, clear causation)
- **Defendant conduct** (negligence vs. deliberate wrongdoing)
- **Plaintiff characteristics** (vulnerability, pre-existing conditions, comparative fault)
- **Jurisdictional factors** (local law, jury tendencies, procedural rules)
- **Insurance availability** (coverage providing settlement funds)
- **Strategic leverage** (punitive exposure, fee-shifting, bad faith claims)
- **Timing and negotiation dynamics** (mediation effectiveness, litigation lifecycle)

No simple formula determines settlement value. But experienced practitioners evaluate these factors systematically, developing realistic ranges and negotiating effectively within them.

Key Takeaways:

1. **Settlement tiers cluster around evidentiary strength** from minimal ($5K-$25K) to major ($400K-$1.5M+)
2. **Documentary evidence of deliberate conduct** multiplies settlement value through punitive exposure
3. **Vulnerable plaintiffs command premium settlements** given jury sympathy
4. **Insurance availability often determines** whether meaningful settlement is feasible
5. **Fee-shifting statutes multiply defendant exposure** by 50-100% or more
6. **Pre-existing conditions and delayed reporting** significantly reduce settlement value
7. **Jurisdictional variations are substantial** requiring local knowledge for accurate valuation
8. **Daubert/Frye rulings are inflection points** fundamentally altering

settlement ranges

9. **Creative settlement structures** can bridge valuation gaps through non-cash components

10. **Economic analysis provides baseline** but non-economic factors influence final resolution

The next and final chapter examines future trends and emerging issues in toxic mold litigation, including climate change impacts, evolving building codes, advanced detection technologies, and regulatory developments. Understanding where mold litigation is headed helps practitioners anticipate and prepare for the next generation of cases.

18

Evidentiary Skepticism and Scientific Resistance

Navigating Judicial Caution in Toxic Mold Cases

I. The Era of Judicial Caution

By 2026, toxic mold litigation no longer benefits from novelty. Courts have witnessed two decades of mold-related claims, and judges have become intimately familiar with the recurring patterns: sensationalized "black mold" narratives promising catastrophic illness, expansive systemic injury theories lacking peer-reviewed support, sharply conflicting expert testimony, and aggressive defense admissibility challenges that have successfully narrowed or eliminated entire categories of claims.

The result is a judicial environment characterized not by hostility, but by disciplined caution, particularly regarding claims of systemic toxicity, neurological impairment, or chronic multi-system illness allegedly caused by residential mold exposure. Understanding this skepticism is not merely useful for litigators; it is essential for realistic case development, honest client counseling, and strategic resource allocation.

Consider what happens in practice: A plaintiff presents photographs of extensive black staining behind drywall, air sampling showing Stachybotrys concentrations forty times outdoor levels, and medical records documenting three emergency room visits for respiratory distress. Yet the case is dismissed at summary judgment. Why? Because the medical expert could not prove, with sufficient scientific reliability, that this specific exposure caused this specific plaintiff's claimed neurological symptoms. The mold was real. The exposure was documented. The symptoms were genuine. But the causal link could not satisfy modern evidentiary standards.

This chapter examines why that happens and how attorneys on both sides navigate an environment where visible contamination no longer guarantees courtroom success.

II. The Collapse of the "Next Asbestos" Prediction

Early commentary in the 2000s confidently predicted that mold would become a mass tort comparable to asbestos litigation. Major insurers reacted by implementing sweeping mold exclusions. Media coverage amplified public fear. Plaintiff attorneys anticipated waves of high-value claims. Defense counsel prepared for decades of litigation.

That prediction has not materialized, and understanding why reveals much about modern judicial attitudes.

Unlike asbestos litigation, mold cases lack several critical elements that sustained decades of mass tort claims:

Ubiquity Without Clear Toxicity Thresholds: Asbestos is a manufactured product with documented dose-response relationships and established exposure limits. Mold is ubiquitous in the natural environment. Every breath of outdoor air contains fungal spores. Indoor air typically contains some level of mold as well. The question is not presence but amplification, and courts struggle to identify the line between normal environmental exposure and dangerous contamination.

Absence of Epidemiological Consensus: Asbestos litigation benefited from decades of epidemiological studies demonstrating clear associations between occupational exposure and specific diseases like mesothelioma. Mold litigation lacks comparable epidemiological support for many claimed conditions. While studies confirm that mold can trigger allergies and asthma, research supporting systemic toxicity, cognitive impairment, or chronic inflammatory syndromes from typical residential exposure remains limited and contested.

Variable Exposure Conditions: Asbestos exposure often occurred in specific occupational settings with relatively consistent conditions. Mold exposure varies dramatically based on building type, climate, maintenance practices, ventilation, occupant behavior, and remediation efforts. This variability makes class certification difficult and forces individualized proof in most cases.

Scientific Community Division: Unlike asbestos, where medical consensus eventually solidified, mold-related illness remains subject to significant scientific debate. Some medical professionals recognize emerging conditions like chronic inflammatory response syndrome. Others dismiss such diagnoses as lacking sufficient validation. This division provides courts with justification for excluding controversial theories.

The mold litigation wave did not collapse because mold is harmless. It narrowed because courts demanded proof that many plaintiffs could not provide under rigorous evidentiary standards. The field survived, but only as a specialized, evidence-driven practice area rather than a sweeping mass tort.

III. The Scientific Dividing Line: What Courts Accept and What They Question

Judicial skepticism in mold litigation tends to follow a predictable and increasingly well-defined pattern. Attorneys who understand this dividing line can frame claims more effectively and avoid the costly mistake of promising outcomes that modern courts will not support.

Generally Accepted Medical Theories

Courts across most jurisdictions readily accept expert testimony supporting the following propositions:

Allergic Reactions: Mold exposure can cause allergic rhinitis, characterized by sneezing, nasal congestion, eye irritation, and throat discomfort. This is well-established in peer-reviewed literature and widely recognized by allergists. Courts rarely exclude testimony linking documented mold exposure to allergic symptoms.

Asthma Exacerbation: Mold can trigger or worsen asthma in sensitized individuals. Numerous studies support this association, and expert testimony connecting mold exposure to asthma flare-ups typically survives admissibility challenges, provided the expert can demonstrate temporal correlation and rule out alternative triggers.

Respiratory Irritation: Prolonged exposure to high concentrations of mold spores can cause irritant effects on the respiratory system even in non-allergic individuals. This mechanism is distinct from allergic response and involves direct irritation of mucous membranes.

Hypersensitivity Pneumonitis: In rare cases, intense mold exposure can cause hypersensitivity pneumonitis, a serious inflammatory lung condition. However, courts require clear clinical diagnosis, objective findings on pulmonary function testing or imaging, and documented exposure to high mold concentrations. Speculative diagnoses fail.

When plaintiffs remain within these established frameworks, courts are generally receptive. Medical experts testifying to these conditions face lower admissibility hurdles, and juries often find such testimony persuasive.

Frequently Challenged Medical Theories

Courts become significantly more skeptical when expert testimony ventures into the following areas:

Systemic Inflammatory Disorders: Claims that residential mold exposure causes chronic inflammatory response syndrome, biotoxin illness, or similar multi-system inflammatory conditions face substantial challenges. While some physicians diagnose and treat these conditions, many courts exclude such testimony as insufficiently validated by peer-reviewed research or general acceptance in the relevant scientific community.

Neurological Impairment Absent Invasive Infection: Plaintiffs sometimes allege that mold exposure caused cognitive dysfunction, memory impairment, brain fog, or other neurological symptoms. Absent invasive fungal infection (which is extraordinarily rare in immunocompetent individuals), courts frequently exclude such testimony. The causal pathway from airborne spore exposure to neurological damage remains poorly established in mainstream medical literature.

Chronic Multi-System Illness from Low-Level Exposure: Some experts testify that even modest indoor mold concentrations can trigger chronic illness affecting multiple organ systems over years. Courts often reject this testimony, particularly when:

- Exposure levels were not measured or were comparable to outdoor concentrations
- Symptoms are nonspecific and subjective
- No objective diagnostic findings support the claims
- Alternative causes were not adequately ruled out
- The theory lacks substantial peer-reviewed support

The difference between accepted and contested theories often determines whether a case proceeds to trial or collapses at the admissibility stage. Plaintiff attorneys who advance only scientifically defensible claims improve their chances significantly. Those who overreach risk losing credible claims along with speculative ones.

IV. The Dose-Response Problem: Courts Demand Measurable Exposure

One of the most persistent and perhaps insurmountable challenges in toxic mold litigation is the absence of defined indoor exposure thresholds. Unlike lead poisoning, where blood lead levels establish dose, or asbestos exposure, where fiber counts and duration create dose metrics, residential mold exposure lacks clear quantitative benchmarks.

The Fundamental Questions Courts Ask

When evaluating toxic exposure claims, courts instinctively ask:

- What concentration of the substance causes harm?
- How much exposure did this plaintiff actually receive?
- Over what duration did exposure occur?
- Compared to what baseline or safe level?

In lead or asbestos cases, experts can answer these questions with data. In mold cases, the answers are often indirect, comparative, or speculative.

Why Federal Standards Do Not Exist

No federal agency has established permissible exposure limits for indoor mold, and this regulatory vacuum creates significant litigation challenges. The reasons for this absence are instructive:

Scientific Uncertainty: Dose-response relationships for mold vary by species, individual sensitivity, exposure route, and co-occurring environmental factors. Establishing a single numerical threshold is scientifically problematic.

Environmental Variability: Outdoor mold concentrations fluctuate dramatically based on season, weather, geography, and time of day. Any indoor standard would need to account for this natural variability.

Measurement Challenges: Air sampling provides only a snapshot in time. Spore concentrations change hourly based on disturbance, ventilation, humidity, and occupant activity. Historical exposure reconstruction is difficult or impossible in most cases.

Species Diversity: Different mold species produce different health effects. A numerical limit based on total spore count may not reflect toxicity if particularly harmful species are present at lower concentrations.

Given these complexities, agencies like the EPA have issued guidance recommending prompt remediation when visible mold is present, but have declined to establish numeric exposure thresholds. This cautious regulatory approach reinforces judicial skepticism.

How Plaintiffs Attempt to Prove Dose

In the absence of defined thresholds, plaintiffs typically rely on comparative analysis:

Indoor vs. Outdoor Comparisons: Environmental consultants compare indoor spore counts to outdoor baseline samples taken the same day. When indoor concentrations significantly exceed outdoor levels, particularly for species not common outdoors, this suggests indoor amplification. Courts sometimes accept this methodology as evidence of contamination, but defendants argue persuasively that elevated indoor counts do not automatically establish toxic dose. The question remains: elevated compared to what harmful level?

Visible Growth as Proxy: Extensive visible mold growth covering significant surface area suggests sustained moisture and likely higher exposure. Some experts testify that visible colonization correlates with higher airborne spore concentrations. However, courts distinguish between evidence of contamination and proof of toxic exposure. Visible growth may establish a habitability violation without proving medical causation.

Duration and Intensity Evidence: Plaintiffs may present evidence of chronic moisture intrusion lasting months or years, arguing that prolonged exposure increases risk even if specific dose cannot be measured. This temporal argument has intuitive appeal but still leaves the fundamental question unanswered: how much exposure over what period causes which specific health effects?

Mycotoxin Testing: Some plaintiffs introduce laboratory testing for mycotoxins in dust samples or air. However, courts have grown increasingly skeptical of such evidence when:

- Testing methods lack standardized validation
- Results cannot be compared to established safe or unsafe levels
- Presence of mycotoxins in samples does not prove biologically significant airborne exposure
- Chain of custody or sampling protocols are questionable

Defense Responses to Dose Arguments

Defense counsel effectively exploit the dose-response gap by emphasizing:

Snapshot Limitations: Air sampling conducted weeks or months after exposure began cannot establish what concentrations existed during the claimed exposure period. Remediation or ventilation may have reduced levels substantially before testing occurred.

Normal Environmental Presence: Mold spores are always present. The plaintiff must prove not just presence but exposure levels sufficient to cause harm, which requires establishing what level causes harm, which does not exist for most species.

Alternative Exposure Sources: Individuals are exposed to mold in many environments: workplaces, vehicles, schools, other residences. Attributing symptoms to one specific indoor environment requires more than general exposure evidence.

Absence of Regulatory Violation: Unlike asbestos or lead cases where regulatory exceedance may establish negligence per se, mold exposure cannot be compared to a violated standard. This weakens the plaintiff's ability to argue that any particular level was unreasonable or dangerous.

The Practical Impact

The dose-response problem has profound practical consequences. It means that even cases with dramatic visual evidence and clear moisture intrusion may fail if the plaintiff cannot bridge the gap between "there was mold" and "the mold made me sick in this specific way."

Plaintiff attorneys must candidly assess whether their expert can articulate a scientifically defensible dose theory. If not, the case may rest primarily on property damage and habitability claims rather than personal injury.

V. Peer-Reviewed Literature and the Gatekeeping Function

Modern judges take their gatekeeping role seriously, particularly in scientifically complex cases. The Daubert framework requires courts to evaluate whether expert testimony is based on reliable principles and methods, and one of the most important reliability factors is grounding in peer-reviewed scientific literature.

What Courts Look For in Scientific Support

Judges evaluating mold-related expert testimony typically examine several key indicators of scientific reliability:

Publication in Respected Journals: Has the expert's theory been published in peer-reviewed medical or scientific journals? Journals with rigorous peer review carry more weight than those with minimal editorial oversight or advocacy-oriented publications.

Reproducibility: Have other researchers been able to reproduce the findings? Single-author studies or isolated case reports carry less weight than replicated research from multiple independent sources.

General Acceptance: Is the theory accepted by a substantial portion of the relevant scientific community? Novel theories may eventually gain acceptance, but courts are cautious about permitting testimony based on minority or emerging views.

Error Rate and Standards: Does the methodology have a known error rate? Are there professional standards governing its application? Well-established diagnostic criteria and testing protocols enhance reliability.

Appropriate Application: Even if a theory is valid in one context, is the expert applying it appropriately to this case? Extrapolating from high-dose occupational exposure studies to low-level residential settings may be problematic.

Common Grounds for Exclusion in Mold Cases

Courts have identified several recurring weaknesses that frequently lead to exclusion of expert testimony in toxic mold litigation:

Selective Literature Citation: Experts who cite only studies supporting their position while ignoring substantial contradictory research face credibility challenges. Courts expect balanced consideration of the relevant scientific literature.

Example: An expert testifies that mold causes neurological damage, citing three case reports, while ignoring multiple epidemiological studies finding no association between residential mold exposure and cognitive impairment.

Reliance on Anecdotal Evidence: Case reports and clinical anecdotes can suggest hypotheses but do not constitute robust scientific evidence. Courts are skeptical of experts who base opinions primarily on their own clinical observations rather than controlled research.

Novel Syndromes Lacking Diagnostic Consensus: When an expert diagnoses a condition that lacks clear diagnostic criteria, validated testing, or recognition by major medical organizations, courts often exclude the testimony. The condition itself becomes the subject of scientific debate, and courts hesitate to let juries resolve contested scientific questions.

Inadequate Methodology: Experts who fail to conduct proper differential diagnosis, who assume causation without investigating alternative causes, or who reach conclusions not supported by their own data face exclusion.

Cherry-Picked Testing: Reliance on laboratory tests that lack standardization, FDA approval, or peer-reviewed validation is increasingly problematic. Courts question testing that appears designed to generate favorable results rather than accurate assessment.

The Impact of Exclusion

When a court excludes a plaintiff's medical causation expert, the practical effect is often case-ending. Without admissible testimony linking mold exposure to the claimed injury, specific causation cannot be proven, and personal injury damages collapse.

However, exclusion is not always total. Courts may permit testimony regarding certain conditions (allergies, asthma exacerbation) while excluding testimony about others (cognitive impairment, systemic toxicity). Partial exclusion narrows damages but may allow the case to proceed on limited theories.

Plaintiff Strategies to Survive Gatekeeping

Experienced plaintiff counsel improve admissibility outcomes by:

Retaining Highly Credentialed Experts: Board-certified specialists with academic appointments, peer-reviewed publications, and respected reputations face lower exclusion risk than general practitioners or physicians known primarily for litigation work.

Thorough Literature Review: Ensuring the expert has reviewed and can address the full scope of relevant literature, including studies that might undercut the opinion.

Conservative Theory Selection: Focusing on scientifically accepted conditions rather than pushing boundaries with novel syndromes increases the likelihood of admission.

Documented Methodology: Ensuring the expert followed established diagnostic protocols, conducted comprehensive examinations, ordered appropriate testing, and documented reasoning clearly.

Anticipating Challenges: Preparing the expert to explain limitations, acknowledge areas of scientific uncertainty, and distinguish between what is proven and what is suspected.

Defense Strategies to Exclude Testimony

Defense counsel seeking exclusion typically focus on:

Literature Gaps: Identifying peer-reviewed studies that contradict or fail to support the expert's theory, then questioning why the expert disregarded them.

Methodology Critique: Demonstrating that the expert's diagnostic process deviated from accepted standards or failed to rule out obvious alternative causes.

Bias Evidence: Highlighting the expert's history of testifying primarily for plaintiffs, earning substantial litigation income, or holding views outside mainstream medical practice.

Dose-Response Failure: Emphasizing that the expert cannot articulate what level of exposure causes harm or prove that the plaintiff received such exposure.

Effective Daubert challenges narrow or eliminate personal injury claims in a significant percentage of mold cases, fundamentally altering settlement dynamics.

VI. Chronic Inflammatory Response Syndrome and Similar Contested Diagnoses

Perhaps no single medical theory has generated more judicial division in toxic mold litigation than chronic inflammatory response syndrome (CIRS) and related diagnoses attributed to "biotoxin" exposure from water-damaged buildings.

The Theory Behind CIRS

Proponents of CIRS theory argue that certain individuals have genetic susceptibilities that prevent them from properly eliminating biotoxins produced by mold and bacteria in water-damaged environments. According to this theory, biotoxins trigger chronic inflammatory responses affecting multiple body systems, producing symptoms including:

- Fatigue and weakness
- Cognitive dysfunction and memory problems

- Respiratory symptoms
- Muscle aches and joint pain
- Gastrointestinal disturbances
- Neurological symptoms
- Visual disturbances
- Sensitivity to light and noise

CIRS advocates use specific laboratory testing panels, including visual contrast sensitivity testing, certain inflammatory markers, and genetic testing for HLA-DR gene patterns. Treatment typically involves removal from the contaminated environment, binders to eliminate toxins, and sometimes cholestyramine or other medications.

The Scientific Controversy

CIRS remains deeply controversial within the medical community:

Supporters Argue:

- Clinical observations demonstrate consistent symptom patterns in patients exposed to water-damaged buildings
- Laboratory testing shows objective abnormalities
- Patients often improve when removed from the environment and treated
- Genetic susceptibility explains why some individuals develop illness while others do not
- Peer-reviewed publications support the syndrome

Critics Counter:

- Symptoms are nonspecific and overlap with many common conditions
- Laboratory testing lacks standardized validation and reference ranges
- No large-scale epidemiological studies confirm the syndrome

- Improvement may reflect placebo effects or natural symptom fluctuation
- Diagnostic criteria are too broad and may pathologize normal variation
- The theory relies heavily on work by a limited number of researchers
- Major medical organizations have not recognized CIRS as an established diagnosis

How Courts Have Responded

Judicial treatment of CIRS testimony varies significantly by jurisdiction and specific case facts:

Some courts have permitted CIRS testimony when:

- The expert was highly credentialed (board-certified, academic appointment)
- The plaintiff underwent comprehensive diagnostic evaluation
- Laboratory results showed abnormalities
- Temporal correlation between exposure and symptoms was documented
- Improvement after environmental intervention was observed
- The expert could cite peer-reviewed publications
- The testimony was framed as differential diagnosis rather than absolute certainty

Other courts have excluded CIRS testimony when:

- The syndrome lacked general acceptance in the medical community
- Diagnostic testing was not adequately validated
- Symptoms were too subjective and nonspecific
- Alternative causes were not thoroughly investigated
- The expert appeared to diagnose CIRS in most or all mold exposure cases

- The theory relied heavily on unpublished or non-peer-reviewed sources
- Causation claims exceeded what published research supported

The jurisdictional divide is significant. In some states, plaintiffs can expect CIRS testimony to survive Daubert challenges if properly supported. In others, such testimony is routinely excluded as scientifically unreliable.

Strategic Implications

The contested status of CIRS creates difficult strategic decisions for both plaintiffs and defendants:

For Plaintiffs:

Should you advance a CIRS theory knowing it faces significant exclusion risk? The answer depends on several factors:

- Jurisdiction and local judicial precedent
- Strength of alternative theories (allergies, asthma)
- Severity of symptoms and disability
- Quality of expert credentials and methodology
- Whether CIRS is the only plausible explanation or merely one possibility

Some plaintiff attorneys avoid CIRS entirely, focusing on more accepted respiratory conditions. Others pursue CIRS claims aggressively, viewing the potential upside as worth the exclusion risk.

The risk is that aggressive pursuit of a contested theory may undermine credibility regarding accepted conditions. If a judge excludes CIRS testimony, the jury may hear that the plaintiff's expert was deemed unreliable, potentially tainting even valid asthma or allergy claims.

For Defendants:

Should you challenge CIRS testimony or concede some elements? Defense strategies include:

- Moving to exclude the testimony entirely

- Seeking to limit testimony to specific, validated elements
- Allowing the testimony but vigorously cross-examining
- Retaining defense experts to explain scientific weaknesses

Some defense counsel believe aggressive exclusion motions backfire by making CIRS seem more threatening than warranted. Others view exclusion as essential to preventing runaway damages.

The Broader Pattern

CIRS exemplifies a broader pattern in toxic mold litigation: medical theories that have passionate advocates and significant clinical followings but lack the robust epidemiological support and general acceptance that courts increasingly demand.

Other contested diagnoses that follow similar patterns include:

- Multiple chemical sensitivity attributed to mold exposure
- Mold-induced autoimmune conditions
- Electromagnetic hypersensitivity allegedly triggered by mold
- Mycotoxin-induced cognitive impairment

Courts are more receptive when such conditions are presented as working diagnoses or differential considerations rather than certainties, when experts acknowledge scientific limitations, and when testimony focuses on documented symptoms rather than theoretical mechanisms.

VII. The Risk of Overreach: How Aggressive Claims Undermine Credible Ones

One of the most counterproductive mistakes in toxic mold litigation is overstatement. When plaintiffs assert expansive injury theories that cannot withstand scientific scrutiny, they risk not only exclusion of those specific claims but potential damage to the entire case.

How Overreach Backfires

Consider a case with strong facts:

- Documented moisture intrusion lasting eighteen months
- Multiple tenant complaints ignored
- Visible mold growth covering significant areas
- Plaintiff with well-documented asthma exacerbation
- Clear temporal correlation between exposure and symptoms
- Credible medical expert prepared to testify

This is a viable case that could settle for meaningful damages or survive summary judgment. But then plaintiff's counsel decides to add claims for:

- Permanent neurological damage
- Immune system dysfunction
- Future increased cancer risk
- Cognitive impairment preventing the plaintiff from working

The expert retained to support these additional claims relies on controversial testing, unvalidated laboratory panels, and theories not widely accepted in mainstream medicine. Defense counsel moves to exclude the testimony entirely.

Three Possible Outcomes, All Bad

Outcome 1: Total Exclusion

The court finds the expert's methodology so unreliable that it excludes all testimony, including the well-supported asthma claims. The baby goes out with the bathwater. What was a strong respiratory case collapses because it was bundled with speculative systemic claims.

Outcome 2: Partial Exclusion with Taint

The court excludes the systemic claims but permits testimony regarding asthma. However, the jury hears that the plaintiff's expert testimony was deemed partially unreliable. The credibility damage affects even the admissible claims. Jurors wonder: if the expert was wrong about neurological damage, why should we trust the asthma opinion?

Outcome 3: Admission with Devastating Cross-Examination

The testimony survives the admissibility challenge, but defense counsel methodically demolishes the expert's systemic injury opinions on cross-examination, highlighting:

- Lack of peer-reviewed support
- Reliance on invalidated testing
- Failure to rule out alternative causes
- Financial incentive from litigation work
- Previous testimony excluded in other cases

The expert's credibility is destroyed, and again, even valid opinions suffer guilt by association.

Why Attorneys Overreach

Understanding why overreach occurs helps prevent it:

Client Pressure: Clients experiencing genuine suffering want validation and compensation. They may pressure attorneys to pursue every possible theory. Saying "no" to a client in distress is difficult but sometimes necessary.

Economic Incentives: Larger claimed damages create larger potential fees. The temptation to inflate claims can override disciplined case assessment.

Optimism Bias: Attorneys may convince themselves that emerging theories will gain acceptance or that their particular expert will survive challenges that have failed elsewhere.

Competitive Dynamics: When other plaintiffs' firms advertise aggressive mold litigation, conservative case selection may seem like leaving money on the table.

Lack of Scientific Literacy: Some attorneys lack the background to distinguish between emerging theories with potential merit and fringe theories that courts will reject.

The Discipline of Restraint

Experienced toxic mold litigators know that less is often more. Strategic restraint involves:

Limiting Claims to Scientifically Defensible Theories: Focus on conditions with established peer-reviewed support: allergies, asthma exacerbation, respiratory irritation, documented hypersensitivity pneumonitis. These claims survive admissibility challenges and resonate with juries.

Candid Case Assessment: Honestly evaluate whether systemic injury claims have sufficient scientific support in your jurisdiction. If not, do not pursue them.

Conservative Damages Projections: Claim medical expenses you can prove, lost wages you can document, and emotional distress proportional to the documented suffering. Speculative future damages invite skepticism.

Expert Vetting: Retain experts who can withstand rigorous cross-examination, who acknowledge scientific limitations, and whose opinions remain within the mainstream of their specialties.

Transparent Client Counseling: Explain to clients why certain theories, however appealing, will not survive modern evidentiary standards. Manage expectations early.

When Limited Claims Succeed

Paradoxically, narrower claims often produce better results:

Higher Settlement Value: Defense counsel knows that focused, scientifically sound claims are more likely to survive summary judgment and persuade juries. Settlement offers increase when liability and damages are defensible.

Judicial Respect: Judges appreciate attorneys who make realistic claims. That credibility benefits future motions and settlement discussions.

Jury Persuasion: Jurors are more likely to believe modest, well-supported claims than dramatic assertions that strain credulity.

A plaintiff who seeks $150,000 for documented asthma treatment, relocation expenses, and reasonable emotional distress often recovers more than one who seeks $5 million for speculative neurological damage that gets excluded.

Discipline beats drama in the modern mold courtroom.

VIII. Defense Strategy: Narrow and Concede

While plaintiff overreach creates problems, disciplined defense strategy creates opportunities. The most effective defense approach in toxic mold litigation has evolved toward a model that can be characterized as "narrow and concede."

The Strategic Framework

Rather than denying that mold can cause any harm whatsoever (a position that strains credibility and irritates courts), sophisticated defense counsel now typically:

Concede Limited Harm: Acknowledge openly that mold can cause allergic reactions, irritant symptoms, and asthma exacerbation. This concession costs little because damages for these conditions are typically modest, especially when exposure was limited in duration.

Challenge Systemic Claims Aggressively: Focus all resources on excluding or limiting testimony regarding neurological damage, immune dysfunction, cognitive impairment, and other systemic conditions that drive large damage awards.

Emphasize Dose-Response Gaps: Repeatedly highlight that the plaintiff cannot prove exposure levels sufficient to cause serious harm.

Leverage Absence of Standards: Point out that no federal or state agency has established what concentration of mold is dangerous, making claims of "toxic" exposure speculative.

Attack Causation, Not Condition: Rather than arguing that the plaintiff is not really sick, argue that mold exposure did not cause the illness. Alternative causes, pre-existing conditions, and subsequent exposures become the focus.

Why This Approach Works

The narrow-and-concede strategy is effective for several reasons:

Credibility Enhancement: Judges and juries respond better to defendants who acknowledge obvious truths. Admitting that mold can cause allergies makes the defense seem reasonable and science-based rather than obstinate.

Focused Resources: Rather than fighting every element of causation, defense counsel concentrates expertise and litigation resources on the claims that matter most to damages exposure.

Settlement Leverage: When defendants concede respiratory claims but successfully exclude systemic injury testimony, settlement values often drop dramatically. The plaintiff may accept a modest settlement rather than proceed to trial on limited damages.

Judicial Receptiveness: Courts appreciate focused legal arguments. Motions that do not ask judges to accept that mold is completely harmless but instead identify specific scientific weaknesses in systemic injury claims tend to succeed.

Tactical Implementation

In Pleadings:

Rather than categorical denials, defenses admit that mold may cause irritation while specifically denying systemic toxicity, neurological harm, or permanent injury.

In Discovery:

Focus interrogatories and document requests on exposure measurement, alternative causes, pre-existing conditions, and the scientific basis for systemic injury claims. Do not waste resources litigating whether mold can cause sneezing.

In Daubert Motions:

Target the weakest link in plaintiff's causation chain, which is typically specific causation for systemic conditions. Draft motions that acknowledge general causation for allergies while challenging the scientific basis for neurological or immune claims.

At Mediation:

Frame settlement discussions around a realistic assessment of likely trial outcomes. Concede that some damages are likely (property loss, temporary respiratory treatment) while emphasizing that systemic injury claims will likely fail.

At Trial:

Defense opening statements often sound remarkably reasonable: "We acknowledge this was an unfortunate maintenance problem that caused temporary discomfort. What we dispute is the claim that it caused permanent neurological damage. The science simply does not support that conclusion."

The Economic Impact

This strategic approach fundamentally alters case economics:

Before Exclusion:

Plaintiff demands $2 million based on claimed permanent neurological damage, cognitive impairment, and immune dysfunction. Defense evaluation is high because systemic injury claims create jury verdict risk.

After Successful Daubert Motion:

Systemic claims are excluded. Remaining damages include $15,000 in documented respiratory treatment, $8,000 in relocation costs, and potential emotional distress. Settlement value drops to $50,000-$100,000 range.

This $1.9+ million difference in exposure explains why defendants invest heavily in admissibility challenges and why the narrow-and-concede approach dominates modern defense practice.

Limitations and Risks

The strategy is not without risks:

Concession Liability: Acknowledging that mold caused some harm may strengthen liability findings, even if damages are limited.

Partial Settlement Pressure: Once defendants concede respiratory harm, plaintiffs may push for immediate partial settlement of those claims while continuing to litigate systemic theories.

Appeal Complications: Concessions made at trial can complicate appellate arguments if defendants later seek to challenge even limited liability findings.

Public Perception: In high-profile cases, acknowledging harm (even limited harm) may generate negative publicity that corporations wish to avoid.

Despite these limitations, the narrow-and-concede approach has become the dominant defense posture in toxic mold litigation because it aligns defense strategy with scientific reality and judicial expectations.

IX. Plaintiff Adaptation: Evidence-Based Case Development

As defense strategies have evolved toward disciplined narrowing, successful plaintiff attorneys have adapted by embracing evidence-based case development from the outset. The days of filing mold cases based primarily on photographs and client complaints are over. Modern plaintiff practice requires front-end investment in scientific credibility.

The New Plaintiff Practice Model

Leading plaintiff firms in toxic mold litigation now approach cases systematically:

Phase 1: Scientific Screening Before Filing

Before accepting a mold case, evaluate:

Environmental Documentation: Has meaningful testing occurred? Are spore counts, moisture readings, and source identification documented? Or will you need to invest $5,000-$15,000 in environmental assessment before understanding exposure?

Medical Records Review: Do medical records support a plausible causal connection? Are symptoms documented during the exposure period? Did symptoms improve after remediation or relocation? Or are you relying solely on the client's current self-reporting?

Expert Feasibility: Can you retain a credible expert willing to testify in your jurisdiction that the documented exposure caused the claimed condition? Have you had preliminary discussions confirming this before investing significant resources?

Jurisdictional Analysis: How does your jurisdiction treat mold causation testimony? What theories have survived Daubert challenges locally? What damage caps or limitations apply?

Economic Viability: Even if liability and causation are defensible, do the damages justify the litigation costs? Mold cases require $30,000-$100,000+ in expert fees, testing, and trial preparation. Will potential recovery exceed costs by a sufficient margin?

This front-end screening prevents the costly mistake of developing cases that cannot succeed under modern standards.

Phase 2: Early Expert Retention and Integration

Rather than retaining experts after the complaint is filed, sophisticated plaintiff practice now involves:

Medical Expert Involvement Pre-Litigation: Engage a qualified physician to review records and provide a preliminary opinion on causation before filing. This ensures you are not pursuing a theory that your own expert will later abandon.

Environmental Consultant Selection: Retain consultants who follow established protocols, use accredited laboratories, and can withstand cross-examination on methodology. Avoid consultants known primarily for plaintiff work who may face bias challenges.

Building Science Expertise: In construction defect or design failure cases, involve building envelope specialists early to identify moisture intrusion pathways and establish preventability.

Expert Coordination: Ensure your environmental, medical, and building science experts can tell a coherent story. Inconsistencies between experts undermine credibility.

Phase 3: Focused Discovery Targeting Defendant Conduct

Modern plaintiff discovery in mold cases focuses less on proving toxicity and more on proving neglect:

Complaint Documentation: Obtain all tenant complaints, work orders, maintenance requests, and inspection reports. Patterns of ignored complaints drive settlement value.

Internal Communications: Subpoena emails and internal memos discussing the moisture problem, remediation delays, budget constraints, or cosmetic concealment efforts. These documents often prove knowledge and unreasonable response better than any expert testimony.

Prior Incidents: Identify whether the defendant had similar problems in other units, buildings, or properties. Systematic failures increase exposure and settlement leverage.

Insurance Communications: In bad faith cases, obtain claim files, reservation letters, adjuster notes, and coverage analysis. The defendant's own insurance evaluation often reveals liability awareness.

Phase 4: Conservative Case Framing and Damage Presentation

Successful plaintiff attorneys now frame cases around defensible theories:

Lead with Property and Habitability: Emphasize documented moisture intrusion, habitability violations, and property damage. These claims survive regardless of medical causation controversies.

Present Respiratory Claims Conservatively: Focus on allergies, asthma exacerbation, and irritant symptoms supported by mainstream medical literature. Avoid speculative systemic claims unless absolutely necessary and scientifically defensible.

Demonstrate Temporal Correlation: Present clear timelines showing symptom onset during exposure and improvement after remediation. Temporal association strengthens plausibility even when dose cannot be precisely measured.

Rule Out Alternatives Proactively: Anticipate defense arguments about alternative causes and address them through thorough differential diagnosis. Show that your expert investigated and excluded other explanations.

Quantify Damages Specifically: Provide itemized medical expenses, receipts for relocation costs, contractor estimates for remediation, and documented lost wages. Avoid speculative future damages that invite skepticism.

Why This Approach Succeeds

Evidence-based plaintiff practice succeeds because it aligns with how modern courts evaluate mold cases:

Improved Admissibility Outcomes: Well-supported expert testimony survives Daubert challenges, keeping cases viable.

Enhanced Settlement Leverage: Defense counsel knows that disciplined plaintiff cases are more likely to reach juries, increasing settlement pressure.

Judicial Credibility: Judges appreciate attorneys who make realistic claims supported by solid evidence. That credibility benefits all aspects of case management.

Jury Persuasion: Jurors are more likely to award substantial damages when they trust the plaintiff's presentation as honest and scientifically grounded.

The Investment Required

This approach requires significant front-end investment:

- Environmental testing: $3,000-$10,000
- Expert retainers: $10,000-$30,000 pre-trial
- Medical record review and analysis: $2,000-$5,000
- Building science evaluation: $5,000-$15,000

Many cases cannot justify this investment. But cases that can are far more likely to produce meaningful recoveries.

The modern toxic mold plaintiff's bar has split into two groups: attorneys who screen cases rigorously and invest heavily in strong ones, and attorneys who file many cases hoping defendants will settle nuisance value. The first group succeeds. The second increasingly faces summary judgment and sanctions for frivolous claims.

X. The Summary Judgment Battleground: Where Cases Live or Die

Summary judgment motions have become perhaps the most consequential phase of toxic mold litigation. Many cases that survive initial pleading challenges and expensive discovery ultimately fail at summary judgment, making this the critical battleground where evidentiary standards determine outcomes.

The Standard and Its Application

Under Federal Rule of Civil Procedure 56 and similar state standards, summary judgment is appropriate when "there is no genuine dispute as to any material fact and the movant is entitled to judgment as a matter of law." In toxic mold cases, this typically means defendants argue that even viewing evidence in the plaintiff's favor, no reasonable jury could find causation or substantial damages.

The motion typically follows this structure:

Defendant's Opening Salvo:

"Plaintiff cannot establish specific medical causation through admissible evidence. Without causation, personal injury claims must fail as a matter of law."

Plaintiff's Response Challenge:

Plaintiff must demonstrate that admissible expert testimony creates a triable issue on causation. General statements that "mold can cause illness" are insufficient. Specific testimony that "this exposure caused this plaintiff's condition based on reliable methodology" is required.

The Court's Analysis:

Did the plaintiff's expert use reliable scientific methodology? Does the testimony create a genuine factual dispute about whether this specific exposure caused this specific injury? Or are the expert's conclusions speculative, unsupported, or based on unreliable methods?

Common Grounds for Summary Judgment in Mold Cases

Defense motions for summary judgment typically succeed on one or more of these bases:

Failure to Establish Exposure

Even if mold was present, the plaintiff cannot prove exposure levels sufficient to cause harm:

- No air sampling was conducted during the exposure period
- Testing occurred after remediation had begun

- Spore counts were comparable to outdoor concentrations
- Visual evidence shows minor growth insufficient to generate significant airborne exposure

Courts frequently grant summary judgment when exposure is assumed rather than measured.

Insufficient Expert Methodology

The plaintiff's medical expert:

- Failed to conduct differential diagnosis
- Relied on unvalidated laboratory testing
- Did not review complete medical records
- Based opinions on patient history alone without objective findings
- Extrapolated from irrelevant literature
- Could not explain the biological mechanism

Daubert-based summary judgment effectively ends the case by excluding the only evidence that could prove causation.

Alternative Causation Not Ruled Out

The plaintiff's medical condition can be explained by:

- Pre-existing conditions documented in medical records
- Subsequent exposures or injuries
- Other environmental factors (smoking, occupational exposures, pet allergies)
- Common illnesses unrelated to mold

When defense experts identify plausible alternative causes that plaintiff's expert did not adequately address, summary judgment often follows.

Speculative or Conclusory Causation

The expert's opinion amounts to "it could have been mold" rather than "it was more likely than not mold." Courts require affirmative proof, not mere possibility.

Example of insufficient testimony: "Mold exposure can cause respiratory symptoms, and the plaintiff had respiratory symptoms, so mold probably caused them."

Example of sufficient testimony: "I examined the plaintiff, reviewed environmental testing showing Aspergillus concentrations 30 times outdoor levels, documented the temporal correlation between exposure and symptom onset, ruled out seasonal allergies through testing, confirmed improvement after remediation, and concluded to a reasonable medical probability that this specific mold exposure caused this plaintiff's documented asthma exacerbation."

Damages Too Speculative

Even if causation survives, damages claims may fail when:

- Medical expenses are not documented
- Future care projections lack foundation
- Lost wage claims are not supported by employment records
- Emotional distress claims are not tied to documented impact

Partial Summary Judgment: The Common Outcome

Total summary judgment dismissing all claims is less common than partial summary judgment narrowing the case:

Typical Pattern:

- Systemic injury claims: GRANTED (excluded)
- Neurological damage: GRANTED (excluded)
- Future medical monitoring: GRANTED (speculative)
- Respiratory injury (allergies/asthma): DENIED (triable issue)
- Property damage: DENIED (damages disputed)
- Emotional distress: DENIED (factual question)
- Punitive damages: GRANTED (insufficient evidence of malice)

This winnowing fundamentally changes case value. What began as a $5 million demand drops to a $200,000 realistic settlement range.

Strategic Implications

For Plaintiffs:

Summary judgment risk requires:

Robust Expert Reports Early

Provide detailed expert reports during discovery that demonstrate methodology, rule out alternatives, and establish causation clearly. Do not wait until deposition to develop the opinion.

Document Everything

Medical records, environmental reports, photographs, complaint logs, and remediation invoices must be organized and authenticated. Gaps in documentation invite summary judgment.

Address Weaknesses Proactively

If your case has problems (late testing, alternative causes, mild symptoms), address them in your expert's report and deposition testimony. Hoping defense counsel will not notice guarantees failure.

Prepare for Daubert

Assume your expert will face a Daubert challenge. Ensure methodology can withstand scrutiny. If it cannot, the case will not survive summary judgment.

For Defendants:

Summary judgment should be the goal in most mold cases involving systemic injury claims:

- **Move Early and Comprehensively:** File summary judgment motions addressing all weak causation links. Do not assume plaintiffs will voluntarily narrow claims.
- **Focus on Methodology:** Attack the scientific foundation of expert opinions. Courts grant summary judgment when methodology is unreliable, even if the expert is credentialed.
- **Highlight Evidence Gaps:** Emphasize what plaintiff cannot prove: dose, mechanism, exclusion of alternatives. Absence of evidence becomes evidence supporting summary judgment.

- **Seek Partial Relief:** Even if some claims survive, eliminating high-value systemic injury claims through partial summary judgment changes settlement dynamics dramatically.

The Evolving Standard

Courts have become increasingly willing to grant summary judgment in mold cases as the scientific issues have become familiar. Early mold litigation benefited from judicial uncertainty; judges hesitated to exclude novel claims. By 2026, mold causation theories are no longer novel. Courts have seen the same arguments repeatedly and have become comfortable distinguishing between scientifically supported claims and speculative ones.

This evolution means that summary judgment success rates for defendants have increased substantially over the past decade. Plaintiffs can no longer rely on dramatic photos and sympathetic clients to survive summary judgment. Scientific proof is required, and courts will enforce that requirement at the summary judgment stage rather than allowing questionable claims to reach juries.

XI. Judicial Attitudes Toward Emotional Distress: The Safety Valve When Medical Claims Fail

Even when courts exclude or limit systemic medical injury testimony, many jurisdictions remain receptive to emotional distress claims arising from living in mold-contaminated conditions. This creates an interesting dynamic: plaintiffs may lose the battle over toxic injury but win compensation for the psychological impact of contamination.

The Doctrinal Framework

Emotional distress claims in toxic mold cases typically arise under several theories:

Negligent Infliction of Emotional Distress

Some jurisdictions permit recovery for emotional distress caused by defendant's negligent conduct, even absent physical injury. The plaintiff must typically prove:

- Defendant owed a duty of care

- Defendant breached that duty
- Plaintiff suffered serious emotional distress
- The distress was a foreseeable result of the breach

In mold cases, this might involve a landlord's prolonged failure to remediate despite knowledge of tenant distress.

Intentional Infliction of Emotional Distress

Where defendant's conduct was particularly egregious, plaintiffs may assert intentional infliction claims. This requires proof that:

- Defendant's conduct was extreme and outrageous
- Defendant intended to cause emotional distress or acted with reckless disregard
- Plaintiff suffered severe emotional distress
- Defendant's conduct was the cause

Documented internal communications showing deliberate concealment or callous indifference can support these claims.

Habitability-Based Distress: In landlord-tenant cases, emotional distress may flow directly from habitability violations. Some courts allow distress damages as a component of habitability breach without requiring separate proof under tort standards.

Fraud-Based Distress: In nondisclosure cases, emotional distress may accompany fraud claims, particularly where buyers discover they were misled about serious contamination.

The Physical Injury Requirement: Jurisdictional Variation

Perhaps the most significant jurisdictional divide concerns whether physical injury is required to recover emotional distress damages:

Physical Injury Required Jurisdictions: Some states require plaintiffs to prove physical injury before recovering emotional distress damages in negligence cases. This requirement serves to:

- Limit speculative claims
- Ensure objective verification of harm

- Prevent trivial complaints from generating damages

In these jurisdictions, documented respiratory symptoms, even if mild, may satisfy the physical injury threshold and open the door to substantial emotional distress damages.

The strategic implication: even when systemic injury claims fail, proving minor physical manifestations (allergic rhinitis, occasional wheezing, irritated eyes) becomes critical because it unlocks emotional distress recovery.

No Physical Injury Required Jurisdictions: Other states permit emotional distress recovery based solely on the distress itself, provided it is serious and reasonable under the circumstances. Courts in these jurisdictions may award substantial emotional distress damages even when medical causation for physical injury fails entirely.

Contract vs. Tort Distinctions: Some jurisdictions that limit emotional distress damages in tort actions permit them more liberally in contract cases. Habitability claims, being quasi-contractual, may therefore support distress damages even where pure negligence claims would not.

What Courts Consider Reasonable Distress in Mold Cases

Judicial attitudes toward the reasonableness of emotional distress in mold cases have evolved through recurring fact patterns:

Generally Accepted Bases for Distress:

Courts typically find emotional distress reasonable when based on:

- **Fear for Children's Health:** Parents' anxiety about exposing children to contaminated environments resonates strongly with courts and juries. Even when medical proof of actual harm is weak, courts often find parental distress foreseeable and compensable.

- **Displacement and Loss of Home:** The disruption of being forced to relocate, live in temporary housing, and lose the sense of home security causes genuine distress that courts recognize as legitimate.

- **Visible Contamination:** Living with visible mold growth, persistent musty odors, and obvious water damage creates reasonable distress about health and safety, even if actual medical injury cannot be proven.

- **Institutional Indifference:** When landlords or property managers ignore repeated complaints, dismiss concerns, or delay remediation unreasonably, the resulting sense of helplessness and frustration constitutes compensable distress.

- **Financial Stress**
  The costs of temporary housing, property replacement, medical evaluation, and legal fees create genuine anxiety that courts may compensate.

Generally Rejected Bases for Distress:

Courts are more skeptical of distress claims based on:

- **Speculative Future Illness:** Fear of developing cancer, neurological disease, or other serious conditions years in the future generally fails without credible scientific support that such risks are real.

- **Media-Fueled Panic:** Distress based primarily on sensationalized media coverage about "toxic black mold" rather than actual conditions in the plaintiff's residence may be deemed unreasonable.

- **Minor, Temporary Exposure:** Brief exposure to limited mold growth that was promptly remediated typically does not support substantial distress damages.

- **Self-Inflicted Prolongation:** When plaintiffs refuse reasonable remediation offers, decline to relocate despite available alternatives, or otherwise prolong their exposure unnecessarily, distress damages may be reduced or denied.

Quantifying Emotional Distress: The Practical Challenge

Unlike medical expenses or property damage, emotional distress has no objective market value. Courts and juries must assess damages based on:

- **Severity and Duration:** How serious was the distress and how long did it last? Temporary anxiety resolves differently than ongoing trauma requiring therapy.

- **Objective Manifestations:** Did the plaintiff seek counseling? Take medication for anxiety or depression? Experience documented sleep disturbance, panic attacks, or other objective symptoms?

- **Impact on Daily Life:** Did the distress interfere with work, relationships, parenting, or normal activities? Testimony from family members, employers, or therapists can establish impact.

Proportionality to Conditions
Is the claimed distress proportional to the actual conditions experienced? Courts are skeptical when claimed distress seems exaggerated relative to exposure.

Typical Range in Mold Cases

Emotional distress damages in mold litigation typically range from:

- Minor claims: $5,000 - $15,000 for temporary, mild distress
- Moderate claims: $20,000 - $75,000 for significant, documented distress lasting months
- Substantial claims: $100,000 - $300,000 for severe, prolonged distress with objective manifestations and therapeutic intervention
- Extraordinary claims: $500,000+ reserved for truly egregious cases involving vulnerable plaintiffs and extreme defendant misconduct

Strategic Use of Emotional Distress Claims

For Plaintiffs:

Emotional distress claims serve several strategic functions:

- **Backup Recovery When Medical Claims Fail:** When Daubert challenges eliminate systemic injury claims, emotional distress may preserve meaningful damages. A case that loses $2 million in medical damages may retain $150,000 in distress damages.
- **Leverage in Settlement:** Defendants cannot easily predict what juries will award for emotional distress. This unpredictability creates settlement pressure even when medical causation is weak.
- **Humanizing the Case:** Emotional distress testimony allows plaintiffs to describe their experience in personal, relatable terms rather than through sterile medical records. Jurors connect with fear, frustration, and helplessness.
- **Aggregating Damages:** In family cases, each family member may claim individual emotional distress, multiplying damages even when property and medical damages are fixed.

- **Avoiding Expert Battles:** Unlike medical causation, emotional distress typically does not require expert testimony. Plaintiff testimony, corroborated by family and circumstantial evidence, may suffice.

Best Practices for Plaintiff Counsel:

- **Document Contemporaneously:** Encourage clients to keep journals documenting their emotional state, sleep patterns, anxiety triggers, and daily impact. Contemporary documentation is more credible than retrospective testimony.
- **Seek Therapeutic Support:** Referrals to counselors or therapists create objective records of distress and demonstrate severity. Treatment records provide powerful corroboration.
- **Avoid Exaggeration:** Moderate, honest testimony about genuine distress is more persuasive than dramatic claims that seem rehearsed or inflated.
- **Connect to Defendant Conduct:** Emphasize not just the presence of mold but the defendant's response. Distress from ignored complaints and institutional indifference resonates more than distress from contamination alone.

For Defendants:

Defendants approach emotional distress claims with several tactics:

- **Minimize Through Quick Remediation:** Prompt, thorough remediation limits the duration and severity of distress. Evidence that defendants acted reasonably once aware reduces damages.
- **Challenge Objective Evidence:** If plaintiffs claim severe distress but never sought counseling, never missed work, and continued normal activities, defendants argue the distress was minor.
- **Comparative Fault:** When plaintiffs refused remediation access, delayed notification, or contributed to conditions through poor housekeeping, defendants seek to reduce distress damages proportionally.
- **Highlight Alternative Stressors:** Financial problems, relationship issues, employment difficulties, or health conditions unrelated to mold may explain emotional symptoms better than contamination.

- **Proportionality Arguments:** Defendants emphasize that distress damages should be proportional to actual conditions. Minor, brief exposure should not generate major emotional distress awards.

Motion Practice
In jurisdictions requiring physical injury, defendants may move to exclude emotional distress claims entirely when no physical manifestation exists.

The Compensation Function

Emotional distress damages in mold litigation serve an important compensation function that courts increasingly recognize. Even when toxic injury claims fail scientifically, genuine suffering occurs when:

- Families are displaced from their homes
- Parents fear for children's safety
- Tenants feel trapped in unhealthy conditions
- Property owners discover they were deceived

This suffering deserves recognition and compensation, even if it does not fit neatly into traditional toxic tort frameworks.

The challenge is distinguishing between:

- Reasonable distress warranting compensation
- Speculative fear unsupported by actual risk
- Exaggerated claims designed to inflate damages

Courts navigate this distinction case by case, examining credibility, proportionality, and objective corroboration. The result is a somewhat unpredictable but generally workable system that provides a safety valve when medical causation fails but genuine harm occurred.

XII. The Appellate Influence: How Higher Courts Have Shaped Evidentiary Standards

While trial courts make initial admissibility and summary judgment decisions, appellate courts have played a crucial role in shaping the evidentiary landscape of toxic mold litigation. Over two decades, patterns have emerged in how appellate courts review mold-related expert testimony, and these patterns now guide trial court decision-making.

The Appellate Standard of Review

Appellate courts typically review evidentiary rulings for abuse of discretion, meaning trial courts have substantial latitude in admissibility decisions. However, appellate opinions still influence the field by:

- **Identifying Common Errors:** Appellate decisions catalog mistakes that trial courts should avoid, creating practical guidance.
- **Clarifying Legal Standards:** When trial courts misapply Daubert or similar standards, appellate correction establishes clearer frameworks.
- **Signaling Skepticism:** Even when affirming trial court decisions, appellate opinions may signal skepticism toward certain theories, influencing future litigation.
- **Creating Precedent:** Published appellate decisions become binding or persuasive authority, shaping how future cases are evaluated.

Key Themes in Appellate Mold Decisions

Reviewing appellate case law from 2005-2026, several consistent themes emerge:

Theme 1: Affirming Exclusion of Speculative Causation

Appellate courts have consistently upheld exclusion of expert testimony when:

The expert assumed exposure without measurement: Courts have repeatedly held that expert opinions based on assumptions about exposure levels, rather than actual testing data, are inadmissible. The absence of air sampling or other objective exposure measurement is often fatal to causation testimony.

Example pattern from decisions: "The expert testified that plaintiff was exposed to 'high levels' of mold based solely on photographs of visible growth. Without air sampling, moisture testing, or other objective measurement, this conclusion was speculative and properly excluded."

The expert failed to rule out alternative causes: Differential diagnosis requires more than listing possible causes; it requires investigating and eliminating alternatives through appropriate testing and analysis. Appellate courts have affirmed exclusion when this process was inadequate.

The expert relied on unreliable testing: Urinary mycotoxin panels, certain inflammatory marker tests, and visual contrast sensitivity testing have faced particular skepticism. When trial courts exclude testimony based on such testing, appellate courts typically affirm if the trial court articulated valid reliability concerns.

Theme 2: Deference to Trial Court Gatekeeping

Appellate courts have generally deferred to trial court admissibility decisions, whether excluding or admitting expert testimony, as long as the trial court:

- Conducted a proper Daubert hearing or analysis
- Considered the relevant reliability factors
- Explained its reasoning adequately
- Did not rely on clearly erroneous findings

This deference means that outcomes often depend more on trial court judges than appellate review. However, it also means that well-reasoned trial court exclusions are likely to survive appeal.

Theme 3: Distinguishing Between Accepted and Novel Theories

Appellate courts have drawn clear lines between:

Accepted: Testimony that mold caused or exacerbated allergies, asthma, or respiratory irritation receives favorable appellate treatment. Courts affirm admission of such testimony when based on proper methodology.

Novel: Testimony about systemic toxicity, neurological damage, or emerging syndromes faces greater scrutiny. Appellate courts affirm exclusion when trial courts find insufficient peer-reviewed support or general acceptance.

Theme 4: Emphasizing Dose-Response Requirements

Multiple appellate decisions have emphasized that toxic exposure claims require proof of dose sufficient to cause injury. Courts have affirmed summary judgment or exclusion when plaintiffs could not establish:

- What concentration of mold causes the alleged condition
- What concentration the plaintiff was exposed to
- Why that exposure was sufficient to cause harm

One recurring appellate statement: "The expert's inability to articulate a dose-response relationship or to establish that plaintiff's exposure exceeded any identified threshold rendered the causation opinion unreliable."

Theme 5: Rejecting Temporal Correlation Alone

While temporal correlation (symptoms began during exposure, improved after removal) is relevant to causation, appellate courts have consistently held that temporal association alone is insufficient without additional scientific support.

Appellate decisions affirm exclusion when experts rely primarily on "post hoc ergo propter hoc" reasoning (after this, therefore because of this) without connecting temporal correlation to biological mechanism, dose, or differential diagnosis.

Influential Appellate Decisions

While specific case citations would require current legal research, certain types of appellate decisions have been particularly influential:

- **Construction Defect Cases:** Appellate decisions in construction defect mold litigation have often focused on economic loss doctrine, statute of repose issues, and allocation of liability among multiple defendants. These decisions shape whether mold claims can proceed as pure property damage claims or require personal injury.
- **Insurance Coverage Cases:** Appellate interpretation of mold exclusions, resulting loss provisions, and anti-concurrent causation clauses has created a body of law that insurance carriers and policyholders both rely on when assessing coverage.
- **Daubert Applications:** State appellate courts applying Daubert to mold cases have created frameworks that trial courts follow when evaluating expert reliability. These decisions identify which factors matter most in mold-specific contexts.
- **Summary Judgment Standards:** Appellate review of summary judgment in mold cases has clarified what level of expert support is

necessary to create a triable issue of fact on causation.

The Cumulative Effect

The cumulative effect of appellate decisions over two decades has been to:

- **Narrow Viable Claims:** Each appellate decision affirming exclusion of speculative theories makes trial courts more willing to exclude similar testimony in future cases.
- **Raise Evidentiary Bars:** As appellate courts identify methodological deficiencies, trial courts demand more rigorous expert support to avoid reversal.
- **Create Predictability:** Patterns in appellate decisions allow attorneys to predict with reasonable accuracy which claims will survive and which will fail.
- **Discourage Marginal Cases:** When appellate courts consistently affirm summary judgment in weak cases, plaintiff attorneys become more selective about which cases to file.

Strategic Implications

For Trial Courts:

Trial judges now have substantial appellate guidance on mold causation issues. This reduces uncertainty and provides confidence when excluding questionable expert testimony.

For Litigants:

Understanding appellate patterns allows both sides to assess case strength more accurately. Plaintiffs can identify which theories have appellate support. Defendants can predict which exclusion arguments are likely to succeed.

For Settlement:

Appellate precedent creates baseline expectations that guide settlement negotiations. When appellate courts in a jurisdiction consistently exclude systemic injury claims, settlement values adjust accordingly.

The Ongoing Evolution

Appellate influence continues to evolve as new issues emerge:

- **Emerging Science:** As new research is published on mold-related illness, appellate courts will address whether it provides sufficient support for previously rejected theories.
- **Technology and Testing:** New testing methodologies and environmental monitoring technologies will require appellate courts to evaluate their reliability.
- **Insurance Innovation:** As insurers develop new exclusion language, appellate courts will interpret its scope and effect.

The appellate process ensures that toxic mold litigation does not remain static. Each decision adds to the body of law, creating an increasingly sophisticated framework for evaluating these scientifically complex claims.

XIII. The Balance Between Skepticism and Access to Justice

The judicial caution documented throughout this chapter raises an important question: Has the pendulum swung too far? In demanding rigorous scientific proof, do courts risk denying legitimate claims by families genuinely harmed by substandard housing conditions?

This tension between preventing junk science and ensuring access to justice defines much of the modern debate about toxic mold litigation.

The Case for Judicial Skepticism

Proponents of strict evidentiary standards argue that judicial gatekeeping serves essential functions:

- **Protecting Jury Competence:** Juries are ill-equipped to resolve contested scientific disputes. When experts disagree fundamentally about whether mold can cause systemic illness, asking laypersons to decide which scientist is correct invites arbitrary verdicts based on sympathy rather than evidence.
- **Preventing Speculative Damages:** Allowing claims based on unproven theories creates risk of substantial damages awards for injuries that may not exist or may have other causes. This punishes defendants for harm they did not cause.

- **Maintaining Scientific Integrity:** Courts should not validate fringe medical theories by allowing them to reach juries. Doing so gives credence to unproven concepts and may encourage development of dubious diagnostic industries.
- **Ensuring Fairness to Defendants:** Property owners should not face liability for causing injuries that mainstream science does not recognize. Liability should be based on breach of known duties, not evolving theories that lack consensus.
- **Resource Allocation:** Judicial resources should focus on claims with scientific merit rather than processing speculative lawsuits that cannot survive rigorous review.

The Case for Greater Access

Critics of strict gatekeeping argue that judicial skepticism creates unfair barriers:

- **Legitimate Harms Go Uncompensated:** Families living in objectively substandard, contaminated housing suffer genuine harm even if precise biological mechanisms cannot be proven with scientific certainty. Requiring proof beyond current scientific consensus denies recovery to victims of clear negligence.
- **Scientific Knowledge Is Incomplete:** Medicine does not fully understand all mold-related health effects. Demanding peer-reviewed consensus before allowing recovery means early victims cannot be compensated until science catches up, which may take decades.
- **Economic Barriers to Expert Testimony:** The cost of retaining highly credentialed experts who can survive Daubert challenges creates a wealth-based barrier to justice. Lower-income plaintiffs cannot afford the expert investments required under strict standards.
- **Imbalance Favors Institutional Defendants:** Large landlords, corporations, and insurers can afford sophisticated defense experts and aggressive motion practice. Strict evidentiary standards disproportionately benefit well-resourced defendants over individual plaintiffs.
- **Ignoring Common Sense:** Sometimes the connection between exposure and harm is obvious even without perfect scientific proof.

A child who was healthy, lived in mold-contaminated housing, became ill, improved after moving, and worsened upon return has an intuitively clear causal story even if dose-response relationships are undefined.

Finding the Middle Ground

The most thoughtful judicial approaches attempt to balance these competing concerns by:

- **Accepting Well-Established Conditions:** Courts should readily admit testimony regarding allergies, asthma, and respiratory irritation where peer-reviewed support is strong. Skepticism should not extend to well-accepted medical knowledge.
- **Requiring but Not Overemphasizing Dose Evidence:** While perfect dose measurement may be impossible, plaintiffs should demonstrate meaningful exposure through some objective evidence (environmental testing, moisture documentation, visible growth extent). Complete absence of exposure evidence should be fatal, but imperfect measurement should not be.
- **Evaluating Methodology, Not Conclusions:** Focus Daubert analysis on whether the expert used reliable methods, not whether the conclusion seems correct to the judge. An expert using proper differential diagnosis, appropriate testing, and thorough alternative cause investigation should be heard even if the condition diagnosed is not universally recognized.
- **Considering Vulnerable Populations:** Children, elderly, and immunocompromised individuals may experience effects not seen in healthy adults. Courts should account for heightened susceptibility rather than requiring proof based on general population studies.
- **Allowing Property-Based Claims:** Even when medical causation fails, courts should permit claims based on property damage, habitability violations, and nondisclosure. These theories do not require contested medical proof and ensure accountability for objective failures.
- **Proportionality in Damages:** Allow cases to proceed but carefully scrutinize damages claims. A plaintiff who cannot prove serious systemic injury may still recover for documented property loss, temporary respiratory symptoms, and reasonable emotional

distress.

The Practical Reality

In practice, most jurisdictions have found workable compromises:

- **Respiratory Claims Usually Survive:** Courts generally admit testimony regarding allergies and asthma, ensuring plaintiffs are not completely barred from recovery.
- **Systemic Claims Face Scrutiny:** Claims of neurological damage or chronic multi-system illness face higher bars, preventing speculative theories from reaching juries.
- **Property Claims Remain Viable:** Habitability, negligence, and nondisclosure claims based on property conditions proceed regardless of medical causation disputes.
- **Settlement Occurs:** Most cases settle for amounts reflecting this middle ground: meaningful compensation for respiratory effects and property damage, but not windfalls based on unproven systemic illness.

This practical compromise may not satisfy either extreme. Plaintiffs' advocates argue it undercompensates victims. Defense advocates worry it still allows questionable claims to extract nuisance settlements.

The Philosophical Question

Ultimately, the balance between skepticism and access reflects competing visions of law's purpose:

- **Law as Truth-Seeking:** Under this view, courts should determine what actually happened based on reliable evidence. Compensation should follow only when causation is proven with confidence approaching scientific certainty.
- **Law as Harm-Redressing:** Under this view, courts should compensate victims of negligence and ensure accountability, even when causation cannot be proven with scientific precision. Probability and reasonableness should suffice.

Neither vision is wholly right or wrong. Both serve important functions. The challenge is finding the appropriate balance in specific contexts.

The Current Equilibrium

As of 2026, judicial attitudes reflect a middle position that has stabilized:

Courts reject: Speculative systemic toxicity claims lacking scientific support

Courts accept: Respiratory injury claims based on established medical knowledge

Courts evaluate: Emerging theories on methodology and credibility rather than categorical acceptance or rejection

Courts preserve: Property-based claims ensuring accountability for maintenance and disclosure failures

This equilibrium is unlikely to shift dramatically absent major scientific developments or legislative intervention. It represents judicial pragmatism: protecting against junk science while ensuring that genuine harms find legal remedy.

The question is not whether this balance is perfect. It is whether it is workable. Most participants in the system, even those dissatisfied with aspects of it, would likely concede that it functions reasonably well given the competing pressures.

XIV. The 2026 Reality: Where Judicial Skepticism Has Settled

After two decades of evolution, toxic mold litigation in 2026 reflects several settled realities that define the judicial landscape:

What Courts Now Accept Without Controversy

Mold as a Legitimate Environmental Concern: Courts no longer question whether indoor mold can create health and property problems. Judicial skepticism focuses on specific causation and injury theories, not whether mold matters at all.

Respiratory Effects are Real: Allergies, asthma exacerbation, and irritant effects from mold exposure are universally recognized. Testimony supporting these conditions typically survives admissibility challenges.

Property Damage is Compensable: Remediation costs, structural repairs, and property value loss from mold contamination are legitimate damages requiring no medical proof.

Habitability Violations Exist: Courts readily find that chronic moisture intrusion and extensive mold growth can constitute habitability violations, triggering landlord liability.

Disclosure Duties Apply: Sellers and landlords must disclose known mold problems in most jurisdictions, and failure to do so supports fraud or concealment claims.

What Courts Remain Skeptical About

Systemic Toxicity from Typical Exposure: Claims that routine residential mold exposure causes neurological damage, immune dysfunction, or chronic multi-system illness face substantial hurdles absent extraordinary proof.

Causation Without Dose: Courts remain unwilling to accept causation testimony that cannot explain exposure levels or dose-response relationships.

Novel Syndromes: Conditions lacking general medical acceptance or validated diagnostic criteria face exclusion in many jurisdictions.

Speculative Future Harms: Claims about increased future disease risk (cancer, neurological disease) without current manifestation rarely survive.

Invisible Injury: Subjective complaints without objective findings or corroborating test results generate skepticism, particularly regarding permanent injury.

The Practical Consequences

This settled landscape creates predictable patterns:

Case Selection: Plaintiff attorneys screen cases more rigorously, pursuing only those with documented respiratory injury, substantial property damage, or egregious defendant conduct.

Settlement Values: Ranges have stabilized based on injury type:

- Pure respiratory/allergy cases: $25,000 - $150,000

- Property damage dominant cases: $50,000 - $500,000
- Combined respiratory and property with strong neglect evidence: $150,000 - $750,000
- Extraordinary cases with vulnerable plaintiffs and systemic failures: $1 million+

Litigation Strategy: Both sides now understand the evidentiary battlefield and tailor strategies accordingly, focusing resources on admissibility fights rather than assuming all claims reach juries.

Expert Markets: Experts who can survive modern scrutiny command premium fees. Those with histories of exclusion struggle to find work. The expert witness market has professionalized.

Insurance Responses: Carriers have refined exclusions and adjusted reserves based on realistic exposure, reducing the panic-driven overcorrection of the early 2000s while maintaining protective policy language.

The Stability Factor

Perhaps most significantly, the field has achieved stability. The wild swings from "next asbestos" predictions to defense victories excluding all claims have moderated into a steady state where:

- Legitimate claims based on accepted science succeed
- Speculative claims lacking scientific support fail
- Property-based accountability continues regardless of medical disputes
- Settlement values reflect realistic assessment of trial outcomes

This stability benefits the legal system, litigants, insurers, and property owners by creating predictability and discouraging both frivolous claims and unreasonable denials.

XV. Conclusion: Discipline Through Skepticism

Evidentiary skepticism has fundamentally reshaped toxic mold litigation. The field has matured from early sensationalism through judicial overcorrection toward a disciplined, evidence-based practice area.

Courts now approach mold cases with informed caution, neither dismissing all claims as junk science nor accepting expansive toxic injury theories without rigorous proof. This skepticism serves important functions: protecting juries from unreliable expert testimony, ensuring compensation is based on proven harm, and preventing speculative theories from generating arbitrary verdicts.

But skepticism is not hostility. Courts still recognize that:

- Mold contamination causes genuine respiratory harm
- Property damage from moisture intrusion deserves compensation
- Habitability failures breach landlord duties
- Nondisclosure of known problems constitutes fraud
- Institutional neglect warrants accountability

The result is a field defined by proof over panic, methodology over speculation, and discipline over drama.

The Central Lessons for Practitioners

For Plaintiff Attorneys: Success requires accepting judicial skepticism as a permanent feature of the landscape and adapting by:

- Screening cases for scientific viability before filing
- Retaining highly credentialed experts using mainstream methodology
- Focusing on well-accepted conditions rather than pushing boundaries
- Emphasizing property damage and habitability violations
- Documenting exposure and defendant conduct thoroughly
- Managing client expectations about systemic injury claims

For Defense Counsel: Effective defense requires understanding which battles to fight:

- Conceding respiratory effects that are scientifically established
- Challenging aggressively on systemic toxicity and novel syndromes
- Exploiting dose-response gaps in causation testimony
- Moving for summary judgment on weak causation evidence
- Settling cases with strong liability evidence before trial

For Judges: The gatekeeping role requires balancing access to justice with scientific reliability:

- Applying Daubert factors consistently but not mechanically
- Distinguishing between accepted and novel medical theories
- Evaluating methodology rather than prejudging outcomes
- Allowing legitimate claims while excluding junk science
- Explaining exclusion decisions with sufficient detail to guide future litigation

The Path Forward

Judicial skepticism in toxic mold cases will likely persist because it serves legitimate purposes. Courts have learned from two decades of litigation that:

- Mold fears can be exaggerated
- Expert testimony can be unreliable
- Damages can be speculative
- Scientific uncertainty invites exploitation

But courts have also learned that:

- Indoor air quality matters
- Moisture intrusion causes real harm
- Negligent property management deserves accountability

- Families living in substandard housing suffer genuine injury

The challenge is honoring both realities: maintaining rigorous standards while ensuring access to justice for legitimate claims.

By 2026, courts have largely succeeded in striking that balance. The toxic mold courtroom rewards careful preparation, scientific credibility, honest presentation, and realistic claims. It punishes speculation, exaggeration, methodological sloppiness, and overreach.

This is not a field for attorneys seeking quick settlements on fear-based claims. It is a field for practitioners willing to master complex science, invest in credible experts, document thoroughly, and frame claims conservatively.

Scientific resistance has not killed toxic mold litigation. It has refined it into a disciplined specialty where evidence determines outcomes.

The next chapter turns from courtroom battles to jury persuasion, examining how attorneys translate complex environmental science, building failures, and medical causation into compelling trial narratives that resonate with everyday citizens tasked with deciding these technically demanding cases.

19

Trial Practice in Toxic Mold Litigation

Presenting Science, Human Impact, and Responsibility

I. When Mold Cases Reach the Jury: The Paradox of Trial in a Settlement-Driven Field

Most toxic mold cases resolve before trial. Settlement rates in this field exceed 90%, driven by evidentiary uncertainty, expert costs, insurance dynamics, and the unpredictability of jury verdicts. Yet the relatively small percentage of cases that do proceed to trial play an outsized role in shaping the entire field.

Trial verdicts establish valuation benchmarks. Trial outcomes influence settlement negotiations in pending cases. Trial strategies tested in court become templates for future litigation. And trial results generate appellate decisions that refine evidentiary standards.

When settlement fails, it typically fails for identifiable reasons that make trial particularly challenging:

1. **Disputed Causation:** The parties fundamentally disagree about whether mold exposure caused the plaintiff's condition, and neither side believes the risk of an adverse ruling exceeds the cost of trying the case.
2. **Coverage Disputes:** Insurance carriers contest coverage, leaving defendants without settlement funds and forcing trial on both liability and coverage issues simultaneously.
3. **Punitive Exposure:** Evidence of egregious conduct creates potential for punitive damages that defendants refuse to settle but plaintiffs believe a jury will award.
4. **Principle Over Economics:** Occasionally, institutional defendants try cases on principle, seeking to establish precedent or resist what they view as extortionate demands.
5. **Unrealistic Expectations:** One or both parties misjudge case value, creating a settlement gap that cannot be bridged through negotiation.

These selection pressures mean that cases reaching trial tend to be harder, more contested, and more uncertain than the average mold dispute. Trial attorneys must navigate not only the inherent scientific complexity of mold litigation but also the additional challenges that prevented settlement.

This chapter examines how experienced litigators present toxic mold cases to juries, balancing scientific credibility with human impact, technical accuracy with accessible narrative, and legal precision with persuasive storytelling.

II. The Fundamental Challenge: Translating Complexity Into Clarity

Toxic mold trials present a unique communications challenge. Jurors must understand:

- **Building Science:** How water intrudes through building envelopes, why certain construction details fail, what drainage planes and flashing systems do, and how HVAC systems affect humidity.
- **Microbiology:** What mold is, how it reproduces, why certain species proliferate in specific conditions, and what spore counts mean.

- **Medical Causation:** How mold affects the respiratory system, what dose-response relationships exist, why some individuals are more susceptible, and how physicians differentiate mold-related illness from other conditions.

- **Environmental Testing:** How air sampling works, what laboratory analysis reveals, why outdoor comparisons matter, and what testing limitations exist.

- **Insurance Coverage:** How policies define covered perils, what exclusions mean, how resulting loss provisions operate, and when carriers act in bad faith.

Jurors bring no specialized knowledge to these topics. Most have never heard of Stachybotrys chartarum, cannot define hypersensitivity pneumonitis, and have never considered how window flashing prevents water intrusion.

Yet attorneys must convey sufficient understanding for jurors to make informed decisions about technical causation disputes while maintaining engagement and avoiding information overload that produces confusion or disengagement.

The Translation Imperative

Successful trial attorneys in mold cases become translators, converting technical concepts into accessible language without oversimplifying to the point of inaccuracy.

This requires several skills:

- **Metaphor and Analogy:** Complex scientific concepts become comprehensible through comparison to familiar experiences. Mold spore reproduction might be explained by analogy to dandelion seeds spreading in wind. Building envelope failures might be compared to a leaky umbrella that seems fine until rain tests it.

- **Visual Communication:** Diagrams, photographs, demonstrative exhibits, and animations convey information more efficiently than verbal explanation alone. A simple cross-section diagram showing how water travels through a wall assembly may communicate in seconds what would take minutes to explain verbally.

- **Progressive Building:** Rather than presenting all information at once, effective attorneys build understanding progressively, establishing foundational concepts before advancing to more complex ideas.

- **Repetition Through Variation:** Key concepts must be repeated multiple times through different witnesses and exhibits, but repetition must vary presentation to maintain engagement.
- **Ruthless Editing:** Not every technical detail matters to the jury's decision. Attorneys must identify which information is essential and eliminate distracting complexity.

The attorney who masters translation without condescension, who respects juror intelligence while recognizing knowledge gaps, who educates without lecturing, gains significant advantage in mold trials.

III. Theme Development: The Narrative Foundation of Trial Strategy

Before addressing specific trial components, successful attorneys develop overarching themes that organize all evidence and argument. In toxic mold litigation, theme selection determines how jurors process complex information and make ultimate decisions.

Effective Plaintiff Themes: Responsibility and Prevention

The most persuasive plaintiff themes in mold cases focus less on mold's scientific characteristics and more on human responsibility:

"This Was Preventable"

This theme emphasizes that moisture intrusion results from human decisions: design choices, construction shortcuts, deferred maintenance, ignored complaints. Mold becomes evidence of preventable failure rather than the primary focus.

Implementation: Every witness and exhibit reinforces preventability. The building inspector testifies that proper flashing would have prevented intrusion. The contractor explains that waterproofing was omitted to save costs. The maintenance logs show that leak reports were ignored for months. The theme shifts responsibility from natural occurrence to human negligence.

"They Knew and Did Nothing"

In cases with strong documentation of ignored complaints, this theme proves particularly powerful. It transforms the case from a technical dispute about mold species into a narrative about institutional indifference.

Implementation: Present a timeline showing escalating tenant complaints met with delays, dismissals, or superficial responses. Internal emails acknowledging the problem but deferring action become centerpiece exhibits. The theme resonates because jurors understand what it feels like to be ignored by unresponsive institutions.

"Our Home Became Unsafe"

This theme emphasizes loss of the fundamental security that homes should provide. It works particularly well when children are involved.

Implementation: Testimony focuses on the family's experience: the smell that wouldn't go away, the stains that kept spreading, the fear of letting children play in their own bedrooms, the humiliation of hosting guests in contaminated space. Medical testimony supports this lived experience but does not dominate it.

"Simple Maintenance Would Have Stopped This"

This theme works when liability evidence is strong but damages are moderate. It portrays defendants as having created significant harm through trivial neglect.

Implementation: Expert testimony establishes that prompt response to initial moisture intrusion would have prevented mold amplification. Contrast the defendant's actual response time (months) with professional standards (48-72 hours). Show that minimal investment would have prevented substantial harm.

Effective Defense Themes: Perspective and Proportion

Defense themes must acknowledge reality while limiting liability:

"Mold Exists Everywhere; What Matters Is Response"

This theme accepts that mold was present but emphasizes the defendant's reasonable response once aware.

Implementation: Environmental experts testify that mold spores are ubiquitous in all indoor environments. The focus shifts to whether the defendant acted reasonably after discovering amplification. Maintenance logs, contractor invoices, and remediation protocols demonstrate prompt, professional response. The theme concedes the problem while defending the handling.

"Discomfort Is Not Permanent Injury"

This theme accepts temporary inconvenience while challenging claims of lasting harm.

Implementation: Acknowledge that the situation was unpleasant and required remediation. Challenge medical testimony regarding permanent injury. Emphasize that plaintiff's current symptoms have other explanations. The theme validates the plaintiff's experience while limiting damages to what was actually proven.

"Science Requires Proof, Not Fear"

This theme addresses the emotional resonance of "toxic mold" while requiring scientific rigor.

Implementation: Defense experts explain that responsible medicine requires reliable methodology, measurable exposure, and differential diagnosis. The theme does not dismiss plaintiff's concerns but insists that compensation requires proof. It positions the defense as advocating for scientific integrity rather than corporate indifference.

"We Fixed the Problem Promptly"

When liability is weak and response was reasonable, this simple theme can be effective.

Implementation: Timeline exhibits show rapid response after notification. Contractor testimony establishes that remediation met professional standards. Post-remediation testing confirms successful abatement. The theme asks: what more should the defendant have done?

Theme Consistency: The Golden Rule

Once selected, themes must permeate every aspect of trial presentation:

- Opening statement introduces the theme explicitly
- Direct examination reinforces it through witness testimony

- Cross-examination undermines opposing themes
- Exhibits are selected and designed to support it
- Closing argument returns to it repeatedly

Jurors will not remember every technical detail presented during trial. They will remember compelling narratives that organized information coherently. Effective theme development provides that organizational structure.

IV. Jury Selection in Mold Cases: Identifying Bias and Building Rapport

Voir dire in toxic mold litigation serves critical functions beyond simply identifying jurors with disqualifying bias. It begins the education process, introduces key concepts, and establishes rapport between attorneys and jurors who will decide scientifically complex issues.

The Unique Challenges of Mold Case Voir Dire

Unlike many tort cases where jurors arrive with established attitudes about car accidents or medical malpractice, most jurors have limited preconceptions about toxic mold litigation. This creates both opportunity and challenge.

Opportunity: Attorneys can shape initial understanding rather than overcoming existing bias.

Challenge: Jurors may have absorbed sensationalized media coverage about "toxic black mold" without understanding scientific nuance, or may view mold as trivial because they have personally experienced minor growth without serious consequence.

Key Areas of Inquiry

Effective voir dire explores several critical areas:

Personal Experience with Mold or Water Damage

Questions to explore:

- Has anyone dealt with mold or water damage in their home?
- How did you handle it?

- Did you or family members experience any health issues you associated with it?
- How was the problem resolved?

Why this matters: Personal experience shapes perspective powerfully. A juror who discovered minor mold, cleaned it with bleach, and had no issues may view plaintiff claims skeptically. A juror who experienced serious water damage and difficult remediation may be more sympathetic. Neither automatically disqualifies, but understanding these experiences allows informed peremptory challenges and theme adjustment.

Employment in Relevant Industries

Questions to explore:

- Does anyone work in construction, property management, real estate, or insurance?
- Do you have professional knowledge about building science, environmental testing, or remediation?
- Has anyone worked as a landlord or property manager?

Why this matters: Industry professionals may bring expertise that influences deliberations, sometimes helpfully, sometimes problematically. A building inspector may educate other jurors about proper construction practices, potentially helping either side depending on facts. A property manager might sympathize with maintenance challenges defendants face. An insurance adjuster understands coverage disputes deeply.

Attitudes Toward Environmental Illness

Questions to explore:

- Has anyone heard of conditions like multiple chemical sensitivity or chronic fatigue syndrome?
- Do you believe environmental exposures can cause long-term health problems?
- Do you think some people are more sensitive to environmental factors than others?

Why this matters: Jurors with strong opinions about environmental illness, either believing it is underrecognized or believing it is overdiagnosed, bring those perspectives to mold causation disputes. Neither view automatically disqualifies, but extreme positions may warrant challenge.

Experience with Asthma or Allergies

Questions to explore:

- Does anyone in your family have asthma or serious allergies?
- Have you dealt with identifying triggers for allergic reactions?
- Do you understand that different people react differently to the same exposure?

Why this matters: Personal experience with respiratory conditions often makes jurors more receptive to testimony about mold-triggered allergies and asthma. It also helps them understand individual susceptibility variations.

Attitudes Toward Landlords and Tenants

In landlord-tenant mold cases, explore:

- Has anyone rented property or been a landlord?
- What was your experience?
- Do you have strong feelings about landlord-tenant relationships?

Why this matters: Jurors with negative landlord experiences may approach defense arguments skeptically. Landlords may empathize with maintenance challenges. Both perspectives influence deliberation.

Views on Corporate Responsibility

Questions to explore:

- Do you believe large companies sometimes prioritize profits over safety?
- Do you think lawsuits against corporations are usually justified or usually excessive?
- How do you feel about punitive damages?

Why this matters: In cases involving institutional defendants, attitudes about corporate responsibility shape receptiveness to punitive damage arguments and credibility assessments of corporate witnesses.

Scientific and Medical Literacy

Questions to explore:

- Does anyone have scientific or medical training?
- Are you comfortable evaluating conflicting expert testimony?
- How do you typically decide between competing scientific claims?

Why this matters: Scientifically literate jurors may demand higher proof standards or may better understand methodology issues. Some may be helpful during deliberation; others may overvalue their own expertise.

Tactical Approaches

For Plaintiffs:

Ideally seek jurors who:

- Have experienced similar frustrations with unresponsive institutions
- Have personal experience with allergies or asthma
- Are comfortable with environmental health concepts
- View corporate accountability as important
- Can empathize with vulnerable plaintiffs (particularly children)

Avoid jurors who:

- Work in property management or insurance and may identify with defendants
- View environmental illness claims skeptically
- Had minor mold experiences without consequence
- Express strong anti-litigation views
- Seem impatient with scientific complexity

For Defendants:

Ideally seek jurors who:

- Understand practical maintenance challenges

- Value scientific rigor and methodology
- Have dealt with minor mold without serious impact
- Are skeptical of expansive injury claims
- Respect expertise and professional standards

Avoid jurors who:

- Have had negative experiences with landlords or corporations
- Express strong environmental concerns
- Seem predisposed to believe "toxic mold" claims
- Show hostility toward property owners or insurers
- Lost family members to respiratory illness

Educating During Voir Dire

Beyond identifying bias, effective voir dire begins educating jurors:

Introducing Key Concepts

Sample question: "This case will involve testimony about something called 'differential diagnosis,' which is how doctors rule out various possible causes of symptoms. Has anyone heard of this concept? Do you understand that diagnosing what caused someone's illness requires eliminating other possibilities?"

This question serves dual purposes: identifying jurors with relevant knowledge and introducing a concept that will be important during trial.

Managing Expectations About Science

Sample question: "You'll hear from experts who disagree about whether the mold in this case caused the plaintiff's health problems. Are you comfortable with the idea that scientists can look at the same evidence and reach different conclusions? How would you decide which expert to believe?"

This prepares jurors for conflicting testimony and establishes that credibility assessment will be required.

Humanizing Without Prejudging

Sample question: "Imagine discovering that your family has been living in a home with a serious mold problem for months. How would that make you feel? Now imagine being the property owner who didn't know about the problem until tenants complained. Can you see both perspectives?"

This acknowledges emotional elements while encouraging balanced consideration.

Building Rapport

Effective voir dire also builds connection between attorney and jurors:

- **Respect Intelligence:** Never talk down to jurors. Acknowledge complexity while expressing confidence they can understand it.
- **Show Genuine Interest:** Listen carefully to responses. Ask follow-up questions that demonstrate engagement with individual jurors' experiences.
- **Be Authentic:** Jurors detect phoniness instantly. Genuine concern for fair jury selection reads very differently than manipulative questioning.
- **Acknowledge Burden:** Recognize that jury service is challenging and that this will be a demanding case requiring attention to technical detail.

Jurors who feel respected and whose intelligence is acknowledged are more likely to engage seriously with complex evidence.

V. Opening Statements: Setting the Scientific and Emotional Tone

Opening statements in toxic mold trials must accomplish multiple objectives: introducing the case narrative, establishing themes, previewing evidence, managing expectations about scientific disputes, and beginning the process of building credibility. The challenge is achieving all this while avoiding promises that evidence cannot fulfill.

The Dual Nature of Mold Cases

Effective openings acknowledge that mold cases exist on two planes simultaneously:

The Scientific Plane: Did exposure occur? Was it significant? Did it cause injury? What does reliable methodology require?

The Human Plane: How did it feel to live in contaminated housing? What did it do to family life? How did defendants respond to complaints?

The best openings integrate both planes, using human experience to give meaning to scientific evidence and using scientific evidence to validate human experience.

Opening Statement Structure for Plaintiffs

A strong plaintiff opening might follow this pattern:

Begin With Impact, Not Background

Weak opening: "This case involves alleged exposure to toxic mold in a rental property between 2023 and 2024."

Strong opening: "For eighteen months, the Rodriguez family lived with a secret hidden behind the walls of their children's bedrooms: black mold spreading across studs and drywall, fed by water that leaked through defective windows every time it rained. For eighteen months, Maria Rodriguez watched her seven-year-old daughter cough through the night, struggling to breathe. For eighteen months, she complained to the property manager, filed work orders, sent emails, made phone calls. And for eighteen months, the landlord did nothing."

The strong opening establishes stakes, introduces plaintiffs as real people, and creates narrative momentum.

Introduce Your Theme Early

After the impact opening, state your theme explicitly: "This case is about a simple truth: when property owners know about dangerous conditions and choose to do nothing, they are responsible for the harm that follows. That is what happened here."

Tell the Story Chronologically

Walk through the narrative:

- When the family moved in, the apartment seemed fine
- Problems began during the first winter

- Complaints were filed and ignored
- Conditions worsened
- Health problems developed
- Eventual discovery of the extent of contamination
- The family's displacement and remediation

Chronological storytelling is easiest for jurors to follow and creates narrative cohesion.

Preview the Evidence Without Over-Promising

"You will see photographs of what was hidden behind those walls. You will hear from Dr. Martinez, an allergist who treated Emma Rodriguez and will explain how mold exposure triggered her asthma attacks. You will see the work orders that went unfulfilled. You will read the emails where the property manager acknowledged the problem but said fixing it would be too expensive."

This promises specific evidence jurors will actually see, building credibility.

Acknowledge Challenges Honestly

"The defense will argue that we cannot prove exactly how many mold spores Emma was exposed to, because testing wasn't done until months later. That's true. But Dr. Martinez will explain why precise spore counts aren't necessary to determine that this environment made Emma sick. You will have to decide whether her doctor's opinion, based on her examinations, testing, and treatment, is reliable."

Acknowledging challenges inoculates against defense arguments and demonstrates honesty.

End With What You're Asking For

"At the end of this trial, we will ask you to hold the landlord accountable for what happened to this family. That means compensating them for Emma's medical treatment, for the costs of finding new housing, for their property that was damaged, and for the fear and stress of living in unsafe conditions. And it means sending a message through punitive damages that ignoring tenant complaints about health hazards has consequences."

Clear articulation of requested relief gives jurors a framework for deliberation.

Opening Statement Structure for Defense

Defense openings must establish credibility while limiting liability:

Accept Reality Before Challenging Causation

Weak opening: "The mold in this case was not dangerous, and the plaintiffs' claims are exaggerated."

Strong opening: "No one disputes that the Rodriguez family experienced a moisture problem in their apartment. No one disputes that mold grew in areas affected by that moisture. What you will need to decide is whether the evidence proves that this mold caused Emma Rodriguez serious, permanent injury, or whether she experienced temporary allergy symptoms that resolved completely after the problem was fixed."

The strong opening concedes undisputed facts, demonstrating reasonableness before framing the actual dispute.

Introduce Your Theme

"This case is about the difference between inconvenience and injury, between temporary problems and permanent harm. Science requires proof, not assumption. Medicine requires methodology, not speculation. You will decide whether the plaintiffs have met their burden of proving their claims with reliable evidence."

Frame the Scientific Dispute

"You will hear from two medical experts who examined the same records and reached different conclusions. Dr. Chen, the plaintiffs' expert, believes Emma's asthma was caused by mold. Dr. Patterson, a board-certified allergist with 25 years of experience, reviewed those same records and concluded that Emma had pre-existing seasonal allergies that would have caused her symptoms regardless of any mold exposure. You will have to evaluate which doctor's opinion is more reliable."

This prepares jurors for conflicting testimony and establishes defense expert credentials.

Emphasize What Was Done Right

"You will see evidence that when the property manager learned about the extent of the problem, remediation began within two weeks. A licensed contractor performed the work. The apartment was tested afterward and cleared. The landlord paid for the family's temporary housing. Were mistakes made initially? Perhaps. But did this landlord respond appropriately once the scope of the problem was understood? The evidence will show yes."

This focuses jurors on defendant conduct rather than just plaintiff harm.

Address Damages Proportionally

"Even if you find that some inconvenience and temporary symptoms occurred, you must ensure that any damages awarded are proportional to the actual harm proven. The plaintiffs are asking for millions of dollars for permanent injury. The evidence will show that Emma's symptoms resolved, that she is healthy now, and that the family received compensation for their actual losses at the time."

This primes jurors to scrutinize damages claims carefully.

Close Confidently

"At the end of this case, we will ask you to return a verdict that reflects what the evidence actually proves, not what fear or sympathy might suggest. We trust that you will carefully evaluate the science, assess the credibility of the experts, and reach a fair conclusion based on proof."

Common Opening Statement Mistakes

Several errors appear repeatedly in mold case openings:

- **Over-Promising on Causation:** Promising to prove specific causation "beyond any doubt" or representing that experts will provide "absolute certainty" sets standards that cannot be met. Medical testimony provides opinions to "reasonable medical probability," not certainty.
- **Drowning in Technical Detail:** Opening statements that attempt to explain mold biology, building science, and medical causation comprehensively lose juror attention. Save detailed technical explanation for witness testimony.
- **Ignoring the Other Side:** Failing to acknowledge obvious defense arguments or weaknesses in plaintiff's case creates appearance of

hiding problems. Similarly, defense openings that ignore legitimate plaintiff harms seem callous.

- **Argument Instead of Preview:** Opening statements should preview evidence, not argue about its meaning. "The evidence will show X" is appropriate. "X proves the defendant is lying" is argumentative and objectionable.

- **Lack of Structure:** Rambling chronologies without clear themes or conclusions fail to organize information for jurors. Structure matters.

- **The Lasting Impact:** Opening statements disproportionately influence trial outcomes because they provide the framework through which jurors process all subsequent evidence. Information presented later will be understood through the lens of opening narratives.

Therefore, crafting openings with precision, honoring promises made, and establishing credibility through honest, organized presentation may be the most important trial skill in toxic mold litigation.

VI. Direct Examination: Building the Foundation Through Witness Testimony

Direct examination in toxic mold trials serves to establish facts, introduce evidence, educate jurors, and build credibility. The challenge is accomplishing this while maintaining engagement and avoiding the dry, leading-question style that characterizes poor direct examination.

Lay Witness Direct: Humanizing the Case

Plaintiff testimony in mold cases must balance several objectives:

Establishing Chronology and Facts

- Take the plaintiff through the story systematically:
- When did you move into the property?
- Describe its condition initially
- When did you first notice problems?

- What did you observe?
- When did you report it?
- To whom?
- What response did you receive?

This factual foundation is essential but can be tedious if not handled skillfully.

Techniques for Engaging Factual Direct:

- Use present tense where appropriate: "Describe what you see when you walk into Emma's bedroom that morning" feels more immediate than "What did you see?"
- Encourage specific sensory detail: "What did it smell like?" "What did the walls feel like when you touched them?" "What sounds did Emma make when she was coughing at night?"
- Break monotony with exhibits: Introduce photographs, work orders, or emails at natural points in the chronology rather than in a separate exhibit dump.

Conveying Emotional Impact Without Melodrama

The plaintiff must communicate genuine distress without appearing rehearsed or exaggerated:

Good questions:

- "How did you feel when the third work order went unanswered?"
- "What went through your mind when the doctor said Emma needed to leave the apartment?"
- "Describe what it was like packing up your home in the middle of the night to move to a hotel."

These open-ended questions allow authentic emotional expression.

Avoid:

- "Were you terrified?" (Leading and melodramatic)
- "Did this devastate your family?" (Conclusory)
- "Tell the jury how awful this was." (Too obvious)

Establishing Knowledge and Notice

Plaintiff testimony must document what defendants knew and when:

- "Did you provide written notice of the water intrusion?"
- "Let me show you Exhibit 12. Is this the email you sent to the property manager?"
- "What did he say when you called?"
- "Did he promise to fix it?"
- "How long did you wait?"

This builds the neglect narrative systematically.

Avoiding Common Plaintiff Testimony Problems

- **Over-rehearsal:** Witnesses who sound scripted lose credibility. Prepare content, not specific wording.
- **Exaggeration:** Testimony that every surface was covered in "thick black mold" when photographs show limited growth undermines credibility.
- **Speculation:** Plaintiffs should testify to what they observed, not what they think the mold was doing biologically.
- **Inconsistency:** Ensure testimony aligns with prior statements, work orders, and contemporaneous emails.
- **Defendant/Corporate Representative Direct:** Defense witness examination must establish reasonable conduct:

Showing Maintenance Systems

For property managers:

- "Describe your maintenance request system."
- "How are work orders prioritized?"
- "What happened when this work order was received?"
- "Walk me through your response."

This demonstrates orderly processes rather than chaotic neglect.

Documenting Response Timeline

Use exhibits chronologically:

- "Exhibit 23 shows the work order dated March 15. What action was taken?"
- "Exhibit 24 is the contractor invoice dated March 22, one week later. What work was performed?"
- "Exhibit 25 shows the clearance testing. What did it reveal?"

Visual timeline demonstratives reinforce prompt response.

Explaining Constraints or Challenges

Where appropriate, explain practical difficulties:

- "Did weather conditions affect when work could be performed?"
- "Did you need tenant cooperation to access the apartment?"
- "What coordination was required among different contractors?"

This humanizes defendants without making excuses.

Avoiding Defensive Posture

Witnesses who appear hostile, dismissive, or defensive alienate jurors. Better approaches:

- Acknowledge that the situation was serious
- Express appropriate concern for tenants
- Focus on what was done, not on blaming others
- Accept responsibility for any actual failures

Environmental Expert Direct Examination

Structure environmental testimony to build understanding progressively:

Phase 1: Establish Credentials and Methodology

Brief but sufficient credential review:

- Education and training

- Professional certifications
- Relevant experience
- Publications if significant

Then establish methodology:

- "What standards govern environmental sampling for indoor mold?"
- "Describe the protocol you followed in this case."
- "Why is that protocol reliable?"

Phase 2: Explain Findings Accessibly

Use visual aids extensively:

- Photographs of sampling locations
- Laboratory reports with key findings highlighted
- Comparison charts showing indoor vs. outdoor spore counts
- Building diagrams showing moisture pathways

Questions that aid understanding:

- "Let's start with what mold actually is. Can you explain in simple terms?"
- "You found elevated Aspergillus concentrations. What does that mean to someone who isn't a scientist?"
- "This chart shows indoor counts of 15,000 spores per cubic meter and outdoor counts of 300. Help the jury understand that comparison."

Phase 3: Connect Findings to Causation (Carefully)

Environmental experts typically cannot offer medical opinions but can establish exposure:

- "Based on your testing, was mold growing inside this apartment?"
- "Was the concentration you measured higher than typical outdoor levels?"
- "How long would conditions need to exist for this level of

colonization to develop?"

Avoid overreach:

- Do not ask environmental experts whether mold "caused" health problems
- Do not ask them to diagnose medical conditions
- Do not ask them whether exposure was "dangerous" without scientific foundation

Medical Expert Direct Examination

Medical testimony requires even greater care in translation:

Phase 1: Establish Expertise Relevant to This Case

Beyond general credentials, establish specific relevant expertise:

- "How many patients with mold-related respiratory conditions have you treated?"
- "Are you board-certified in allergy and immunology?"
- "Have you published research on environmental triggers for asthma?"

Phase 2: Explain Medical Concepts

Before testifying about this plaintiff, educate about medical principles:

- "Explain how allergic asthma develops."
- "What is the difference between allergies and irritant reactions?"
- "How do physicians determine what triggered an asthma attack?"

Use demonstratives:

- Anatomical diagrams showing respiratory system
- Charts explaining immune response
- Timelines showing symptom correlation with exposure

Phase 3: Describe Examination and Diagnosis

Establish thorough evaluation:

- "When did you first examine the plaintiff?"
- "What tests did you perform?"
- "What did those tests reveal?"
- "What medical records did you review?"
- "What was your differential diagnosis process?"

Phase 4: Explain Causation Opinion

This is the critical testimony:

- "Based on your examination, testing, and review of records, do you have an opinion to a reasonable degree of medical probability about what caused Emma's asthma attacks?"
- "What is that opinion?"
- "What is the basis for that opinion?"

Then systematically walk through:

- Temporal correlation between exposure and symptoms
- Improvement after removal from environment
- Test results ruling out other triggers
- Literature supporting mold as asthma trigger
- Absence of alternative explanations

Phase 5: Address Anticipated Challenges

Inoculate against cross-examination:

- "Did you consider other possible causes?"
- "How did you rule those out?"
- "Are there any uncertainties in your opinion?"
- "What would change your opinion?"

Acknowledging limitations builds credibility.

Building Science Expert Direct Examination

In construction defect cases, building science experts bridge engineering and causation:

Phase 1: Explain Building Systems

Use models and diagrams:

- "Show the jury how this wall assembly is supposed to work."
- "Point out where the flashing should be installed."
- "Explain what happens when water enters here."

Phase 2: Identify Failures

With photographs and site inspection reports:

- "What did you observe during your inspection?"
- "Is this the proper way to install this component?"
- "What was the consequence of this installation error?"

Phase 3: Establish Preventability

Connect failures to professional standards:

- "Does the building code address this issue?"
- "What is the industry standard of care?"
- "Could this failure have been prevented?"
- "How?"

Common Direct Examination Mistakes

Leading Questions: Direct examination should generally use open-ended questions. Leading questions (those suggesting their answer) are typically objectionable and make testimony seem scripted.

Weak: "The mold was black, wasn't it?" Strong: "What color was the mold you observed?"

Information Overload: Attempting to cover every detail exhausts juror attention. Focus on key facts that advance your narrative.

Lack of Visual Support: Technical testimony without visual aids loses effectiveness. Use photographs, diagrams, charts, and demonstratives liberally.

Failing to Translate Jargon: Experts must define technical terms as they use them or jurors will disengage.

Ignoring Engagement: Watch jurors during direct examination. If attention wanders, adjust pacing, introduce exhibits, or shift topics.

The Goal

Effective direct examination builds a coherent, credible case through witness testimony that educates jurors, establishes necessary facts, and maintains engagement. In toxic mold cases, this requires patient development of complex scientific and technical concepts while never losing sight of the human narrative that gives those concepts meaning and importance.

VII. Cross-Examination Strategy: Narrowing Claims and Exposing Weaknesses

Cross-examination in toxic mold litigation must accomplish specific objectives: undermining opponent's causation evidence, limiting damages, establishing alternative explanations, and highlighting methodological weaknesses. Effective cross in these cases is rarely dramatic confrontation; more often it is methodical demonstration of gaps in proof.

Cross-Examination of Plaintiff

Plaintiff cross-examination in mold cases typically focuses on several key areas:

Establishing Alternative Causes of Symptoms

The goal is not to prove the plaintiff is lying about symptoms but to show other explanations exist:

Q: "You've had seasonal allergies since childhood, correct?"

A: "Yes."

Q: "Spring and fall have always been difficult for you?"

A: "Yes."

Q: "Your symptoms include sneezing, congestion, and itchy eyes?"

A: "Yes."

Q: "Those are the same symptoms you experienced in the apartment?"

A: "Well, they were worse."

Q: "But the same types of symptoms?"

A: "Yes."

This establishes that symptoms are not unique to mold exposure.

Continue:

Q: "You also have a cat, correct?"

A: "Yes."

Q: "You've never been tested for cat allergies?"

A: "No."

Q: "So we don't know if you're allergic to your cat?"

A: "I guess not."

Multiple alternative causes create reasonable doubt about specific causation.

Timeline and Symptom Inconsistencies

If medical records show symptoms predated mold exposure or persisted after remediation:

Q: "Let me show you your medical records from 2022, before you moved into this apartment."

Q: "Your doctor noted respiratory complaints in March 2022?"

A: "I had a cold."

Q: "The record says 'chronic respiratory symptoms.' That's more than a cold, isn't it?"

A: "I don't remember exactly."

Q: "You also saw the doctor in June 2022 for breathing difficulties?"

A: "Maybe."

Q: "That was eight months before you claim mold exposure started causing problems?"

A: "Yes, but it got worse in the apartment."

This does not eliminate the claim but weakens temporal causation arguments.

Exaggeration or Inconsistency

When testimony conflicts with prior statements or physical evidence:

Q: "You testified that every room had visible mold?"

A: "Yes."

Q: "Let me show you the photographs taken by the environmental consultant."

Q: "These are photos of your living room, correct?"

A: "Yes."

Q: "Do you see visible mold in these photographs?"

A: "Not in those."

Q: "What about the dining room photos? Any visible mold there?"

A: "Not that I can see in the photos."

Q: "So it wasn't actually every room?"

A: "Well, the bedrooms had it."

Establishing exaggeration on one point creates doubt about other testimony.

Knowledge and Responsibility

When plaintiffs contributed to conditions:

Q: "You were responsible for maintaining the apartment in good condition under your lease?"

A: "Yes."

Q: "That included reporting problems promptly?"

A: "Yes."

Q: "You noticed water staining in February?"

A: "Yes."

Q: "But you didn't report it until April?"

A: "I thought it was minor."

Q: "Two months passed before you told anyone?"

A: "I wasn't sure what to do."

Establishing plaintiff delay complicates neglect claims.

Avoiding Common Plaintiff Cross-Examination Mistakes

Being Perceived as Bullying: Aggressive cross-examination of sympathetic plaintiffs, particularly children or elderly victims, backfires spectacularly. Maintain respectful tone even when challenging testimony.

Relitigating Undisputed Facts: Do not cross-examine about facts you cannot contest. Spending thirty minutes establishing that mold was present when photographs prove it wastes time and suggests weakness.

Allowing Plaintiff to Re-Explain: Ask focused, closed-ended questions. Avoid "why" or "explain" questions that let plaintiffs rehabilitate testimony.

Fighting Over Minor Points: Choose battles carefully. Impeaching the plaintiff on trivial inconsistencies seems petty and may generate sympathy.

Cross-Examination of Plaintiff's Medical Expert

Medical expert cross-examination often determines trial outcome in mold cases:

Establishing Lack of Dose Evidence

This is frequently the strongest cross-examination line:

Q: "Doctor, you testified that mold exposure caused the plaintiff's condition?"

A: "Yes."

Q: "You cannot tell this jury what concentration of mold causes asthma, can you?"

A: "It varies by individual."

Q: "I understand it varies. But you cannot identify a specific exposure level that causes harm?"

A: "Sensitive individuals react to lower levels."

Q: "That's not my question. Can you tell the jury: 'X spores per cubic meter causes asthma'?"

A: "No, there's no universal threshold."

Q: "And you cannot tell the jury how many spores the plaintiff actually inhaled, can you?"

A: "The environmental testing showed elevated levels."

Q: "The testing occurred three months after the alleged exposure ended?"

A: "Yes."

Q: "So you're estimating what exposure was?"

A: "Based on the data available, yes."

Q: "You're assuming?"

A: "Making a reasonable inference."

This establishes that causation opinion rests on assumptions rather than measurements.

Challenging Differential Diagnosis

Show that alternative causes were not adequately investigated:

Q: "Differential diagnosis requires ruling out other possible causes?"

A: "Yes."

Q: "Did you test the plaintiff for cat allergies?"

A: "No."

Q: "For dust mite sensitivity?"

A: "No, but the history suggested mold."

Q: "You didn't actually rule those out through testing?"

A: "The temporal correlation was clear."

Q: "Symptoms occurred in spring and fall?"

A: "Yes."

Q: "Those are peak allergy seasons for pollen?"

A: "They are."

Q: "But you didn't test for pollen allergies either?"

A: "The patient's report pointed to mold."

Q: "So you relied on what the patient told you, not on testing that ruled out alternatives?"

A: "I considered the entire clinical picture."

This suggests confirmation bias rather than thorough differential diagnosis.

Highlighting Literature Gaps

When expert opinions exceed peer-reviewed support:

Q: "Doctor, you testified that mold caused cognitive impairment?"

A: "Yes."

Q: "Can you cite a single peer-reviewed study showing that residential mold exposure causes permanent cognitive damage in otherwise healthy individuals?"

A: "There are case reports."

Q: "Case reports aren't controlled studies, are they?"

A: "No, but they document clinical observations."

Q: "Are there any epidemiological studies supporting your opinion?"

A: "The research is still developing."

Q: "So the answer is no?"

A: "Not to my knowledge."

Q: "Are there any controlled clinical trials?"

A: "No."

Q: "Any research published in major medical journals?"

A: "Some smaller journals have published on this."

Q: "But none of the major journals like JAMA or The New England Journal of Medicine?"

A: "Not specifically on mold and cognition."

This exposes the gap between expert opinion and scientific consensus.

Financial Bias

While potentially risky, establishing litigation income can be effective:

Q: "Doctor, what percentage of your income comes from legal testimony?"

A: "I'm not sure exactly."

Q: "More than half?"

A: "Possibly."

Q: "How many times have you testified in mold cases?"

A: "Forty or fifty."

Q: "Always for plaintiffs?"

A: "Usually, yes."

Q: "Have you ever testified that mold did not cause a plaintiff's condition?"

A: "I only take cases wherc I believe the claims are valid."

Q: "So that's a no?"

A: "Correct."

This suggests the expert always reaches plaintiff-favorable conclusions.

Previous Excluded Testimony

If the expert has had testimony excluded in other cases:

Q: "Have you had your testimony excluded in mold cases before?"

A: "Occasionally judges have made that decision."

Q: "In the Smith case, your testimony was excluded as unreliable?"

A: "The judge there applied a different standard."

Q: "The same Daubert standard applies everywhere, doesn't it?"

A: "Judges interpret it differently."

Q: "In the Jones case, different judge, same result?"

A: "Yes."

Q: "And in the Garcia case?"

A: "That's three out of perhaps fifty cases."

Multiple exclusions damage credibility significantly.

Cross-Examination of Plaintiff's Environmental Expert

Environmental expert cross-examination focuses on methodology and interpretation:

Testing Protocol Deficiencies

Q: "How many air samples did you collect?"

A: "Three."

Q: "From a 1,200-square-foot apartment?"

A: "Yes."

Q: "The industry standard recommends one sample per room?"

A: "Ideally, yes."

Q: "This apartment had five rooms?"

A: "Yes."

Q: "So you sampled 60% of what the standard calls for?"

A: "Budget constraints limited sampling."

This suggests incomplete evaluation.

Continue:

Q: "You did one outdoor sample for comparison?"

A: "Yes."

Q: "At what time of day?"

A: "2 PM."

Q: "Outdoor spore counts vary dramatically by time of day?"

A: "They can."

Q: "Peak outdoor counts often occur in morning and evening?"

A: "Sometimes."

Q: "You sampled at the time of day when outdoor counts are typically lowest?"

A: "I sampled when I was there."

Q: "That would make the indoor-outdoor comparison appear more dramatic than if you'd sampled during peak outdoor spore times?"

A: "Potentially."

This undermines the reliability of indoor-outdoor comparisons.

Interpretation Bias

Q: "You described Aspergillus concentrations as 'elevated'?"

A: "Yes."

Q: "Aspergillus is one of the most common molds found in all buildings?"

A: "It's common, yes."

Q: "Indoor Aspergillus levels frequently exceed outdoor levels even in buildings without moisture problems?"

A: "That can happen."

Q: "So 'elevated' doesn't necessarily mean 'dangerous'?"

A: "It suggests amplification."

Q: "But you used language suggesting danger?"

A: "I characterized the findings accurately."

Chain of Custody

If sampling or laboratory procedures were questionable:

Q: "Who collected the samples?"

A: "My technician."

Q: "What are her qualifications?"

A: "She's completed training."

Q: "Is she certified?"

A: "Not currently."

Q: "How were samples stored before laboratory analysis?"

A: "In our office."

Q: "In a refrigerator?"

A: "No."

Q: "At room temperature?"

A: "Yes."

Q: "For how long?"

A: "About a week."

Q: "Can mold grow on samples during storage?"

A: "If conditions allow."

This raises questions about sample reliability.

Cross-Examination of Defense Witnesses

Plaintiff cross-examination of defendants focuses on knowledge, delay, and indifference:

Establishing Notice

Force acknowledgment of when defendant knew:

Q: "The tenant sent a work order on March 15?"

A: "Yes."

Q: "You received it that day?"

A: "Within a day or two."

Q: "It described water staining?"

A: "Yes."

Q: "You knew water staining could indicate leaks?"

A: "Generally, yes."

Q: "You knew leaks could cause mold?"

A: "Potentially."

Q: "How many days passed before anyone inspected?"

A: "About three weeks."

Q: "Twenty-one days?"

A: "Approximately."

This establishes unreasonable delay despite knowledge.

Internal Contradictions

Use defendant's documents against them:

Q: "Let me show you this email you sent to the regional manager."

Q: "You wrote: 'The apartment has significant moisture damage that will require extensive repairs'?"

A: "Yes."

Q: "You knew the damage was significant?"

A: "Yes."

Q: "The email is dated April 1?"

A: "Yes."

Q: "But repairs didn't begin until June?"

A: "We had to get contractor bids."

Q: "It took two months to get bids?"

A: "And schedule the work."

Q: "During those two months, a family was living there?"

A: "Yes."

Internal communications often contradict defendant testimony about urgency.

Budget vs. Safety

Establish cost considerations affected decisions:

Q: "The contractor recommended replacing all affected drywall?"

A: "Yes."

Q: "That would have cost $8,000?"

A: "Approximately."

Q: "You chose instead to clean and paint?"

A: "We thought that would address it."

Q: "That cost $1,200?"

A: "Yes."

Q: "Saving $6,800?"

A: "It wasn't about cost."

Q: "But you chose the less expensive option?"

A: "We chose what seemed appropriate."

This suggests financial considerations drove inadequate response.

Cross-Examination of Defense Medical Expert

Plaintiff cross-examination of defense medical experts challenges minimization:

Conceding General Causation

Force acknowledgment of basic principles:

Q: "Mold can cause allergic reactions?"

A: "Yes."

Q: "It can trigger asthma in sensitized individuals?"

A: "Yes."

Q: "Children are more susceptible than adults?"

A: "Generally."

Q: "Prolonged exposure increases risk?"

A: "It can."

Establishing these concessions limits how far the expert can minimize harm.

Highlighting Lack of Personal Examination

Q: "You never examined the plaintiff?"

A: "I reviewed records."

Q: "You didn't take her medical history personally?"

A: "No."

Q: "Didn't conduct physical examination?"

A: "No."

Q: "Didn't order any tests?"

A: "No, I reviewed existing tests."

Q: "Dr. Martinez, who did examine her, reached a different conclusion?"

A: "Yes."

Q: "She actually treated the patient?"

A: "Yes."

This emphasizes that treating physician has superior information.

Financial Bias (Both Directions)

Q: "How often do you testify for insurance companies?"

A: "Regularly."

Q: "More than half your cases?"

A: "Possibly."

Q: "Have you ever testified that an insured's claim was valid against your retaining insurer?"

A: "My opinions are independent."

Q: "That's not my question. Have you?"

A: "I don't recall specific cases."

This suggests defense bias, though must be handled carefully to avoid appearing to attack expert credibility unfairly.

The Art of Cross-Examination

Effective cross in toxic mold cases requires:

- **Preparation:** Know the expert's publications, prior testimony, and methodological weaknesses before beginning.
- **Focus:** Limit cross-examination to points that matter. Avoid exhaustive coverage of every issue.
- **Control:** Use leading questions that permit only yes/no answers. Never ask "why" questions that allow the witness to explain.
- **Brevity:** Make your points efficiently. Long cross-examinations lose juror attention and give witnesses opportunities to rehabilitate.
- **Strategic Concessions:** Do not fight every point. Concede what you cannot contest and focus on what matters.
- **Know When to Stop:** Once you have made your point, stop. Additional questions risk allowing the witness to undo damage.
- **Listen to Answers:** Be prepared to abandon prepared questions when unexpected answers create new opportunities or dangers.

In toxic mold litigation, cross-examination is rarely the dramatic confrontation depicted in legal fiction. More often, it is patient, methodical demonstration that:

- The plaintiff cannot prove what concentration caused harm
- The expert assumed rather than measured exposure
- Alternative causes were not adequately investigated
- The defendant responded reasonably once aware
- Damages are not as severe as claimed

These incremental victories accumulate during deliberation, creating reasonable doubt about causation or damages even when liability for some environmental problem is established.

VIII. Demonstrative Exhibits and Visual Communication: Making Science Accessible

Toxic mold trials depend heavily on visual communication. Jurors processing testimony about spore counts, building envelope failures, and medical causation need visual aids to understand and retain complex information.

Categories of Visual Exhibits in Mold Cases

Photographs

The most basic but often most powerful exhibits:

Property Condition Photos

- Visible mold growth (showing extent and location)
- Water staining and damage
- Structural deterioration
- Comparison photos showing progression over time

Presentation Tips:

- Use high resolution images that display clearly on screens
- Include scale references (rulers, common objects) to show size
- Take photos from multiple angles
- Date and label all images clearly
- Create before/after sequences showing deterioration or remediation

Environmental Sampling Photos

- Sample collection locations
- Sampling equipment and methodology
- Laboratory analysis (when helpful)

Plaintiff Impact Photos

- Medical equipment (inhalers, nebulizers)
- Packed belongings during displacement
- Temporary housing conditions

- Damaged personal property

Common Mistakes:

- Photos so graphic they are excluded as prejudicial
- Poor quality images that do not display well
- Unlabeled photos that confuse rather than clarify
- Excessive quantity that overwhelms rather than educates

Building Diagrams and Cross-Sections

Essential for explaining construction defects and moisture intrusion:

What to Include:

- Wall assembly cross-sections showing: Exterior cladding; Weather-resistant barrier; Structural framing; Insulation; Interior finish
- Water intrusion pathways highlighted in color
- Proper installation details compared to actual installation
- Flashing and drainage plane locations

Design Principles:

- Use color coding consistently (blue for water, red for errors)
- Label all components clearly
- Simplify to essential elements (avoid overwhelming detail)
- Create progressive reveals (show proper installation, then show what actually happened, then show consequences)

Roof and Window Details

- Close-up details of critical intersections
- Animation showing how water travels through defective assemblies
- Comparison of code-compliant vs. actual installation

Timeline Exhibits

Chronological organization clarifies complex sequences:

Complaint and Response Timeline

Vertical timeline showing:

- When tenant reported problems
- When defendant acknowledged
- When inspections occurred
- When repairs were promised
- When repairs actually happened
- Gaps highlighted in color

Medical Timeline

Correlation between exposure and symptoms:

- Move-in date
- First symptoms
- Medical visits
- Medication changes
- Remediation
- Symptom improvement
- Return/relapse if applicable

Design Elements:

- Use consistent time scale
- Color code different types of events
- Highlight critical gaps or correlations
- Include supporting photographs or documents at key points

Charts and Graphs

Quantitative data requires visual representation:

Spore Count Comparisons

Bar graphs comparing:

- Indoor vs. outdoor concentrations
- Different rooms within property
- Pre and post-remediation
- Normal ranges vs. measured levels

Medical Data

- Symptom frequency over time
- Medication usage patterns
- Pulmonary function test results
- Emergency room visits correlated with exposure

Property Value Impact

- Appraisal data showing diminution
- Comparable sales analysis
- Remediation cost breakdowns

Design Principles:

- Keep axes clearly labeled
- Use color strategically to highlight key comparisons
- Avoid 3D effects that distort data
- Include data source citations
- Make numbers large enough to read from jury box

ANIMATIONS AND VIDEO

Dynamic exhibits can illustrate processes:

Moisture Intrusion Animation

- Show water entering through defective window

- Traveling behind wall assembly
- Accumulating in hidden areas
- Creating conditions for mold growth

Ventilation and HVAC

- Demonstrate air flow patterns
- Show condensation formation
- Illustrate humidity distribution

Medical Illustrations

- Respiratory system anatomy
- How allergic response develops
- Asthma attack mechanism

Critical Requirements:

- Ensure scientific accuracy (inaccurate animations do more harm than good)
- Keep duration short (30-60 seconds typically)
- Focus on single concept per animation
- Avoid gratuitous special effects
- Have expert testify that animation accurately represents the process

DOCUMENT ENLARGEMENTS

Key documents deserve visual emphasis:

Work Orders and Complaints

- Blow up critical language
- Highlight key dates
- Show progression of urgency

Email Communications

- Display internal acknowledgments of problems
- Highlight dismissive or cost-focused language
- Show decision-making process

Medical Records

- Enlarge diagnostic findings
- Highlight temporal correlations
- Show prescription changes

Laboratory Reports

- Make findings readable to jury
- Highlight abnormal results
- Show comparison to normal ranges

Presentation Methods:

- Large foam board enlargements for key documents
- Digital display for others
- Color highlighting of critical text
- Side-by-side comparisons when contrasts are important

Strategic Use of Demonstrative Exhibits

Progressive Complexity

Introduce simple concepts before complex ones:

1. Start with photographs showing visible mold
2. Progress to diagrams explaining why it grew there
3. Advance to scientific data quantifying exposure
4. Conclude with medical evidence connecting exposure to injury

This builds understanding rather than overwhelming with complexity.

Repetition Through Multiple Modalities

Key concepts should appear in multiple exhibit types:

- Moisture intrusion explained verbally by expert
- Shown in photographs
- Illustrated in building cross-section
- Demonstrated in animation
- Documented in contractor reports

Repetition through variation reinforces without boring.

Thematic Consistency

Maintain visual themes throughout:

- Consistent color coding (water = blue, mold = green, problem areas = red)
- Consistent timeline format
- Consistent labeling conventions
- Consistent design aesthetic

This creates subconscious organization in jurors' understanding.

Technology Considerations

Modern courtrooms support various presentation technologies:

Advantages of Digital Presentation:

- Can zoom into details
- Can overlay exhibits for comparison
- Can play video and animation
- Can annotate during testimony
- Professional appearance

Disadvantages:

- Technical failures during trial

- Jury may focus on technology rather than content
- Some jurors prefer physical exhibits
- Cost of creation and equipment

Best Practice: Prepare both digital and backup physical exhibits for critical items.

Common Demonstrative Exhibit Mistakes

- **Overly Complex Diagrams:** Including every technical detail overwhelms rather than educates. Simplify ruthlessly to essential elements.
- **Inconsistent Scaling:** Diagrams that are not to scale can mislead. Either maintain accurate scale or clearly label as "not to scale."
- **Advocacy Disguised as Education:** Demonstratives should illustrate facts, not argue conclusions. An exhibit titled "Defendant's Negligent Indifference" is argumentative. "Timeline of Complaint and Response" is factual.
- **Poor Quality Production:** Hand-drawn exhibits or low-resolution images appear unprofessional and suggest the case lacks merit. Invest in professional quality.
- **Excessive Quantity:** Fifty exhibits dilute impact. Ten powerful exhibits used strategically outperform fifty mediocre ones.
- **Failure to Practice:** Attorneys must practice using exhibits with witnesses before trial. Fumbling with technology or exhibits undermines credibility.
- **Evidentiary Foundation:** All demonstrative exhibits require proper foundation:

For Photographs:

- Witness testifies they recognize the location
- Photograph fairly and accurately represents what witness saw
- Relevant to issues in case

For Diagrams and Illustrations:

- Expert testifies diagram accurately represents the concept
- Based on reliable data or accepted principles
- Helpful to jury understanding

For Animations:

- Expert testifies animation accurately depicts the process
- Based on evidence in the case
- Does not include speculation

For Summaries:

- Underlying documents are in evidence or available
- Summary fairly represents the underlying evidence
- Helpful to jury understanding of voluminous material

Failure to establish proper foundation results in exclusion, wasting preparation time and weakening presentation.

The Impact of Visual Communication

Well-designed demonstrative exhibits transform toxic mold trials:

- **Comprehension:** Jurors understand technical concepts they would not grasp from testimony alone.
- **Retention:** Visual information is retained far better than verbal testimony. Jurors remember what they saw during deliberation.
- **Persuasion:** Powerful images influence decisions more than words. A photograph of a child's mold-covered bedroom wall resonates emotionally in ways that verbal description cannot match.
- **Credibility:** Professional presentation suggests thorough preparation and case strength. Poor visuals suggest weak case.

Investment in high-quality demonstrative exhibits is not optional in modern toxic mold litigation. Cases with superior visual presentation win more often, settle for higher amounts, and withstand appellate review more successfully than cases relying primarily on verbal testimony.

IX. Jury Instructions and the Law: Framing Deliberation

Jury instructions in toxic mold cases provide the legal framework within which jurors evaluate evidence. While attorneys cannot draft instructions from scratch, they must carefully propose, argue for, and preserve objections to instructions that shape how the jury approaches its decision.

Standard Instructions in Mold Cases

BURDEN OF PROOF

Standard civil burden instruction: "The plaintiff has the burden of proving each element of their claim by a preponderance of the evidence. This means the evidence must show that it is more likely than not that the claim is true. It does not require proof beyond all doubt, but it requires more than speculation or possibility."

Strategic Implications: Plaintiffs want this instruction to emphasize that certainty is not required. Defense wants emphasis on "more than speculation."

Proposed plaintiff variation: "The law does not require absolute certainty or proof beyond all doubt. If you find the evidence shows it is more probable than not, that is sufficient."

Proposed defense variation: "Mere possibility or suspicion is not enough. The plaintiff must prove each element is more likely true than not true."

CAUSATION

Critical instruction in toxic mold cases: "To establish causation, the plaintiff must prove that the defendant's conduct was a substantial factor in causing the plaintiff's harm. The defendant's conduct need not be the only cause, but it must be a substantial factor."

Variations by jurisdiction: Some states use "proximate cause" language. Others use "substantial factor." Some require "more likely than not" causation. Understanding jurisdictional standards is essential.

Special causation instructions for toxic exposure:

In cases involving alleged toxic exposure, the plaintiff must prove both:

1. That the substance is capable of causing the type of harm alleged (general causation), and
2. That exposure to the substance did in fact cause this plaintiff's specific harm (specific causation)."

This instruction, when given, helps defense by requiring distinct proof of both general and specific causation.

EXPERT TESTIMONY

Standard instruction about evaluating experts: You are not required to accept expert testimony.

In evaluating expert testimony, you may consider:

- The expert's qualifications and experience
- The facts or data the expert relied upon
- The reasoning the expert used to reach conclusions
- Whether the expert's opinion is supported by adequate reasons
- Any bias or interest the expert may have
- The consistency of the expert's testimony"

Strategic use:

Both sides reference this instruction in closing, emphasizing factors favoring their expert.

DAMAGES

Itemizing potential damages:

If you find for the plaintiff, you may award damages for:

- Past and future medical expenses
- Past and future pain and suffering
- Emotional distress
- Property damage
- Loss of enjoyment of life

- [Other applicable damages]

You may not award damages based on speculation or sympathy. Awards must be based on evidence presented."

Contested damages instructions:

Jurisdictions vary on whether emotional distress damages require physical injury. Plaintiffs may request special instructions allowing emotional distress in habitability cases without physical manifestation.

Special Instructions in Mold Litigation

Absence of Regulatory Standards

Defense may request instruction emphasizing no federal exposure limits exist:

"There are no federal or state regulations establishing permissible exposure limits for indoor mold. The absence of such standards does not relieve the defendant of the duty to maintain safe premises, but you should consider this when evaluating evidence about whether exposure was harmful."

Plaintiffs typically oppose this as emphasizing facts rather than law, but some courts permit it.

Vulnerable Populations

Plaintiffs may request instruction about susceptibility:

"Different individuals may react differently to the same environmental conditions. Children, elderly persons, and individuals with pre-existing respiratory conditions may be more susceptible to environmental triggers than healthy adults. You should consider the specific characteristics of the plaintiff when evaluating causation."

Defense opposes as highlighting facts rather than stating law, but plaintiffs argue it prevents jurors from applying their own health as the standard.

Multiple Causes

When alternative causes are significant:

"The plaintiff need not prove that the defendant's conduct was the only cause of harm. However, the plaintiff must prove that the defendant's conduct was a substantial contributing factor. If you find that other factors fully explain the plaintiff's condition without any contribution from the defendant's conduct, you must find for the defendant."

This balanced instruction acknowledges both multiple causation and the need for defendant's conduct to contribute meaningfully.

Property Owner Duties

In habitability cases, instruction clarifying duty:

"A landlord has a duty to maintain rental premises in a habitable condition. This includes promptly addressing moisture intrusion and mold growth that materially affects the health or safety of tenants. The landlord must respond within a reasonable time after receiving notice of the condition."

Definition of "reasonable time" is often contested. Plaintiffs want specific timeframes mentioned. Defense wants flexibility recognized.

Insurance Bad Faith (if applicable)

Special instructions when insurance bad faith is alleged:

"An insurer must investigate claims promptly and thoroughly. An insurer acts in bad faith if it denies a claim or delays payment without a reasonable basis for doing so. However, the mere fact that you may find coverage existed does not automatically establish bad faith. The question is whether the insurer's actions were unreasonable under the circumstances."

Instruction Conferences

Jury instruction conferences occur outside the jury's presence, typically after evidence concludes. This is where attorneys:

Propose Instructions: Submit written proposed instructions with legal citations supporting their use. Courts typically require these proposals before trial begins.

Argue for Inclusion: Explain why proposed instructions are legally correct and necessary for the jury to properly decide the case.

Object to Opponent's Proposals: Preserve objections to instructions you believe are improper, prejudicial, or not supported by law or evidence.

Preserve the Record: Ensure all objections are clearly stated and recorded. Failure to object waives appellate review of instruction errors.

Strategic Considerations

Simplicity vs. Detail: Courts prefer standard pattern instructions over custom language. When requesting special instructions, attorneys must balance:

- Specificity that favors your position
- Simplicity that courts will accept
- Clarity that jurors will understand

Sequence: Instruction order matters. Jurors remember first and last instructions best. When possible, argue that favorable instructions should come early or late in the charge.

Emphasis: Some instructions can be given multiple times or emphasized. For example, causation instructions might appear in general principles and again when specifically addressing plaintiff's claims.

Negative Instructions: Sometimes what is not instructed matters as much as what is. If the court refuses to instruct on punitive damages, that tells the jury punitives are not available.

Consistency with Argument: Plan closing argument around the instructions you expect to receive. Quote key instruction language in closing. Frame evidence in terms that map onto instruction elements.

Common Instruction Disputes in Mold Cases

Whether to give CIRS or contested syndrome instructions

Plaintiffs may request instructions defining specific conditions like CIRS. Defense typically objects that this elevates disputed expert opinion to legal status.

Resolution usually: Court declines to define specific medical conditions, leaving that to expert testimony.

Whether physical injury is required for emotional distress damages

Varies by jurisdiction. In disputed jurisdictions, this becomes a key instruction fight with major damages implications.

Whether to instruct on statute of limitations issues

If defendant raises statute of limitations defense, instructions on when claims accrue and what constitutes discovery become necessary.

Whether to give "eggshell plaintiff" instruction

Plaintiffs want: "You take the plaintiff as you find them. If the plaintiff was more susceptible to harm due to pre-existing conditions, that does not reduce the defendant's liability."

Defense opposes: "This case doesn't involve an injury that made plaintiff more vulnerable; it involves disputed causation about whether defendant caused any injury at all."

The Impact of Instructions

Jury instructions profoundly influence verdicts:

- **Framing:** Instructions frame how jurors think about evidence. An instruction emphasizing "substantial factor" causation feels more plaintiff-friendly than one emphasizing "more likely than not" causation, even though they may be legally equivalent.
- **Legitimacy:** Instructions give legal legitimacy to arguments. When an attorney quotes jury instructions in closing argument, it carries the court's authority.
- **Deliberation:** During deliberation, instructions guide discussion. Jurors return to instruction language when disagreeing about what must be proven.
- **Verdict Forms:** Instructions connect directly to verdict forms, creating a logical progression from legal standards to fact-finding to verdict.

Attorneys who understand instruction battles and fight them strategically gain significant advantage. Conversely, attorneys who treat instructions as afterthought or accept boilerplate without consideration may lose cases during instruction conference rather than during evidence presentation.

X. Closing Arguments: Synthesis, Persuasion, and the Call to Action

Closing argument is the attorney's final opportunity to speak directly to the jury, synthesizing weeks of evidence into coherent narrative and persuading jurors that the evidence compels a specific verdict. In toxic mold cases, effective closing must integrate complex science, human impact, and legal standards while maintaining clarity and emotional resonance.

The Structure of Effective Closing

Opening: Returning to Theme

Begin by returning to the theme introduced in opening statement:

Plaintiff example: "Three weeks ago, I told you this case is about a simple truth: when property owners know about dangerous conditions and choose to do nothing, they are responsible for the harm that follows. You've now heard all the evidence. And the evidence proves exactly that."

This creates satisfying narrative closure and reminds jurors of the organizing principle.

Defense example: "At the beginning of this trial, I told you this case is about the difference between discomfort and injury, between temporary problems and permanent harm. After all the evidence, that remains the central question: Did the plaintiffs prove real injury, or have they asked you to compensate them based on fear and speculation?"

Body: Walking Through Evidence

The core of closing argument systematically reviews evidence:

For Plaintiffs:

Organize around elements that must be proven:

"Let me walk you through what the law requires us to prove and how the evidence proves each element.

First, duty. Did the landlord owe a duty to maintain safe, habitable housing? You heard expert testimony that landlords must address moisture problems promptly. You heard the lease agreement itself promises habitable conditions. There's no dispute about duty.

Second, breach. Did the landlord breach that duty? Look at Exhibit 23, the work order from March 15. Mrs. Rodriguez reported water staining. Now look at Exhibit 31, the email from April 20, where the property manager admits he knew about the problem. Finally, look at Exhibit 47, the invoice showing repairs didn't begin until June 10. Eighty-seven days. Nearly three months. That's not reasonable response. That's breach.

Third, causation. Did that breach cause harm? Dr. Martinez testified that Emma's asthma attacks correlated directly with her time in that apartment. Look at Exhibit 52, the medical timeline. Emma was healthy when she moved in. Within two months, first attack. The attacks continued as long as she lived there. Within a week of moving out, they stopped. That's not coincidence. That's causation.

Fourth, damages. What harm did this family suffer? You heard testimony about medical bills totaling $15,000. You saw receipts for the emergency housing. You heard Mrs. Rodriguez describe the fear of watching her daughter struggle to breathe. That's real harm requiring real compensation."

This methodical review maps evidence onto legal requirements.

For Defense:

Challenge the weakest links in plaintiff's proof:

"The plaintiffs want you to believe a simple story: mold made Emma sick. But the evidence shows the truth is more complicated.

Yes, there was mold. We've never denied that. But presence doesn't equal causation. Dr. Patterson testified that Emma had seasonal allergies long before moving to this apartment. Look at the medical records from 2022, before she lived there. Same symptoms. Same medications. Same time of year.

Dr. Martinez, the plaintiffs' expert, never explained why Emma's symptoms occurred in spring and fall, the exact times when pollen allergies peak. He never tested her for pollen allergies. Never tested for dust mite sensitivity. Never tested for cat allergies, even though she has a cat. That's not differential diagnosis. That's assumption.

And ask yourselves: if the mold was so toxic, why did symptoms continue after remediation? Emma was still using her inhaler six months after the mold was gone. If mold caused the problem, wouldn't removing the mold solve it? The continued symptoms tell you something else is causing Emma's asthma."

This creates reasonable doubt about causation without denying sympathy for the child.

Addressing Weaknesses

Both sides must address their case weaknesses in closing:

Plaintiff acknowledging weakness:

"The defense will tell you we can't prove exactly how many mold spores Emma inhaled. That's true. But Dr. Martinez explained why that doesn't matter. You don't need a spore count to diagnose mold-triggered asthma any more than you need a pollen count to diagnose hay fever. You look at the exposure, the symptoms, the timing, and the response to treatment. All of that evidence supports Dr. Martinez's conclusion."

This inoculates against defense argument by acknowledging and explaining the limitation.

Defense acknowledging weakness:

"Was our initial response as fast as it should have been? In hindsight, probably not. Once the problem was fully understood, we acted quickly. Professional remediation. Clearance testing. Compensation for temporary housing. But yes, we could have moved faster at first. That doesn't mean we caused permanent injury or owe millions of dollars. It means there was temporary inconvenience that we've already addressed."

This acknowledges fault on timing while limiting damages implications.

Emotional Resonance vs. Legal Arguments

Effective closing balances emotional appeal with legal argument:

Appropriate Emotional Appeal:

"Imagine being a parent. Your child is struggling to breathe. You report the problem to your landlord. You wait. You call again. You wait more. You send emails. Nothing happens. Week after week, watching your daughter suffer, knowing someone else could fix this but won't. That's what this family endured. That's what you're here to remedy."

This emotional content connects to legal duty (landlord's obligation to act) and damages (emotional distress).

Inappropriate Emotional Appeal:

"Look at this precious child. How can the defense sit there and deny she suffered? What kind of person puts profits over children's health?"

This strays into personal attack and emotional manipulation unsupported by evidence.

Using Jury Instructions

Quote and explain instructions in closing:

"Judge Williams will instruct you that the plaintiff must prove causation by a preponderance of the evidence. That means more likely than not. Not absolute certainty. Not beyond all doubt. More likely than not. Given the timeline correlation, given the medical testimony, given Emma's improvement after leaving, is it more likely than not that mold triggered her asthma? The evidence clearly shows yes."

This connects evidence to the legal standard jurors will apply.

Damages Argument

Plaintiff damages argument must be specific:

"What is fair compensation for what this family endured?

Medical expenses: The bills are in evidence. $15,240. That's not speculation. That's documented.

Housing displacement: Six months in temporary housing while remediation occurred and Emma recovered. The receipts total $8,500.

Property damage: Furniture, clothing, and belongings that had to be discarded. $3,200.

Emotional distress: How do you value eighteen months of fear? Watching your child struggle to breathe? Feeling helpless because the landlord won't help? The evidence shows Mrs. Rodriguez sought counseling. The therapist's records document anxiety and sleep disruption. This was real, serious distress. We ask $100,000 for this component.

Total: $127,000 in actual damages.

Punitive damages: Finally, the evidence of delay despite knowledge warrants punitive damages to deter this conduct. We ask for $300,000 in punitive damages, triple the actual harm, to send the message that ignoring tenant health for months has consequences."

This specific breakdown is more persuasive than asking for a "fair amount."

Defense damages argument creates perspective:

"Even if you find some liability, damages must be proportional to actual harm proven.

The plaintiffs ask for $100,000 for emotional distress. But Mrs. Rodriguez testified she saw a counselor four times. Four sessions over six months. The therapist's notes describe 'mild anxiety.' That's not the severe, debilitating distress that warrants six figures.

Emma's medical expenses are documented at $15,240. Not trivial, but not catastrophic. Her asthma is now well-controlled. She's active, healthy, living a normal life.

The plaintiffs received $8,500 for temporary housing. That's already been paid.

If you find any damages are warranted, they should reflect the temporary nature of the problems and the successful remediation that followed. Tens of thousands, not hundreds of thousands, and certainly not the millions being requested."

The Call to Action

Close with clear direction:

Plaintiff: "When you deliberate, you'll have a verdict form asking whether the landlord breached his duty to maintain habitable housing. The evidence proves he did. It asks whether that breach caused harm to this family. The evidence proves it did. It asks what compensation is fair. I've suggested amounts based on the evidence. You'll decide the exact figures, but justice requires meaningful compensation and accountability. Thank you for your service."

Defense: "When you look at the verdict form, you'll see it asks whether the plaintiffs proved their case. That's their burden. They must prove it. If you have reasonable doubt about whether mold caused Emma's condition, the verdict must be for the defense. If you find the damages requested are excessive and disproportionate, award only what the evidence actually supports. Thank you."

Common Closing Argument Mistakes

Reading from Notes: Closing should be delivered extemporaneously from outline, not read. Reading diminishes eye contact, engagement, and persuasive power.

Arguing Facts Not in Evidence: Statements like "everyone knows mold is toxic" when no evidence established that universal knowledge constitute arguing facts not in evidence and draw objections.

Personal Opinion: "I believe" or "I think" statements are improper. Arguments must be based on evidence, not attorney's personal views.

Misstating Evidence: Claiming a witness said something they did not, or that an exhibit shows something it does not, destroys credibility when jurors review evidence during deliberation.

Improper Appeals: References to insurance coverage, wealth or poverty of parties (unless relevant to punitive damages), or asking jurors to "send a message" to all landlords (rather than holding this defendant accountable) often draw objections and may constitute misconduct.

Excessive Length: Closing arguments that exceed two hours lose juror attention. Focus and brevity demonstrate confidence and respect for jurors' time.

The Final Word

Closing argument is the culmination of trial preparation and strategy. It is where complex evidence becomes accessible narrative, where scientific data becomes human story, where legal standards become calls to justice.

In toxic mold litigation, effective closing acknowledges scientific complexity while insisting that common sense and careful evaluation of evidence lead to clear conclusions. It respects juror intelligence while providing the organization and emphasis needed to navigate technical disputes.

The attorney who delivers closing argument that is clear, honest, well-organized, emotionally resonant without manipulation, legally grounded, and respectful of the jury's task maximizes the chance of favorable verdict regardless of which side they represent.

XI. Deliberation, Verdict, and Post-Trial Motions

After closing arguments and jury instructions, the case passes to the jury for deliberation. While attorneys wait, they must prepare for various post-verdict scenarios and potential motions that may follow.

The Deliberation Process

Jurors retire to deliberate with:

- Jury instructions
- Verdict forms
- Admitted exhibits
- Their notes (if note-taking was permitted)

What Jurors Typically Do:

- **Select a foreperson** to organize discussion and communicate with the court.
- **Review instructions** to understand what must be decided.
- **Discuss evidence** systematically, often following the order of elements in instructions.
- **Request exhibits** they want to review more carefully. Popular requests in mold cases include: Photographs of conditions; Timeline exhibits; Medical records; Correspondence showing notice and response
- **Ask questions** of the court if confused about instructions or procedures. Courts typically answer legal questions but cannot answer factual questions.
- **Take preliminary votes** to gauge where jurors stand.
- **Discuss disagreements** attempting to reach consensus.

Length of Deliberation:

Mold cases typically deliberate longer than simple car accident cases due to scientific complexity. Deliberations lasting several days are not uncommon in complex toxic exposure cases.

Quick deliberations (under two hours) often favor defendants, suggesting jurors found causation or damages lacking.

Extended deliberations suggest serious consideration of competing evidence, which can favor either side depending on case facts.

Verdict Forms

Verdict forms in mold cases typically present questions sequentially:

Special Verdict Form Example:

1. Do you find that the defendant breached a duty to maintain habitable housing? ☐ Yes ☐ No : If No, your deliberations end. Sign and return. If Yes, continue.
2. Do you find that the breach was a substantial factor in causing harm to the plaintiffs? ☐ Yes ☐ No : If No, your deliberations end. If Yes, continue.
3. What damages do you award? Medical expenses: $___________ Property damage: $___________ Emotional distress: $___________ Total compensatory damages: $___________
4. Do you find that the defendant's conduct warrants punitive damages? ☐ Yes ☐ No : If Yes, what amount? $___________

General Verdict Form Alternative:

Some jurisdictions use simpler forms:

1. Do you find for plaintiff or defendant? ☐ Plaintiff ☐ Defendant : If for plaintiff, what amount? $___________

Strategic Implications: Special verdicts force jurors to articulate reasoning step by step, potentially helping defendants by requiring proof of each element. General verdicts give jurors more flexibility to reach compromise outcomes without explaining specific reasoning.

Reading the Verdict

When the jury signals it has reached verdict, all parties return to court for the reading.

The Moment of Truth: The clerk or foreperson reads the verdict. Attorneys watch juror faces and body language for clues about how deliberation went, but the written verdict controls regardless of juror demeanor.

Polling the Jury: Either party may request the jury be polled, meaning each juror individually confirms agreement with the verdict. This occasionally reveals a juror who felt pressured and did not truly agree, potentially causing a mistrial, but more often simply confirms the verdict.

Immediate Reactions: Attorneys must maintain composure regardless of outcome. Visible disappointment or excessive celebration appears unprofessional and may be remembered if the case proceeds to appeal or retrial.

Post-Trial Motions

Win or lose, post-trial motions may be appropriate:

JUDGMENT NOTWITHSTANDING THE VERDICT (JNOV)

Also called Judgment as a Matter of Law, this motion asks the court to enter judgment contrary to the jury verdict because no reasonable jury could have reached that conclusion based on the evidence.

When filed: Typically by defendants after plaintiff verdict when they believe evidence did not support the verdict.

Standard: Very difficult to win. Courts are reluctant to overturn jury verdicts and will do so only when the evidence, viewed most favorably to the prevailing party, could not support the verdict.

Example in mold case: Defense might argue that exclusion of medical causation expert required JNOV because without that testimony, no evidence supported causation.

MOTION FOR NEW TRIAL

Requests the court order a new trial based on errors during the first trial.

Grounds include:

- Erroneous evidentiary rulings
- Improper jury instructions

- Jury misconduct
- Newly discovered evidence
- Damages award that is excessive or inadequate

Example in mold case: Plaintiff might move for new trial arguing that exclusion of certain expert testimony was erroneous and prejudicial.

Remittitur or Additur

Court reduces (remittitur) or increases (additur) damages award.

Remittitur scenario: Jury awards $5 million in emotional distress damages. Defense moves for remittitur arguing the award is excessive and unsupported by evidence. Court reduces to $500,000 or offers plaintiff choice between accepting reduced amount or facing new trial on damages only.

Additur scenario: Jury awards $5,000 in damages when medical bills alone were $50,000. Plaintiff moves for additur. Court increases award or grants new trial on damages.

Note: Many jurisdictions do not permit additur, viewing it as violating the Seventh Amendment right to jury trial.

Motion for Attorneys' Fees and Costs

In jurisdictions allowing fee-shifting in habitability or consumer protection cases, prevailing party may seek attorneys' fees.

Requirements:

- Statutory authorization for fee award
- Prevailing party status
- Reasonable fee calculation

Amount: Based on reasonable hourly rates multiplied by time spent, potentially adjusted by success achieved.

Settlement After Verdict

Even after verdict, settlement may occur:

- **Post-verdict settlement scenarios:**
- **Plaintiff wins but defendant appeals:** Plaintiff may accept reduced settlement to avoid delay and risk of reversal.
- **Defendant wins but plaintiff plans to appeal:** Defendant may pay nuisance settlement to avoid appeal costs and risk of reversal and retrial.
- **Damages verdict is unclear:** Parties may settle rather than litigate post-trial motions and appeals.
- **Economic factors:** Insurance policy limits, bankruptcy concerns, or desire for finality may motivate post-verdict settlement.

The Appeals Process

If post-trial motions fail and no settlement occurs, the losing party may appeal.

- **Notice of Appeal:** Must be filed within strict deadlines (often 30 days from entry of judgment).
- **Appellate Briefing:** Appellant briefs arguing trial court errors. Appellee responds defending the judgment.
- **Standard of Review:** Appellate courts review different issues under different standards: Legal questions ("De novo" - fresh review); Evidentiary rulings ("Abuse of discretion")
- **Jury verdicts:** Substantial evidence support

Outcome possibilities:

- Affirmance (judgment stands)
- Reversal (judgment overturned, may order entry of opposite judgment)
- Reversal and remand (judgment overturned, case sent back for new trial)
- Modification (damages adjusted, otherwise affirmed)

Timeline: Appeals in complex civil cases often take 12-24 months from notice of appeal to decision.

The Human Element: Post-Trial Attorney Duties

To Clients: Win or lose, attorneys must:

- Explain the verdict and what it means
- Discuss post-trial motion options realistically
- Advise on appeal prospects honestly
- Handle final financial matters (disbursing awards, settling costs)
- Ensure clients understand finality if no appeal is pursued

Professional Reflection: Post-trial is the time for honest self-assessment:

- What worked in presentation?
- What could have been done differently?
- What lessons apply to future cases?
- Were case evaluation and settlement recommendations accurate?

Relationship with Opposing Counsel: Professional courtesy continues after trial. Future cases may involve the same opposing counsel or judge.

XII. Conclusion: The Art and Science of Trial Practice in Mold Litigation

Trial practice in toxic mold litigation demands mastery of diverse skills: scientific translation, visual communication, witness examination, strategic positioning, and persuasive storytelling. Success requires attorneys who can simultaneously function as educators, scientists, storytellers, and advocates.

The Fundamental Balancing Act

Throughout trial, effective attorneys balance competing demands:

- **Science and Accessibility:** Present complex technical information accurately while making it comprehensible to lay jurors.
- **Emotion and Evidence:** Connect jurors emotionally to clients'

experiences while grounding arguments in admissible evidence.

- **Aggression and Respect:** Advocate vigorously while maintaining professional demeanor and respect for court, opposing counsel, and witnesses.
- **Comprehensiveness and Focus:** Present complete cases while avoiding information overload that confuses rather than clarifies.
- **Confidence and Humility:** Project confidence in case strength while acknowledging weaknesses honestly.

The Enduring Principles

Certain principles transcend specific tactical choices:

Credibility Is Currency: Jurors decide cases based substantially on which attorneys and witnesses they trust. Credibility once lost is rarely regained. Every decision during trial should be evaluated through the lens of: Does this enhance or undermine credibility?

Clarity Beats Complexity: In disputes between experts offering dueling complex methodologies, jurors often favor the side whose presentation was clearer and more accessible. The attorney who translates science effectively wins more often than the attorney with marginally stronger science presented incomprehensibly.

Preparation Shows: Jurors perceive and appreciate thorough preparation. Fumbling with exhibits, searching for documents, or appearing surprised by testimony suggests inadequate preparation and weakens credibility.

Theme Discipline Matters: Cases with clear, consistent themes that organize all evidence persuade more effectively than cases presenting evidence without coherent narrative structure.

Honesty Pays: Acknowledging case weaknesses, conceding opponent's strong points, and presenting evidence fairly builds trust that enhances advocacy when arguing contested issues.

The Reality of Modern Mold Trials: By 2026, toxic mold trials reflect the maturation of the field:

Judges Are Informed: Judges have seen these cases before, understand the scientific issues, and apply evidentiary standards rigorously. Attorneys cannot rely on judicial uncertainty or unfamiliarity with mold litigation.

Juries Are Skeptical: Public awareness of "toxic mold" claims has created some skepticism. Juries are sophisticated consumers of information who demand proof, not assumptions.

Standards Are High: Expert testimony faces stringent admissibility requirements. Property and medical causation must be proven with reliable methodology. Damages require documentation.

Stakes Are Significant: For plaintiffs, trials represent the culmination of years of illness, displacement, and financial stress. For defendants, trials create potential for substantial judgments and reputational harm. These stakes demand attorneys at the top of their craft.

The Path to Victory

Victory in toxic mold trials comes from:

1. **Early Case Assessment:** Recognizing strong cases from weak ones, investing in strong cases, and resolving or declining weak ones.

2. **Strategic Expert Selection:** Retaining credentialed experts who use reliable methodology and can withstand rigorous cross-examination.

3. **Thorough Preparation:** Mastering every exhibit, document, test result, and testimony before trial begins.

4. **Clear Presentation:** Organizing complex information into accessible narratives supported by powerful visual exhibits.

5. **Disciplined Execution:** Following trial plans while remaining flexible enough to adapt to unexpected developments.

6. **Professional Persistence:** Maintaining focus, energy, and professionalism through weeks of demanding trial work.

Toxic mold litigation will never be simple. The science is complex. The medicine is contested. The causation is difficult to prove. The damages are hard to quantify. The insurance is complicated. The emotions are raw.

But attorneys who master the intersection of building science, environmental testing, medical causation, insurance coverage, and persuasive advocacy can succeed in this challenging field. They can achieve justice for families harmed by substandard housing. They can hold institutional defendants accountable for neglect. They can defend property owners from speculative claims. They can ensure that compensation is based on proof rather than fear.

Trial remains the ultimate accountability mechanism in toxic mold litigation. While most cases settle, the possibility of trial shapes every settlement negotiation. Trial outcomes establish the valuation benchmarks that guide future cases. Trial verdicts create the precedents that define the field.

The attorneys who try these cases well, who translate science into story, who balance emotion with evidence, who prepare thoroughly and execute skillfully, determine not only the outcomes of their specific cases but the evolution of toxic mold litigation as a whole.

As the field continues to mature, as climate change increases moisture-related disputes, as building science advances, and as medical understanding evolves, trial practice in toxic mold litigation will continue to develop. But the fundamental skills of clear communication, strategic thinking, thorough preparation, and persuasive advocacy will remain central to success.

The courtroom is where proof meets narrative, where science becomes accessible, where responsibility is determined, and where justice is achieved or denied. For attorneys practicing in this demanding field, excellence in trial practice is not optional. It is essential.

The next and final chapter examines the future of toxic mold litigation, considering how climate change, evolving insurance markets, technological advances in environmental testing, and shifting legal standards will shape the field in the coming decade and whether mold litigation will remain a specialized niche or expand into broader environmental reform and public health accountability.

PART VI: The Future

20

The Future of Toxic Mold Litigation

Climate, Insurance, Technology, and the Next Decade

I. The Field at an Inflection Point

As of 2026, toxic mold litigation is no longer speculative, sensational, or emergent. It is established, but it remains profoundly dynamic.

Over the past two decades, the field has traveled a remarkable trajectory. It survived early "next asbestos" predictions that proved hyperbolic. It withstood scientific scrutiny that narrowed but did not eliminate viable claims. It adapted to tightening insurance exclusions that reshaped but did not destroy coverage. It expanded beyond simple landlord-tenant disputes into construction defect, nondisclosure, bad faith, and institutional accountability litigation. And it matured into a technically sophisticated practice area requiring integration of building science, environmental assessment, medical causation, insurance analysis, and trial advocacy.

The question facing practitioners, judges, insurers, property owners, and policymakers is no longer whether mold litigation will continue. It will. The volume of moisture-driven disputes, the aging of housing infrastructure, and the increasing volatility of climate patterns ensure ongoing litigation for the foreseeable future.

The essential questions are different: How will the field evolve? What external forces will reshape it? Which legal theories will expand and which will contract? How will technology change environmental assessment and proof? Will insurance markets stabilize or continue restricting coverage? And perhaps most significantly, will toxic mold litigation remain a specialized niche practice or expand into broader environmental justice and public health reform?

This final chapter examines the forces likely to shape toxic mold litigation over the next decade, analyzes emerging trends, identifies potential inflection points, and offers predictions about where the field is heading.

II. Climate Change as the Primary Litigation Driver

Perhaps the most significant force that will shape toxic mold litigation in the coming decade is climate change. The relationship between climate volatility and moisture intrusion is direct, measurable, and accelerating.

The Scientific Reality

Climate patterns across the United States are shifting in ways that increase moisture-related building failures:

Increased Precipitation Intensity
While total annual rainfall may not increase dramatically in all regions, precipitation is increasingly concentrated in extreme events. Instead of steady, moderate rain, many areas experience intense downpours that overwhelm drainage systems, exceed building envelope design assumptions, and create saturation conditions that promote mold growth.

Atmospheric River Events
The West Coast, particularly California, is experiencing more frequent and intense atmospheric river events. These moisture-laden storm systems can deliver months' worth of precipitation in days, causing flooding, overwhelming aging infrastructure, and creating widespread moisture intrusion in buildings not designed for such extremes.

Hurricane Intensification
Atlantic and Gulf Coast regions face increasingly powerful hurricanes with greater rainfall totals. Hurricane-related flooding causes immediate moisture problems, but the litigation often follows months or years later as hidden water intrusion manifests as mold growth.

Freeze-Thaw Cycles
Northern regions are experiencing more variable winter temperatures, creating repeated freeze-thaw cycles that stress building envelopes, crack foundations, damage roofing systems, and create pathways for water intrusion that accumulate over time.

Humidity Pattern Changes
The Southeast is experiencing prolonged periods of elevated humidity that stress HVAC systems, promote condensation in wall assemblies, and create ideal conditions for mold amplification even without obvious water intrusion events.

Coastal Flooding and Sea Level Rise
Low-lying coastal areas face increasing tidal flooding, storm surge, and rising groundwater tables that create chronic moisture problems in buildings that previously experienced only occasional water exposure.

Litigation Implications

These climate-driven changes will manifest in several litigation trends:

Increased Case Volume
More moisture events inevitably produce more mold disputes. The baseline volume of toxic mold litigation is likely to increase by 15-25% over the next decade simply due to increased moisture intrusion frequency.

Geographic Shifts
Litigation hot spots will evolve. Regions previously experiencing modest mold litigation may see substantial increases. Florida, Louisiana, and Texas have long been active mold litigation jurisdictions. But expect significant growth in:

- Mid-Atlantic states facing increased hurricane exposure
- Mountain West regions experiencing atmospheric river flooding
- Northern tier states with aging housing stock stressed by freeze-thaw cycles

- Low-lying coastal communities from South Carolina to Maine

Design and Construction Standard Evolution
As climate patterns shift, building codes developed for historical weather patterns become inadequate. Construction defect litigation will increasingly focus on whether builders and designers should have anticipated more extreme moisture conditions than codes required.

Questions that will drive litigation:

- Should designers in 2026 account for 100-year storms that now occur every 25 years?
- Do builders have duties to exceed code minimums when codes lag behind climate reality?
- Are moisture management systems adequate for historical conditions but inadequate for projected future conditions negligent?

Courts will grapple with whether reasonable professional practice requires forward-looking climate-adaptive design or merely compliance with existing codes based on historical data.

Insurance Pressure
Climate-driven moisture claims will stress insurance markets, likely producing:

- Further coverage restrictions in high-risk regions
- Increased premiums for comprehensive water damage coverage
- More aggressive coverage litigation as insurers seek to limit exposure
- Potential market withdrawal from certain coastal and flood-prone areas

Systemic Infrastructure Cases
Expect increasing litigation against municipalities and public housing authorities whose aging infrastructure cannot handle more intense precipitation. Storm water management failures, inadequate drainage systems, and overwhelmed sewage systems create moisture intrusion that may generate governmental liability claims.

Resilience and Adaptation Litigation

A new category of claims may emerge: failure to adapt known infrastructure to documented climate risks. Property owners who ignore recommendations to upgrade drainage, improve waterproofing, or enhance moisture management systems may face heightened liability when predictable climate-driven failures occur.

The Ten-Year Climate Litigation Prediction

By 2035, climate change will have fundamentally altered toxic mold litigation:

Volume: Total mold-related cases will increase 20-30% above 2026 levels.

Complexity: Cases will increasingly involve expert testimony about changing climate patterns, evolving building standards, and whether reasonable professional practice requires climate-adaptive rather than merely code-compliant design.

Damages: Aggregate damages will increase as more severe moisture events cause more extensive contamination and longer displacement periods.

Defendants: Expanded liability theories will draw in municipal defendants for infrastructure failures, product manufacturers for systems inadequate for new climate realities, and designers who failed to account for projected rather than historical conditions.

Geographic Distribution: The litigation map will shift toward previously moderate-activity jurisdictions experiencing climate-driven moisture stress.

Climate change is not merely a background factor in toxic mold litigation's future. It is the primary driver that will determine case volume, geographic distribution, liability theories, and damages exposure for the next generation.

III. Aging Infrastructure and Deferred Maintenance: The Crisis Accelerates

While climate change creates new moisture challenges, aging housing stock and deferred maintenance amplify vulnerability. The United States faces an infrastructure crisis that extends beyond roads and bridges to include the buildings where people live and work.

The Scope of the Problem

Housing Age
The median age of U.S. housing stock continues to increase. By 2026, nearly 40% of all housing units are more than 40 years old. Building components have finite lifespans:

- Roofing systems: 15-30 years depending on material
- Window seals: 10-20 years
- Exterior cladding: 20-50 years depending on material and installation
- Plumbing systems: 20-50 years
- HVAC systems: 15-20 years

As these systems age beyond their design life without replacement, failure rates increase exponentially.

Deferred Capital Expenditure
Particularly in rental housing, public housing, and institutionally-owned properties, capital improvement budgets have not kept pace with building needs. Property owners defer expensive roof replacements, postpone window system upgrades, and delay waterproofing repairs until failures become acute.

This deferred maintenance creates a growing inventory of buildings one storm away from significant moisture intrusion and mold contamination.

Multi-Family Concentration
The problem is most acute in multi-family housing where:

- Ownership is often remote from occupancy
- Profit margins incentivize deferred maintenance
- Complex building systems require coordinated repair
- Tenant turnover reduces pressure for long-term investment
- Affordable housing faces chronic underfunding

Geographic Vulnerability
Certain regions face particular infrastructure challenges:

Rust Belt Cities: Post-industrial urban areas with large inventories of aging housing, declining property values that discourage investment, and population loss that reduces political pressure for enforcement.

Sun Belt Boom Areas: Rapid growth regions where construction in the 1980s-2000s used moisture-management systems now reaching end of design life. Stucco-clad construction in humid climates, in particular, faces widespread moisture intrusion as sealants fail and drainage planes degrade.

Coastal Resort Areas: Properties experiencing intense seasonal use, salt air exposure, and hurricane stress age faster than similar buildings in benign climates.

Affordable Housing Nationally: Public housing authorities and affordable housing providers face chronic underfunding, creating systematic deferred maintenance across millions of units.

Litigation Implications

The collision between aging infrastructure and climate-driven moisture stress will produce several litigation trends:

Systemic Failure Cases

Expect more cases involving multiple units or entire buildings where aging building envelope systems fail comprehensively. These cases generate:

- Higher aggregate damages
- More complex allocation questions among multiple defendants
- Greater institutional defendant exposure
- Increased insurance coverage disputes

Habitability Class Actions

Conditions may ripen for class certification in certain contexts. While medical causation remains individualized and difficult to certify, property-based habitability claims affecting many similarly-situated tenants may overcome certification barriers.

Scenarios likely to generate class litigation:

- Public housing developments with systematic moisture management failures

- Large apartment complexes with design defects affecting multiple buildings
- Manufactured housing communities with endemic moisture problems

Governmental Liability
Public housing authorities and governmental landlords face particular vulnerability. Chronic underfunding combined with aging infrastructure creates conditions ripe for major litigation when:

- Deferred maintenance leads to catastrophic failures
- Documentation shows knowledge of problems but budget-driven inaction
- Vulnerable populations (families with children, elderly, disabled) experience extended exposure

Regulatory Enforcement
Increased litigation may produce enhanced regulatory response. Jurisdictions experiencing mold litigation spikes may adopt:

- Mandatory inspection regimes for aging rental housing
- Required capital reserve funding for multi-family properties
- Enhanced habitability enforcement with meaningful penalties
- Moisture management standards for older buildings

Insurance Market Stress
As aging infrastructure claims increase, insurers may:

- Require infrastructure inspections before issuing coverage
- Exclude coverage for buildings over certain ages without upgrade documentation
- Implement aggressive reserve policies anticipating higher claim frequency
- Increase premiums substantially for older buildings

Market-Driven Obsolescence
Buildings with chronic moisture problems may become economically

ms may become economically obsolete. When remediation costs approach or exceed property value, ownership becomes untenable. This creates:

- Abandonment in low-value markets
- Demolition and redevelopment in high-value markets
- Potential for environmental justice concerns when affordable housing is demolished rather than repaired

The Maintenance Crisis Timeline

Looking forward to 2035:

Phase 1 (2026-2029): Accumulating Problems
Deferred maintenance continues. Building systems age beyond design life. Failure rates accelerate. Litigation increases but remains manageable within existing frameworks.

Phase 2 (2030-2033): Crisis Recognition
Major failures in public housing and large multi-family properties generate headlines. Regulatory attention increases. Insurance costs spike. Property values in vulnerable areas decline.

Phase 3 (2034-2035): System Response
Policy interventions emerge. Funding mechanisms for infrastructure upgrade develop. Building codes modernize. Insurance markets partially stabilize with new risk assessment models.

Throughout this timeline, toxic mold litigation serves as the accountability mechanism forcing attention to problems that market forces and political processes fail to address proactively.

IV. Insurance Market Evolution: Contraction, Innovation, and Coverage Wars

The insurance industry's response to toxic mold exposure has profoundly shaped litigation, and insurance evolution will continue driving the field's future trajectory.

The Current Insurance Landscape

By 2026, mold-related insurance coverage reflects two decades of exclusion development:

Comprehensive Mold Exclusions: Most standard homeowners and commercial property policies include absolute mold exclusions or sub-limits (typically $5,000-$15,000) for mold remediation.

Anti-Concurrent Causation Clauses: Modern policies bar coverage when excluded perils (like mold) contribute concurrently with covered perils (like water damage).

Pollution Cross-References: Many policies treat mold as a pollutant, incorporating mold into broad pollution exclusions.

Reduced Resulting Loss Coverage: The doctrine that mold resulting from covered water damage remains covered has been narrowed through careful policy drafting.

This restrictive environment creates two consequences: reduced settlement resources in underlying liability cases and increased insurance bad faith litigation as policyholders challenge coverage denials.

Emerging Insurance Trends

Several developments will shape insurance's role in mold litigation over the next decade:

Climate-Based Underwriting Refinement
Insurers are developing increasingly sophisticated models that assess property-specific moisture risk based on:

- Microclimate precipitation patterns
- Flood zone proximity
- Building age and construction type
- Historical claims data
- Topography and drainage
- Coastal exposure

This risk modeling will produce:

- Highly differentiated premiums based on moisture exposure

- Coverage unavailability in highest-risk areas
- Reduced coverage limits even when available
- Mandatory risk mitigation requirements (upgraded drainage, moisture monitoring systems) as conditions of coverage

Parametric Insurance Products

Expect development of parametric insurance that pays pre-determined amounts when objective triggers occur (e.g., precipitation exceeds X inches in Y time period) rather than traditional indemnity coverage requiring proof of covered loss.

For mold, parametric products might trigger payment when:

- Flooding reaches certain depth
- Humidity levels exceed thresholds for defined periods
- Precipitation intensity exceeds design standards

These products avoid coverage litigation by eliminating interpretation questions, but they may not align coverage with actual mold-related losses.

Mold Endorsement Evolution

Some insurers are developing affirmative mold coverage endorsements for higher premiums. These endorsements may cover:

- Remediation costs beyond standard policy sub-limits
- Displacement expenses during extensive remediation
- Property damage resulting from mold growth
- Limited personal injury coverage for documented respiratory effects

Endorsement availability will vary dramatically by region, building type, and demonstrated risk management.

Technology Integration Requirements

Insurers may begin requiring (or offering premium discounts for) installation of:

- Moisture monitoring systems that alert to water intrusion
- Smart home technology tracking humidity levels
- Automatic water shut-off systems

- Real-time building health monitoring

This technology-driven underwriting shifts some risk management burden to insureds while providing earlier intervention that reduces ultimate severity.

Coverage Litigation Intensification

As exclusions tighten and climate-driven claims increase, expect intensified litigation over:

Ambiguity Interpretation: Whether specific policy language clearly excludes claims or contains interpretive ambiguities that courts should resolve in favor of coverage.

Efficient Proximate Cause vs. Anti-Concurrent Causation: Whether anti-concurrent causation clauses effectively override traditional efficient proximate cause doctrines that would provide coverage when covered perils predominate.

Bad Faith Standards: Whether coverage denials based on mold exclusions constitute bad faith when insurers knew or should have known that covered water damage predominated.

Regulatory Challenges: Whether mold exclusions are so broad they render policies illusory, violating public policy or insurance regulatory principles.

Some jurisdictions may develop case law limiting mold exclusion scope. Others may uphold exclusions as written. This jurisdictional variation will influence forum selection in cases involving national insurers.

Insurance Market Predictions for 2035

Market Segmentation: Insurance will bifurcate into limited, inexpensive coverage for standard risks and comprehensive, expensive coverage for those willing to pay premiums reflecting full moisture exposure.

Geographic Withdrawal: Expect partial or complete market withdrawal from highest-risk coastal and flood-prone areas, creating residual market or governmental backstop coverage needs.

Mandatory Climate Disclosure: Insurers will require detailed climate risk assessments before issuing coverage for commercial properties and high-value residential properties in vulnerable areas.

Bad Faith Evolution: Courts will develop more sophisticated standards for evaluating insurer conduct in climate-driven mold claims, potentially creating heightened duties to investigate thoroughly and interpret coverage reasonably when climate change creates novel exposure scenarios.

Legislative Intervention: Some states may regulate mold exclusions more aggressively, requiring minimum coverage levels or prohibiting certain exclusion types in residential policies.

The insurance dimension of toxic mold litigation will not simplify. It will become more complex, more contentious, and more central to case outcomes as coverage availability determines whether meaningful settlement funds exist.

V. Technological Advances: Transforming Environmental Assessment and Proof

Technology is reshaping how moisture intrusion and mold contamination are detected, documented, measured, and proven in litigation.

Current Technology Applications

As of 2026, several technologies are already influencing mold litigation:

Infrared Thermography: Identifies temperature differentials indicating moisture behind walls and ceilings without destructive testing.

Moisture Meters: Provide non-invasive readings of moisture content in building materials.

Thermal Imaging Drones: Allow roof and building envelope inspection without scaffolding or physical access.

Air Sampling Evolution: Laboratory analysis has become more sophisticated, with genus and species-level identification and quantification.

Environmental DNA (eDNA) Analysis: Emerging technology that identifies mold species from dust samples or surface swabs with greater precision than traditional culture methods.

These technologies have already changed litigation by:

- Providing earlier detection of hidden problems

- Creating more objective documentation of extent
- Reducing destructive testing requirements
- Generating more precise exposure data

Emerging Technologies (2026-2035)

Several technological developments will significantly impact mold litigation:

Artificial Intelligence and Machine Learning

AI applications in mold litigation will include:

Predictive Moisture Modeling: AI systems analyzing building characteristics, weather data, construction details, and historical patterns to predict moisture intrusion risk with high precision. These models may become evidence of notice (defendant should have known building was high-risk) or foreseeability (reasonable design requires systems adequate for predicted conditions).

Image Analysis: AI-powered analysis of photographs and infrared images to identify moisture intrusion patterns, quantify mold extent, and assess remediation completeness. This may reduce reliance on human expert interpretation and create more objective assessment standards.

Claims Pattern Recognition: Insurance companies will use AI to identify suspicious mold claim patterns, potentially leading to more aggressive coverage denials but also revealing systemic building failures when multiple claims cluster.

Automated Building Health Monitoring

Real-Time Sensor Networks: Buildings increasingly incorporate networks of sensors monitoring:

- Humidity levels in wall cavities
- Moisture content of building materials
- Temperature differentials indicating water intrusion
- Air quality including mold spore concentrations

These systems create continuous data streams replacing snapshot environmental testing.

Litigation Implications:

- Defendants with monitoring systems have earlier notice, reducing response time defenses but also demonstrating diligence
- Absence of monitoring in high-risk buildings may suggest negligence
- Continuous data provides objective exposure timelines, strengthening or weakening causation arguments
- Data preservation and production create new discovery challenges

Blockchain and Documentation

Immutable Maintenance Records: Blockchain technology may create tamper-proof documentation of:

- Inspection dates and findings
- Work order submissions and completions
- Contractor certifications
- Remediation protocols and clearances

This technology prevents post-hoc document alteration while creating discoverable audit trails.

Smart Contract Remediation: Automated systems might trigger remediation protocols when sensors detect moisture conditions, creating documentation of response or failure to respond without human intervention.

Advanced Biological Testing

Mycotoxin Quantification: Laboratory methods for accurately measuring mycotoxin concentrations in air, dust, and biological samples are improving. If these methods achieve validation and standardization, they may provide the dose evidence currently lacking in toxic exposure claims.

Biomarker Development: Research into biological markers of mold exposure may eventually provide objective evidence of exposure levels and physiological response, strengthening specific causation arguments.

Genetic Susceptibility Testing: As understanding of genetic factors affecting mold sensitivity improves, testing may identify individuals at heightened risk, supporting vulnerability arguments while also creating defenses (genetic predisposition rather than exposure caused illness).

Virtual and Augmented Reality

Site Documentation: VR capture of contaminated properties creates immersive documentation allowing remote inspection and jury "walk-throughs" of conditions.

Expert Demonstration: AR presentations allow experts to overlay building diagrams onto photographs, animate water intrusion pathways, and demonstrate concepts interactively.

Remote Testimony: VR courtrooms may permit more engaging remote expert testimony when travel is impossible or impractical.

Technology's Impact on Proof Standards

Technological advances will influence evidentiary standards:

Increased Precision Demands: As measurement technologies improve, courts may demand more precise dose evidence. The excuse that precise exposure measurement is impossible weakens when continuous monitoring technology exists.

Objective Data Over Expert Opinion: Courts may prefer objective sensor data to expert interpretation, reducing some expert battles while creating new disputes about sensor accuracy, calibration, and data interpretation.

Real-Time Notice: Automated monitoring systems create documented notice of problems immediately upon occurrence, eliminating delayed-discovery arguments but also potentially shortening response times courts deem reasonable.

Validation Requirements: New technologies create new Daubert battles. AI-generated risk assessments, eDNA analysis results, and biomarker testing will face admissibility challenges until methodologies become generally accepted.

The Digital Divide Concern

Technology advances create potential inequities:

Access Disparity: Sophisticated monitoring, testing, and documentation technologies are expensive. Well-funded institutional defendants can deploy comprehensive technology while individual plaintiffs cannot. This may create evidentiary imbalances favoring wealthy parties.

Expertise Requirements: Interpreting complex technological data requires specialized expertise, increasing litigation costs and potentially favoring parties who can afford top-tier technological experts.

Data Privacy: Continuous monitoring systems create privacy concerns. Tenants may resist sensor installation that documents their activities. Employees may object to workplace air quality monitoring that tracks their presence.

Courts and legislatures will need to address whether technology creates unfair advantages and whether minimum technological standards should apply to certain building types or ownership categories.

Technology Trajectory to 2035

By 2035, toxic mold litigation will be technologically transformed:

Standard of Care Evolution: Reasonable property management will include technology-assisted moisture monitoring in many contexts.

Evidence Expectations: Courts will expect objective sensor data when available, viewing subjective assessment as insufficient when technology could have provided precision.

Causation Proof: Improved biological testing may finally provide the dose-response data currently lacking, potentially expanding viable personal injury claims or definitively limiting them based on measured safe thresholds.

Efficiency Gains: Technology will accelerate case development, reduce inspection costs, and provide earlier clarity about liability and damages, potentially increasing settlement rates.

Technology is neither inherently pro-plaintiff nor pro-defendant. It is a tool that increases precision, creates objective documentation, and raises evidentiary standards. Attorneys who master technological evidence will have significant advantages over those practicing as if environmental assessment were still limited to visual inspection and basic air sampling.

VI. Legislative and Regulatory Evolution: From Recognition to Reform

Statutory and regulatory responses to toxic mold have thus far emphasized recognition rather than comprehensive reform. The next decade may produce more substantive legislative intervention.

Current Legislative Landscape

As of 2026, mold-specific statutes remain limited:

State-Level Approaches:

- California's foundational but limited Toxic Mold Protection Act
- Texas's former licensing framework for remediation professionals
- Scattered disclosure requirements in real estate transactions
- Building code amendments addressing moisture management in some jurisdictions

Federal Inaction:

- No comprehensive federal mold statute
- No EPA exposure standards
- No OSHA residential mold limits
- Limited HUD guidance for public housing

This legislative vacuum leaves mold litigation primarily governed by common law tort and contract principles, creating jurisdictional variation and uncertainty.

Potential Legislative Developments

Several legislative trends may emerge:

Mandatory Disclosure Expansion

More states may adopt comprehensive disclosure requirements for:

Residential Sales: Requiring sellers to disclose:

- Known moisture intrusion history
- Previous mold remediation
- Ongoing moisture problems
- Building envelope defects affecting moisture management

Rental Housing: Requiring landlords to disclose:

- Moisture problems in prior 12-24 months
- Mold complaints from previous tenants
- Remediation conducted
- Known building envelope vulnerabilities

Commercial Leasing: Extending disclosure requirements to commercial properties, particularly regarding HVAC adequacy and moisture management.

Disclosure statutes create strict liability frameworks reducing litigation uncertainty while ensuring transparency.

Habitability Codification

States may codify habitability standards regarding moisture and mold:

Response Timeframes: Statutory requirements that landlords:

- Inspect within 48-72 hours of moisture complaint
- Begin remediation within defined periods (5-14 days)
- Complete work within reasonable timeframes based on scope

Tenant Remedies: Clear statutory remedies including:

- Rent abatement during contamination
- Relocation assistance during remediation
- Termination rights for serious habitability failures
- Attorney fee recovery for prevailing tenants

Administrative Enforcement: Enhanced housing code enforcement with:

- Meaningful penalties for violation
- Inspection authority
- Emergency remediation powers
- Receivership options for chronic violators

Such statutes reduce litigation by creating clear standards while enhancing enforcement beyond private lawsuits.

Building Code Modernization

Climate-Adaptive Standards: Building codes may begin requiring:

- Drainage systems designed for projected rather than historical precipitation
- Enhanced waterproofing in flood-prone areas
- Moisture-resistant materials in high-humidity climates
- HVAC systems adequate for projected future temperature and humidity patterns

Retrofit Requirements: Older buildings may face mandatory upgrades:

- Moisture barrier installation during renovations
- Drainage system improvements
- Ventilation upgrades

Technology Integration: Codes may eventually require:

- Moisture monitoring systems in certain building types
- Smart home water shut-off technology
- Building health monitoring in large multi-family properties

Insurance Regulation

State insurance commissioners may regulate mold coverage more actively:

Minimum Coverage Standards: Requiring minimum mold remediation coverage in homeowners policies (e.g., $25,000-$50,000) rather than permitting nominal sub-limits.

Disclosure Requirements: Mandating clear, plain-language disclosure of mold exclusions and coverage limitations.

Bad Faith Standards: Establishing statutory bad faith standards for mold claim handling, including:

- Mandatory investigation timelines
- Prohibited claim practices
- Policyholder bill of rights

Rate Regulation: Reviewing mold-related premium increases for reasonableness and actuarial support.

Public Housing Reform

Federal and state legislation may address systemic public housing mold problems:

Capital Funding: Dedicated funding for:

- Building envelope repairs
- Moisture management system upgrades
- Comprehensive mold remediation
- Preventive maintenance programs

Inspection Mandates: Required regular inspections with:

- Public reporting of conditions
- Mandatory remediation timelines
- Enforcement mechanisms

Tenant Protections: Enhanced rights for public housing residents including:

- Right to habitability enforcement without eviction retaliation
- Relocation assistance during remediation

- Health monitoring for affected residents

Environmental Justice Integration

Mold litigation increasingly intersects with environmental justice concerns. Legislation may emerge recognizing:

Disproportionate Impact: Low-income communities and communities of color experience higher rates of substandard housing with moisture problems.

Health Equity: Children in affordable housing face elevated respiratory illness rates partly attributable to poor indoor air quality.

Climate Vulnerability: Low-income housing often occupies flood-prone areas with inadequate infrastructure.

Environmental justice frameworks may produce:

- Targeted enforcement in historically neglected communities
- Funding priorities for affordable housing infrastructure
- Enhanced monitoring and reporting requirements

Barriers to Legislative Reform

Despite potential benefits, comprehensive legislative reform faces obstacles:

Industry Opposition: Property management associations, builder groups, and insurance industry lobbies oppose regulations increasing compliance costs or liability exposure.

Cost Concerns: Mandatory upgrades, enhanced enforcement, and coverage requirements create costs ultimately passed to consumers through higher rents, home prices, and insurance premiums.

Jurisdictional Variation: Federal legislation faces states' rights resistance. State legislation creates compliance complexity for national operators.

Scientific Uncertainty: Absence of established exposure thresholds makes standard-setting difficult. Legislators hesitate to mandate specific remediation protocols when scientific consensus is incomplete.

Competing Priorities: Housing affordability, climate adaptation, and infrastructure funding compete for limited legislative attention and resources.

Legislative Trajectory to 2035

Realistic expectations for legislative evolution:

Incremental Reform: Expect gradual adoption of disclosure requirements, modest building code updates, and limited habitability codification rather than comprehensive federal mold legislation.

Crisis-Driven Response: Major reforms will likely follow high-profile tragedies (child deaths, catastrophic building failures) that generate political pressure for action.

Jurisdictional Variation: Blue states will adopt more comprehensive tenant protections and stricter building standards. Red states will favor market-based approaches and liability limits. Variation will increase rather than harmonize.

Soft Law Development: Industry standards, professional guidelines, and voluntary best practices will evolve faster than binding legislation, creating de facto standards that influence litigation even without statutory force.

Legislation will shape mold litigation's future, but the pace will be measured and the scope limited. Common law development through case-by-case adjudication will remain the primary mechanism for defining duties, standards, and remedies.

VII. Medical and Scientific Research: The Knowledge Frontier

The evolution of medical and scientific understanding of mold-related illness will profoundly influence litigation's future trajectory.

Current State of Scientific Knowledge

As of 2026, scientific consensus exists regarding:

Well-Established Effects:

- Allergic reactions (rhinitis, conjunctivitis)
- Asthma exacerbation in sensitized individuals
- Respiratory irritation from high-concentration exposure
- Hypersensitivity pneumonitis in rare, intense exposure scenarios

Contested or Emerging Theories:

- Chronic inflammatory response syndrome (CIRS)
- Cognitive impairment from residential exposure
- Immune dysfunction from mycotoxin exposure
- Multi-system illness from routine exposure levels

This division between accepted and contested science creates the courtroom battles over expert admissibility and causation proof.

Research Directions

Several research areas may produce findings that reshape litigation:

Dose-Response Studies

What's Needed: Large-scale epidemiological studies establishing relationships between measured mold exposure levels and specific health outcomes across general populations and vulnerable subgroups.

Challenges: Expense, difficulty measuring historical exposure, confounding environmental factors, and variability in individual susceptibility make such studies difficult.

If Developed: Reliable dose-response data would transform causation litigation by providing objective thresholds. Claims below threshold levels would fail; claims above would succeed. Uncertainty would decrease dramatically.

Timeline: Unlikely before 2030 given study design and funding challenges. Possible by 2035 if research prioritization increases.

Biomarker Validation

What's Needed: Validated, standardized tests that objectively measure:

- Mycotoxin exposure levels in biological samples
- Physiological responses to mold exposure
- Biomarkers distinguishing mold-related illness from similar conditions

Challenges: Developing tests with adequate sensitivity, specificity, and reproducibility. Establishing normal reference ranges. Gaining FDA approval and medical community acceptance.

If Developed: Objective biomarkers would reduce reliance on subjective symptom reporting and expert opinion, making causation more provable or disprovable based on test results.

Timeline: Some tests may achieve preliminary validation by 2030, widespread acceptance by 2035.

Genetic Susceptibility Research

What's Needed: Identification of genetic markers predicting heightened mold sensitivity, helping explain why some individuals develop serious illness while others exposed similarly do not.

Challenges: Genetic complexity, population diversity, interaction with environmental factors, and ethical concerns about genetic testing in litigation.

If Developed: Genetic susceptibility evidence could:

- Support plaintiffs showing they are genetically vulnerable
- Support defendants showing plaintiffs would have developed symptoms from any environmental trigger
- Create complex causation allocation questions

Timeline: Basic research exists but clinical application likely 2030-2040.

Mechanism of Action Studies

What's Needed: Clear understanding of biological pathways through which mold exposure produces systemic effects beyond allergic and irritant responses.

Challenges: Complexity of immune system, difficulty isolating mold effects from other environmental exposures, and variability in individual responses.

If Developed: Understanding mechanisms would either validate emerging illness theories (strengthening plaintiff claims) or definitively establish that proposed mechanisms are biologically implausible (strengthening defense positions).

Timeline: Ongoing research may produce clarifying findings by 2030-2033.

Long-Term Outcome Studies

What's Needed: Longitudinal studies following individuals after mold exposure to determine whether effects are transient or persistent, whether removal from exposure produces full recovery, and what factors predict long-term outcomes.

Challenges: Long study duration, participant retention, and difficulty controlling for confounding factors.

If Developed: Outcome data would inform damages by establishing what percentage of exposed individuals experience lasting effects and what severity of exposure predicts long-term harm.

Timeline: Results from studies beginning now might be available 2030-2035.

Potential Scenarios

Scientific research could produce three broad outcomes:

Scenario 1: Validation of Emerging Theories

Research establishes that mold exposure at levels commonly found in water-damaged buildings causes systemic illness in susceptible individuals through identifiable biological mechanisms.

Litigation Impact:

- Expansion of viable personal injury claims
- Higher settlement values
- More aggressive plaintiff litigation
- Insurance industry crisis requiring regulatory intervention

- Potential mass tort development if exposure is sufficiently widespread

Probability: Low to moderate. Current scientific trajectory does not strongly suggest this outcome, but research could produce surprises.

Scenario 2: Definitive Limitation of Health Effects

Research establishes clear thresholds below which mold exposure does not cause serious illness, validates reliable testing methods for determining exposure levels, and demonstrates that systemic illness theories lack biological plausibility.

Litigation Impact:

- Narrowing of viable claims to clearly documented high-exposure scenarios
- Decreased settlement values for residential exposure claims
- More successful defense motions for summary judgment
- Shift of litigation focus from personal injury to property damage
- Stabilization of insurance markets

Probability: Moderate. Current scientific trends suggest gradual consensus developing that severe systemic effects require exposure levels uncommon in residential settings.

Scenario 3: Continued Uncertainty

Research continues producing mixed results. Some studies suggest broader health effects; others find limited impact. Consensus remains elusive.

Litigation Impact:

- Continued reliance on expert battles
- Continued jurisdictional variation in outcomes
- Continued settlement value unpredictability
- Continued insurance industry caution
- Field remains specialized and scientifically contentious

Probability: High. Scientific complexity and individual variability may prevent definitive resolution of contested questions for decades.

The Realistic Prediction

The most likely scenario is gradual clarification rather than dramatic breakthrough. By 2035:

Accepted: Respiratory effects, allergic reactions, and asthma exacerbation will be even more firmly established as clearly caused by mold exposure.

Better Understood: Dose-response relationships for allergic and respiratory effects will be clearer, though not reduced to simple numeric thresholds.

Still Contested: Systemic illness theories will remain controversial but may gain some additional peer-reviewed support, creating jurisdictional splits in admissibility.

Emerging: Genetic susceptibility markers may be identified, creating new causation complexities.

Improved Testing: Better environmental and biological testing will provide more objective data without fully resolving causation disputes.

Scientific progress will shape but not revolutionize toxic mold litigation. The field will remain scientifically sophisticated, expert-driven, and factually intensive.

VIII. The Future of Settlement: Valuation Evolution and ADR Innovation

As the field matures, settlement practices and alternative dispute resolution mechanisms continue evolving.

Settlement Valuation Trends

Several factors will influence how mold cases are valued:

Narrowing Personal Injury Values

As courts consistently exclude or limit systemic illness claims, settlement values based primarily on personal injury will compress. The range for well-documented respiratory injury claims will stabilize in relatively narrow bands:

2035 Predicted Ranges:

- Mild allergic reactions, fully resolved: $10,000-$30,000
- Moderate asthma exacerbation requiring treatment: $30,000-$100,000
- Severe respiratory injury with lasting effects: $100,000-$300,000
- Exceptional cases with permanent respiratory damage: $300,000-$750,000

Values exceeding $1 million will be rare, limited to cases with devastating permanent injury, vulnerable plaintiffs (children with lifelong complications), and egregious defendant conduct.

Expanding Property Damage Values

As buildings age and climate-driven moisture events increase in severity, property damage components will expand:

Remediation Costs: Increasing due to:

- More extensive contamination requiring comprehensive remediation
- Stricter clearance standards
- Technology requirements (post-remediation monitoring)
- Labor cost inflation

Structural Damage: Water intrusion causing mold often causes concurrent structural damage, increasing total property loss.

Diminution in Value: Growing recognition that mold history affects property values even after remediation, particularly in competitive markets.

Business Interruption: Commercial cases involving displacement and lost revenue during extended remediation.

Property damages in major cases may routinely reach $500,000-$2 million, particularly in commercial properties or large multi-family developments.

Insurance Bad Faith Premium

Where insurance bad faith claims are viable, settlement values increase substantially:

Bad Faith Multiplier Effect:

- Underlying damages: $100,000
- Bad faith exposure (including punitive damages): $500,000-$2 million
- Total settlement leverage: $600,000-$2.1 million

Insurance bad faith will drive the highest-value settlements, particularly when carrier conduct is documented as unreasonable.

Alternative Dispute Resolution Evolution

ADR mechanisms will become more sophisticated:

Specialized Mold Mediators

Expect development of mediator specialization in toxic mold cases. Effective mold mediators will understand:

- Building science and remediation costs
- Medical causation standards and evidentiary hurdles
- Insurance coverage interpretation
- Jurisdiction-specific valuation norms
- Technology-driven assessment methods

Specialized mediators facilitate settlement more effectively than generalist mediators lacking technical knowledge.

Early Neutral Evaluation

Insurance carriers and sophisticated defendants may increasingly use early neutral evaluation where:

- Parties jointly retain neutral expert (building scientist, environmental consultant)
- Neutral conducts independent assessment

- Neutral provides non-binding evaluation of liability and damages
- Parties use evaluation to inform settlement negotiations

This process reduces dueling expert costs while providing objective baseline.

Binding Arbitration with Expert Arbitrators

Some parties may agree to binding arbitration before retired judges with scientific backgrounds or arbitrators with building science expertise, avoiding jury unpredictability while ensuring technical sophistication.

Structured Settlements

Complex mold cases may increasingly resolve through structured settlements including:

Remediation Oversight: Defendant funds remediation but plaintiff retains consultant to ensure adequacy.

Medical Monitoring: Periodic health evaluations for affected children funded by settlement.

Property Value Guarantees: Defendant guarantees to make up difference if property sells below appraised value within defined period.

Phased Payments: Initial payment for documented losses, subsequent payments contingent on medical outcomes or clearance testing results.

Technology-Enhanced Mediation

Virtual reality, demonstrative technology, and real-time data analysis will enhance mediation:

- VR property walk-throughs during mediation
- Live moisture monitoring data reviewed by parties
- AI-assisted valuation tools providing settlement ranges based on case characteristics

Settlement Practice Predictions for 2035

Increased Settlement Rates: As case outcomes become more predictable through accumulated precedent and improved assessment technology, settlement rates will exceed 95%.

Earlier Settlement: Technology-driven early assessment will facilitate settlement before expensive expert development, reducing litigation costs.

Bifurcated Approach: Simple cases settle quickly based on standardized valuations. Complex cases with novel issues proceed to developed motion practice before settling.

Insurance-Driven Dynamics: Insurance coverage positions will determine settlement timing and amounts more than underlying liability strength in many cases.

The settlement landscape will favor parties with access to sophisticated assessment technology, quality expert relationships, and understanding of jurisdiction-specific valuation norms.

IX. Will Mold Litigation Expand or Stabilize?

A central question about the field's future: Will toxic mold litigation expand into broader categories or stabilize as a specialized niche?

Expansion Scenarios

Several developments could expand the field:

Climate-Driven Volume Growth

Increasing moisture events could expand case volume by 30-50% over current levels, drawing in less specialized attorneys and creating pressure for procedural innovations (specialized dockets, case management protocols).

Environmental Justice Integration

Toxic mold litigation could merge with broader environmental justice movements, producing:

- Public interest litigation targeting systematic housing failures
- Government enforcement actions in environmental justice communities
- Federal intervention if mold in affordable housing becomes civil rights issue

Mass Tort Development

If research establishes clear causation for serious systemic illness at exposure levels common in certain building types (e.g., particular manufactured housing, specific multi-family construction), mass tort litigation could develop around:

- Defective building products
- Systematic construction practices
- Manufactured housing design failures

Regulatory Expansion Creating Private Rights

If states enact comprehensive mold statutes with private rights of action, citizen suit provisions, and statutory damages, litigation could expand beyond current tort frameworks.

Stabilization Scenarios

Alternatively, forces may limit growth:

Scientific Consensus Narrowing Claims

If research definitively establishes that serious systemic illness is rare or requires exposure levels uncommon in typical residential settings, viable claims narrow to well-documented respiratory injury, limiting potential case universe.

Insurance Market Adjustment

If insurance exclusions become universal and courts consistently uphold them, reduced settlement resources may discourage case filings.

Legislative Caps or Limitations

Some states may enact tort reform specifically addressing mold litigation, implementing:

- Damage caps
- Statutes of repose
- Heightened expert qualification requirements

- Pleading specificity requirements

Economic Barriers

Increasing expert costs and technology requirements may price out all but highest-value cases, limiting access to justice but reducing total case volume.

Alternative Dispute Resolution Mandates

Mandatory mediation or arbitration for mold cases below certain damage thresholds could divert cases from traditional litigation.

The Realistic Prediction

The most likely future is moderate expansion combined with continued specialization:

Volume: 20-30% increase by 2035 driven by climate and aging infrastructure.

Specialization: Increasing concentration in specialized plaintiff and defense firms rather than general practice expansion.

Bifurcation: Small cases (under $100,000 exposure) handled through streamlined ADR. Large cases (over $500,000 exposure) receiving full litigation development.

Geographic Concentration: Growth concentrated in climate-vulnerable regions (coastal areas, flood zones, hurricane-prone states) while remaining stable or declining in regions with stable climate patterns.

Subject Matter Evolution: Shift from pure toxic injury claims toward integrated claims combining property damage, habitability, nondisclosure, and insurance bad faith.

Toxic mold litigation will not become the next asbestos (mass tort with hundreds of thousands of claims) nor will it disappear (specialized practice remaining viable for select cases). It will remain a substantial but manageable category within environmental and property litigation.

X. Emerging Trends to Watch

Several developing trends bear monitoring:

Coronavirus Pandemic Legacy Effects

COVID-19 produced several consequences affecting mold litigation:

Remote Work and Commercial Real Estate

Reduced office occupancy means:

- Less frequent building inspection and maintenance
- HVAC systems running less, potentially creating humidity problems
- Deferred capital improvements as office values decline
- Moisture problems developing undetected in vacant or underutilized buildings

Expect spike in commercial mold claims as buildings return to full occupancy or are repurposed.

Residential Ventilation Concerns

Pandemic-driven attention to indoor air quality may produce:

- Increased awareness of mold as air quality issue
- More sophisticated tenant expectations about ventilation
- Enhanced building code ventilation requirements
- Greater use of air quality monitoring technology

Economic Displacement

Pandemic-related economic stress forced deferred maintenance in rental housing, creating inventory of deteriorating buildings likely to experience moisture failures in coming years.

Cryptocurrency and Digital Assets

The blockchain-based digital economy may influence mold litigation through:

Smart Contracts for Property Management

Automated lease agreements and maintenance protocols creating immutable records of obligations and performance.

Digital Property Records

Blockchain-based property histories including comprehensive moisture intrusion and remediation documentation, making concealment more difficult.

Cryptocurrency-Based Settlements

International parties or privacy-concerned defendants may offer cryptocurrency settlements, creating new valuation and enforcement challenges.

Artificial Intelligence in Legal Practice

AI will transform mold litigation practice:

Predictive Analytics

AI systems will analyze case characteristics and predict outcomes with increasing accuracy, informing settlement positions and case selection.

Document Review

AI document review will efficiently identify relevant emails, maintenance records, and communications in large discovery sets.

Legal Research

AI-powered research will quickly identify relevant precedent across jurisdictions, improving brief quality and strategic decision-making.

Expert Matching

AI systems may match cases with appropriate experts based on case characteristics, expert credentials, and historical testimony patterns.

Climate Refugees and Displacement

As climate change renders some areas increasingly uninhabitable:

Managed Retreat Litigation

Property owners in flood-prone areas may sue governmental entities that failed to implement managed retreat strategies, allowing continued development in areas destined for catastrophic moisture failures.

Adaptation Duty Cases

Claims that property owners knew of changing climate risks but failed to adapt infrastructure, constituting negligence or nuisance.

Insurance Allocation Disputes

When properties experience multiple moisture events over years, allocation disputes between successive insurers will generate complex coverage litigation.

Generational Wealth Transfer

As baby boomers transfer wealth to younger generations:

Property Condition Disputes

Heirs inheriting properties with hidden moisture problems may sue executors, trustees, or sellers for nondisclosure or inadequate property management.

Institutional Landlord Concentration

Younger generations less likely to own investment properties may accelerate shift toward institutional landlords, potentially changing litigation dynamics as individual landlords are replaced by corporate entities with sophisticated risk management.

XI. Practice Predictions: How Attorneys Will Practice Mold Litigation in 2035

Toxic mold litigation practice will look substantially different in 2035:

Plaintiff Practice Evolution

Technology Investment Requirements

Successful plaintiff firms will invest heavily in:

- Environmental assessment technology
- Data analysis tools
- Virtual documentation systems
- AI-powered case evaluation

Screening Rigor

Front-end case screening will become even more sophisticated, with firms declining 70-80% of potential cases after preliminary evaluation.

Specialization Depth

Leading plaintiff firms will subspecialize (construction defect mold vs. residential habitability vs. commercial exposure vs. insurance bad faith), recognizing that expertise depth matters more than practice breadth.

Collaborative Practice Models

Plaintiff attorneys may increasingly co-counsel cases, combining environmental expertise, medical causation experience, insurance coverage knowledge, and trial skills in case-specific teams.

Contingency Fee Structures

Fees will continue trending toward higher percentages for smaller cases (40-45%) reflecting increased costs, with sophisticated staged percentages for larger cases.

Defense Practice Evolution

Early Assessment Protocols

Defense firms will develop standardized early assessment checklists enabling rapid evaluation of exposure and settlement authority recommendations.

Technology-Driven Defense

Defendants will leverage monitoring technology, AI pattern recognition, and predictive analytics to identify fraudulent claims, assess risk, and optimize settlement strategy.

National Coordination

Institutional defendants and insurers will retain coordinated national defense counsel who understand jurisdiction-specific nuances while maintaining strategic consistency.

Offensive Claim Prevention

More sophisticated defendants will invest in preventive technology and protocols, reducing claim frequency while creating strong defenses when claims arise.

ADR Preferences

Defense practice will increasingly favor early mediation to avoid expert costs and jury unpredictability in cases with coverage or clear liability.

Judicial Administration

Specialized Dockets

Some jurisdictions may create environmental torts or toxic exposure dockets with judges developing mold litigation expertise.

Case Management Orders

Courts may implement standardized case management orders for mold cases, streamlining discovery, requiring early expert disclosure, and setting firm trial dates.

Science Advisors

Courts may increasingly appoint neutral scientific advisors to assist in evaluating conflicting expert testimony.

Mandatory Settlement Conferences

Early mandatory settlement conferences may become standard in mold litigation, particularly in jurisdictions with heavy dockets.

Expert Witness Evolution

Credentials Arms Race

Expert qualification requirements will escalate, with parties seeking:

- Multiple board certifications
- Academic appointments
- Extensive peer-reviewed publications
- National recognition

Specialization

Generic environmental consultants or general practitioners will become inadequate. Successful experts will have deep specialty credentials specifically in mold-related assessment or illness.

Technology Integration

Experts will be expected to utilize and explain sophisticated technology, AI-driven analysis, and continuous monitoring data.

Early Engagement

Experts will be retained earlier in case development, providing pre-litigation assessment and steering case strategy from inception.

XII. The Role of Mold Litigation in Broader Housing Policy

Toxic mold litigation exists within larger conversations about housing policy, affordability, climate adaptation, and environmental justice. The field's future depends partly on how these broader issues evolve.

Housing Affordability Tensions

Mold litigation creates tension with affordable housing goals:

Regulatory Compliance Costs

Enhanced mold standards, disclosure requirements, and remediation mandates increase housing costs, potentially:

- Raising rents beyond affordability for low-income tenants
- Reducing affordable housing supply as marginal properties become economically unviable
- Creating barriers to housing development

Litigation Risk Premium

Landlords in high-litigation jurisdictions charge rent premiums reflecting litigation risk, raising costs for all tenants regardless of whether problems exist.

Remediation-Driven Displacement

Aggressive mold enforcement can force temporary or permanent displacement of low-income tenants lacking alternative housing options.

Policy Responses:

Policymakers may need to balance habitability enforcement against affordability by:

- Funding remediation assistance for affordable housing providers
- Creating safe harbors for landlords implementing technology-based preventive systems
- Providing tax incentives for building envelope upgrades
- Ensuring displaced tenants have relocation assistance and return rights

Climate Adaptation Integration

Mold litigation may accelerate climate adaptation:

Market Signal Function

Litigation costs signal that certain building practices are inadequate for changing climate, driving innovation and practice improvement faster than regulation alone.

Risk Disclosure

Litigation forces disclosure of climate-related moisture risks, improving market information and potentially redirecting development away from highest-risk areas.

Infrastructure Investment

Lawsuit exposure may drive both public and private infrastructure investment that regulatory pressure alone could not compel.

Adaptation Litigation Theory

Mold cases may evolve into climate adaptation failure claims, holding parties liable for failing to adapt known infrastructure to documented changing risks.

Environmental Justice Dimensions

Mold litigation intersects with environmental justice:

Disparate Impact

Low-income communities and communities of color experience disproportionate exposure to substandard housing with moisture problems, raising environmental justice concerns.

Access to Justice Questions

High litigation costs may prevent residents of affordable housing from pursuing claims, creating justice gaps.

Systemic Reform Potential

Large-scale public housing mold litigation may drive systemic reforms benefiting vulnerable populations beyond individual case outcomes.

Policy Integration Needed:

Environmental justice principles should inform:

- Enforcement priorities targeting worst actors in low-income communities
- Funding mechanisms ensuring adequate housing infrastructure in environmental justice communities
- Community-based monitoring and advocacy support
- Protection against displacement following enforcement actions

Public Health Integration

Mold litigation may increasingly be viewed as public health intervention:

Disease Prevention

Reducing mold exposure through litigation-driven remediation prevents respiratory illness, particularly in children.

Healthcare Cost Reduction

Preventing mold-related asthma reduces healthcare costs, emergency room visits, and lost school/work time.

Environmental Health Tracking

Litigation data may inform public health surveillance, identifying geographic clusters of poor housing conditions.

Collaborative Approaches:

Public health and legal systems may collaborate through:

- Joint inspection and enforcement programs
- Health department support for litigation evidence development
- Epidemiological studies informing causation standards
- Medical-legal partnerships addressing housing health hazards

The future of mold litigation cannot be separated from these broader policy contexts. The field will be shaped by and will shape housing policy, climate adaptation strategy, environmental justice advocacy, and public health priorities.

XIII. Conclusion: A Mature Field Facing Dynamic Future

Toxic mold litigation has traveled far from its early-2000s origins. The sensationalism has faded. The scientific understanding has deepened. The legal standards have refined. The insurance landscape has transformed. The practice has professionalized.

Yet the field faces a dynamic rather than settled future.

The Certainties

Several aspects of mold litigation's future are reasonably certain:

Climate Change Will Drive Growth

Increasing moisture events will produce more mold disputes. Case volume will grow 20-30% by 2035.

Aging Infrastructure Will Amplify Problems

Deferred maintenance combined with climate stress will generate systematic failures in multi-family and affordable housing.

Insurance Will Remain Constrained

Coverage will contract in high-risk areas while potentially expanding modestly in lower-risk markets through specialized endorsements.

Technology Will Transform Practice

Continuous monitoring, AI analysis, and sophisticated testing will fundamentally change how cases are investigated, evaluated, and proven.

Scientific Understanding Will Improve Gradually

Research will clarify dose-response relationships and mechanisms, but dramatic breakthroughs resolving contested causation questions are unlikely in the next decade.

Specialization Will Deepen

The field will remain technically demanding, rewarding specialists and making general practice increasingly difficult.

Settlement Will Dominate

Trial rates will continue declining as case evaluation becomes more sophisticated and predictable.

The Uncertainties

Several critical uncertainties remain:

Legislative Response

Will governments respond to climate-driven mold problems with comprehensive regulation, modest reforms, or continued inaction? The answer will substantially affect the field.

Medical Breakthroughs

Could research validate emerging illness theories or definitively limit viable claims? Either outcome would reshape litigation dramatically.

Insurance Market Stability

Will insurance markets stabilize with sustainable mold coverage, continue contracting, or face crisis requiring governmental intervention?

Mass Tort Potential

Could certain building types or products generate concentrated claims leading to mass tort development, or will litigation remain individualized?

Environmental Justice Integration

Will mold litigation become integrated into broader environmental justice frameworks, potentially drawing federal attention and resources?

The Likely Trajectory

Synthesizing probable developments, the most likely future for toxic mold litigation is:

Moderate Growth: 25% volume increase by 2035, concentrated in climate-vulnerable regions and aging infrastructure contexts.

Continued Specialization: Practice concentration in sophisticated firms with technology capabilities and expert relationships.

Narrowed Personal Injury, Expanded Property Claims: Medical causation standards will remain strict, limiting systemic illness claims while property damage and habitability claims expand.

Insurance Bad Faith Prominence: Coverage disputes and bad faith claims will drive highest-value settlements.

Technology Integration: Continuous monitoring, AI analysis, and sophisticated testing will become standard in developed cases.

Incremental Legislative Reform: Modest disclosure, habitability, and building code improvements rather than comprehensive federal intervention.

Persistent Scientific Uncertainty: Gradual clarification rather than definitive resolution of contested causation questions.

ADR Dominance: Over 95% settlement rate with early mediation becoming standard practice.

Bifurcated Market: High-value cases receiving comprehensive development; low-value cases resolved through streamlined processes or abandoned as economically infeasible.

The Enduring Lessons

Regardless of how specific uncertainties resolve, certain lessons from two decades of toxic mold litigation endure:

1. **Proof Over Panic:** Fear-based claims without scientific support fail. Evidence-based claims succeed.
2. **Documentation Determines Outcomes:** Cases are won or lost based on contemporaneous records of conditions, complaints, and responses.
3. **Science Matters:** Understanding building science, environmental assessment, and medical causation is essential.
4. **Insurance Drives Economics:** Coverage availability and bad faith exposure often matter more than underlying liability strength.
5. **Prevention Beats Litigation:** Prompt response to moisture problems prevents both mold growth and lawsuits.
6. **Specialization Rewards:** Technical complexity favors attorneys who invest in developing expertise.
7. **Climate Cannot Be Ignored:** Weather patterns are changing, building stress is increasing, and litigation will follow.

Final Reflections

Toxic mold litigation in America stands in 2026 as a mature but evolving field. It is no longer the "next asbestos" of early predictions, nor is it the trivial nuisance some defendants wished it to be. It is a substantial, technically demanding practice area that holds property owners accountable for maintaining safe housing, ensures insurance companies honor coverage obligations, provides remedies for families harmed by substandard conditions, and drives improvements in building practices and moisture management.

The field's future will be shaped by climate science, building technology, medical research, insurance economics, legislative choices, and judicial wisdom. But it will ultimately be shaped by the practitioners who choose to work in this space: the attorneys who master complex science, the experts who provide reliable testimony, the judges who apply rigorous evidentiary standards, and the mediators who facilitate fair resolutions.

For those willing to invest in understanding building envelope science, environmental sampling methodology, medical causation standards, insurance policy interpretation, and persuasive trial advocacy, toxic mold litigation offers a practice that is intellectually demanding, socially important, economically viable, and perpetually evolving.

The next decade will bring challenges: climate stress on aging infrastructure, insurance market contraction, technological disruption, and scientific evolution. But it will also bring opportunities: for attorneys who adapt to changing conditions, for building practices that improve to prevent litigation, for regulations that establish clearer standards, and for outcomes that balance accountability with economic reality.

Toxic mold litigation will not disappear. It will not explode into mass tort. It will continue as a specialized field where evidence matters, science governs, and proof determines outcomes.

The future is neither dystopian nor utopian. It is simply work to be done: families to represent, buildings to inspect, experts to retain, coverage to interpret, cases to evaluate, settlements to negotiate, and occasionally, trials to win.

For practitioners committed to excellence in this demanding field, the future holds both challenge and opportunity. The work continues.

Conclusion: Toxic Mold Litigation in America

Discipline Over Drama

Toxic mold litigation in the United States has traveled a long and instructive path. Once predicted to become the next sweeping environmental mass tort, it instead matured into something more disciplined, more technical, and more exacting.

By 2026, mold litigation is neither fringe science nor runaway liability. It is a specialized field defined by proof.

The Journey From Panic to Precision

In the early 2000s, toxic mold litigation was characterized by sensational headlines warning of "killer mold," predictions of asbestos-scale mass tort litigation, panicked insurance market reactions, and widespread fear among property owners. Media coverage amplified worst-case scenarios. Plaintiffs' attorneys anticipated waves of high-value claims. Insurers rushed to implement sweeping exclusions. The field seemed poised to explode.

That explosion never occurred.

Instead, the field underwent a remarkable transformation. Courts demanded scientific rigor. Judges applied Daubert gatekeeping standards. Defense experts challenged speculative causation theories. Insurance carriers refined exclusion language. Legislatures provided limited regulatory guidance without establishing comprehensive frameworks. And the field gradually sorted itself into viable claims based on accepted science and speculative claims that could not withstand evidentiary scrutiny.

By 2026, toxic mold litigation has achieved a state of disciplined maturity. The path from panic to precision reflects the legal system's capacity for self-correction when faced with scientifically complex claims lacking clear regulatory standards.

The Central Lessons

Across twenty chapters, this book has examined the core realities that shape modern toxic mold claims. Several fundamental lessons emerge:

1. Moisture, Not Mold, Is the Root Cause

Toxic mold litigation is rarely about mold biology. It is about water intrusion.

Roof failures, plumbing leaks, building envelope defects, inadequate drainage, condensation from improperly sized HVAC systems, foundation cracks, window installation errors, and deferred maintenance allowing minor problems to become major failures drive the vast majority of claims.

Mold is the visible manifestation of moisture management failure. Successful litigation focuses not on fungal taxonomy but on demonstrating:

- How water entered the building
- How long intrusion persisted
- Who knew or should have known about the problem
- Why remediation was delayed or inadequate
- What preventive measures would have avoided contamination

Attorneys who understand building science, recognize moisture pathway analysis, and present water intrusion as preventable failure rather than mysterious environmental contamination win more often than those who emphasize mold as exotic toxin.

2. Scientific Rigor Governs Medical Causation

Modern toxic mold litigation demands scientific credibility.

General acknowledgment that mold can cause irritation does not create substantial damages. High-value claims depend on admissible, scientifically grounded proof of specific injury. Courts demand dose evidence, reliable methodology, and defensible differential diagnosis.

The days when photographs of visible growth and plaintiff testimony about symptoms could sustain million-dollar verdicts are over. Contemporary mold litigation requires:

- Measurable exposure through environmental testing
- Medical experts using peer-reviewed methodology
- Differential diagnosis ruling out alternative causes
- Temporal correlation between exposure and symptoms
- Objective findings supporting subjective complaints
- Causation opinions that withstand Daubert scrutiny

Where plaintiffs present respiratory injury claims based on allergies and asthma exacerbation, with credentialed allergist testimony grounded in mainstream medical literature, claims survive and generate meaningful settlements.

Where plaintiffs assert systemic toxicity, neurological damage, or chronic multi-system illness without robust peer-reviewed support, courts exclude testimony and grant summary judgment.

The scientific divide between accepted respiratory effects and contested systemic illness theories defines the modern battlefield.

3. Documentation Is Power

In toxic mold litigation, contemporaneous documentation often determines outcomes more than dramatic trial advocacy.

Maintenance logs, work orders, tenant complaint emails, inspection reports, remediation invoices, internal management communications, insurance claim files, and contractor certifications create the factual record that drives settlement negotiations and trial verdicts.

Cases with clear documentation showing:

- Timely tenant complaints
- Delayed or ignored responses
- Internal acknowledgment of problems
- Cost-driven postponement of repairs
- Cosmetic concealment rather than genuine remediation

settle for substantially higher amounts than cases where documentation is sparse, ambiguous, or suggests prompt reasonable response.

For defendants, documentation demonstrating:

- Inspection protocols followed
- Prompt investigation after notice
- Licensed contractors retained
- Professional remediation standards met
- Clearance testing completed

reduces exposure dramatically even when mold was present.

The lesson is universal: document everything, preserve communications, maintain organized records, and treat every work order as potential litigation evidence.

4. Property Claims Often Anchor Recovery

In many toxic mold cases, personal injury claims fail under strict causation standards while property-based claims sustain liability and drive settlement value.

Remediation costs, structural reconstruction, diminution in value, business interruption, and relocation expenses create quantifiable damages that do not depend on contested medical opinions. A case that loses $2 million in excluded systemic illness damages may retain $400,000 in documented property loss.

This reality shapes litigation strategy:

For Plaintiffs: Frame cases as habitability violations and property damage claims first, with medical damages as enhancement rather than foundation. This provides fallback recovery when causation challenges succeed.

For Defendants: Focus resources on medical causation challenges while acknowledging property damage exposure. Settlements often reflect property loss plus modest respiratory treatment costs rather than speculative toxic injury.

The shift from toxic tort to property and habitability litigation reflects the field's maturation from sensationalism to practical loss assessment.

5. Insurance Is the Economic Engine

Coverage availability, exclusion interpretation, and bad faith exposure frequently determine whether cases settle early, proceed to expensive litigation, or expand into multi-party disputes.

The insurance dimension creates a parallel litigation track:

- Did water damage constitute a covered peril?
- Is mold excluded as a pollutant?
- Do anti-concurrent causation clauses bar coverage entirely?
- Did mold result from covered water damage?
- Did the carrier investigate promptly and thoroughly?
- Was the denial reasonable or does it constitute bad faith?

In many mold cases, these insurance questions drive outcomes more directly than underlying liability strength. A defendant with viable insurance coverage settles differently than one facing uncovered exposure. An insurer with bad faith vulnerability settles more aggressively than one with clear exclusion language.

Attorneys practicing toxic mold litigation without understanding insurance coverage analysis miss critical leverage points and strategic opportunities.

6. Climate and Infrastructure Will Sustain the Field

Unlike asbestos litigation, which involves historical exposure to a product no longer widely used, toxic mold litigation addresses ongoing conditions that will persist and intensify.

Climate-driven moisture events are increasing in frequency and severity. Atmospheric rivers, hurricanes, extreme precipitation, freeze-thaw cycles, and coastal flooding create moisture intrusion that inevitably produces mold disputes.

Simultaneously, aging housing stock deteriorates as building envelope components exceed design life without replacement. Roofing systems, window seals, exterior cladding, and waterproofing membranes fail at accelerating rates.

The collision between climate volatility and infrastructure aging ensures continued litigation volume. Unlike fields dependent on specific historical exposures or finite defendant populations, toxic mold litigation draws from an expanding universe of moisture-compromised buildings.

This structural reality means the field will not disappear. It will evolve, but it will endure.

7. Specialization Rewards Mastery

Toxic mold litigation has become too technically complex for general practice.

Successful attorneys must integrate knowledge from multiple disciplines:

- Building science and construction practices
- Environmental sampling methodology
- Medical causation standards
- Insurance policy interpretation
- Evidentiary admissibility requirements
- Damages valuation strategies
- Trial presentation techniques

Attorneys who invest in developing this multidisciplinary expertise succeed. Those who treat mold cases as generic premises liability fail.

The field rewards specialization through:

- Higher settlement values for well-developed cases
- Lower summary judgment rates when expertise informs strategy
- Efficient case development through established expert relationships
- Enhanced credibility with courts, mediators, and opposing counsel
- Ability to identify viable cases while declining weak ones

Generalist practice in toxic mold litigation becomes increasingly difficult as evidentiary standards tighten and technical requirements expand.

What Courts Have Taught Us

Judicial decisions over two decades have refined the field substantially. Several principles now guide litigation:

Evidentiary Rigor Is Mandatory
Courts demand reliable science, measurable exposure, and defensible methodology. Speculative causation theories fail.

General Causation Does Not Suffice
Establishing that mold can cause a type of injury does not prove it caused this plaintiff's specific injury. Specific causation requires individualized proof.

Dose-Response Evidence Matters
Without evidence of what exposure level causes harm and what level the plaintiff received, causation opinions rest on weak foundations.

Differential Diagnosis Must Be Thorough
Ruling out alternative causes requires investigation, not assumption. Testing matters more than temporal correlation alone.

Habitability Remains Viable
Even when medical causation fails, property-based habitability claims often survive, ensuring accountability for moisture management failures.

Emotional Distress Provides Fallback Recovery
Jurisdictions increasingly permit emotional distress damages for living in contaminated conditions even when systemic illness claims are excluded.

Insurance Exclusions Will Be Enforced
Courts generally uphold mold exclusions as written, though ambiguities are resolved in favor of coverage and bad faith remains viable when carrier conduct is unreasonable.

Punitive Damages Require Egregious Conduct
Ordinary negligence does not support punitive awards. Documented knowledge combined with deliberate inaction creates punitive exposure.

These judicial teachings create the framework within which modern mold litigation operates. Attorneys who understand and work within this framework achieve better outcomes than those fighting battles courts have already decided.

The Strategic Imperatives

For practitioners on both sides, certain strategic imperatives emerge:

For Plaintiff Attorneys

Screen Cases Rigorously
Reject cases lacking documented exposure, credible causation evidence, or adequate damages to justify litigation costs. The field rewards quality over quantity.

Invest in Credible Experts
Retain board-certified specialists with peer-reviewed credentials who use mainstream methodology. Generic experts fail Daubert challenges.

Frame Cases Conservatively
Focus on well-accepted conditions (allergies, asthma) rather than pushing contested systemic illness theories. Credibility lost on overreach damages even valid claims.

Document Thoroughly
Organize maintenance records, complaints, medical records, and correspondence meticulously. Documentation drives settlement leverage.

Address Weaknesses Proactively
Anticipate defense arguments about alternative causes, dose limitations, and damages exaggeration. Inoculate by acknowledging and addressing weaknesses honestly.

Understand Insurance
Analyze coverage early. Bad faith exposure often provides more settlement leverage than underlying liability strength.

Master Building Science
Invest time understanding moisture intrusion pathways, building envelope systems, and remediation protocols. Cases are won through technical credibility.

For Defense Attorneys

Respond Promptly to Moisture Complaints
The best defense is remediation before contamination becomes severe. Document quick, professional response.

Maintain Comprehensive Records
Create and preserve records demonstrating reasonable inspection protocols, prompt investigation, and appropriate remediation.

Challenge Causation Aggressively
Focus Daubert challenges on dose-response gaps, inadequate differential diagnosis, and lack of peer-reviewed support for systemic illness theories.

Concede Strategically
Acknowledge that mold can cause allergies and irritation. Focus defense on proving this plaintiff's condition has other causes or was not severe.

Emphasize Alternative Causes
Seasonal allergies, pet dander, smoking, occupational exposures, and pre-existing conditions often explain symptoms better than mold.

Move for Summary Judgment
When medical experts are excluded or causation proof is weak, seek summary judgment rather than proceeding to trial on limited damages.

Evaluate Bad Faith Exposure
When representing insurers, conduct thorough investigations and document reasoning for coverage positions to minimize bad faith risk.

Invest in Building Science Defense
Retain engineers who can demonstrate code compliance, proper construction practices, and preventable vs. unforeseeable failures.

For Property Owners and Managers

Implement Preventive Protocols
Regular inspections, prompt moisture response (48-72 hours), and documented maintenance prevent most litigation.

Upgrade Aging Infrastructure
Replace building envelope components approaching end of design life before failure occurs.

Install Monitoring Technology
Moisture sensors and building health monitoring systems provide early warning and demonstrate diligence.

Train Staff
Ensure maintenance personnel recognize moisture problems and understand response protocols.

Maintain Documentation
Organized records of inspections, complaints, responses, and remediation efforts provide defense foundation.

Obtain Adequate Insurance
Understand policy exclusions and consider mold endorsements where available and cost-effective.

Respond to Climate Risk
Assess properties for climate-driven moisture vulnerability and upgrade systems inadequate for projected conditions.

For Insurers

Draft Clear Exclusions
Ambiguous policy language creates coverage disputes. Clarity reduces litigation.

Investigate Thoroughly
Prompt, comprehensive investigation with qualified experts reduces bad faith exposure even when coverage is denied.

Distinguish Water Damage from Mold
Analyze whether covered water damage predominates over excluded mold growth. Recognize resulting loss doctrine.

Document Decision Reasoning
Memorialize coverage analysis, investigation findings, and decision rationale to defend against bad faith claims.

Train Adjusters
Ensure claims professionals understand mold coverage complexity and bad faith risks.

Consider Early Settlement
When coverage is ambiguous or bad faith exposure exists, early settlement may cost less than litigation.

The Responsibility Paradigm

At its core, toxic mold litigation is not about fungi. It is about responsibility.

Responsibility to design buildings that manage water properly. Architects and engineers who ignore moisture management principles, fail to specify adequate drainage systems, or design building envelopes inadequate for site conditions create conditions for litigation.

Responsibility to construct buildings according to design and code. Contractors who cut corners on flashing installation, omit waterproofing membranes, install windows improperly, or ignore drainage requirements cause moisture intrusion that manifests as mold.

Responsibility to maintain housing in safe condition. Landlords who defer roof repairs, ignore plumbing leaks, dismiss tenant complaints, or postpone remediation to save costs create habitability violations that expose tenants to contamination.

Responsibility to disclose known defects honestly. Sellers who conceal moisture history, property managers who paint over mold without fixing sources, and real estate professionals who minimize problems commit fraud that justifies liability.

Responsibility to handle insurance claims fairly. Carriers who deny claims without adequate investigation, misapply exclusions, delay unreasonably, or prioritize claim cost savings over policyholder rights commit bad faith warranting consequences.

Responsibility to present scientifically reliable evidence in court. Attorneys who advance speculative causation theories, retain questionable experts, exaggerate damages, or misrepresent evidence undermine judicial integrity and harm clients through excluded testimony and lost credibility.

Where these responsibilities are met, disputes narrow. Where they are ignored, litigation expands.

The legal system's role is enforcing responsibility through liability, damages, and accountability. Toxic mold litigation serves this function effectively when it holds negligent parties responsible while protecting defendants who acted reasonably from speculative claims.

The Field's Enduring Value

Toxic mold litigation serves important social functions beyond resolving individual disputes:

Accountability Mechanism
Litigation provides accountability when regulatory enforcement is inadequate. The threat of substantial damages motivates property maintenance, building quality, and prompt remediation more effectively than modest housing code fines.

Information Forcing
Discovery and trial testimony force disclosure of conditions, conduct, and decision-making that would otherwise remain hidden. Internal communications, inspection reports, and contractor evaluations become public, informing tenants, buyers, and regulators.

Standard Setting
Where legislation and regulation lag, case-by-case adjudication establishes practical standards for reasonable professional conduct, appropriate response times, and adequate remediation protocols.

Resource Allocation
Litigation shifts resources from parties who created problems to those harmed by them, forcing internalization of costs that would otherwise be externalized to vulnerable tenants or taxpayer-funded healthcare systems.

Innovation Driver
Litigation exposure motivates development of better building products, improved construction practices, enhanced monitoring technology, and more effective remediation methods.

Public Health Protection
By providing remedies for substandard housing conditions, mold litigation protects public health, particularly children's respiratory health, reducing asthma prevalence and healthcare costs.

Critics who view toxic mold litigation as frivolous or excessive miss these broader functions. While individual cases may frustrate defendants, the aggregate effect is improved building quality, enhanced property maintenance, and greater accountability for housing conditions affecting millions of Americans.

The Limitations and Challenges

Honesty requires acknowledging the field's limitations and ongoing challenges:

Access to Justice Gaps
High expert costs and lengthy timelines make mold litigation economically infeasible for many low-value claims. Families harmed by substandard housing often cannot afford attorneys willing to invest $50,000-$100,000 in case development.

Scientific Uncertainty Persists
Despite two decades of litigation, fundamental questions about dose-response relationships, systemic toxicity, and long-term health effects remain unresolved. This uncertainty creates inconsistent outcomes and settlement unpredictability.

Insurance Market Dysfunction
Comprehensive mold exclusions leave many property owners without coverage for legitimate moisture damage, creating situations where damaged parties cannot recover because defendants lack resources and insurance won't pay.

Affordable Housing Tension
Strict habitability enforcement can force property rehabilitation costs that make affordable housing economically unviable, potentially reducing housing supply and displacing low-income residents.

Litigation Cost Inefficiency
The expert-intensive, technically complex nature of mold litigation means substantial resources are spent on litigation rather than remediation. Cases sometimes cost more to litigate than the underlying repairs would have cost.

Jurisdictional Inconsistency
Dramatic variation across states in evidentiary standards, damage recoveries, and insurance interpretations creates forum-shopping incentives and outcome unpredictability for parties operating nationally.

Climate Adaptation Lag
Building codes, design practices, and construction standards lag behind climate reality, creating liability exposure for following technically compliant but practically inadequate approaches.

These challenges are real and meaningful. They suggest areas where legislative intervention, regulatory reform, or practice innovation could improve outcomes. But they do not negate the field's value or necessity.

Looking Forward

The future of toxic mold litigation will be shaped by forces examined in Chapter 20: climate change, aging infrastructure, insurance market evolution, technological advancement, scientific research, and legislative response.

Certainties include:

- Climate-driven moisture events will increase case volume
- Aging infrastructure will amplify vulnerability
- Technology will transform assessment and proof
- Insurance will remain constrained
- Scientific understanding will improve gradually
- Specialization will deepen

Uncertainties include:

- Whether comprehensive legislative reform will emerge
- Whether medical research will validate or limit contested illness theories
- Whether mass tort scenarios will develop
- Whether environmental justice integration will expand federal attention

The most likely trajectory is moderate growth, continued specialization, narrowed personal injury claims combined with expanded property-based recovery, insurance bad faith prominence, technology integration, incremental legislative reform, and persistent scientific uncertainty.

Regardless of how uncertainties resolve, the field will continue requiring attorneys who master building science, environmental assessment, medical causation, insurance interpretation, and trial advocacy. Toxic mold litigation will remain intellectually demanding, economically viable, and socially significant.

The Work Continues

For families living in mold-contaminated housing, abstract debates about scientific uncertainty and litigation economics are irrelevant. Their reality is watching children struggle to breathe, fighting with unresponsive landlords, living with the stress of unsafe conditions, and seeking accountability when property owners fail fundamental duties.

For property owners facing catastrophic remediation costs from deferred maintenance or unforeseen building failures, mold litigation creates genuine financial hardship. Many defendants acted reasonably within budget constraints and genuine uncertainty about problem severity.

For attorneys representing either side, toxic mold litigation offers the opportunity to practice law at a high level, integrating technical expertise with advocacy skills to achieve justice as defined by their clients' legitimate interests.

For judges and mediators, mold cases present the challenge of applying rigorous evidentiary standards while ensuring access to justice, balancing scientific skepticism with recognition of genuine harm, and facilitating outcomes that hold negligent parties accountable without punishing reasonable conduct.

For society, toxic mold litigation represents one mechanism among many for addressing indoor environmental quality, housing maintenance standards, climate adaptation, and the tension between property rights and habitability duties.

The work continues because the underlying problems persist. Buildings will leak. Infrastructure will age. Climate will stress building envelopes beyond design assumptions. Some property owners will defer maintenance. Some tenants will encounter unresponsive management. Moisture will create mold. Mold will harm health and property. And legal remedies will be sought.

The Essential Truth

After examining toxic mold litigation from its scientific foundations through trial practice to future evolution, one essential truth emerges:

This field is defined not by fear of fungal organisms but by proof of preventable failure.

Successful toxic mold litigation proves:

- Water entered the building through preventable pathways
- Occupants provided notice of problems
- Responsible parties failed to respond adequately
- Contamination developed as a foreseeable consequence
- Harm resulted that requires compensation

It is not about panic. It is about proof.
It is not about speculation. It is about evidence.
It is not about drama. It is about discipline.

The attorneys who succeed in this field are those who understand that mold litigation is won through:

- Mastery of building science revealing how moisture intrusion occurred
- Environmental testing documenting contamination extent
- Medical evidence demonstrating health impacts
- Documentation proving notice and unreasonable response
- Expert testimony surviving rigorous admissibility challenges
- Trial presentation translating complexity into accessible narrative
- Strategic judgment knowing when claims are viable and when they are not

Two decades of evolution have refined toxic mold litigation from sensational predictions and fear-driven claims into a mature, evidence-based practice area requiring technical sophistication and scientific credibility.

The field has achieved what the legal system at its best accomplishes: it has separated legitimate claims from speculative ones, established standards for proof, created accountability mechanisms, protected genuine victims while rejecting exaggerated allegations, and evolved toward consistency while retaining flexibility to address unique circumstances.

Toxic mold litigation in America is not perfect. No area of law is. But it is functional, meaningful, and important.

It holds property owners accountable for maintaining safe housing.
It ensures insurance companies honor their obligations.
It provides remedies for families harmed by substandard conditions.
It drives improvements in building practices and moisture management.
It protects public health, particularly children's respiratory health.
It forces disclosure of hidden defects and unreasonable conduct.

And it does all this through disciplined application of evidentiary standards, rigorous evaluation of scientific proof, careful damages assessment, and fair adjudication balancing competing interests.

The next decade will bring change: climate stress, technological transformation, scientific advancement, insurance evolution, and legislative development. But the core requirement will remain constant.

Proof over panic. Evidence over emotion. Discipline over drama.

That is the legacy of two decades of toxic mold litigation.
That is the reality of practice in 2026.
That is the path forward.

The work continues for those committed to excellence in this demanding field. The challenges are substantial. The rewards are meaningful. And the impact extends beyond individual cases to influence how millions of Americans experience the safety and quality of their homes.

Toxic mold litigation has matured from sensational beginning to disciplined present. Its future will be determined by the practitioners, judges, experts, insurers, property owners, and policymakers who engage with the field's complexities honestly, balance competing interests fairly, and pursue justice through evidence rather than assumption.

For those willing to do that work with integrity and excellence, the field offers the opportunity to practice law at its most technically demanding and socially significant.

The essential lesson endures: In toxic mold litigation, as in all environmental and public health law, proof determines outcomes, evidence commands respect, and discipline defeats drama.

Glossary of Terms

Legal Terms

Additur
A judicial remedy where a court increases a jury's damage award that is deemed inadequately low. The plaintiff is typically given the choice between accepting the increased amount or facing a new trial on damages. Note: Many jurisdictions do not permit additur, viewing it as violating the Seventh Amendment right to jury trial.

Admissibility
The quality of evidence that allows it to be received and considered by a court. In toxic mold litigation, admissibility of expert testimony is often the central battle, determined through Daubert or Frye hearings.

Alternative Causation
Defense theory that the plaintiff's injuries or symptoms were caused by factors other than the defendant's conduct. Common alternative causes in mold cases include seasonal allergies, pet dander, smoking, occupational exposures, or pre-existing medical conditions.

Anti-Concurrent Causation Clause
Insurance policy language that excludes coverage when an excluded peril (such as mold) contributes to a loss in any way, even if a covered peril (such as water damage) also contributed. These clauses attempt to override traditional efficient proximate cause doctrines.

Bad Faith (Insurance)
An insurer's unreasonable denial of coverage, delay in payment, or failure to

conduct adequate investigation. Bad faith may give rise to damages beyond policy limits, including punitive damages in some jurisdictions.

Breach of Contract
Failure to perform obligations required by a contract. In mold litigation, may involve breach of lease provisions, construction contracts, remediation agreements, or insurance policies.

Breach of Warranty of Habitability
Violation of the implied legal duty that landlords must maintain rental premises in a condition fit for human habitation. Mold contamination and moisture intrusion affecting health or safety may constitute habitability breaches.

Burden of Proof
The obligation to prove facts asserted in litigation. In civil mold cases, plaintiffs bear the burden of proving each element of their claims by a preponderance of the evidence (more likely than not).

Causation
The connection between the defendant's conduct and the plaintiff's harm. Toxic mold cases require proof of both general causation (can mold cause this type of injury?) and specific causation (did mold exposure cause this particular plaintiff's injury?).

Certification (Class Action)
Court approval allowing a lawsuit to proceed as a class action on behalf of multiple plaintiffs. Toxic mold personal injury claims rarely achieve certification due to individualized causation issues, though property damage claims may.

Comparative Fault
Legal doctrine apportioning liability based on each party's degree of fault. In mold cases, defendants may argue plaintiffs contributed to contamination through inadequate ventilation, failure to report problems promptly, or poor housekeeping.

Compensatory Damages
Money awarded to compensate plaintiffs for actual losses, including medical expenses, property damage, lost income, and pain and suffering. Distinguished from punitive damages, which punish rather than compensate.

Concealment
Fraudulent hiding of material facts. In real estate transactions, sellers

ns, sellers who hide known mold problems through cosmetic repairs or omissions in disclosure forms may be liable for concealment.

Constructive Eviction
Legal doctrine allowing tenants to terminate leases and cease rent payments when property conditions become so uninhabitable that they are effectively forced to leave. Severe mold contamination may constitute constructive eviction.

Contribution
Right of a defendant who has paid more than their proportionate share of liability to recover the excess from other liable parties. Common in multi-defendant mold cases involving property managers, contractors, and building product manufacturers.

Damages
Monetary compensation awarded to successful plaintiffs. Categories include economic damages (medical bills, property repair costs), non-economic damages (pain and suffering, emotional distress), and punitive damages (punishment for egregious conduct).

Daubert Standard
Federal standard for admissibility of expert testimony, requiring that testimony be based on sufficient facts or data, be the product of reliable principles and methods, and be properly applied. Named for *Daubert v. Merrell Dow Pharmaceuticals*, Inc., 509 U.S. 579 (1993). Most states follow Daubert or similar standards.

Declaratory Judgment
Court determination of parties' rights and obligations. Insurance companies frequently seek declaratory judgments establishing whether coverage exists before liability is determined in underlying mold cases.

Default Judgment
Judgment entered against a party who fails to respond to a complaint or otherwise participate in litigation. Default judgments may be entered against unresponsive property owners in mold cases.

Deposition
Sworn out-of-court testimony taken during discovery. Expert depositions are critical in mold litigation, often revealing methodology weaknesses that lead to exclusion motions.

Differential Diagnosis
Medical methodology involving systematic consideration and elimination of possible causes of a condition to arrive at the most likely diagnosis. Courts require thorough differential diagnosis in toxic exposure cases, including ruling out alternative causes of symptoms.

Discovery
Pre-trial process where parties exchange information and evidence. In mold cases, discovery typically includes document production (maintenance records, emails, medical records), interrogatories, depositions, and property inspections.

Duty of Care
Legal obligation to exercise reasonable care to avoid causing harm to others. Property owners owe duties to maintain safe premises; contractors owe duties to perform work according to professional standards; insurers owe duties to investigate claims thoroughly.

Economic Loss Doctrine
Legal principle that purely economic losses (such as property repair costs) unaccompanied by personal injury or damage to other property may not be recoverable in tort. Application varies by jurisdiction and may affect construction defect mold claims.

Efficient Proximate Cause
Insurance doctrine holding that when covered and excluded perils combine to cause loss, coverage applies if the covered peril was the predominant or efficient cause. Anti-concurrent causation clauses attempt to override this doctrine.

Exclusion (Insurance)
Policy language removing certain perils or damages from coverage. Mold exclusions are standard in modern property and liability policies, though scope and enforceability vary.

Federal Tort Claims Act (FTCA)
Federal law waiving sovereign immunity for certain tort claims against the United States. FTCA claims face strict procedural requirements and limitations, including no punitive damages and bench trial rather than jury trial. Relevant to military housing mold cases.

Fraud
Intentional misrepresentation or concealment of material facts causing

using harm. Sellers who actively conceal mold problems may face fraud claims supporting actual damages and potentially punitive damages.

Frye Standard
Pre-Daubert standard for expert testimony admissibility, requiring that scientific methods be "generally accepted" in the relevant scientific community. Some states still apply Frye rather than Daubert. Named for *Frye v. United States*, 293 F. 1013 (D.C. Cir. 1923).

General Causation
The question of whether a substance is capable of causing a particular type of harm in any individual. Distinguished from specific causation (whether it caused harm in this particular plaintiff). Both must be proven in toxic exposure litigation.

Indemnification
Contractual or legal obligation of one party to compensate another for losses. Construction contracts often require subcontractors to indemnify general contractors for claims arising from the subcontractor's work.

Interrogatories
Written questions that one party serves on another during discovery, requiring written answers under oath. Standard in mold litigation to identify witnesses, experts, and factual claims.

Joint and Several Liability
Legal doctrine allowing a plaintiff to recover the entire judgment from any defendant found liable, regardless of that defendant's proportionate fault. Defendants may then seek contribution from co-defendants. Some states have modified or eliminated this doctrine.

Judgment Notwithstanding the Verdict (JNOV)
Also called Judgment as a Matter of Law. Court order entering judgment contrary to the jury verdict because no reasonable jury could have reached that conclusion based on the evidence. Extremely difficult standard to meet.

Mediation
Voluntary dispute resolution process where a neutral third party facilitates settlement negotiations. Over 90% of mold cases that do not settle informally resolve through mediation.

Motion for Summary Judgment
Request that the court decide the case (or specific issues) as a matter of law

without trial because no genuine dispute of material fact exists. Common in mold litigation after expert exclusion or when causation proof is inadequate.

Motion in Limine
Pre-trial motion requesting that certain evidence be excluded from trial. Frequently used in mold cases to exclude inflammatory photographs, prejudicial testimony, or references to insurance coverage.

Negligence
Failure to exercise reasonable care, causing harm to another. Elements include duty, breach, causation, and damages. Most mold claims sound in negligence, alleging property owners failed to maintain premises or respond reasonably to moisture problems.

Negligent Infliction of Emotional Distress
Tort claim for emotional harm caused by negligent conduct. Some jurisdictions require physical injury to support such claims; others permit recovery for serious emotional distress alone. Relevant when mold causes psychological harm without provable physical injury.

Per Se Negligence
Negligence established as a matter of law by violation of a statute or regulation. Some jurisdictions treat building code violations as negligence per se; others treat them merely as evidence of negligence.

Pleading
Formal written statements filed with the court. The complaint initiates litigation; the answer responds. Amended pleadings may be filed to add claims, parties, or allegations as cases develop.

Pollution Exclusion
Insurance policy language excluding coverage for pollution-related losses. Some insurers invoke pollution exclusions to deny mold claims, arguing mold constitutes a pollutant. Courts vary in accepting this interpretation.

Preponderance of the Evidence
Standard of proof in civil cases, requiring that evidence show a claim is more likely true than not (greater than 50% probability). Less demanding than criminal law's "beyond a reasonable doubt" standard.

Proximate Cause
Legal causation standard requiring that harm be a foreseeable result of the defendant's conduct. Even if conduct was a factual cause of harm, liability requires that the harm was a reasonably foreseeable consequence.

Punitive Damages
Money awarded to punish defendants for egregious conduct and deter similar future behavior. Requires proof of willful, wanton, malicious, or reckless conduct exceeding ordinary negligence. Many jurisdictions cap punitive damages or tie them to ratios with compensatory damages.

Remittitur
Judicial reduction of a jury's damage award deemed excessively high. Courts may order remittitur or give plaintiffs the choice between accepting reduced damages or facing a new trial.

Rent Abatement
Reduction or elimination of rent obligations due to uninhabitable conditions. Tenants experiencing mold contamination may be entitled to partial rent abatement proportional to the reduced value and utility of the premises.

Repair and Deduct
Tenant remedy allowing deduction of repair costs from rent when landlords fail to address habitability problems. Strict statutory requirements typically apply, and improper use may expose tenants to eviction.

Reservation of Rights
Insurance company letter stating it will defend a claim while reserving the right to later deny coverage or seek reimbursement. Common when coverage is uncertain and investigation is ongoing.

Res Ipsa Loquitur
Doctrine allowing inference of negligence when harm results from instrumentality under defendant's control, the accident type ordinarily doesn't occur without negligence, and plaintiff did not contribute. Rarely applied in mold cases due to alternative causation complexity.

Resulting Loss
Insurance doctrine recognizing that even when mold itself is excluded, damage resulting from a covered cause (such as water damage from a burst pipe) may remain covered. Interpretation varies widely by jurisdiction and policy language.

Sovereign Immunity
Legal doctrine protecting governmental entities from suit. Federal, state, and local governments may assert sovereign immunity in mold cases, though waivers exist through statutes like the FTCA or state tort claims acts.

Specific Causation
The question of whether a substance caused harm in this particular plaintiff. Requires connecting the plaintiff's documented exposure to their specific medical condition through reliable scientific methodology. Distinguished from general causation.

Statute of Limitations
Time period within which a lawsuit must be filed. Mold cases raise complex questions about when the limitations period begins (date of exposure, date of discovery, date of injury manifestation). Missing the deadline bars claims permanently.

Statute of Repose
Absolute time limit barring claims regardless of when injury was discovered. Construction-related mold claims may face statutes of repose (commonly 6-10 years from substantial completion) even if contamination wasn't discovered until later.

Strict Liability
Liability without proof of negligence, imposed for ultrahazardous activities or defective products. Rarely applicable to mold cases, which typically proceed under negligence theories.

Sub-limit
Insurance policy provision capping coverage for specific perils below the overall policy limit. Many policies impose mold sub-limits of $5,000-$15,000 even when property damage coverage is much higher.

Subrogation
Right of an insurer who has paid a claim to pursue recovery from responsible third parties. Insurers who pay mold remediation costs may assert subrogation claims against property owners, contractors, or product manufacturers.

Summary Judgment
See Motion for Summary Judgment.

Tort
Civil wrong (other than breach of contract) for which the law provides a remedy. Negligence, fraud, nuisance, and trespass are torts commonly alleged in mold litigation.

Voir Dire
Jury selection process where attorneys question potential jurors to identify

bias and determine challenges. Also refers to questioning of witnesses to establish qualification to testify (particularly experts).

Warranty of Habitability
See Breach of Warranty of Habitability.

Building Science and Construction Terms

ASHRAE (American Society of Heating, Refrigerating and Air-Conditioning Engineers)
Professional organization that publishes standards for HVAC design, ventilation, and indoor environmental quality. ASHRAE standards are frequently referenced in mold litigation regarding proper ventilation and humidity control.

Building Envelope
The physical barrier between interior conditioned space and exterior environment, including walls, roof, windows, doors, and foundation. Building envelope failures are the primary cause of moisture intrusion leading to mold growth.

Cladding
Exterior covering or skin of a building. Common cladding materials include stucco, vinyl siding, brick veneer, and fiber cement. Improper cladding installation or moisture management behind cladding frequently causes mold problems.

Condensation
Water vapor converting to liquid water when warm, humid air contacts cold surfaces. Condensation within wall cavities or on building surfaces creates ideal conditions for mold growth. Proper vapor barriers and insulation prevent condensation problems.

Drainage Plane
Building envelope component designed to direct water that penetrates exterior cladding down and out of the wall assembly. Absence or improper installation of drainage planes is a common construction defect causing mold.

Drywall (Gypsum Board)
Interior wall and ceiling finish material consisting of gypsum plaster pressed between paper facing. Moisture-damaged drywall provides ideal substrate for mold growth and typically requires replacement rather than cleaning.

Eave
Overhanging edge of a roof extending beyond exterior walls. Properly designed eaves protect walls from direct rain exposure, reducing moisture intrusion risk.

Efflorescence
White crystalline deposit on masonry or concrete surfaces, indicating water movement through the material. While not mold, efflorescence signals moisture problems that may lead to mold growth.

Flashing
Thin material (typically metal or flexible membrane) installed to prevent water penetration at building envelope intersections and transitions. Common flashing locations include windows, doors, roof penetrations, and wall-roof junctions. Improper flashing installation is among the most frequent construction defects causing moisture intrusion.

Grading
Slope of ground surface around a building. Proper grading directs water away from foundations, preventing basement and crawlspace moisture problems. Negative grading (sloping toward building) causes chronic moisture intrusion.

HVAC (Heating, Ventilation, and Air Conditioning)
Building mechanical systems controlling temperature, humidity, and air quality. Improperly sized or maintained HVAC systems contribute to mold problems through inadequate ventilation, excessive humidity, or condensation.

Insulation
Material reducing heat transfer between building interior and exterior. Improper insulation installation can create condensation within wall cavities, promoting mold growth.

Moisture Barrier
Generic term for materials preventing moisture migration. Includes vapor barriers (retarding water vapor diffusion) and waterproofing membranes (preventing liquid water penetration).

Porous Materials
Building materials that absorb and retain water, including drywall, insulation, ceiling tiles, carpet, and wood. Porous materials contaminated with mold generally require removal rather than cleaning.

Relative Humidity (RH)
Ratio of actual water vapor in air to maximum water vapor air can hold at a given temperature, expressed as percentage. Indoor relative humidity above 60% for extended periods promotes mold growth. Optimal indoor RH is typically 30-50%.

Remediation
Process of removing mold contamination and correcting conditions that allowed growth. Professional remediation follows established protocols including containment, negative air pressure, HEPA filtration, and clearance testing.

Sealant
Material used to seal joints, gaps, or seams against water and air infiltration. Sealant failure (due to aging, improper application, or inadequate maintenance) is a common moisture intrusion pathway.

Stucco
Exterior cladding material made from cement, sand, lime, and water. Traditional three-coat stucco applied over weather-resistant barriers with drainage planes performs well. Synthetic stucco (EIFS) and improperly installed systems have caused widespread moisture intrusion and mold problems.

Vapor Barrier
Material retarding water vapor diffusion through building assemblies. Proper vapor barrier location depends on climate; improper placement can trap moisture within walls, promoting mold growth.

Ventilation
Introduction of outdoor air to replace indoor air, controlling humidity and indoor air quality. Inadequate ventilation, particularly in bathrooms and kitchens, contributes to elevated humidity and mold growth.

Weather-Resistant Barrier (WRB)
Membrane installed behind exterior cladding to prevent liquid water penetration while allowing water vapor to escape. Common WRBs include building paper and housewrap. Tears, gaps, or improper installation compromise moisture protection.

Weep Hole
Small opening at the bottom of wall assemblies allowing accumulated water to drain out. Blocked or absent weep holes trap water behind cladding, promoting mold growth.

Environmental Science and Mold Biology Terms

Allergenic Mold
Mold capable of triggering allergic reactions in sensitized individuals. Most indoor molds are allergenic, with symptoms ranging from mild respiratory irritation to severe allergic responses.

Amplification
Significant increase in indoor mold concentrations above outdoor baseline levels, typically indicating water intrusion and active mold growth indoors.

Aspergillus
Extremely common genus of mold found in both indoor and outdoor environments. Some species can cause allergic reactions and, in immunocompromised individuals, invasive infections. Frequently identified in water-damaged buildings.

Bioaerosol
Airborne particles of biological origin, including mold spores, bacteria, pollen, and dust mite fragments. Indoor air quality testing measures bioaerosol concentrations.

Chain of Custody
Documentation tracking possession and handling of samples from collection through laboratory analysis. Proper chain of custody is essential for environmental samples to be admissible as evidence.

Clearance Testing
Environmental testing conducted after remediation to verify that contamination has been successfully removed and spore concentrations have returned to acceptable levels.

Colony
Visible mass of mold growing on a substrate. Colonies may appear in various colors (black, green, white, orange) depending on species.

Colony Forming Unit (CFU)
Measure of viable mold spores or fragments capable of growing into colonies. Laboratory results are often reported as CFU per cubic meter of air or per surface area.

Culture
Laboratory method growing mold samples on nutrient media to identify

species and quantify concentrations. More time-consuming than direct microscopic examination but provides species-level identification.

Fungi (plural); Fungus (singular)
Kingdom of organisms including molds, yeasts, and mushrooms. "Fungi" is often used interchangeably with "mold" in litigation, though fungi encompass broader categories.

Genus (plural: Genera)
Taxonomic rank grouping related species. Common mold genera include *Aspergillus*, *Penicillium*, *Cladosporium*, and *Stachybotrys*.

HEPA (High-Efficiency Particulate Air) Filtration
Filtration system removing 99.97% of particles 0.3 micrometers in diameter. Professional mold remediation uses HEPA-filtered negative air machines and HEPA vacuums to prevent spore dispersal.

Hypha (plural: Hyphae)
Thread-like filaments forming the body of most molds. Hyphal fragments can become airborne during disturbance and may cause allergic reactions.

IICRC (Institute of Inspection, Cleaning and Restoration Certification)
Organization establishing professional standards for cleaning and restoration industries. IICRC S520 provides widely recognized mold remediation standards.

Immunocompromised
Having weakened immune system due to disease, medication, or genetic factors. Immunocompromised individuals face higher risk of serious mold infections that rarely affect healthy people.

Indoor Air Quality (IAQ)
Characteristics of indoor air affecting occupant health and comfort. IAQ encompasses temperature, humidity, ventilation, and contaminants including mold spores.

Infrared Thermography
Imaging technology detecting temperature differences across surfaces. Cooler areas may indicate moisture behind walls or ceilings, as evaporating water cools surfaces.

Moisture Meter
Device measuring moisture content in building materials. Non-invasive meters provide quick readings without damaging materials.

Mycotoxin
Toxic chemical produced by certain mold species as secondary metabolites. Mycotoxins in food can cause illness, but whether airborne mycotoxins from building mold cause serious health effects remains scientifically controversial.

Negative Air Pressure
Containment technique where exhaust fans create lower air pressure inside remediation areas than surrounding spaces, preventing spore migration during cleanup.

Penicillium
Very common mold genus frequently found in water-damaged buildings. Typically appears blue-green. Can cause allergic reactions and produce various mycotoxins, though health risks from indoor exposure remain debated.

Spore
Reproductive structure of molds, roughly analogous to plant seeds. Microscopic spores become airborne and can trigger allergic reactions when inhaled. Spore counts are primary metric in air sampling.

Spore Trap
Device collecting airborne particles (including mold spores) onto sticky surfaces or filters for laboratory analysis. Common tool in indoor air quality assessment.

Stachybotrys chartarum
Species commonly called "black mold" or "toxic black mold." Grows on cellulose-rich materials like drywall when wet. Produces mycotoxins under certain conditions. Often implicated in health claims, though actual health risks remain scientifically controversial.

Surface Sampling
Collection of mold samples from surfaces using tape lifts, swabs, or bulk samples. Confirms mold growth but doesn't necessarily indicate airborne exposure levels.

Viable
Capable of growth and reproduction. Viable spore counts (measured through culture) may differ from total spore counts (measured through direct microscopy).

Water Activity (aw)
Measure of water available for biological processes in materials, ranging from 0 (bone dry) to 1.0 (pure water). Most molds require water activity above 0.70 to grow; some require above 0.85.

Medical and Health Terms

Allergen
Substance triggering allergic immune response in sensitized individuals. Mold spores are common allergens.

Allergic Rhinitis
Inflammation of nasal passages caused by allergic reaction. Symptoms include sneezing, congestion, runny nose, and itchy eyes. Well-established response to mold exposure.

Asthma
Chronic respiratory condition characterized by airway inflammation, narrowing, and hyperresponsivity. Mold exposure can trigger asthma attacks in sensitized individuals.

Asthma Exacerbation
Worsening of asthma symptoms beyond usual control, requiring increased medication or emergency treatment. Mold exposure is a recognized asthma trigger.

Biomarker
Measurable biological indicator of exposure, disease, or physiological state. Research into biomarkers for mold exposure continues, but validated, widely accepted biomarkers do not yet exist for most claimed mold-related illnesses.

Bronchitis
Inflammation of bronchial tubes carrying air to lungs. May be acute (short-term) or chronic (long-term). Mold exposure can cause or worsen bronchitis symptoms.

Chronic Inflammatory Response Syndrome (CIRS)
Controversial medical diagnosis attributed to exposure to water-damaged buildings and biotoxins. Characterized by multiple non-specific symptoms affecting various body systems. Lacks general acceptance in mainstream medical community and faces admissibility challenges in many courts.

Cognitive Impairment
Reduction in mental functions including memory, attention, processing speed, or executive function. Claims that mold exposure causes cognitive impairment face substantial scientific skepticism and admissibility challenges.

Conjunctivitis
Inflammation of conjunctiva (membrane covering the white of the eye). Allergic conjunctivitis with itching and redness is a recognized response to allergen exposure including mold.

Differential Diagnosis
Medical process of identifying disease or condition by systematic consideration and elimination of alternatives. Critical methodology in toxic exposure cases; experts must rule out alternative causes of symptoms.

Dose-Response Relationship
Correlation between exposure level and severity of health effects. Establishing dose-response relationships for mold exposure remains challenging due to lack of standardized exposure metrics and individual variability.

Environmental DNA (eDNA)
DNA extracted from environmental samples rather than directly from organisms. eDNA analysis can identify mold species from dust or surface samples with greater precision than traditional culture methods.

Epidemiology
Study of disease patterns in populations. Epidemiological studies can establish general causation (whether exposure can cause disease) but rarely resolve specific causation (whether it did in a particular individual).

Exacerbation
Worsening of pre-existing condition. Mold may exacerbate asthma or allergies without causing new disease.

Genetic Susceptibility
Inherited variations affecting disease risk. Some individuals may be genetically more susceptible to mold-related illness. HLA-DR gene patterns have been studied in relation to mold sensitivity.

Hypersensitivity Pneumonitis
Rare inflammatory lung disease caused by immune system reaction to inhaled organic particles or chemicals. Can result from intense mold

Can result from intense mold exposure. Requires clinical diagnosis with objective findings; claims based solely on patient history face admissibility challenges.

IgE (Immunoglobulin E)
Antibody type involved in allergic reactions. Elevated IgE levels indicate allergic sensitization. Specific IgE tests can determine sensitization to particular mold species.

Immune System
Body's defense system against pathogens and foreign substances. Some claim mold exposure causes immune dysfunction, but this remains scientifically controversial for typical residential exposure levels.

Inflammation
Immune system response to injury or irritation, characterized by redness, swelling, heat, and pain. Mold-triggered inflammation in airways causes asthma and allergic symptoms.

Irritant
Substance causing non-allergic inflammation of eyes, nose, throat, or respiratory tract through direct physical or chemical effects. High mold concentrations can cause irritant symptoms even in non-allergic individuals.

Mycotoxicosis
Illness caused by mycotoxin exposure. Well-documented from contaminated food ingestion. Whether airborne mycotoxins from building mold cause mycotoxicosis remains scientifically controversial.

Pneumonia
Lung infection causing inflammation and fluid accumulation in air sacs. Certain molds can cause pneumonia in immunocompromised individuals, but mold-caused pneumonia is rare in healthy people.

Pulmonary Function Testing
Diagnostic tests measuring lung capacity, airflow, and gas exchange. Objective findings on pulmonary function tests strengthen claims of respiratory injury from mold exposure.

Sensitization
Development of immune system reactivity to a substance after repeated exposure. Once sensitized, even small mold exposure may trigger allergic reactions.

Temporal Correlation
Time-based relationship between exposure and symptoms (symptoms began during exposure, improved after exposure ended). Temporal correlation supports but does not prove causation without additional evidence.

Toxicology
Study of adverse effects of substances on living organisms. Toxicological principles regarding dose, exposure routes, and mechanisms of action apply to evaluating mold exposure claims.

Insurance Terms

Actual Cash Value (ACV)
Property value accounting for depreciation. Some policies pay ACV rather than replacement cost for damaged property.

Additional Living Expenses (ALE)
Coverage for increased costs of temporary housing when property becomes uninhabitable. ALE disputes are common in mold cases requiring extended remediation.

Anti-Concurrent Causation Clause
See Legal Terms section above.

Claims-Made Policy
Insurance covering claims made during the policy period, regardless of when the underlying event occurred. Contrasts with occurrence policies. Professional liability and some environmental policies are claims-made.

Commercial General Liability (CGL)
Standard business liability insurance covering bodily injury and property damage claims. Construction defect mold litigation often involves CGL coverage disputes.

Coverage
Scope of protection provided by an insurance policy. Coverage disputes in mold cases frequently involve interpretation of exclusions, definitions, and resulting loss provisions.

Deductible
Amount the insured must pay before insurance coverage applies. Higher deductibles for water damage or mold claims are increasingly common.

Duty to Defend
Insurer's obligation to provide legal defense for claims potentially covered by the policy. The duty to defend is typically broader than the duty to indemnify (pay judgments).

Duty to Indemnify
Insurer's obligation to pay covered claims and judgments. Narrower than duty to defend; coverage may not exist even when defense is required.

Exclusion
Policy language removing specific perils, causes, or damages from coverage. Mold exclusions are standard in modern policies but vary in scope and enforceability.

First-Party Coverage
Insurance protecting the policyholder's own property or losses. Homeowners and commercial property policies provide first-party coverage.

Fungi Endorsement
Policy amendment specifically addressing mold coverage, typically limiting or excluding fungi-related claims. May be called "fungi and bacteria endorsement" or similar.

Limits of Liability
Maximum amount an insurer will pay for covered losses. Many policies impose lower sub-limits specifically for mold-related claims.

Loss
Damage or injury giving rise to insurance claim. In mold cases, determining when loss occurred (date of water intrusion vs. date of mold discovery) affects coverage.

Occurrence
Under occurrence-based policies, an accident or continuous exposure resulting in injury or damage during the policy period. Construction defect cases may involve disputes about when occurrence happened.

Peril
Cause of loss or damage. Covered perils typically include wind, fire, lightning, and water damage from certain sources. Mold is commonly an excluded peril.

Policy Period
Time during which insurance coverage is in effect. Long-tail claims involving mold may implicate multiple successive policy periods.

Pollution Exclusion
Policy language excluding coverage for pollution-related losses. Some insurers invoke pollution exclusions to deny mold claims; courts vary in accepting this interpretation.

Premium
Amount paid for insurance coverage. Premiums for properties in high-moisture-risk areas or with mold claim history may be substantially elevated.

Replacement Cost
Cost to replace damaged property with new property of like kind and quality, without depreciation deduction. More favorable to policyholders than actual cash value.

Reservation of Rights
See Legal Terms section above.

Resulting Loss
See Legal Terms section above.

Sub-limit
See Legal Terms section above.

Third-Party Coverage
Insurance protecting against claims brought by others. Liability policies provide third-party coverage.

Trigger of Coverage
Event or circumstance activating insurance coverage. Disputes over trigger timing are common in long-term mold exposure cases implicating multiple policy periods.

Underwriting
Process of evaluating risk and determining coverage terms and pricing. Mold claims history significantly affects underwriting decisions.

Procedural and Trial Terms

Answer
Defendant's formal written response to plaintiff's complaint, admitting or denying allegations and raising defenses.

Appeal
Request that a higher court review and reverse a lower court's decision. Mold cases may be appealed based on evidentiary rulings, jury instructions, or damage awards.

Arbitration
Alternative dispute resolution where a neutral arbitrator hears evidence and renders a binding decision. Some parties agree to arbitrate mold disputes to avoid jury trials.

Bench Trial
Trial before a judge without a jury. FTCA claims against the federal government must be tried to the bench.

Closing Argument
Attorney's final presentation to the jury synthesizing evidence and arguing for a favorable verdict. Opportunity to connect technical evidence to legal standards and human narratives.

Complaint
Initial pleading filed by plaintiff initiating lawsuit, stating claims and relief sought.

Cross-Examination
Questioning of a witness by the opposing party. Effective cross-examination in mold cases exposes gaps in expert methodology, alternative causation, or damages exaggeration.

Demonstrative Exhibit
Visual aid used during trial to illustrate testimony, including diagrams, charts, animations, or models. Particularly important in toxic mold cases for explaining building science and exposure pathways.

Direct Examination
Questioning of one's own witness. Direct examination in mold cases must translate complex science into accessible narrative while establishing foundation for evidence.

Discovery
See Legal Terms section above.

Evidence
Information presented to prove or disprove facts. Categories include

documentary evidence, physical evidence, and testimonial evidence (live testimony and depositions).

Expert Witness
Witness qualified by knowledge, skill, experience, training, or education to provide opinion testimony beyond lay understanding. Essential in mold litigation for environmental assessment, building science, medical causation, and damages valuation.

Jury Instructions
Court's explanation to the jury of applicable law. In mold cases, instructions on burden of proof, causation standards, and damages calculation are particularly contested.

Motion
Formal request to the court for a ruling or order. Common motions in mold litigation include motions to dismiss, for summary judgment, to exclude evidence, and for new trial.

Opening Statement
Attorney's preview of evidence and themes at trial's beginning. Opportunity to frame the case narrative before evidence presentation.

Verdict
Jury's decision on disputed facts. May be general verdict (for plaintiff or defendant with damage amount) or special verdict (answering specific questions about elements of claims).

Verdict Form
Document presenting questions for jury decision. Special verdict forms in mold cases typically ask separately about duty, breach, causation, and damages categories.

Voir Dire
See Legal Terms section above.

Regulatory and Statutory Terms

California Toxic Mold Protection Act
California statute enacted in 2001 directing study of mold health effects and development of remediation standards. Influential model despite not establishing enforceable exposure limits or creating comprehensive private right of action.

Disclosure Statute
Law requiring disclosure of material facts in transactions. Many states require sellers to disclose known moisture problems or mold in real estate sales.

EPA (Environmental Protection Agency)
Federal agency providing mold remediation guidance. EPA guidance is advisory rather than mandatory for residential properties.

Fair Housing Act
Federal law prohibiting housing discrimination based on protected characteristics including disability. May require landlords to accommodate tenants with mold-related respiratory conditions.

HUD (Department of Housing and Urban Development)
Federal agency overseeing public housing. HUD guidance requires public housing authorities to address mold and moisture promptly.

OSHA (Occupational Safety and Health Administration)
Federal agency regulating workplace safety. No specific OSHA residential mold standards exist, though General Duty Clause may apply to extreme workplace mold exposure.

Statute of Repose
See Legal Terms section above.

Warranty of Habitability
See Legal Terms section above.

This glossary provides definitions of terms as used in the context of toxic mold litigation in the United States as of 2026. Meanings may vary in different legal contexts or jurisdictions. For authoritative legal definitions, consult relevant statutes, case law, and legal dictionaries.

About the Author

Ngozi E. Bolin, Esq. brings more than three decades of extensive legal and litigation experience to Toxic Mold Litigation in America. With a distinguished career spanning multiple jurisdictions and diverse areas of civil litigation, Ms. Bolin offers readers the benefit of deep legal knowledge, strategic insight, and practical courtroom wisdom grounded in real-world practice.

Educated under the British Commonwealth legal system and having studied at the Harvard Extension School, Ms. Bolin brings a uniquely global perspective to American law. Her international legal career began with her admission as a Barrister and Solicitor of the Supreme Court of Nigeria in 1989. She later relocated to the United States, where she was admitted to the New York State Bar in 1991, the United States Court of Appeals for the Second Circuit, and the California State Bar in 2013.

Throughout her career as a seasoned trial attorney, Ms. Bolin has remained committed to expanding access to legal knowledge and empowering individuals to navigate complex legal systems with confidence. She has been a strong advocate for unbundled legal services, helping consumers better understand their rights while promoting cost-effective legal representation.

Her practice has encompassed a broad range of areas, including consumer protection, personal injury, contract disputes, employment law, unfair business practices, real estate litigation, toxic mold litigation, bankruptcy, probate matters, and insurance coverage disputes. This multidisciplinary experience informs her analytical approach to toxic mold litigation, an area that intersects with premises liability, construction defect law, insurance coverage battles, disclosure obligations, and environmental claims.

Ms. Bolin has successfully negotiated and litigated numerous cases, consistently emphasizing fair settlements, evidentiary discipline, and practical outcomes. Her professional record includes participation in significant cases such as *Louis Capital Markets, LP v. Refco Group Ltd., LLC, et al.*, (9 Misc.3d 283, 801 N.Y.S.2d 490, N.Y. Co. 2005), addressing corporate misconduct and fiduciary duties; *Giordano v. Thomson, et al.*, (438 F. Supp. 2d 35, E.D.N.Y. 2005); and *Davis v. Commercial Bank of New York*, (275 F. Supp. 2d 418, S.D.N.Y. 2003), involving employee benefits and unjust enrichment.

Through her writing and legal advocacy, Ms. Bolin bridges the gap between complex legal doctrine and practical litigation strategy. In this book, she brings that same clarity and rigor to the evolving field of toxic mold litigation, an area defined not by sensationalism, but by scientific precision, statutory nuance, and disciplined proof.

Made in United States
Orlando, FL
04 November 2026

90207623R00332